尾田栄一郎

If I were to liken creating a manga to a game, I would say it's like *Tetris*. I take all the ideas that are scattered inside my head like pieces of a puzzle and put them together into a story. And whenever I'm having trouble making the pieces fit, I take a break from manga and play some actual *Tetris!* When I envision the blocks building up one after another in my head, I think to myself, *"Tetris is so much fun! Yippee!"*

-Eiichiro Oda, 2003

Eiichiro Oda began his manga career at the age of 17, when his one-shot cowboy manga **Wanted!** won second place in the coveted Tezuka manga awards. Oda went on to work as an assistant to some of the biggest manga artists in the industry, including Nobuhiro Watsuki, before winning the Hop Step Award for new artists. His pirate adventure **One Piece**, which debuted in **Weekly Shonen Jump** in 1997, quickly became one of the most popular manga in Japan.

ONE PIECE VOL. 28
SKYPIEA PART 5

SHONEN JUMP Manga Edition

STORY AND ART BY EIICHIRO ODA

English Adaptation/Jake Forbes
Translation/JN Productions
Touch-up Art & Lettering/John Hunt
Design/Sean Lee
Supervising Editor/Yuki Murashige
Editor/Yuki Takagaki

VP, Production/Alvin Lu
VP, Sales & Product Marketing/Gonzalo Ferreyra
VP, Creative/Linda Espinosa
Publisher/Hyoe Narita

Published by VIZ Media, LLC
P.O. Box 77010
San Francisco, CA 94107

10 9 8 7 6 5 4 3 2 1
First printing, January 2010

PARENTAL ADVISORY
ONE PIECE is rated T for Teen and is recommended
for ages 13 and up. This volume contains fantasy
violence and tobacco usage.
ratings.viz.com

www.viz.com

THE WORLD'S
MOST POPULAR MANGA
SHONEN JUMP
www.shonenjump.com

SHONEN JUMP MANGA

ONE PIECE

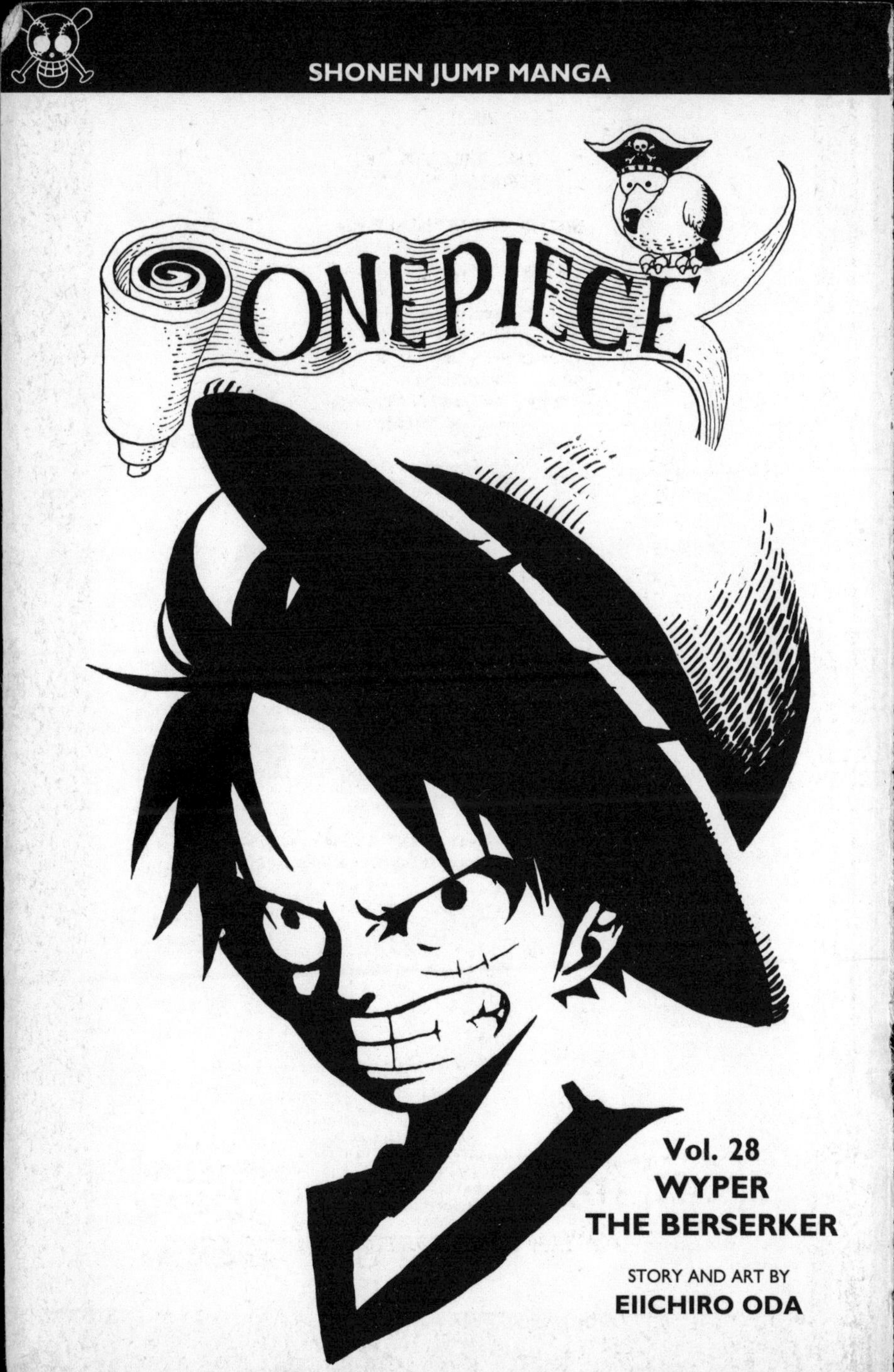

Vol. 28
WYPER THE BERSERKER

STORY AND ART BY
EIICHIRO ODA

The Shandians

The original inhabitants of Upper Yard. Four hundred years ago, their homeland was lifted up into the clouds and conquered by the Skypieans. Now the Shandians fight as guerrilla soldiers to reclaim their ancestral land.

Wyper

Kamakiri

Braham

Genbo

Raki

Aisa

The Former Kami

"Sky Knight" Ganfor

Conis

Pagaya

The Straw Hats

Boundlessly optimistic and able to stretch like rubber, he is determined to become King of the Pirates.

Monkey D. Luffy

A former bounty hunter and master of the "three-sword" style. He aspires to be the world's greatest swordsman.

Roronoa Zolo

A thief who specializes in robbing pirates. Nami hates pirates, but Luffy convinced her to be his navigator.

Nami

A village boy with a talent for telling tall tales. His father, Yasopp, is a member of Shanks's crew.

Usopp

The big-hearted cook (and ladies' man) whose dream is to find the legendary sea, the "All Blue."

Sanji

A blue-nosed man-reindeer and the ship's doctor.

Tony Tony Chopper

A mysterious woman in search of the Ponegliff on which true history is recorded.

Nico Robin

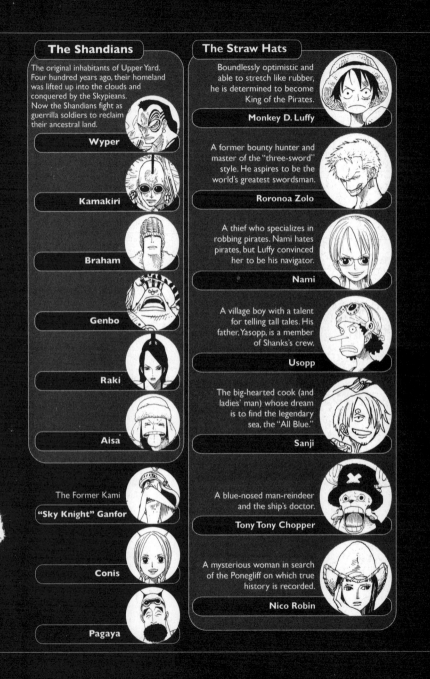

THE STORY OF ONE PIECE

Volume 28

Monkey D. Luffy started out as just a kid with a dream—to become the greatest pirate in history! Stirred by the tales of pirate "Red-Haired" Shanks, Luffy vowed to become a pirate himself. That was before the enchanted Devil Fruit gave Luffy the power to stretch like rubber, at the cost of being unable to swim—a serious handicap for an aspiring sea dog. Undeterred, Luffy set out to sea and recruited some crew-mates—master swordsman Zolo; treasure-hunting thief Nami; lying sharpshooter Usopp; the high-kicking chef Sanji; Chopper, the walkin' talkin' reindeer doctor; and Robin, the cool and crafty archaeologist.

When Robin tells them that there is an island in the sky, Luffy decides to make a detour for this new realm, Skypiea! After surviving a few less-than-warm welcomes, the crew makes an amazing discovery. It turns out Upper Yard, the only place among the sky islands made of soil, is actually the other half of Jaya, the island back on the ground! Which means it's also the location of the fabled city of gold, El Dorado! The search for treasure begins. But Upper Yard is under attack from Shandian guerrilla fighters who seek to reclaim the land from the Skypieans and their tyrant leader Eneru. Worse still, Luffy's crew has been separated!

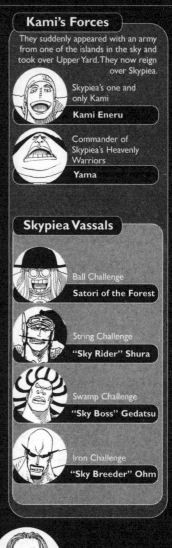

Kami's Forces

They suddenly appeared with an army from one of the islands in the sky and took over Upper Yard. They now reign over Skypiea.

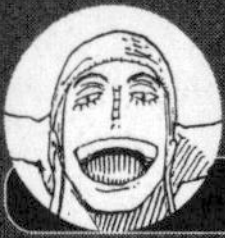

Skypiea's one and only Kami

Kami Eneru

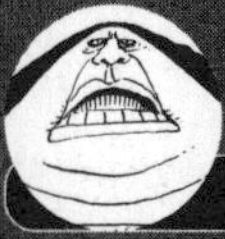

Commander of Skypiea's Heavenly Warriors

Yama

Skypiea Vassals

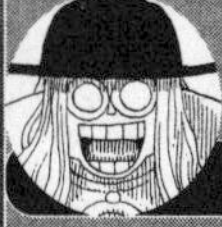

Ball Challenge

Satori of the Forest

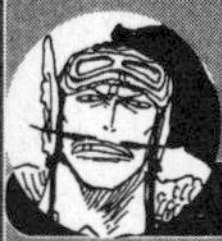

String Challenge

"Sky Rider" Shura

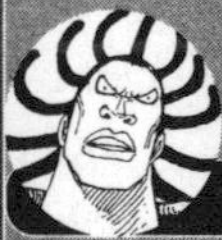

Swamp Challenge

"Sky Boss" Gedatsu

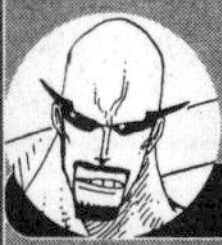

Iron Challenge

"Sky Breeder" Ohm

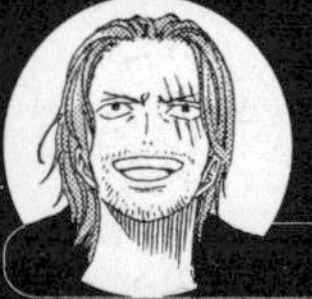

A pirate that Luffy idolizes. Shanks gave Luffy his trademark straw hat.

"Red-Haired" Shanks

SKYPIEA
ONE PIECE

Vol. 28
Wyper the Berserker

CONTENTS

Chapter 256:
WYPER THE BERSERKER

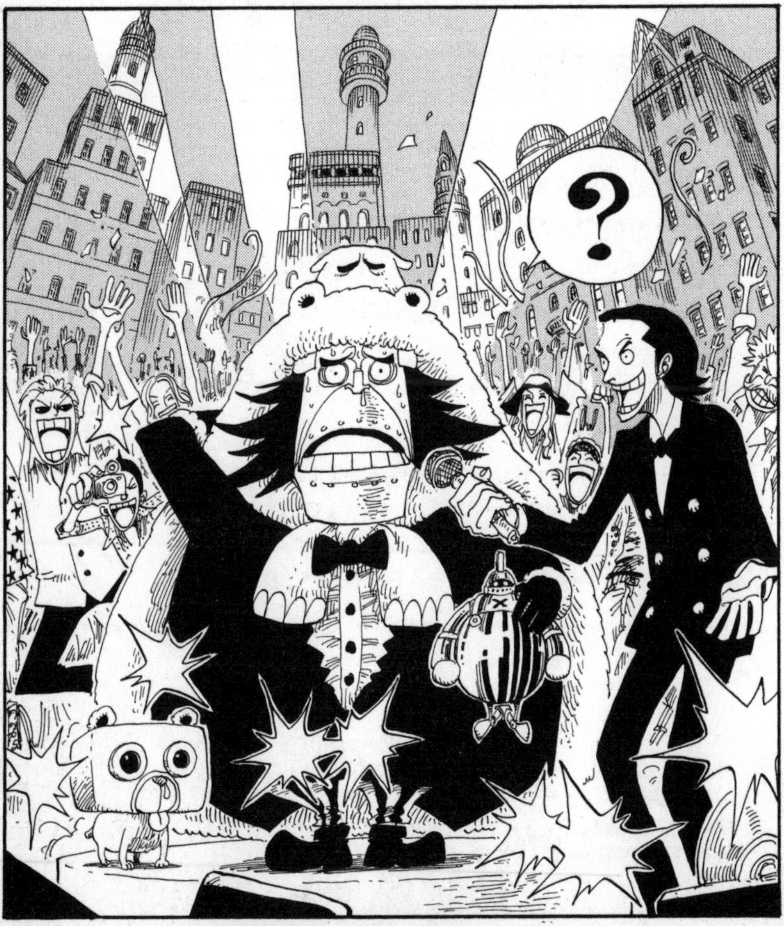
?

WAPOL'S OMNIVOROUS RAMPAGE, VOL. 18:
"DETECTED: A NEW ALLOY CALLED WAPOMETAL"

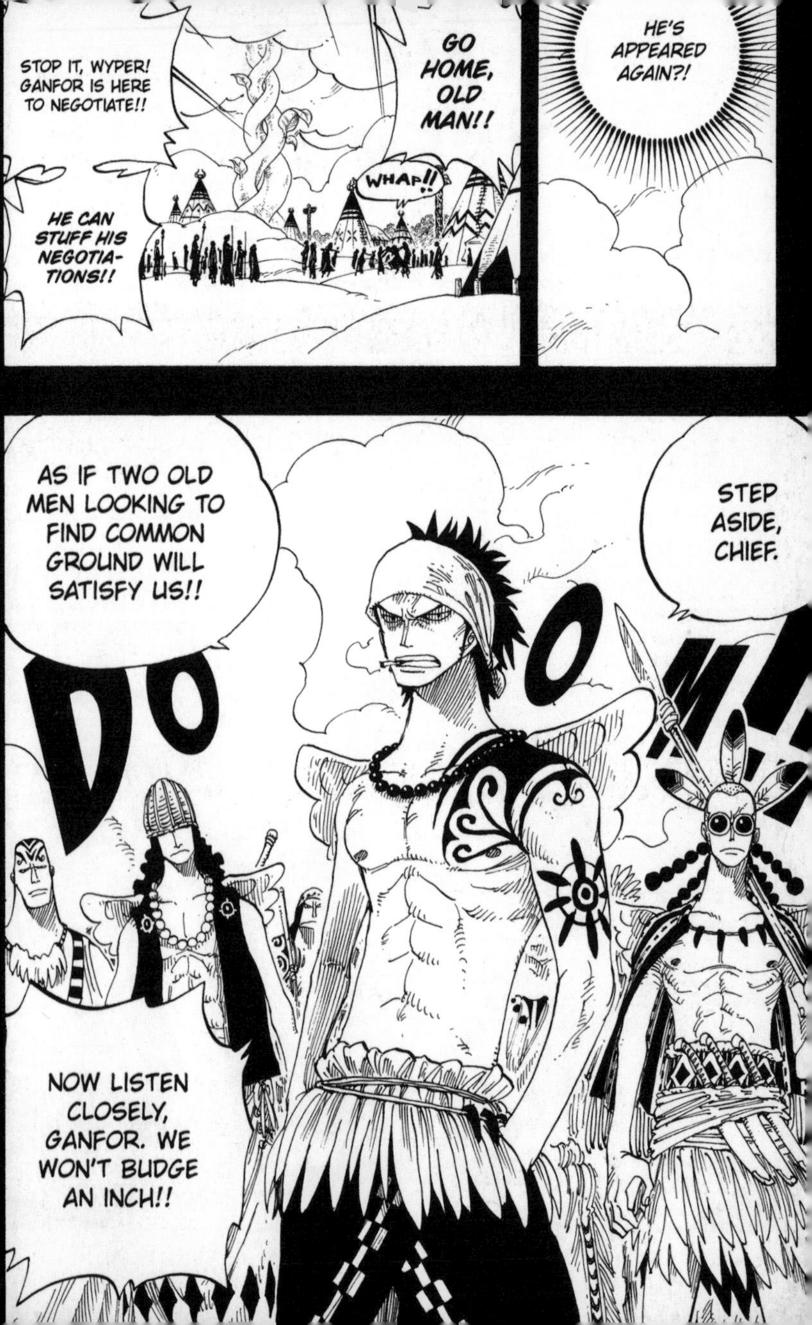
HE'S APPEARED AGAIN?!
GO HOME, OLD MAN!!
STOP IT, WYPER! GANFOR IS HERE TO NEGOTIATE!!
WHAP!!
HE CAN STUFF HIS NEGOTIA-TIONS!!
STEP ASIDE, CHIEF.
AS IF TWO OLD MEN LOOKING TO FIND COMMON GROUND WILL SATISFY US!!
DOOM!!
NOW LISTEN CLOSELY, GANFOR. WE WON'T BUDGE AN INCH!!

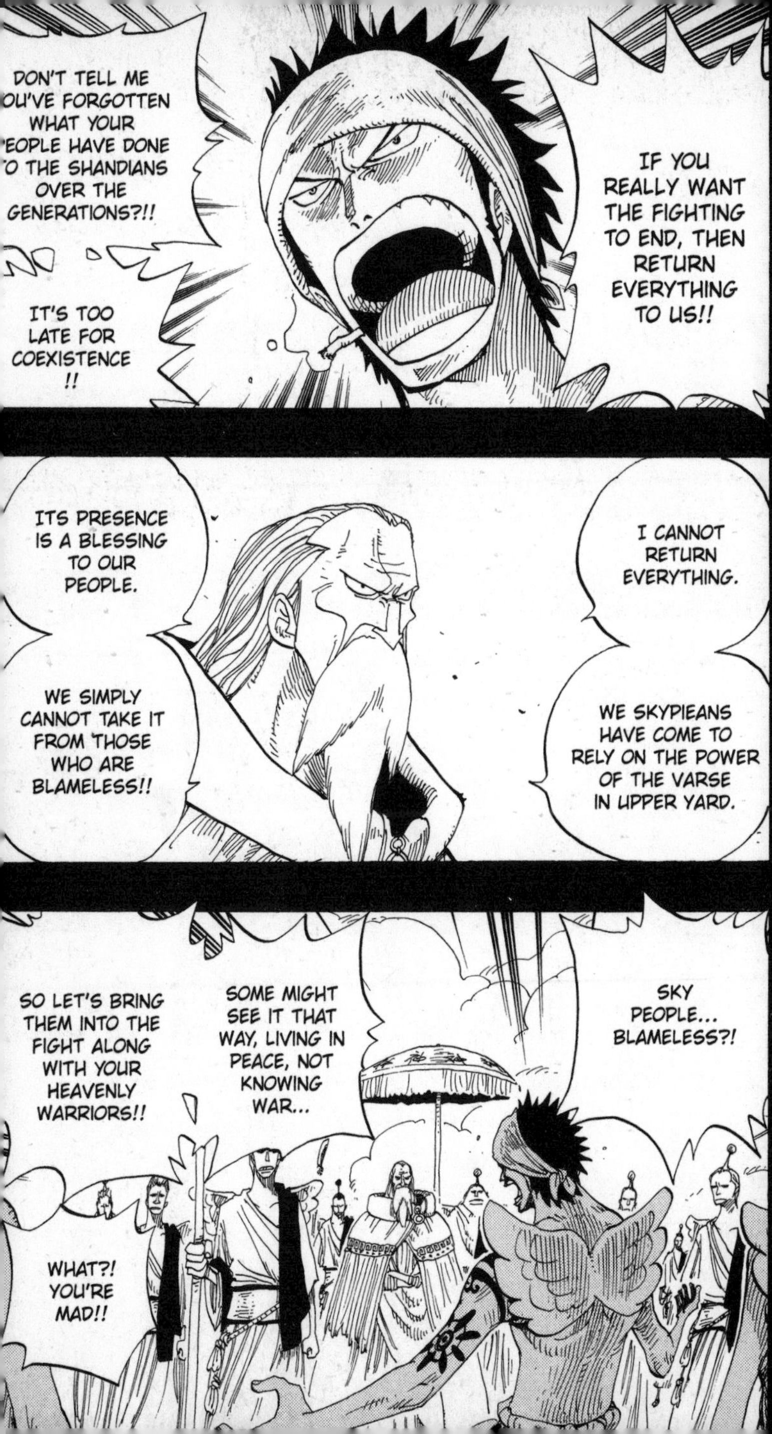
IF YOU REALLY WANT THE FIGHTING TO END, THEN RETURN EVERYTHING TO US!!
DON'T TELL ME OU'VE FORGOTTEN WHAT YOUR EOPLE HAVE DONE O THE SHANDIANS OVER THE GENERATIONS?!!
IT'S TOO LATE FOR COEXISTENCE !!
I CANNOT RETURN EVERYTHING.
WE SKYPIEANS HAVE COME TO RELY ON THE POWER OF THE VARSE IN UPPER YARD.
ITS PRESENCE IS A BLESSING TO OUR PEOPLE.
WE SIMPLY CANNOT TAKE IT FROM THOSE WHO ARE BLAMELESS!!
SKY PEOPLE... BLAMELESS?!
SOME MIGHT SEE IT THAT WAY, LIVING IN PEACE, NOT KNOWING WAR...
SO LET'S BRING THEM INTO THE FIGHT ALONG WITH YOUR HEAVENLY WARRIORS!!
WHAT?! YOU'RE MAD!!

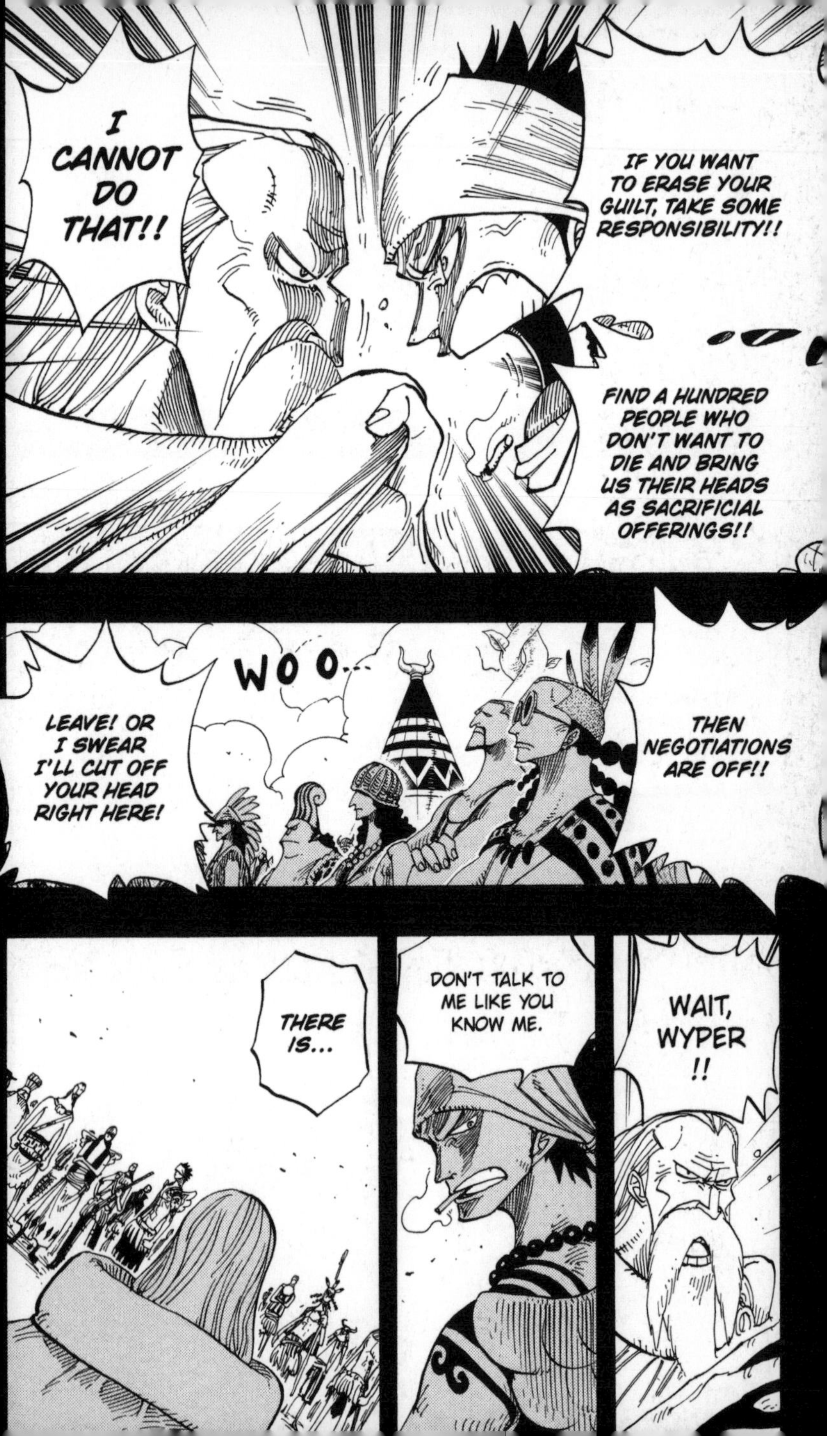
IF YOU WANT TO ERASE YOUR GUILT, TAKE SOME RESPONSIBILITY!!
FIND A HUNDRED PEOPLE WHO DON'T WANT TO DIE AND BRING US THEIR HEADS AS SACRIFICIAL OFFERINGS!!
I CANNOT DO THAT!!
THEN NEGOTIATIONS ARE OFF!!
WOO...
LEAVE! OR I SWEAR I'LL CUT OFF YOUR HEAD RIGHT HERE!
WAIT, WYPER !!
DON'T TALK TO ME LIKE YOU KNOW ME.
THERE IS...

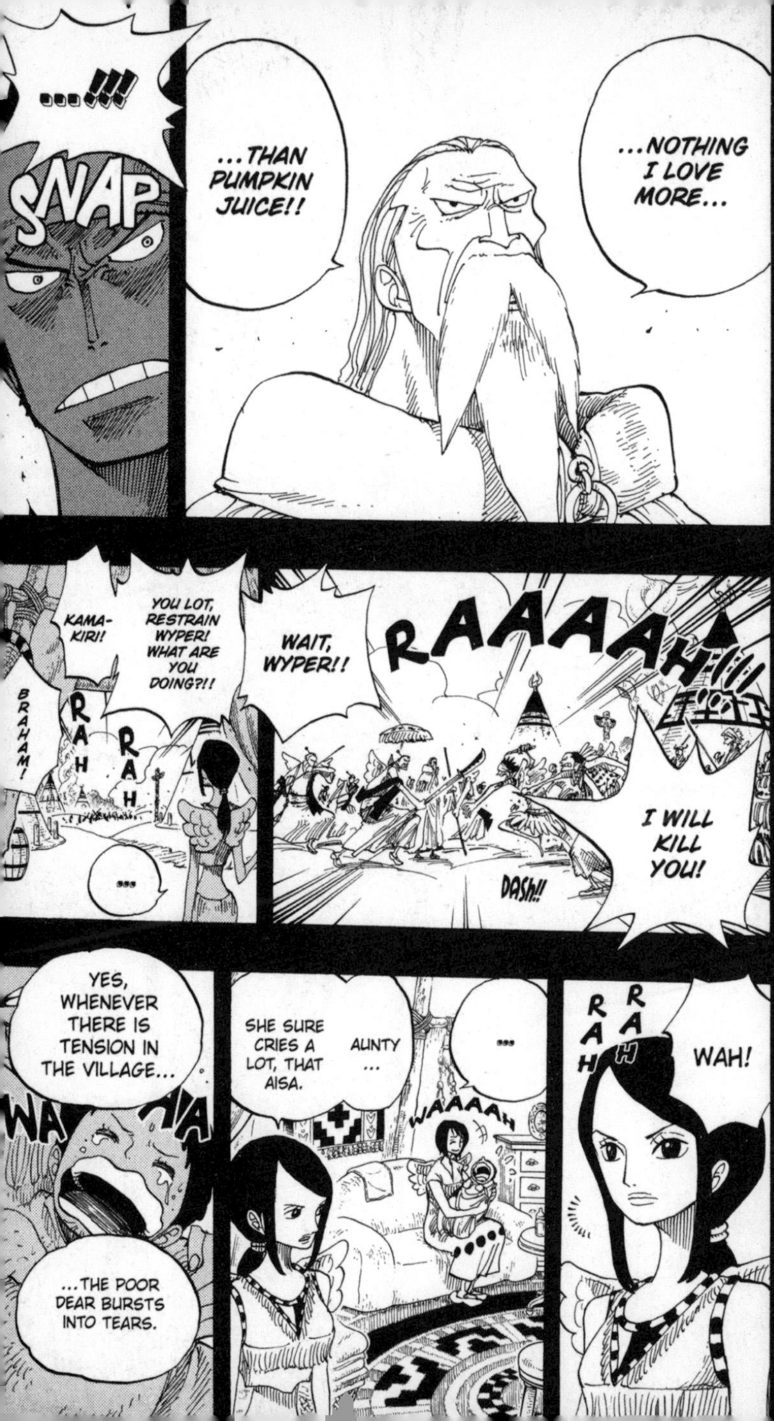
...NOTHING I LOVE MORE...
...THAN PUMPKIN JUICE!!
...!!!
SNAP
RAAAAAH!!!!
I WILL KILL YOU!
DASH!!
WAIT, WYPER!!
YOU LOT, RESTRAIN WYPER! WHAT ARE YOU DOING?!!
KAMA-KIRI!
BRAHAM!
RAH
RAH
...
WAH!
RAH
RAH
...
AUNTY ...
SHE SURE CRIES A LOT, THAT AISA.
WAAAAH
YES, WHENEVER THERE IS TENSION IN THE VILLAGE...
...THE POOR DEAR BURSTS INTO TEARS.

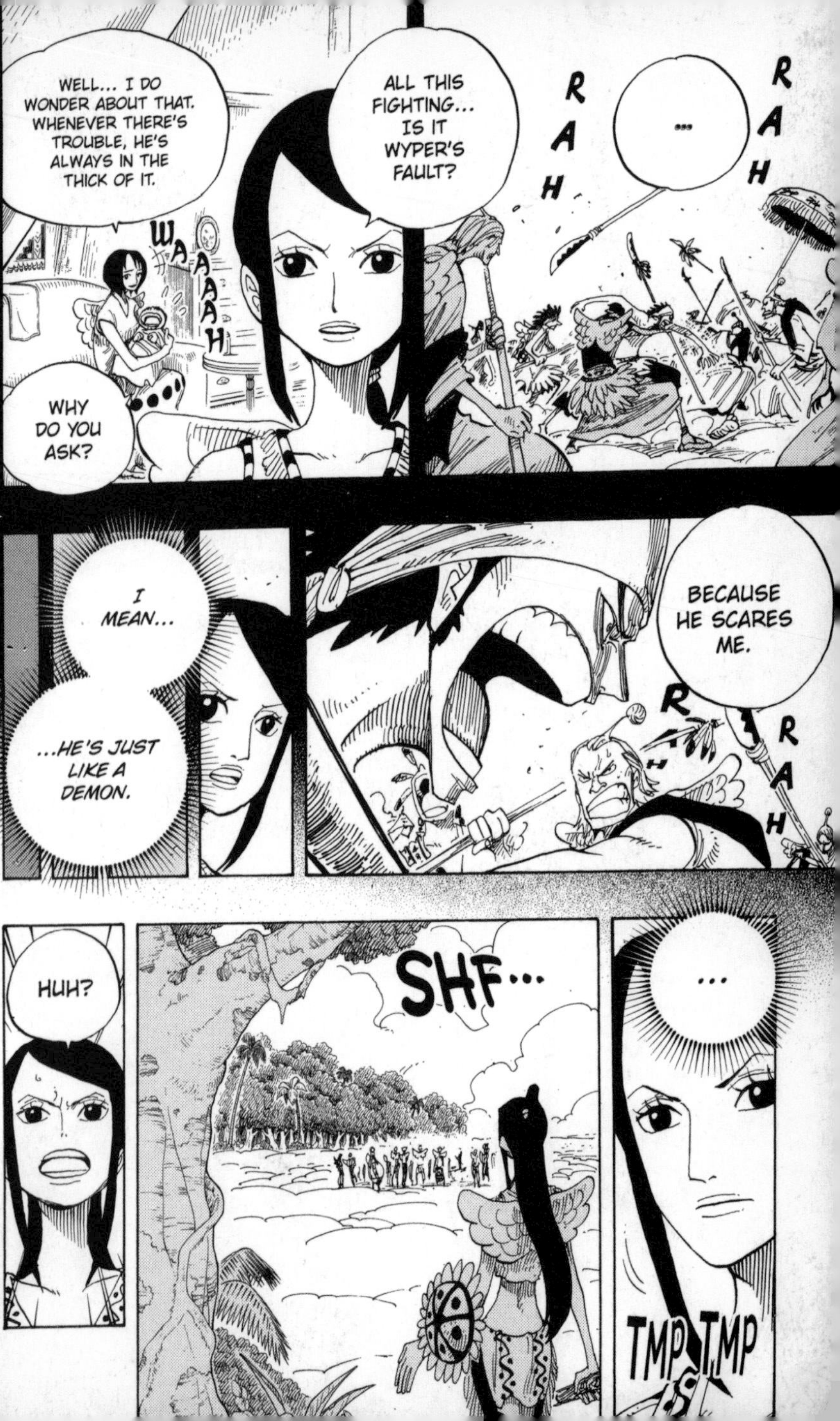
RAH
...
RAH
ALL THIS FIGHTING... IS IT WYPER'S FAULT?
WELL... I DO WONDER ABOUT THAT. WHENEVER THERE'S TROUBLE, HE'S ALWAYS IN THE THICK OF IT.
WAAAAH
WHY DO YOU ASK?
BECAUSE HE SCARES ME.
RAH
RAH
I MEAN...
...HE'S JUST LIKE A DEMON.
...
TMP TMP
SHF...
HUH?

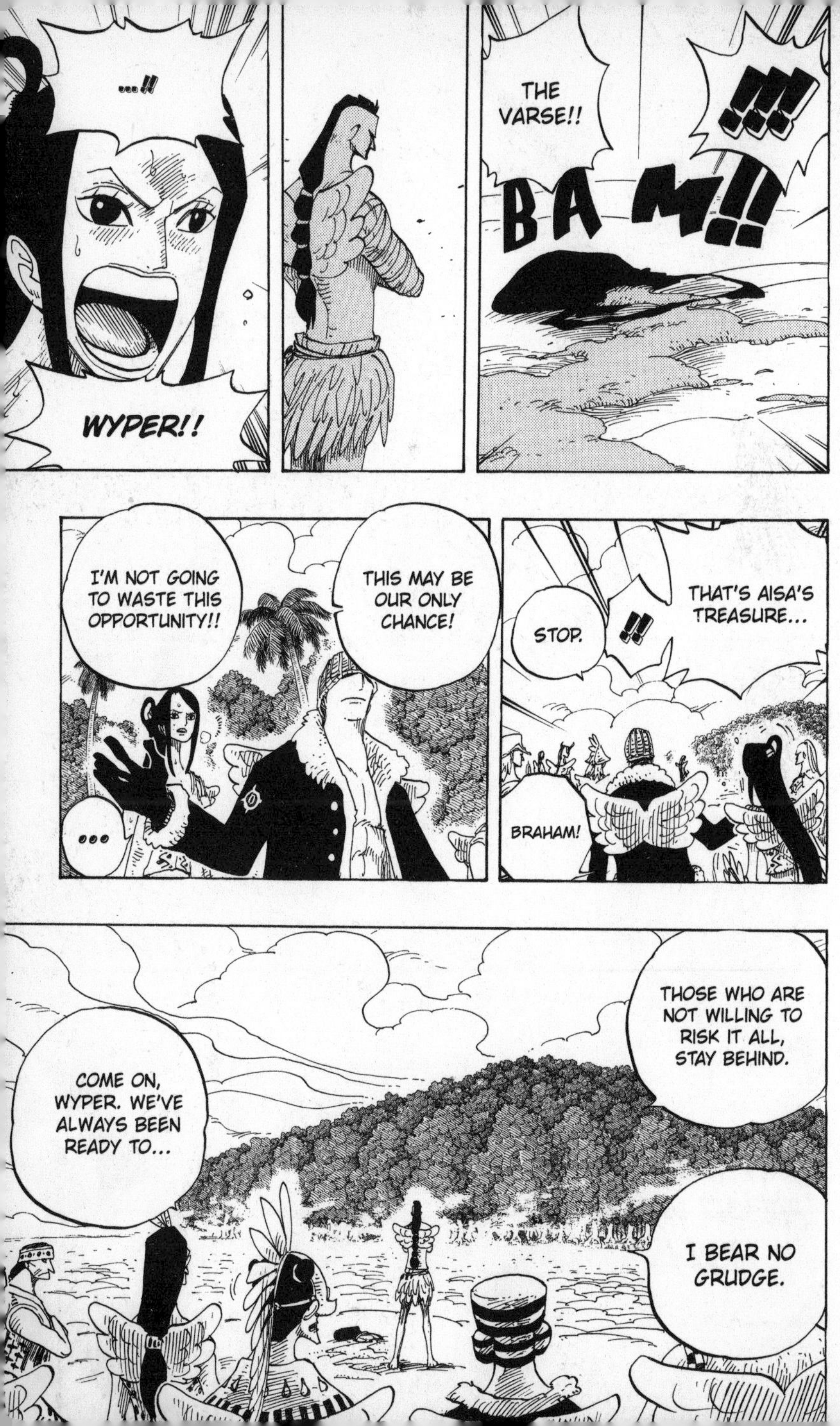
THE VARSE!!
!!!
BAM!!
...!!
WYPER!!
THAT'S AISA'S TREASURE...
!!
STOP.
BRAHAM!
THIS MAY BE OUR ONLY CHANCE!
I'M NOT GOING TO WASTE THIS OPPORTUNITY!!
...
THOSE WHO ARE NOT WILLING TO RISK IT ALL, STAY BEHIND.
I BEAR NO GRUDGE.
COME ON, WYPER. WE'VE ALWAYS BEEN READY TO...

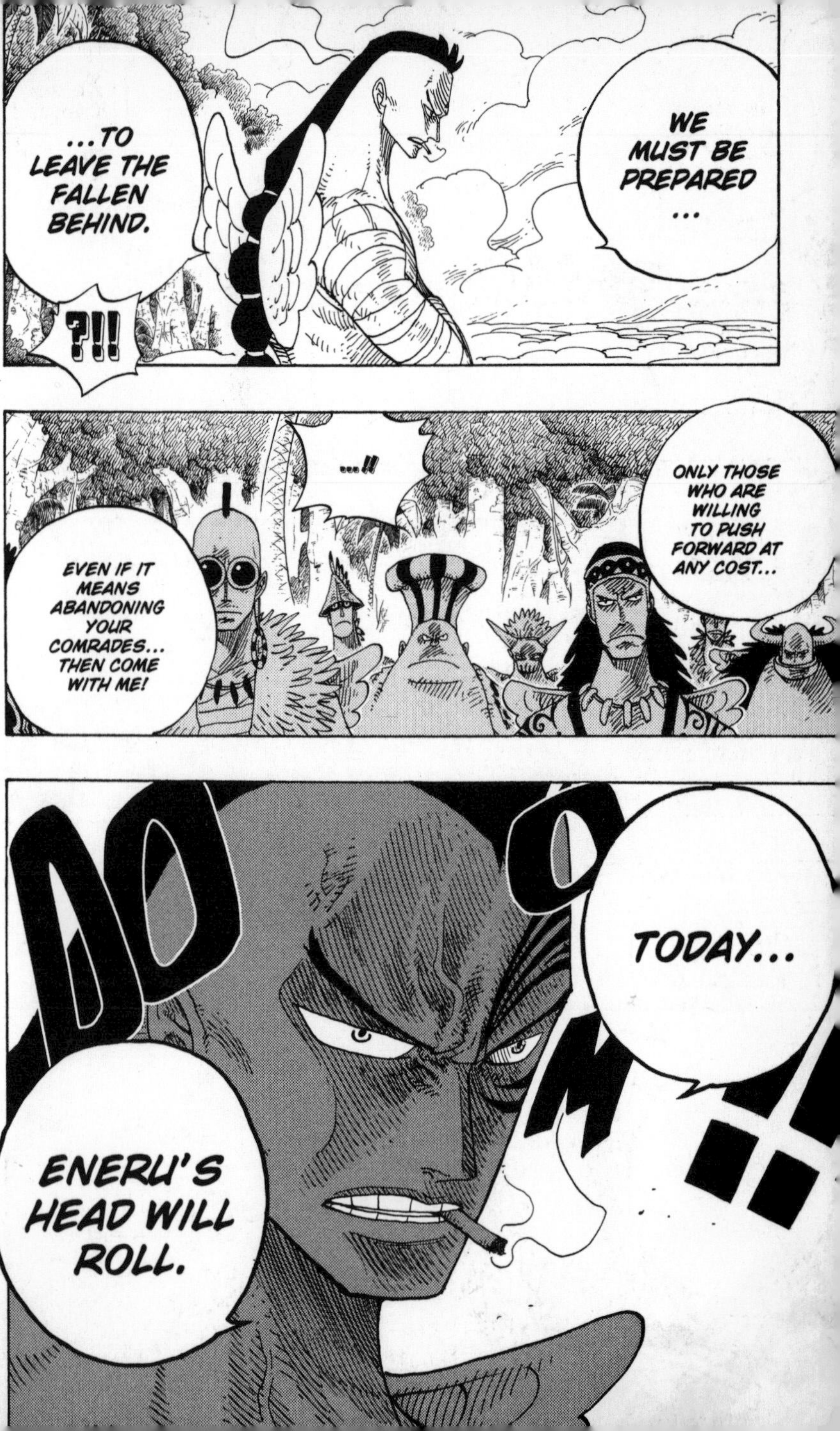
WE MUST BE PREPARED ...
...TO LEAVE THE FALLEN BEHIND.
?!!
ONLY THOSE WHO ARE WILLING TO PUSH FORWARD AT ANY COST...
...!!
EVEN IF IT MEANS ABANDONING YOUR COMRADES... THEN COME WITH ME!
TODAY...
DOOM!!
ENERU'S HEAD WILL ROLL.

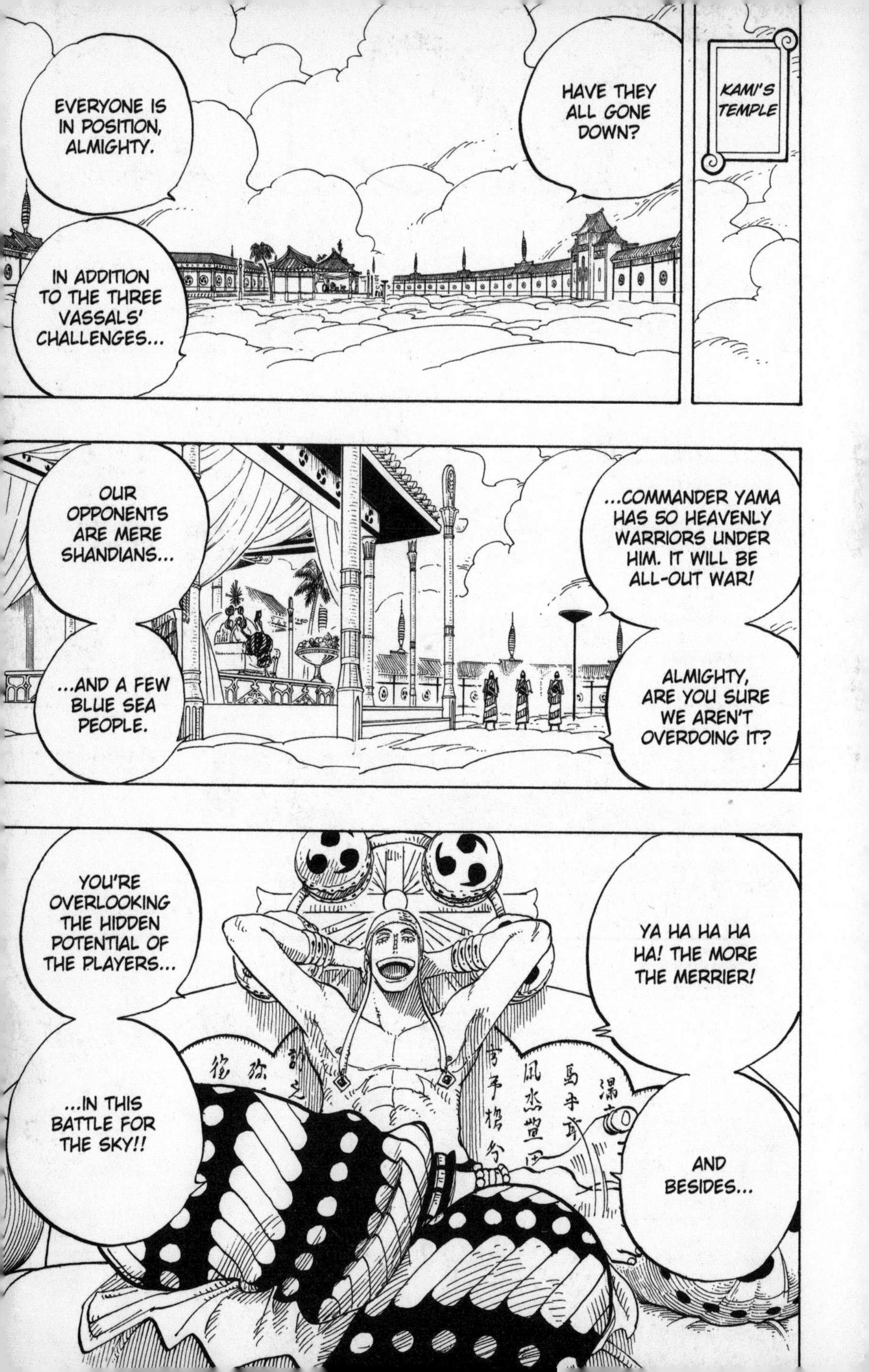
KAMI'S TEMPLE
HAVE THEY ALL GONE DOWN?
EVERYONE IS IN POSITION, ALMIGHTY.
IN ADDITION TO THE THREE VASSALS' CHALLENGES...
...COMMANDER YAMA HAS 50 HEAVENLY WARRIORS UNDER HIM. IT WILL BE ALL-OUT WAR!
ALMIGHTY, ARE YOU SURE WE AREN'T OVERDOING IT?
OUR OPPONENTS ARE MERE SHANDIANS...
...AND A FEW BLUE SEA PEOPLE.
YA HA HA HA HA! THE MORE THE MERRIER!
AND BESIDES...
YOU'RE OVERLOOKING THE HIDDEN POTENTIAL OF THE PLAYERS...
...IN THIS BATTLE FOR THE SKY!!

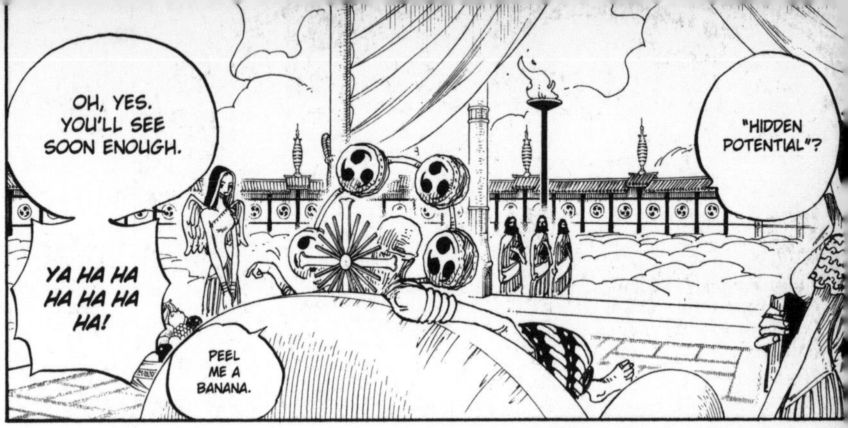
"HIDDEN POTENTIAL"?
OH, YES. YOU'LL SEE SOON ENOUGH.
YA HA HA HA HA HA HA!
PEEL ME A BANANA.

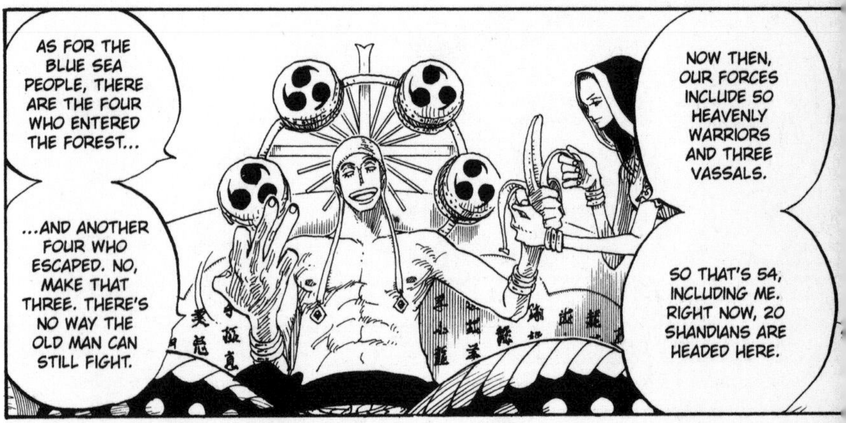
NOW THEN, OUR FORCES INCLUDE 50 HEAVENLY WARRIORS AND THREE VASSALS.
SO THAT'S 54, INCLUDING ME. RIGHT NOW, 20 SHANDIANS ARE HEADED HERE.
AS FOR THE BLUE SEA PEOPLE, THERE ARE THE FOUR WHO ENTERED THE FOREST...
...AND ANOTHER FOUR WHO ESCAPED. NO, MAKE THAT THREE. THERE'S NO WAY THE OLD MAN CAN STILL FIGHT.

THE TEXT ON THE ROOF READS "KAMI." - ED.

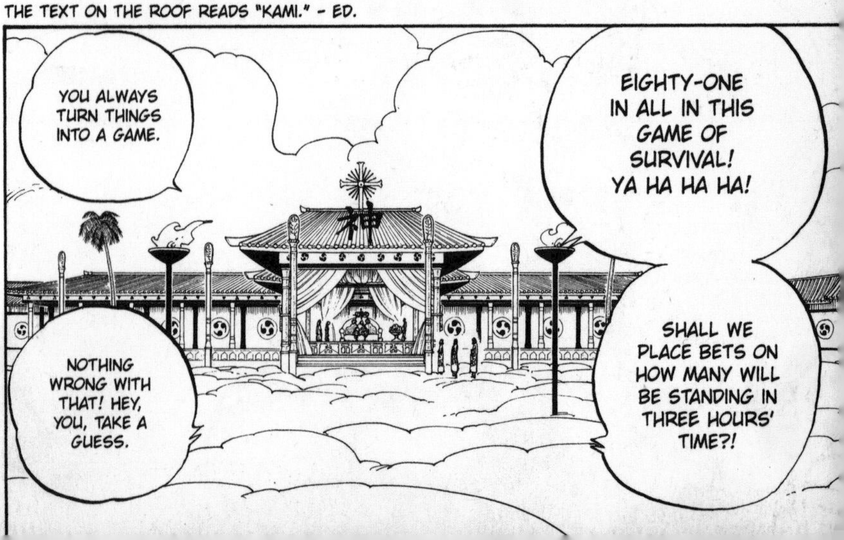
EIGHTY-ONE IN ALL IN THIS GAME OF SURVIVAL! YA HA HA HA!
YOU ALWAYS TURN THINGS INTO A GAME.
SHALL WE PLACE BETS ON HOW MANY WILL BE STANDING IN THREE HOURS' TIME?!
NOTHING WRONG WITH THAT! HEY, YOU, TAKE A GUESS.

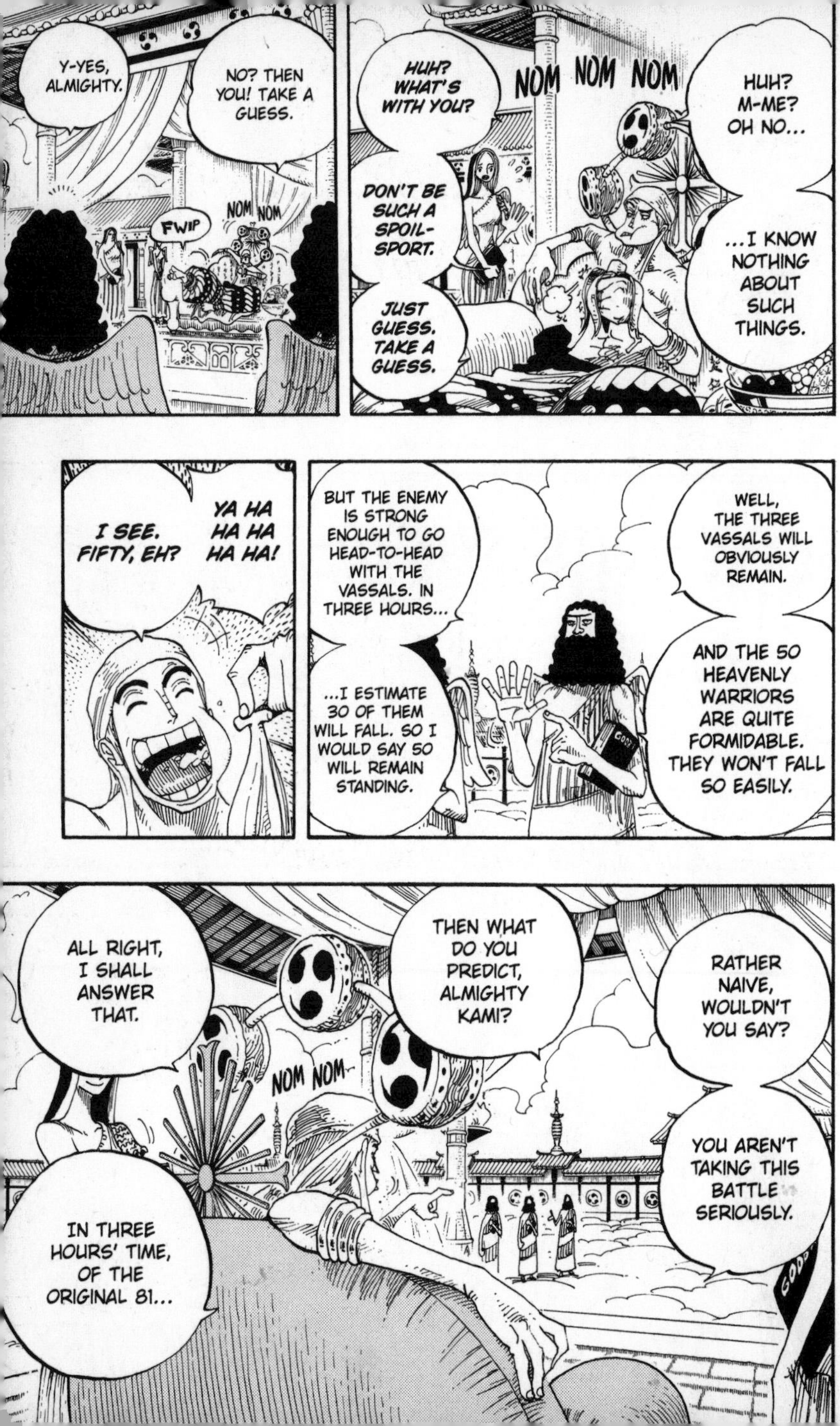
HUH? M-ME? OH NO...
...I KNOW NOTHING ABOUT SUCH THINGS.
NOM NOM NOM
HUH? WHAT'S WITH YOU?
DON'T BE SUCH A SPOIL-SPORT.
JUST GUESS. TAKE A GUESS.
NO? THEN YOU! TAKE A GUESS.
Y-YES, ALMIGHTY.
NOM NOM
FWIP
WELL, THE THREE VASSALS WILL OBVIOUSLY REMAIN.
AND THE 50 HEAVENLY WARRIORS ARE QUITE FORMIDABLE. THEY WON'T FALL SO EASILY.
BUT THE ENEMY IS STRONG ENOUGH TO GO HEAD-TO-HEAD WITH THE VASSALS. IN THREE HOURS...
...I ESTIMATE 30 OF THEM WILL FALL. SO I WOULD SAY 50 WILL REMAIN STANDING.
YA HA HA HA HA HA!
I SEE. FIFTY, EH?
RATHER NAIVE, WOULDN'T YOU SAY?
YOU AREN'T TAKING THIS BATTLE SERIOUSLY.
THEN WHAT DO YOU PREDICT, ALMIGHTY KAMI?
NOM NOM
ALL RIGHT, I SHALL ANSWER THAT.
IN THREE HOURS' TIME, OF THE ORIGINAL 81...

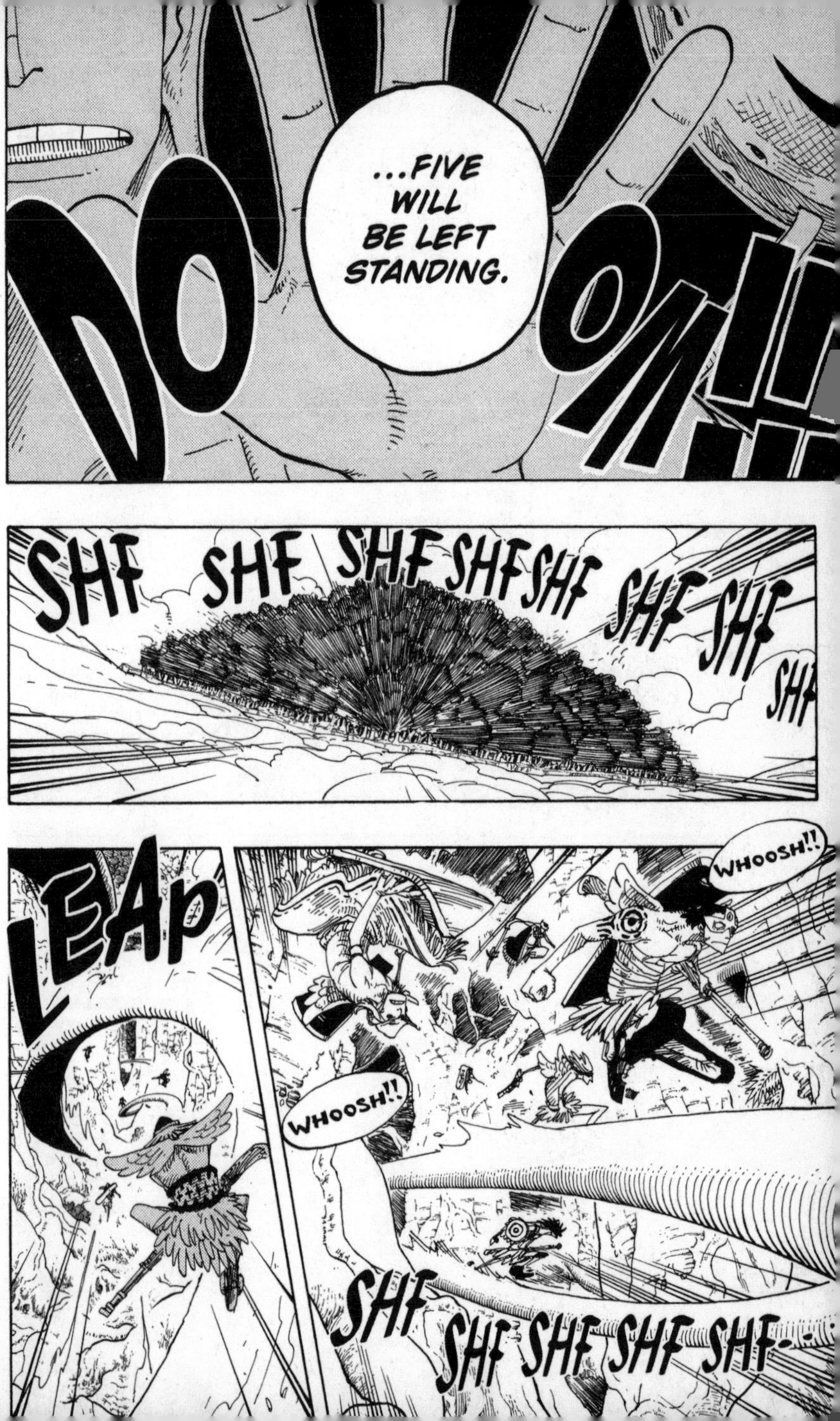
...FIVE WILL BE LEFT STANDING.
SHF SHF SHF SHF SHF SHF SHF
WHOOSH!!
WHOOSH!!
SHF SHF SHF SHF SHF-
LEAP

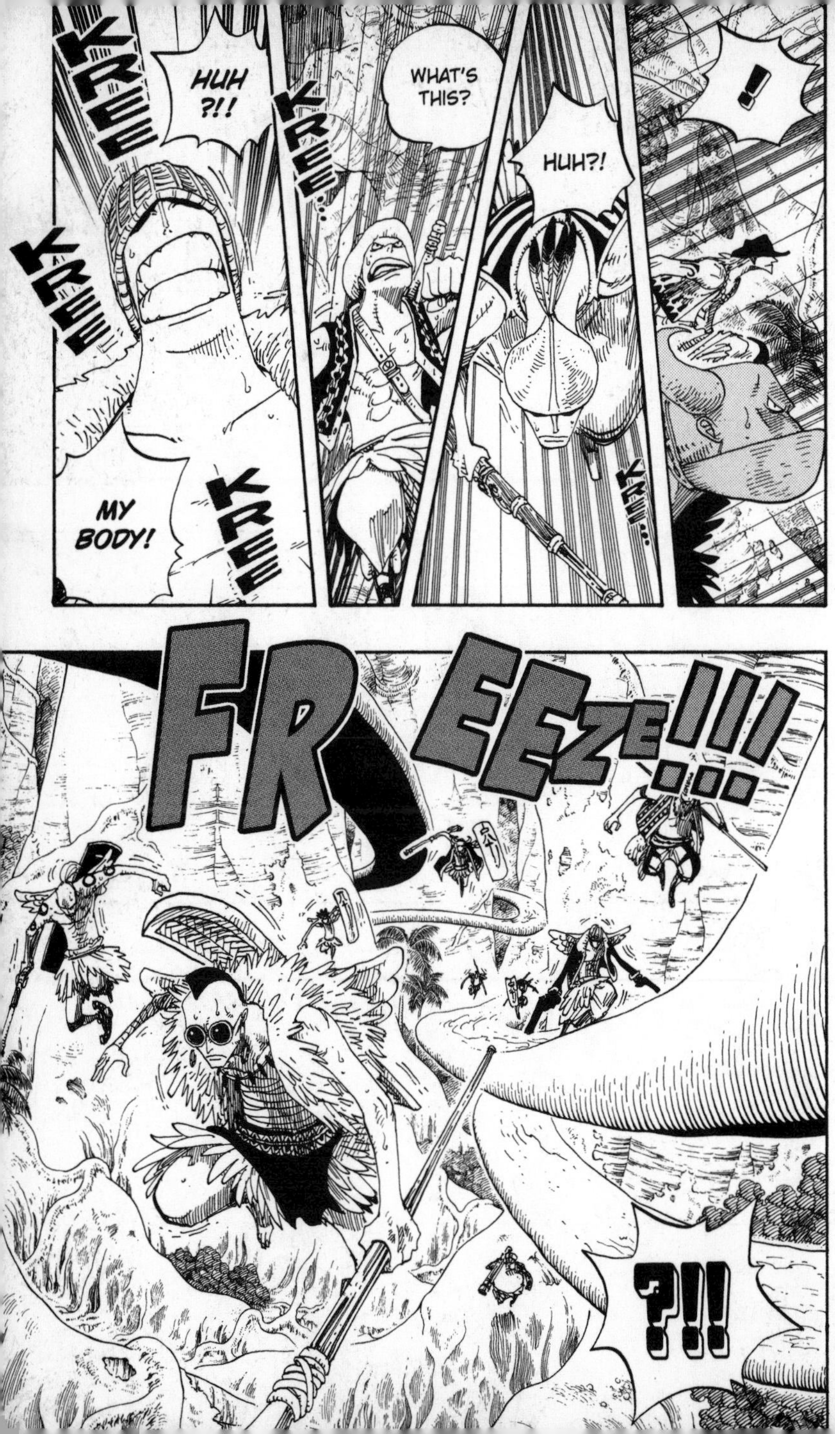
!
HUH?!
KRE...
WHAT'S THIS?
KREE...
HUH ?!!
KREE
KREE
MY BODY!
KREE
FREEZE!!!!...
?!!

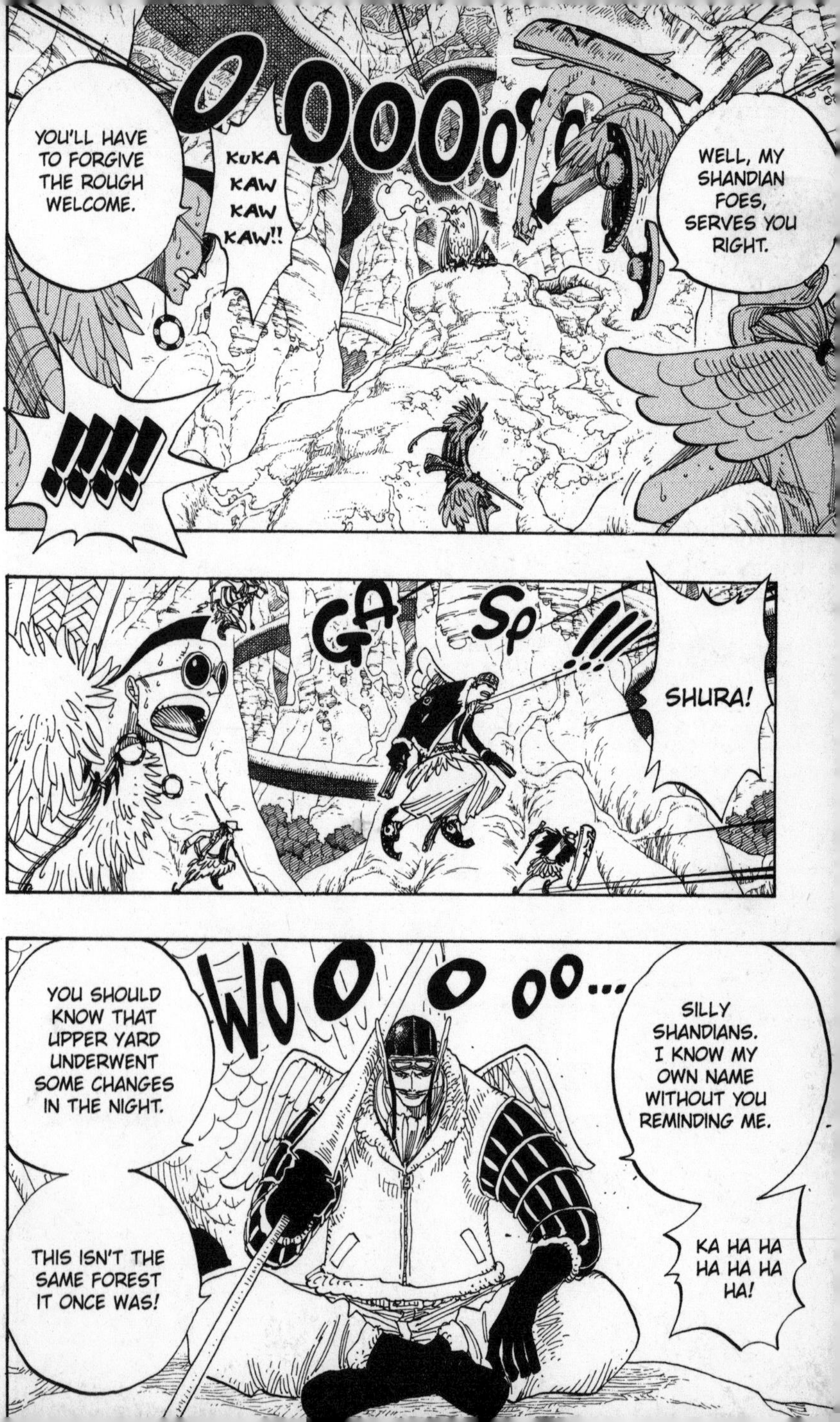
WELL, MY SHANDIAN FOES, SERVES YOU RIGHT.
O OOOOO
KUKA KAW KAW KAW!!
YOU'LL HAVE TO FORGIVE THE ROUGH WELCOME.
!!!!
SHURA!
GA Sp!!!
SILLY SHANDIANS. I KNOW MY OWN NAME WITHOUT YOU REMINDING ME.
KA HA HA HA HA HA HA!
WO O O OO...
YOU SHOULD KNOW THAT UPPER YARD UNDERWENT SOME CHANGES IN THE NIGHT.
THIS ISN'T THE SAME FOREST IT ONCE WAS!

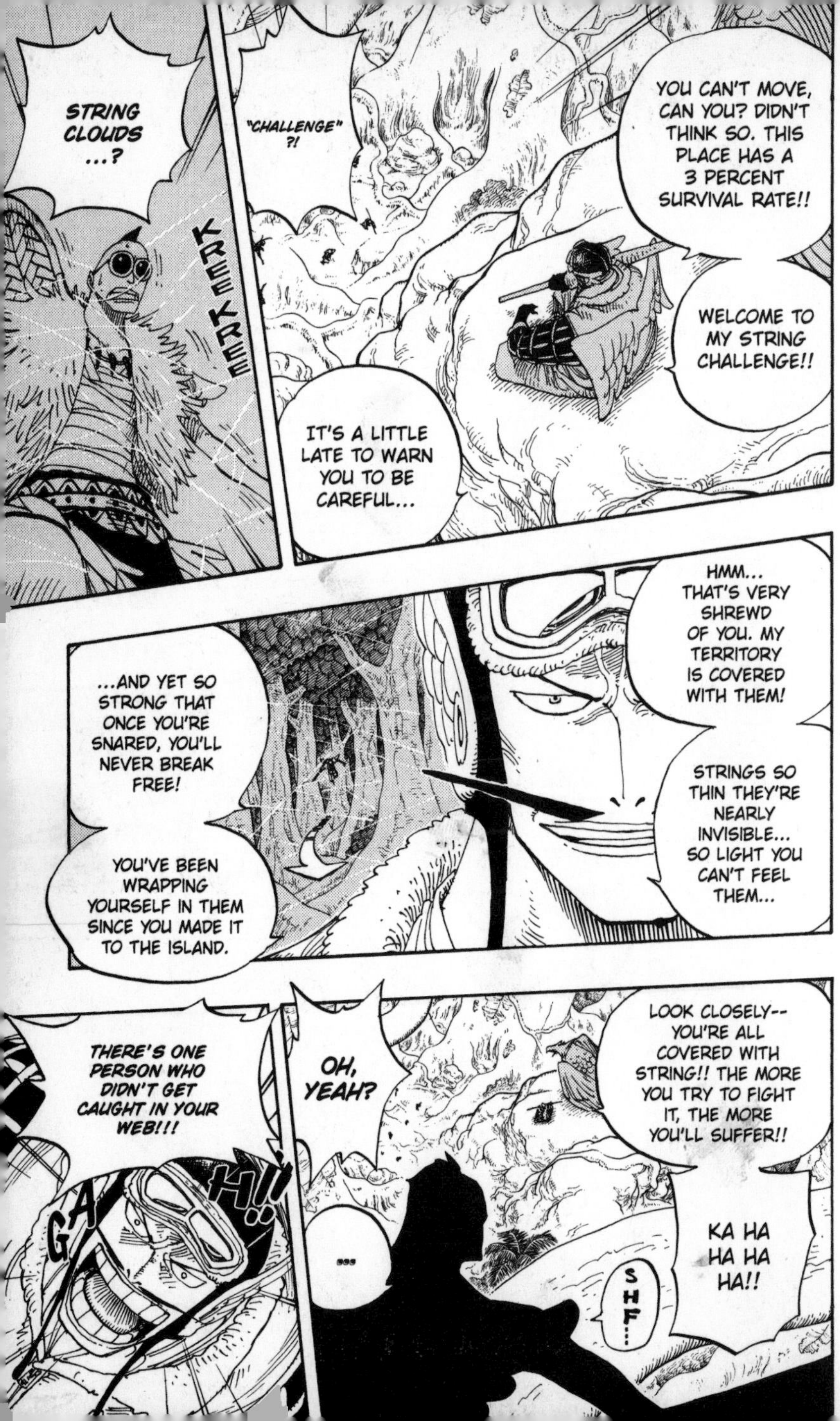
YOU CAN'T MOVE, CAN YOU? DIDN'T THINK SO. THIS PLACE HAS A 3 PERCENT SURVIVAL RATE!!
WELCOME TO MY STRING CHALLENGE!!
IT'S A LITTLE LATE TO WARN YOU TO BE CAREFUL...
"CHALLENGE" ?!
STRING CLOUDS ...?
KREE KREE
HMM... THAT'S VERY SHREWD OF YOU. MY TERRITORY IS COVERED WITH THEM!
STRINGS SO THIN THEY'RE NEARLY INVISIBLE... SO LIGHT YOU CAN'T FEEL THEM...
...AND YET SO STRONG THAT ONCE YOU'RE SNARED, YOU'LL NEVER BREAK FREE!
YOU'VE BEEN WRAPPING YOURSELF IN THEM SINCE YOU MADE IT TO THE ISLAND.
LOOK CLOSELY-- YOU'RE ALL COVERED WITH STRING!! THE MORE YOU TRY TO FIGHT IT, THE MORE YOU'LL SUFFER!!
KA HA HA HA HA!!
SHF...
OH, YEAH?
...
THERE'S ONE PERSON WHO DIDN'T GET CAUGHT IN YOUR WEB!!!
GAH!!

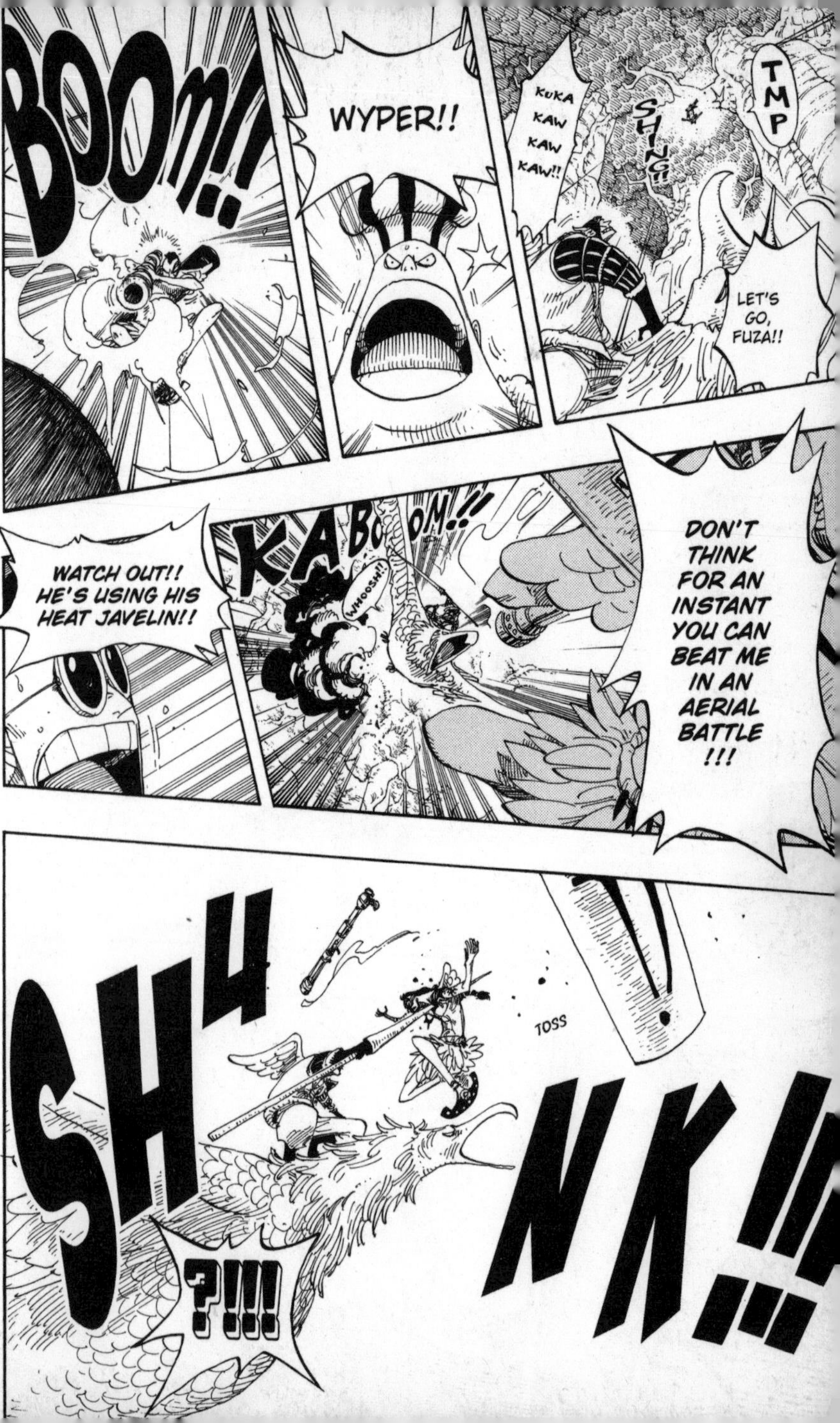
TMP
SHING!!
KUKA KAW KAW KAW!!
LET'S GO, FUZA!!
WYPER!!
BOOM!!
DON'T THINK FOR AN INSTANT YOU CAN BEAT ME IN AN AERIAL BATTLE!!!
KABOOM!!
WHOOSH!!
WATCH OUT!! HE'S USING HIS HEAT JAVELIN!!
TOSS
SHUNK!!
?!!!

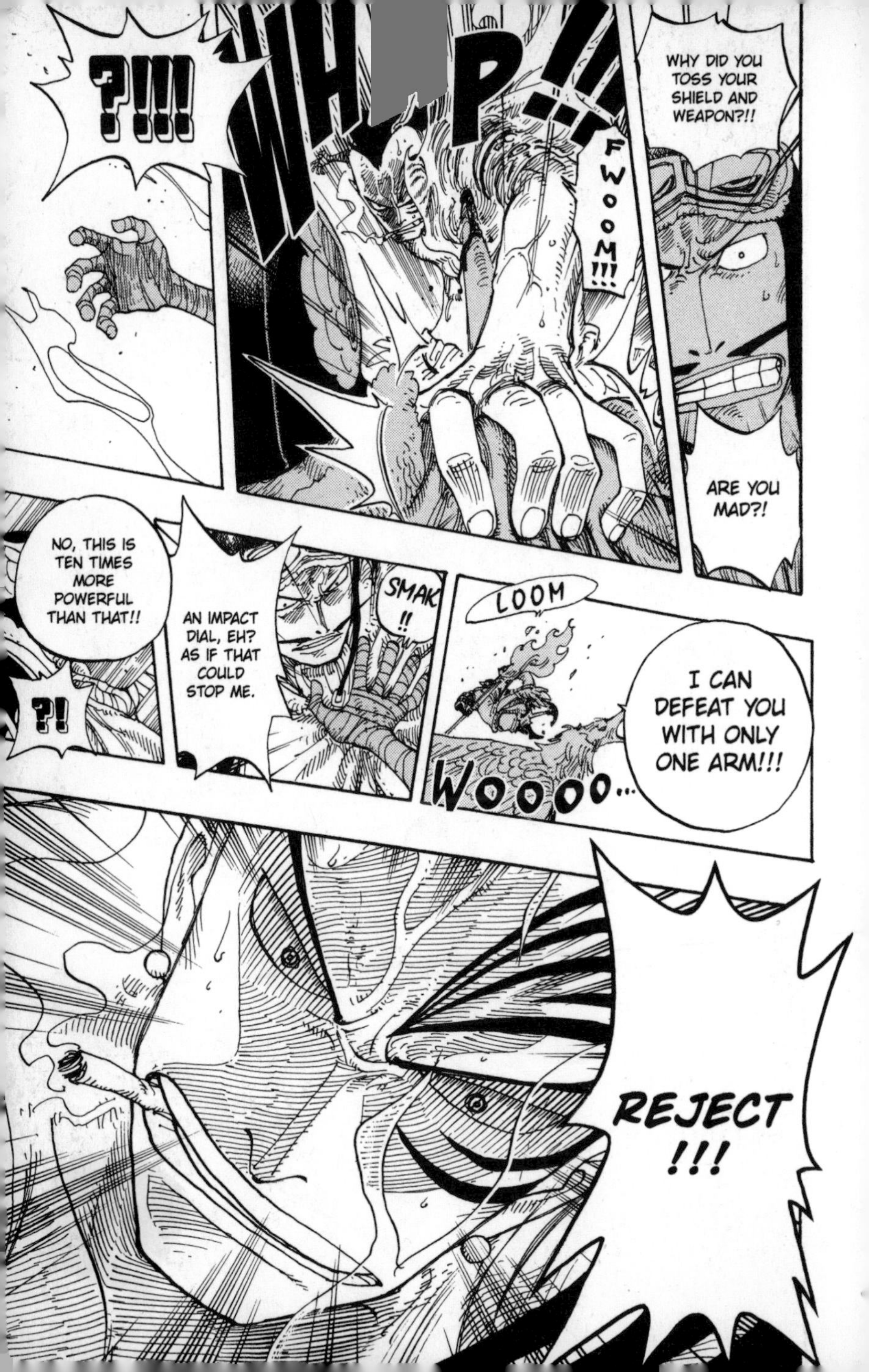
WHY DID YOU TOSS YOUR SHIELD AND WEAPON?!!
ARE YOU MAD?!
WH P!!
FWOOM!!!
?!!!
LOOM
I CAN DEFEAT YOU WITH ONLY ONE ARM!!!
WOOOO...
SMAK!!
AN IMPACT DIAL, EH? AS IF THAT COULD STOP ME.
NO, THIS IS TEN TIMES MORE POWERFUL THAN THAT!!
?!
REJECT!!!

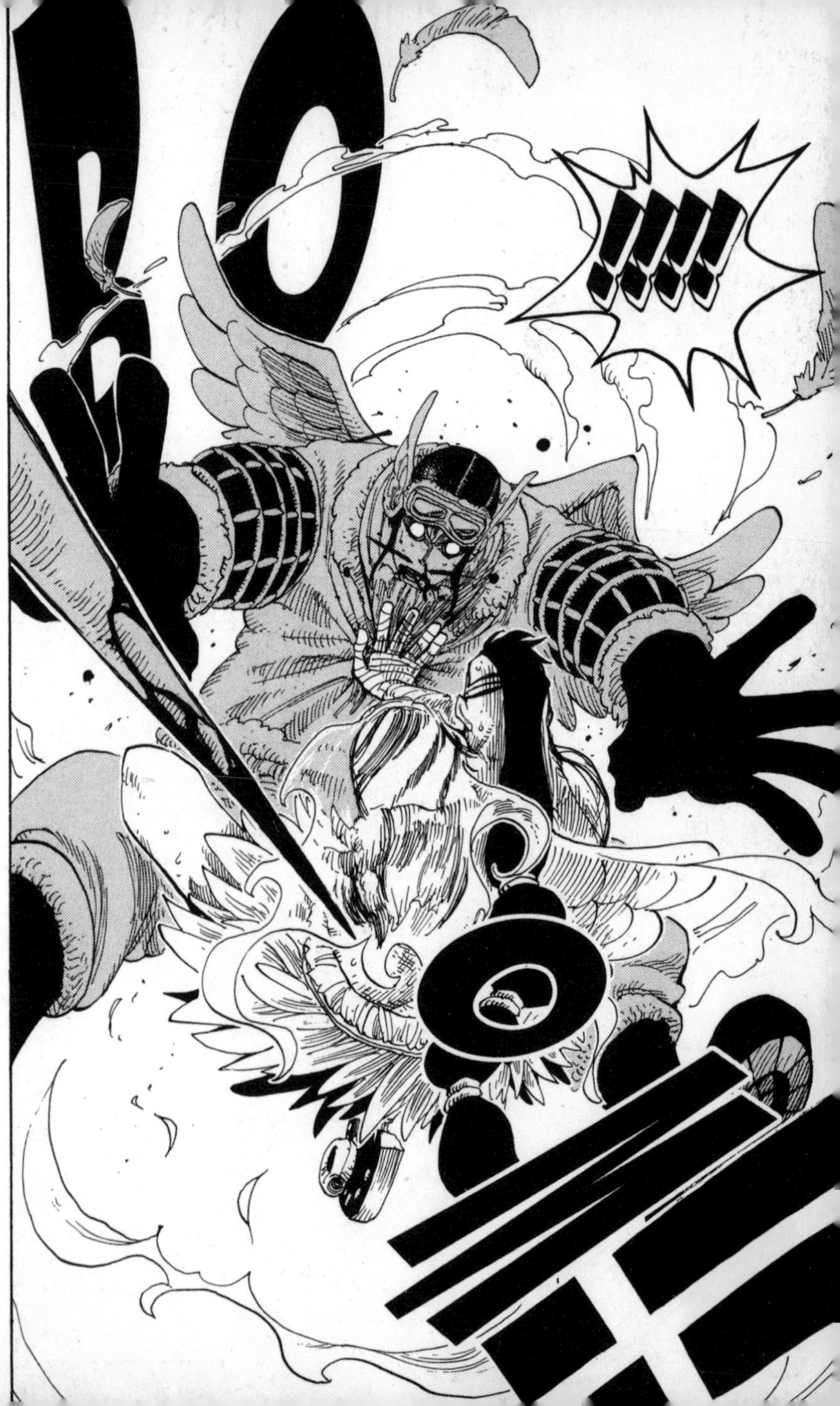
!!!!
BOOM

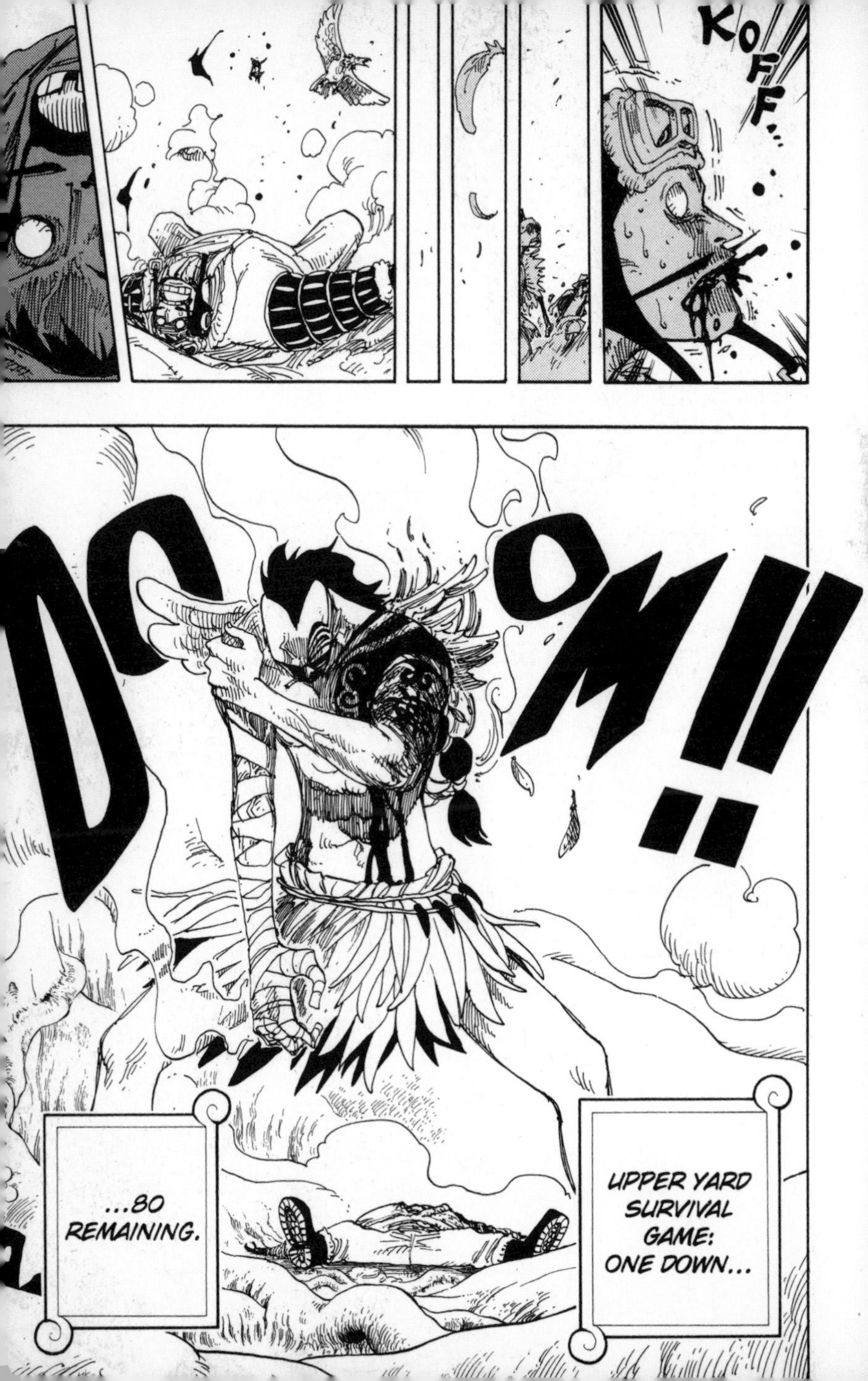
KOFF...
DOOM!!
UPPER YARD SURVIVAL GAME: ONE DOWN...
...80 REMAINING.

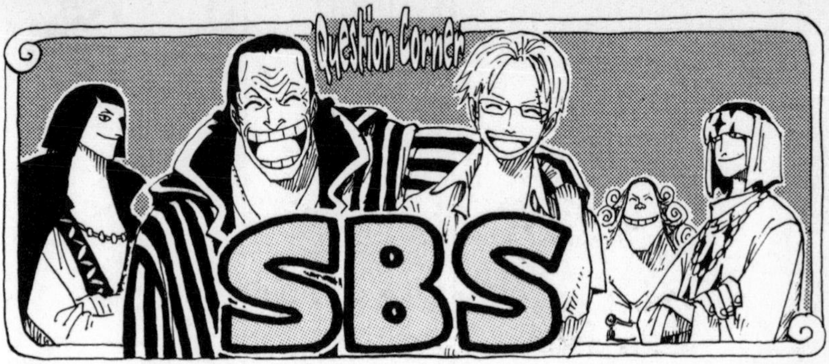
Question Corner
SBS

Reader: Hello, Oda Sensei. Let me tell you about my dream! *One Piece* has inspired me to become an animator. And so it would mean a lot to me if you would let me say it, just this once! Please!! And now… "For all you *One Piece* readers, let's begin the Question Corner!!"
Ahh, I said it. Thank you very much.

-- Octopus Girl

Oda: Choke!! Gasp!! Dah!! Huff Huff...
Whoa, that was close. I nearly couldn't pull my finger out of my nose. Everyone, when picking your nose, be careful not to stick your finger too far up! Anyway, it seems like we've begun the Question Corner!

Q: O great and wise Oda Sensei, May I ask one--JUST ONE--question? Can I? Huh?! Okay?! Yes!! Well then, I humbly ask you this one question: ***WHAT SPECIES ARE YOU?!***

A: I'm human, you idiot! Okay, next!!

Q: Hello!! I know it's sudden, but I came up with a new technique for Luffy. I'm gonna try it out on you, Odacchi, so counter it.
Gum-Gum GUM!! How was that?

-- Gramps

A: Agh! I got hit! It's a bit...gummy!
Hmm. How was that? Okay? Anyway, moving on...

Chapter 257:
DIAL BATTLE

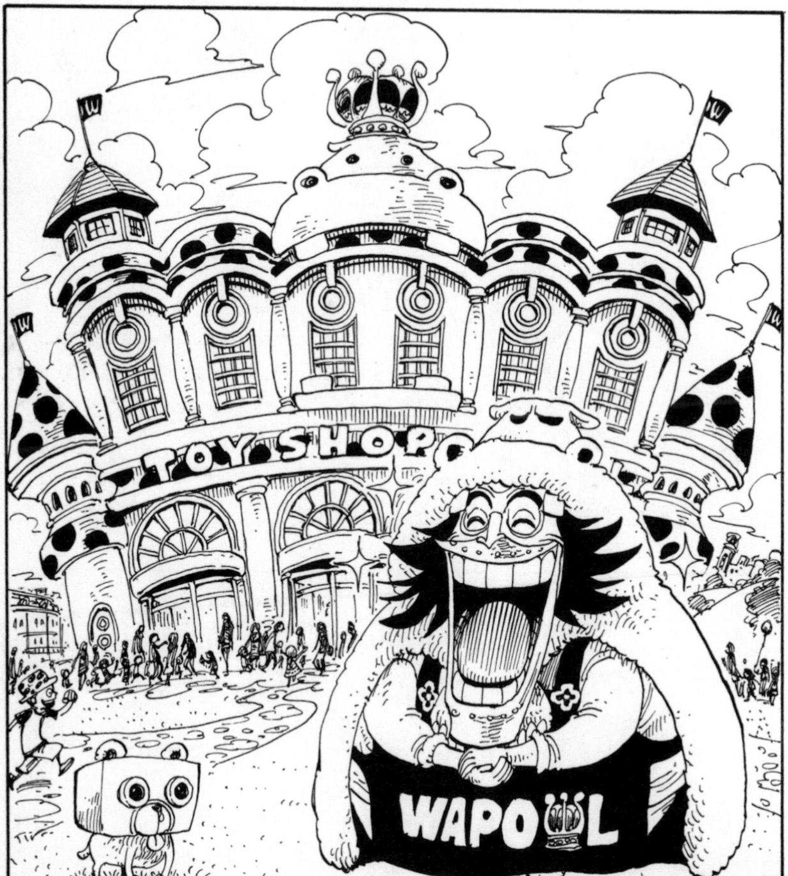
TOY SHOP
WAPOL

WAPOL'S OMNIVOROUS RAMPAGE, VOL. 19:
"WAPOL'S TOY SHOP EXPANDS!"

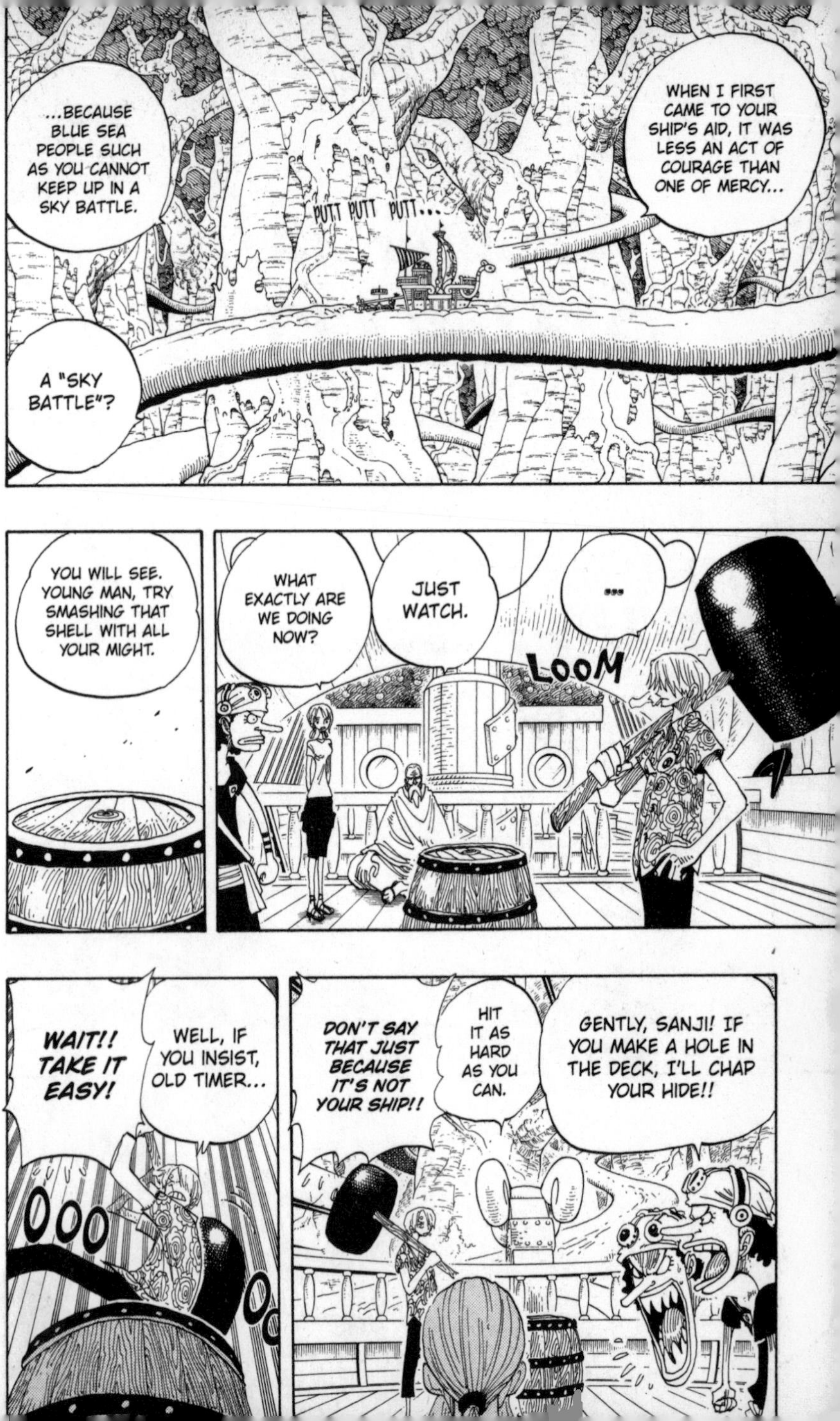
WHEN I FIRST CAME TO YOUR SHIP'S AID, IT WAS LESS AN ACT OF COURAGE THAN ONE OF MERCY...
...BECAUSE BLUE SEA PEOPLE SUCH AS YOU CANNOT KEEP UP IN A SKY BATTLE.
PUTT PUTT PUTT...
A "SKY BATTLE"?
...
LOOM
JUST WATCH.
WHAT EXACTLY ARE WE DOING NOW?
YOU WILL SEE. YOUNG MAN, TRY SMASHING THAT SHELL WITH ALL YOUR MIGHT.
GENTLY, SANJI! IF YOU MAKE A HOLE IN THE DECK, I'LL CHAP YOUR HIDE!!
HIT IT AS HARD AS YOU CAN.
DON'T SAY THAT JUST BECAUSE IT'S NOT YOUR SHIP!!
WELL, IF YOU INSIST, OLD TIMER...
WAIT!! TAKE IT EASY!
OOO

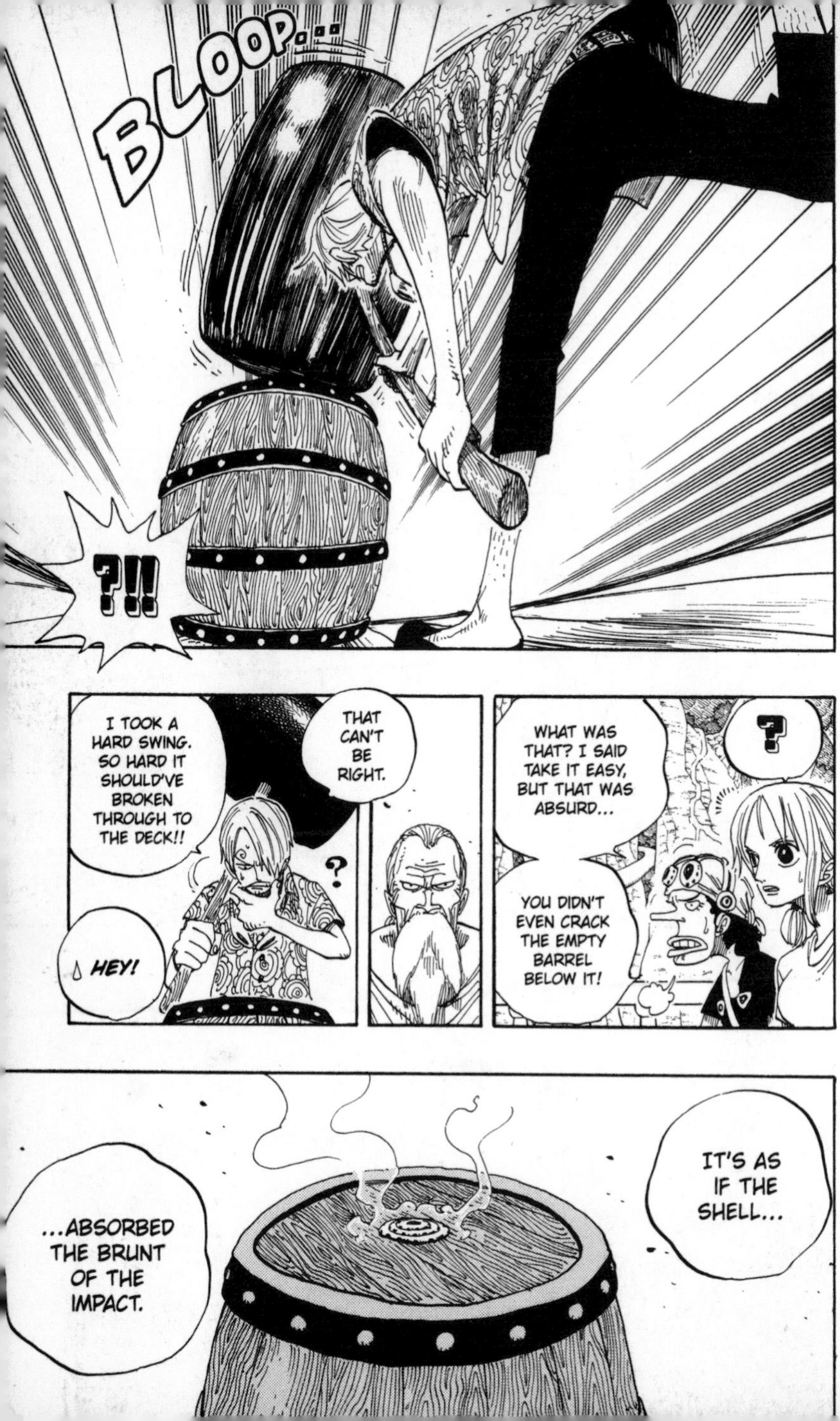
BLOOP...
?!!
?
WHAT WAS THAT? I SAID TAKE IT EASY, BUT THAT WAS ABSURD...
YOU DIDN'T EVEN CRACK THE EMPTY BARREL BELOW IT!
THAT CAN'T BE RIGHT.
I TOOK A HARD SWING. SO HARD IT SHOULD'VE BROKEN THROUGH TO THE DECK!!
?
HEY!
IT'S AS IF THE SHELL...
...ABSORBED THE BRUNT OF THE IMPACT.

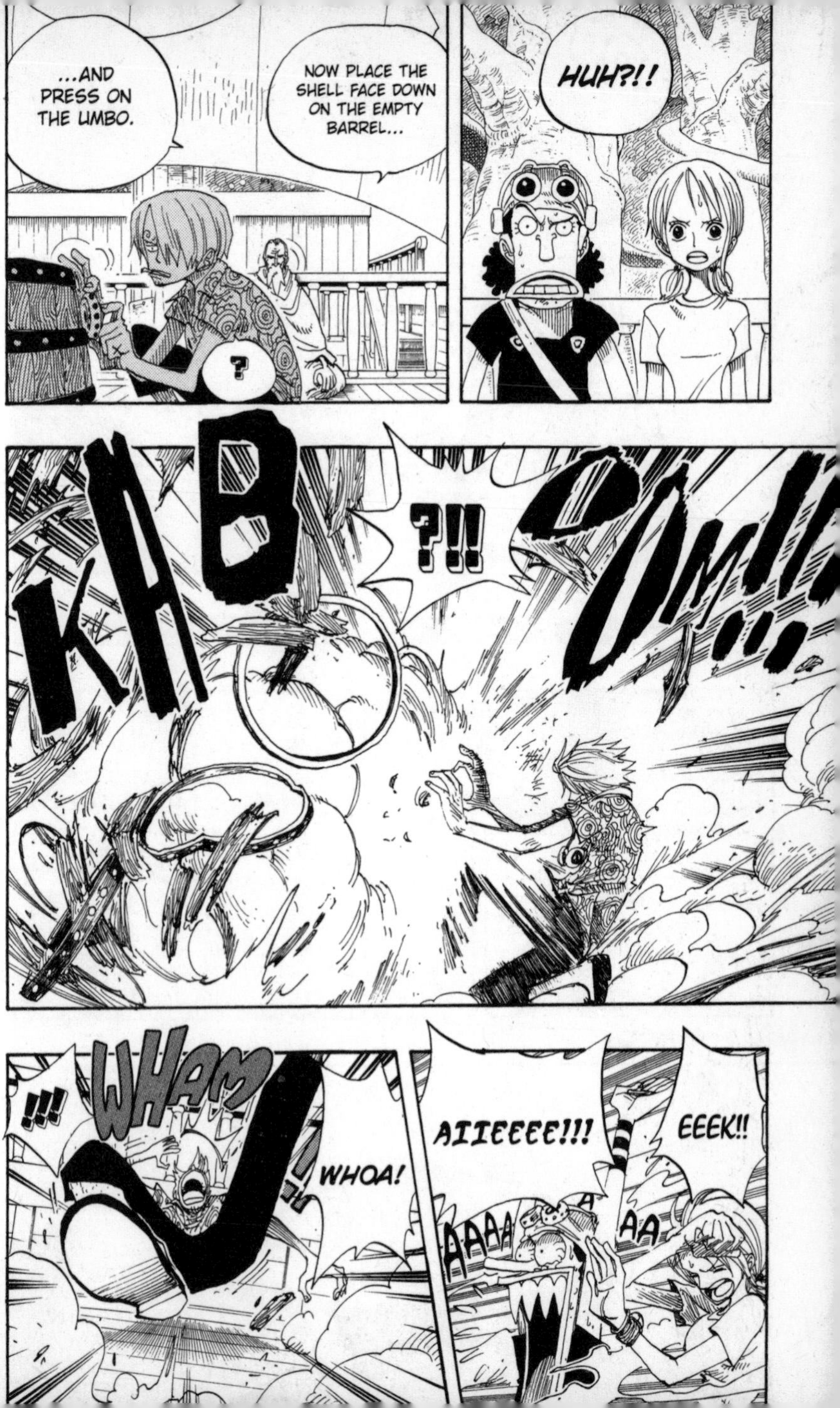
HUH?!!
NOW PLACE THE SHELL FACE DOWN ON THE EMPTY BARREL...
...AND PRESS ON THE UMBO.
?
?!!
KAB
OOM!!!
EEEK!!
AIIEEEE!!!
AA
A
AAAA
WHOA!
WHAM
!!!

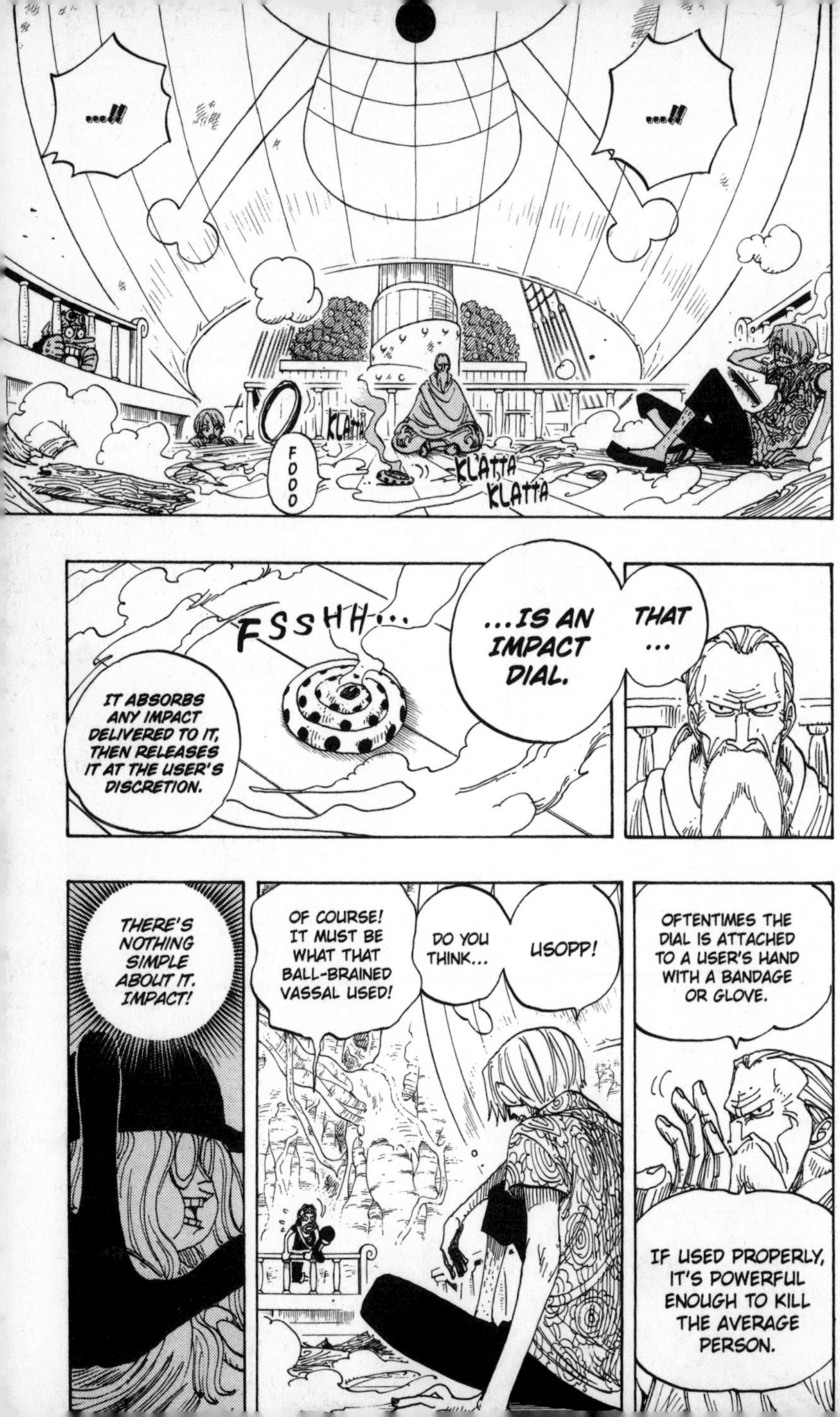
...!!
...!!
KLATTA KLATTA
KLATTA
FOOO
THAT...
...IS AN IMPACT DIAL.
FSSHH...
IT ABSORBS ANY IMPACT DELIVERED TO IT, THEN RELEASES IT AT THE USER'S DISCRETION.
OFTENTIMES THE DIAL IS ATTACHED TO A USER'S HAND WITH A BANDAGE OR GLOVE.
IF USED PROPERLY, IT'S POWERFUL ENOUGH TO KILL THE AVERAGE PERSON.
USOPP!
DO YOU THINK...
OF COURSE! IT MUST BE WHAT THAT BALL-BRAINED VASSAL USED!
THERE'S NOTHING SIMPLE ABOUT IT. IMPACT!

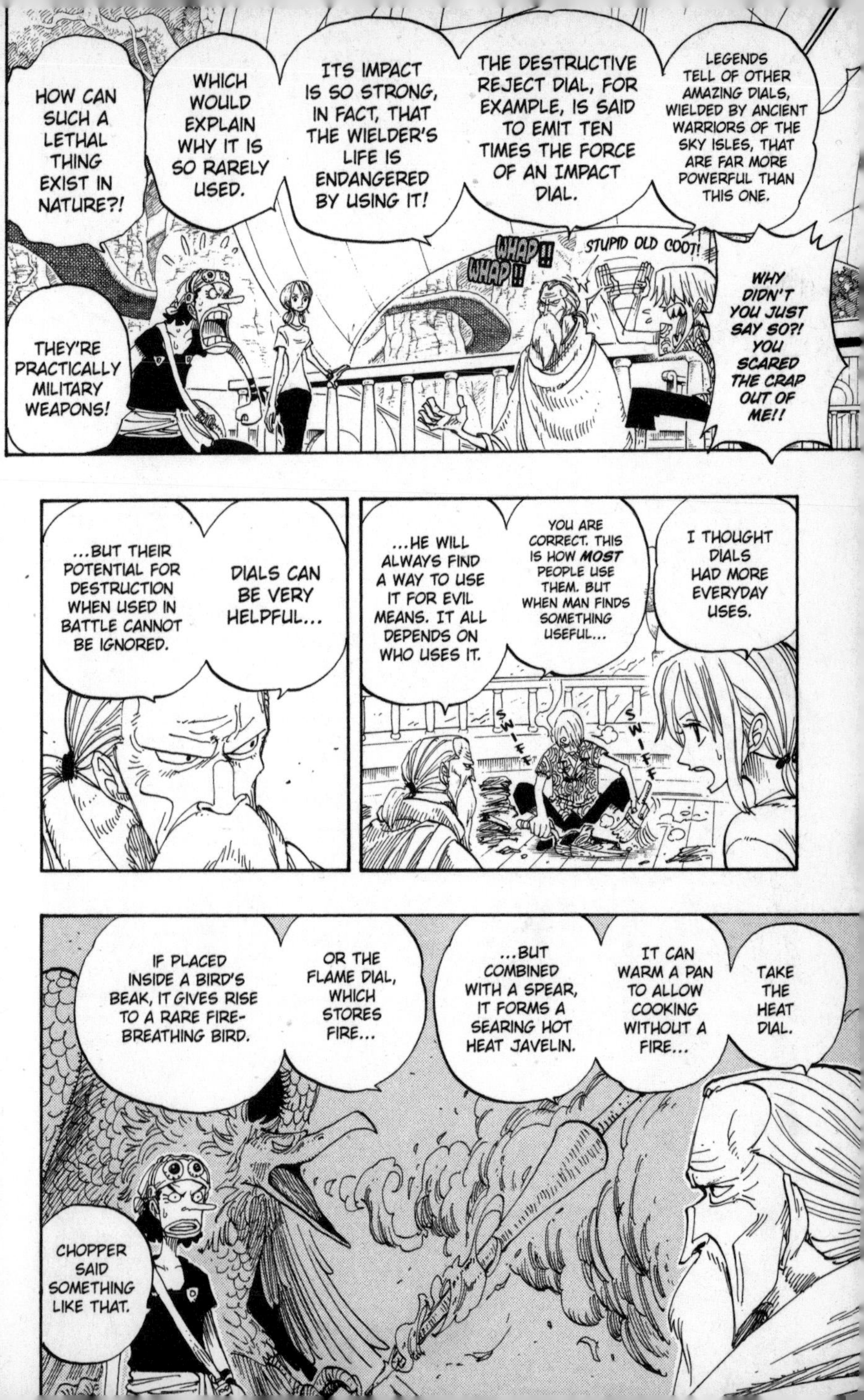
LEGENDS TELL OF OTHER AMAZING DIALS, WIELDED BY ANCIENT WARRIORS OF THE SKY ISLES, THAT ARE FAR MORE POWERFUL THAN THIS ONE.
THE DESTRUCTIVE REJECT DIAL, FOR EXAMPLE, IS SAID TO EMIT TEN TIMES THE FORCE OF AN IMPACT DIAL.
ITS IMPACT IS SO STRONG, IN FACT, THAT THE WIELDER'S LIFE IS ENDANGERED BY USING IT!
WHICH WOULD EXPLAIN WHY IT IS SO RARELY USED.
HOW CAN SUCH A LETHAL THING EXIST IN NATURE?!
WHY DIDN'T YOU JUST SAY SO?! YOU SCARED THE CRAP OUT OF ME!!
STUPID OLD COOT!
WHAP!!
WHAP!!
THEY'RE PRACTICALLY MILITARY WEAPONS!
I THOUGHT DIALS HAD MORE EVERYDAY USES.
YOU ARE CORRECT. THIS IS HOW MOST PEOPLE USE THEM. BUT WHEN MAN FINDS SOMETHING USEFUL...
...HE WILL ALWAYS FIND A WAY TO USE IT FOR EVIL MEANS. IT ALL DEPENDS ON WHO USES IT.
SWIFF
SWIFF
DIALS CAN BE VERY HELPFUL...
...BUT THEIR POTENTIAL FOR DESTRUCTION WHEN USED IN BATTLE CANNOT BE IGNORED.
TAKE THE HEAT DIAL.
IT CAN WARM A PAN TO ALLOW COOKING WITHOUT A FIRE...
...BUT COMBINED WITH A SPEAR, IT FORMS A SEARING HOT HEAT JAVELIN.
OR THE FLAME DIAL, WHICH STORES FIRE...
IF PLACED INSIDE A BIRD'S BEAK, IT GIVES RISE TO A RARE FIRE-BREATHING BIRD.
CHOPPER SAID SOMETHING LIKE THAT.

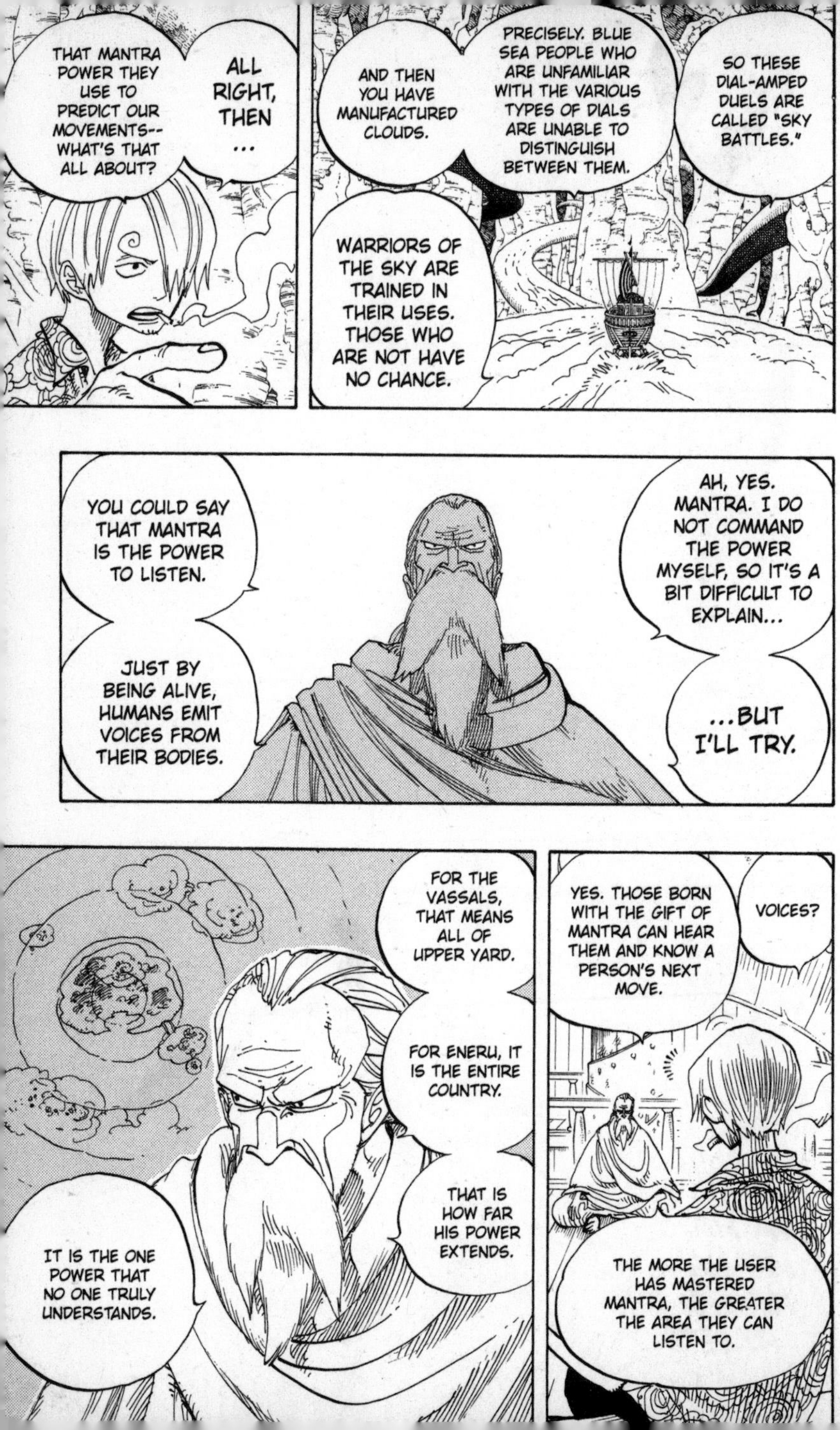
SO THESE DIAL-AMPED DUELS ARE CALLED "SKY BATTLES."
PRECISELY. BLUE SEA PEOPLE WHO ARE UNFAMILIAR WITH THE VARIOUS TYPES OF DIALS ARE UNABLE TO DISTINGUISH BETWEEN THEM.
AND THEN YOU HAVE MANUFACTURED CLOUDS.
WARRIORS OF THE SKY ARE TRAINED IN THEIR USES. THOSE WHO ARE NOT HAVE NO CHANCE.
ALL RIGHT, THEN ...
THAT MANTRA POWER THEY USE TO PREDICT OUR MOVEMENTS-- WHAT'S THAT ALL ABOUT?
AH, YES. MANTRA. I DO NOT COMMAND THE POWER MYSELF, SO IT'S A BIT DIFFICULT TO EXPLAIN...
...BUT I'LL TRY.
YOU COULD SAY THAT MANTRA IS THE POWER TO LISTEN.
JUST BY BEING ALIVE, HUMANS EMIT VOICES FROM THEIR BODIES.
VOICES?
YES. THOSE BORN WITH THE GIFT OF MANTRA CAN HEAR THEM AND KNOW A PERSON'S NEXT MOVE.
THE MORE THE USER HAS MASTERED MANTRA, THE GREATER THE AREA THEY CAN LISTEN TO.
FOR THE VASSALS, THAT MEANS ALL OF UPPER YARD.
FOR ENERU, IT IS THE ENTIRE COUNTRY.
THAT IS HOW FAR HIS POWER EXTENDS.
IT IS THE ONE POWER THAT NO ONE TRULY UNDERSTANDS.

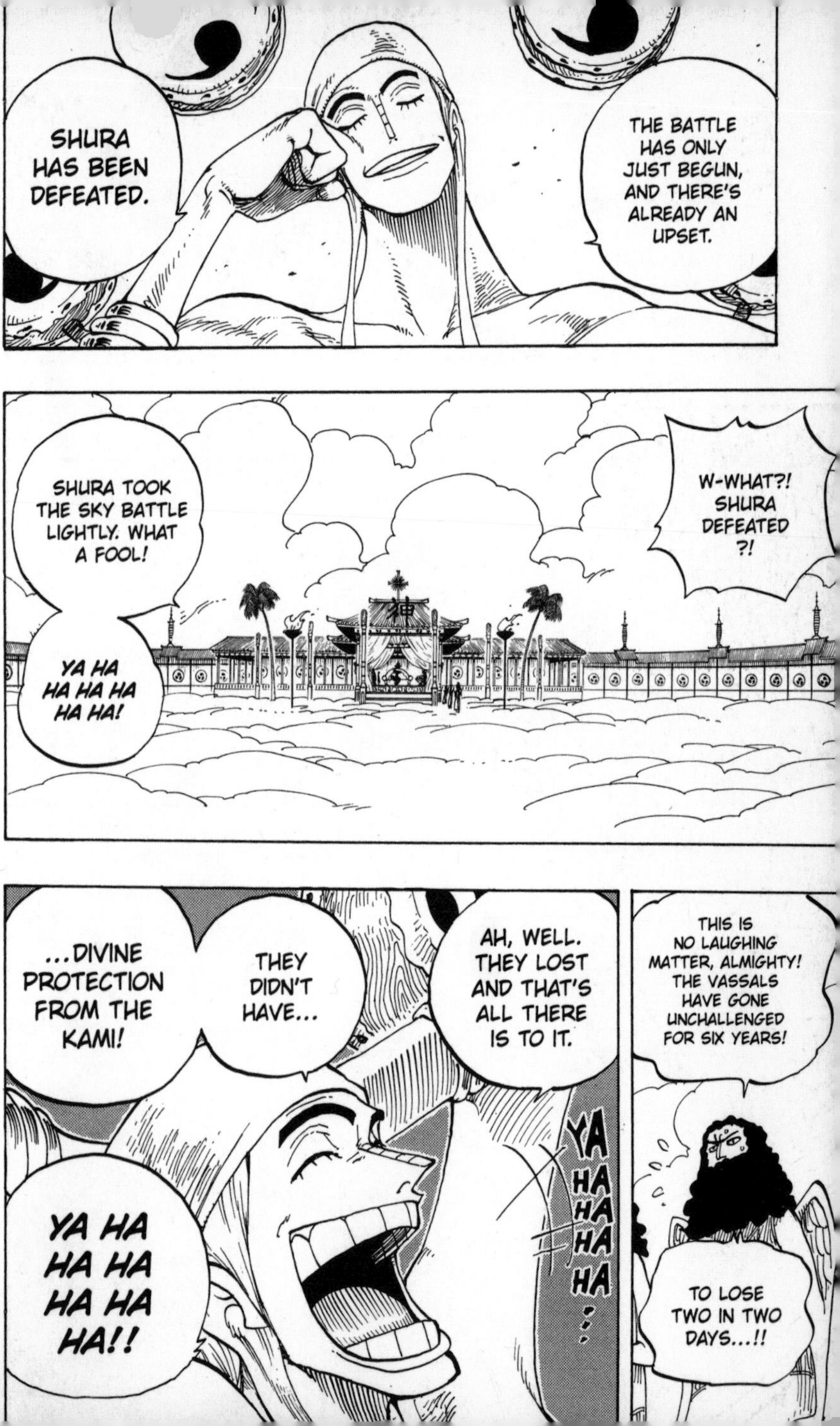
THE BATTLE HAS ONLY JUST BEGUN, AND THERE'S ALREADY AN UPSET.
SHURA HAS BEEN DEFEATED.
W-WHAT?! SHURA DEFEATED?!
SHURA TOOK THE SKY BATTLE LIGHTLY. WHAT A FOOL!
YA HA HA HA HA HA HA!
神
THIS IS NO LAUGHING MATTER, ALMIGHTY! THE VASSALS HAVE GONE UNCHALLENGED FOR SIX YEARS!
TO LOSE TWO IN TWO DAYS...!!
AH, WELL. THEY LOST AND THAT'S ALL THERE IS TO IT.
THEY DIDN'T HAVE...
...DIVINE PROTECTION FROM THE KAMI!
YA HA HA HA HA HA HA!!
YA HA HA HA HA HA...

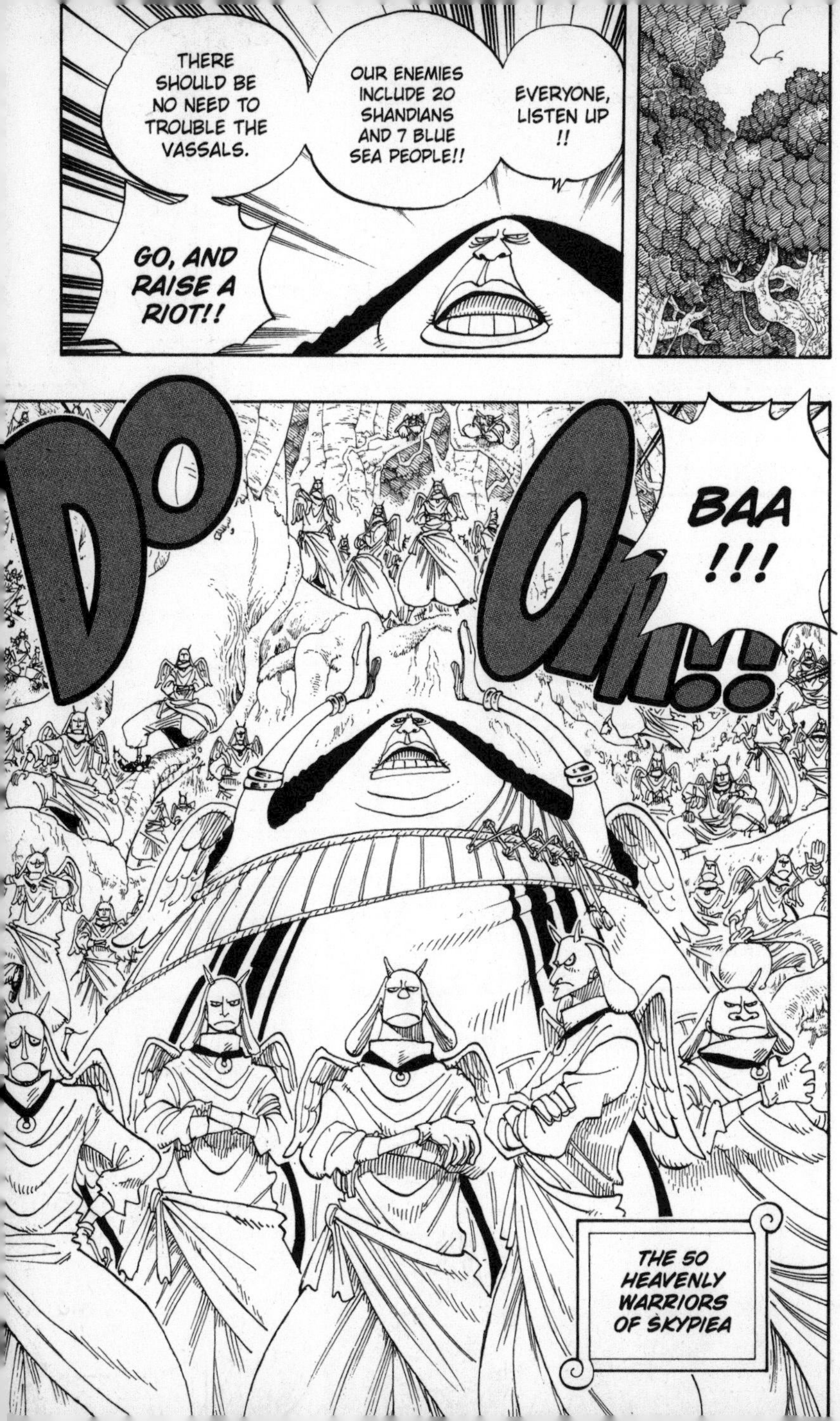
EVERYONE, LISTEN UP!!
OUR ENEMIES INCLUDE 20 SHANDIANS AND 7 BLUE SEA PEOPLE!!
THERE SHOULD BE NO NEED TO TROUBLE THE VASSALS.
GO, AND RAISE A RIOT!!
BAA!!!
THE 50 HEAVENLY WARRIORS OF SKYPIEA

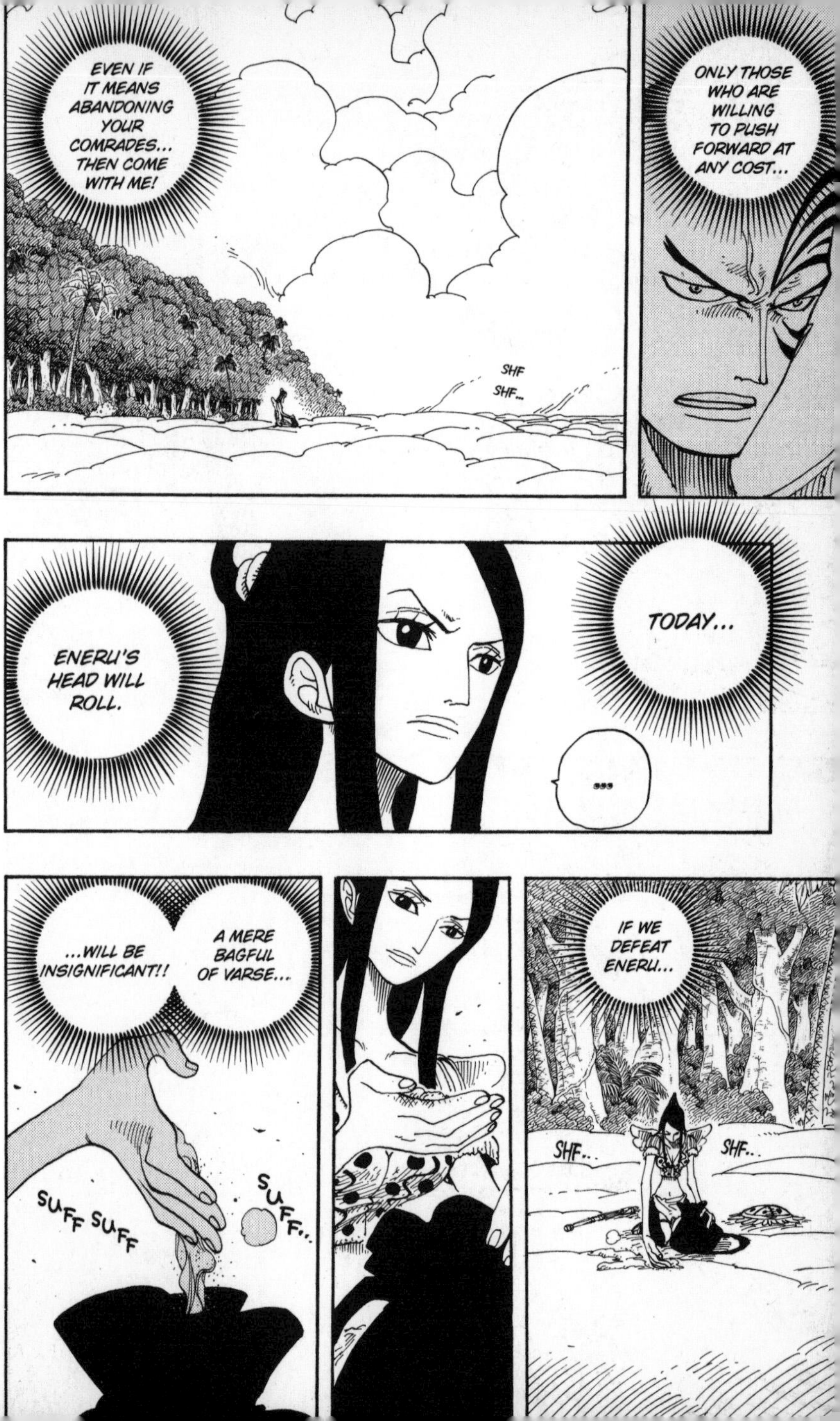
ONLY THOSE WHO ARE WILLING TO PUSH FORWARD AT ANY COST...
EVEN IF IT MEANS ABANDONING YOUR COMRADES... THEN COME WITH ME!
SHF SHF...
TODAY...
ENERU'S HEAD WILL ROLL.
...
IF WE DEFEAT ENERU...
SHF...
SHF...
A MERE BAGFUL OF VARSE...
...WILL BE INSIGNIFICANT!!
SUFF...
SUFF SUFF

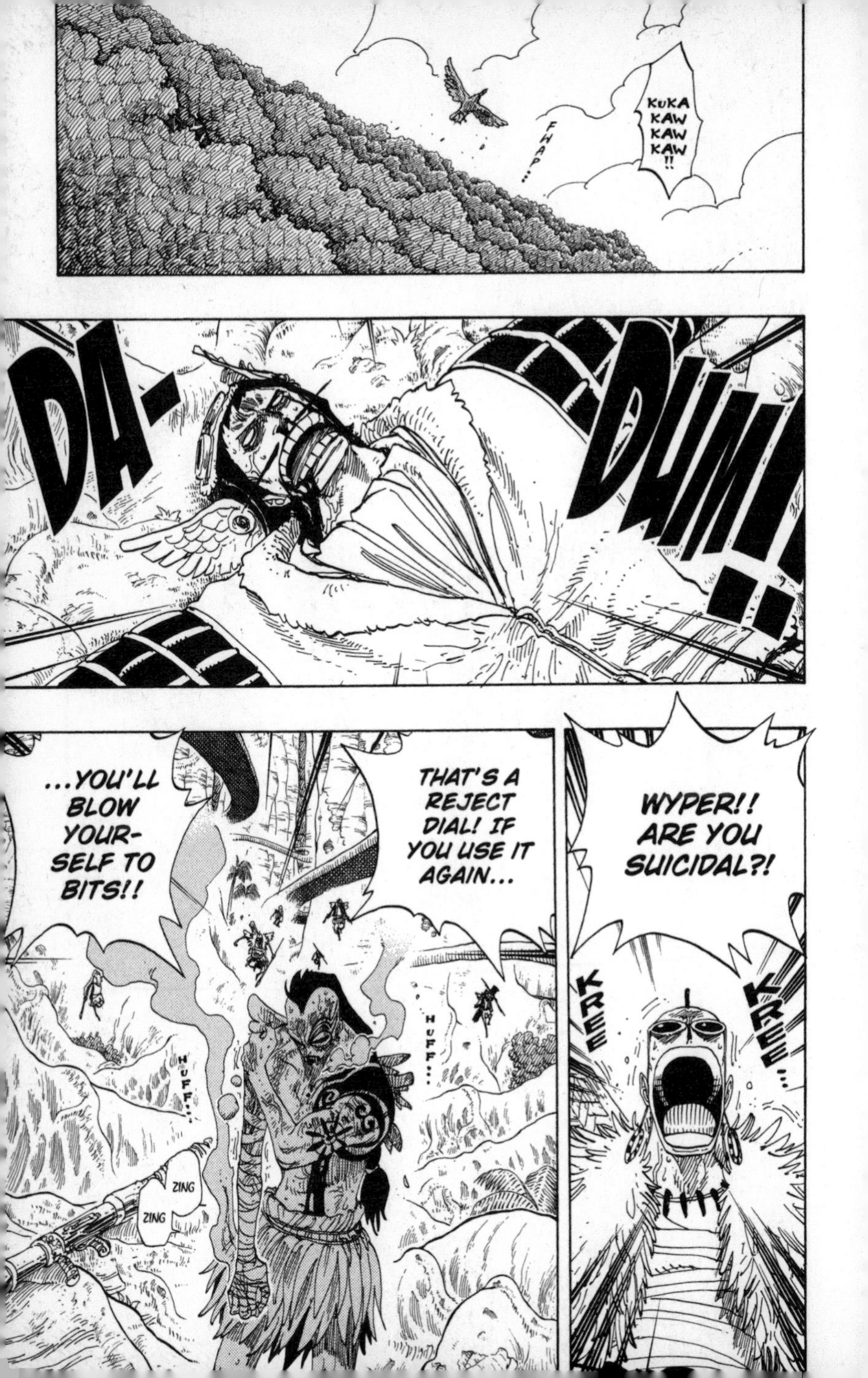
KUKA KAW KAW KAW!!
FWAP...
DA-DUM!!
WYPER!! ARE YOU SUICIDAL?!
KREE
KREE...
THAT'S A REJECT DIAL! IF YOU USE IT AGAIN...
...YOU'LL BLOW YOUR-SELF TO BITS!!
HUFF...
HUFF...
ZING
ZING

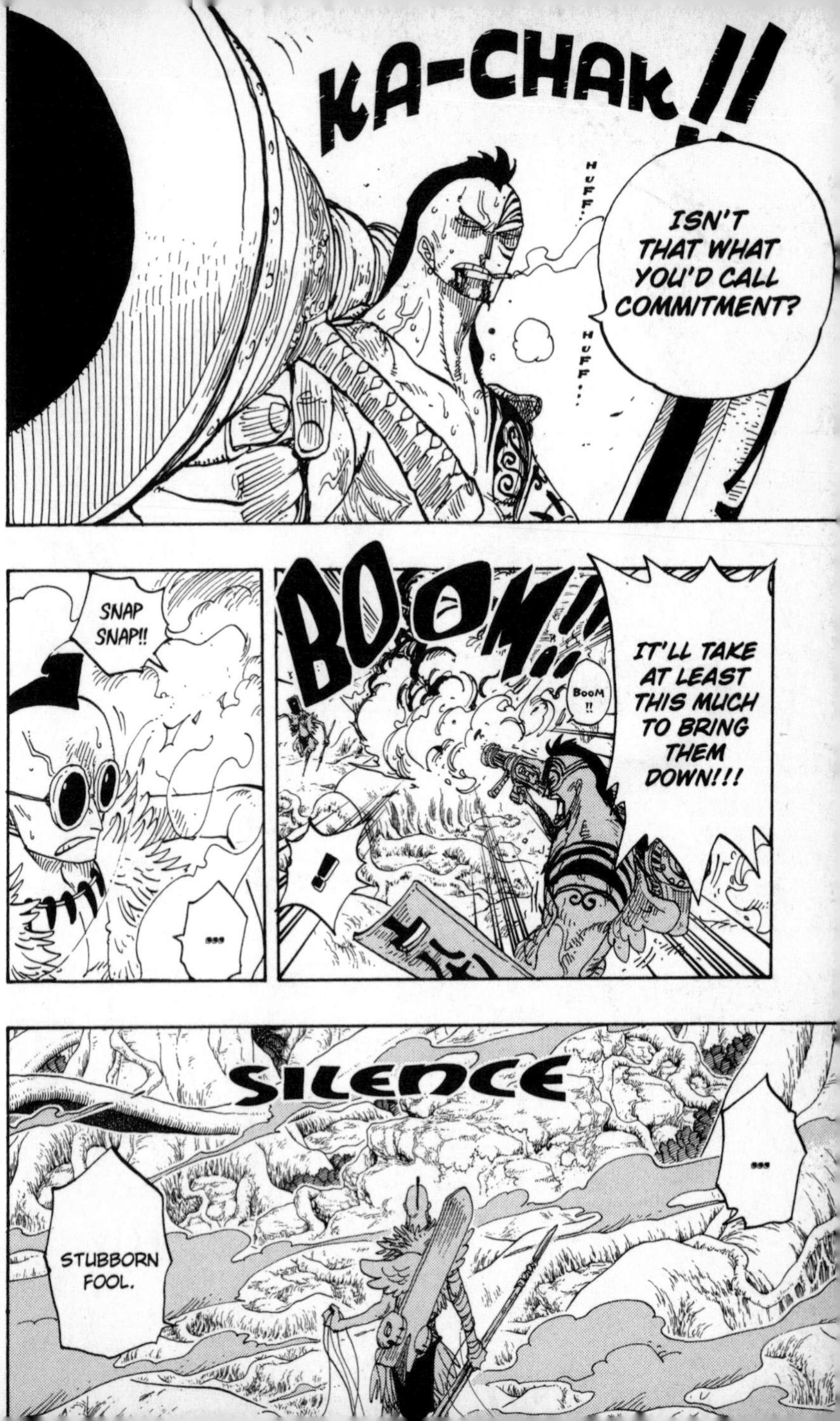
KA-CHAK!!
HUFF...
ISN'T THAT WHAT YOU'D CALL COMMITMENT?
HUFF...
BOOM!!
IT'LL TAKE AT LEAST THIS MUCH TO BRING THEM DOWN!!!
BOOM!!
!
SNAP SNAP!!
...
SILENCE
...
STUBBORN FOOL.

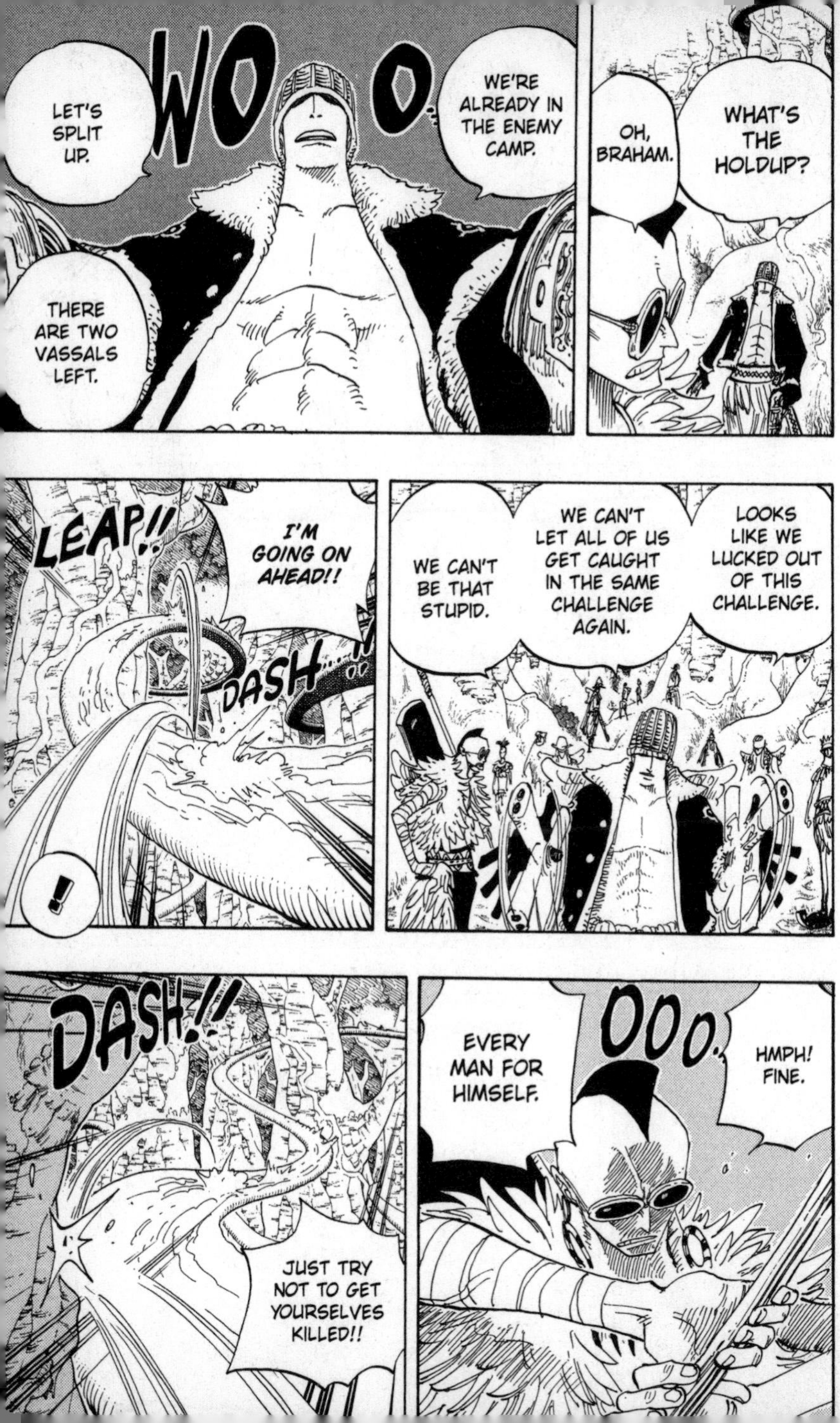
WHAT'S THE HOLDUP?
OH, BRAHAM.
WE'RE ALREADY IN THE ENEMY CAMP.
WOO..
LET'S SPLIT UP.
THERE ARE TWO VASSALS LEFT.
LOOKS LIKE WE LUCKED OUT OF THIS CHALLENGE.
WE CAN'T LET ALL OF US GET CAUGHT IN THE SAME CHALLENGE AGAIN.
WE CAN'T BE THAT STUPID.
LEAP!!
I'M GOING ON AHEAD!!
DASH......
!
HMPH! FINE.
OOO.
EVERY MAN FOR HIMSELF.
DASH!!
JUST TRY NOT TO GET YOURSELVES KILLED!!

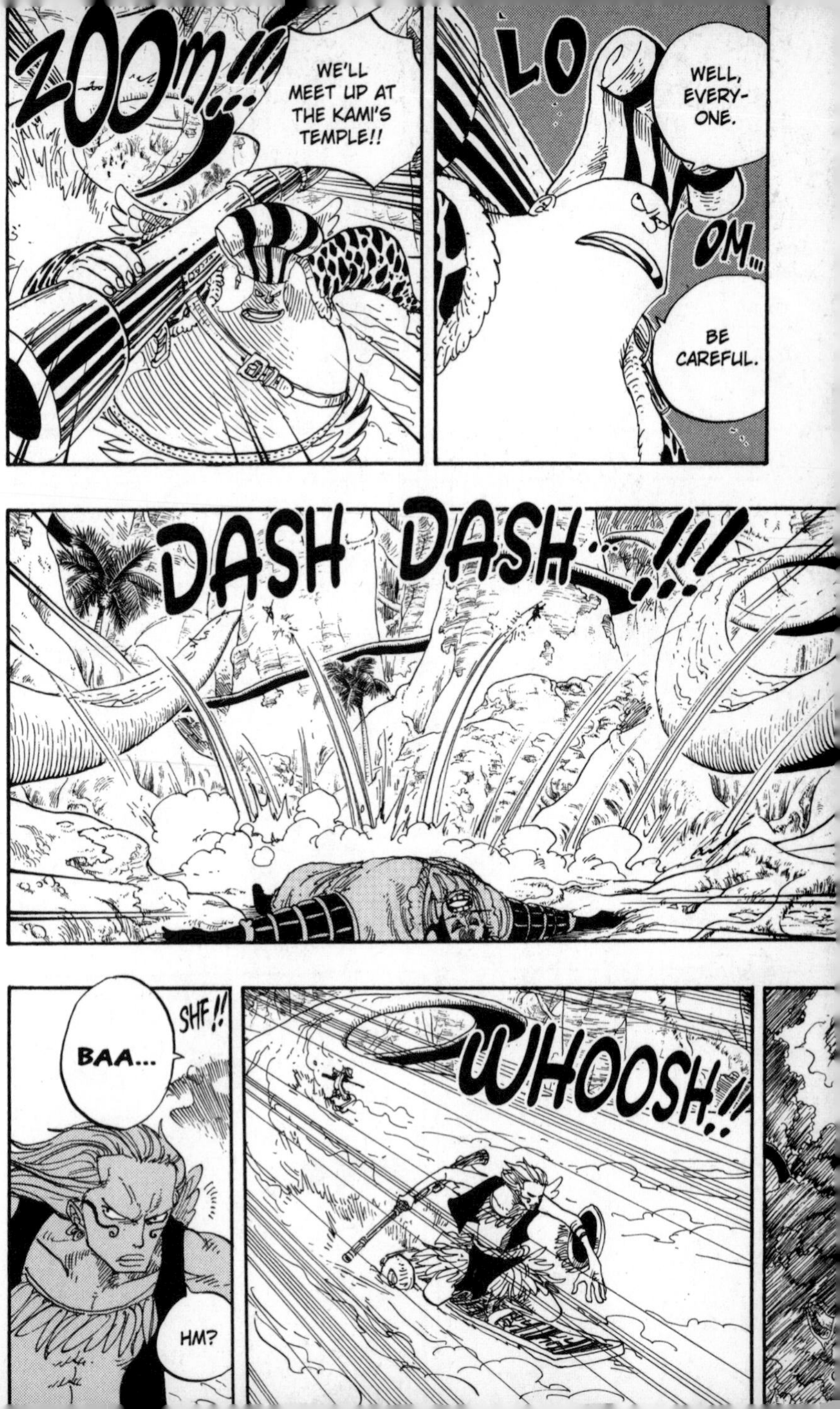
LO
WELL, EVERY-ONE.
OM...
BE CAREFUL.
ZOOM...!!
WE'LL MEET UP AT THE KAMI'S TEMPLE!!
DASH DASH...!!!
WHOOSH!!
SHF!!
BAA...
HM?

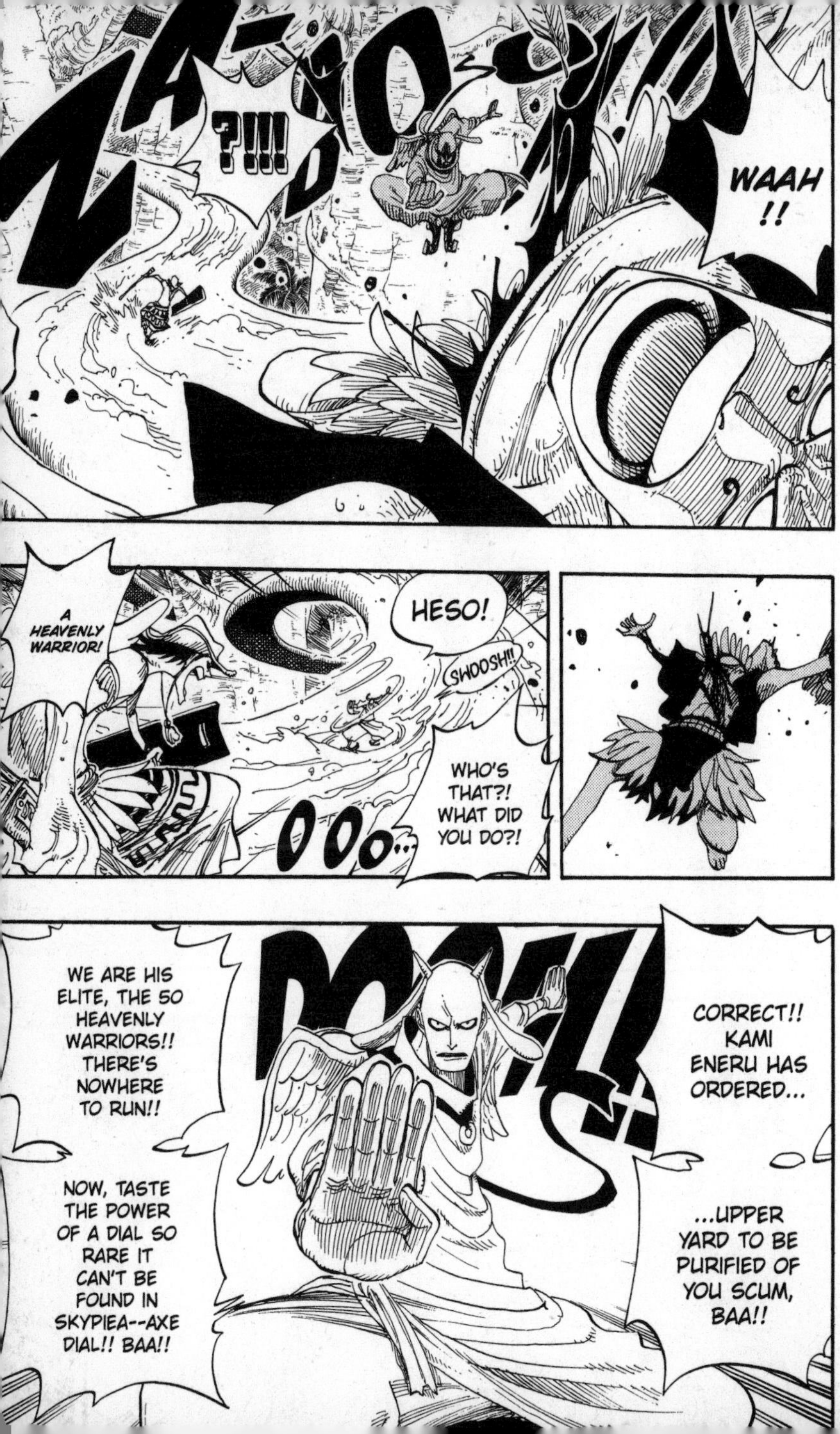
?!!!
WAAH !!
HESO!
SWOOSH!!
WHO'S THAT?! WHAT DID YOU DO?!
A HEAVENLY WARRIOR!
CORRECT!! KAMI ENERU HAS ORDERED...
...UPPER YARD TO BE PURIFIED OF YOU SCUM, BAA!!
WE ARE HIS ELITE, THE 50 HEAVENLY WARRIORS!! THERE'S NOWHERE TO RUN!!
NOW, TASTE THE POWER OF A DIAL SO RARE IT CAN'T BE FOUND IN SKYPIEA--AXE DIAL!! BAA!!

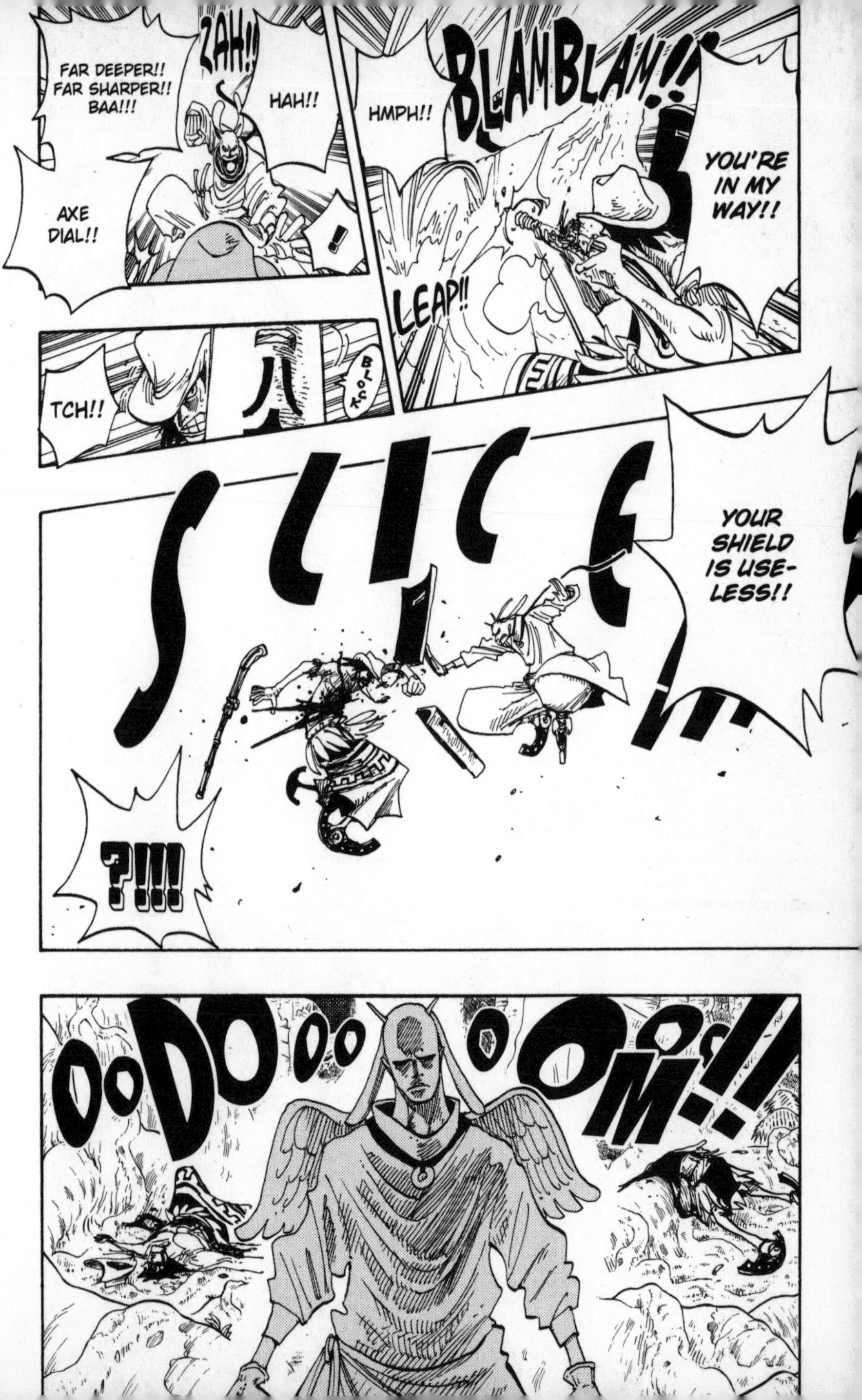

BLAMBLAM!!
YOU'RE IN MY WAY!!
HMPH!!
LEAP!!
HAH!!
ZAH!!
FAR DEEPER!! FAR SHARPER!! BAA!!!
AXE DIAL!!
!
BLOCK
TCH!!
YOUR SHIELD IS USELESS!!
SLICE
?!!!
OODOOOOOOM!!

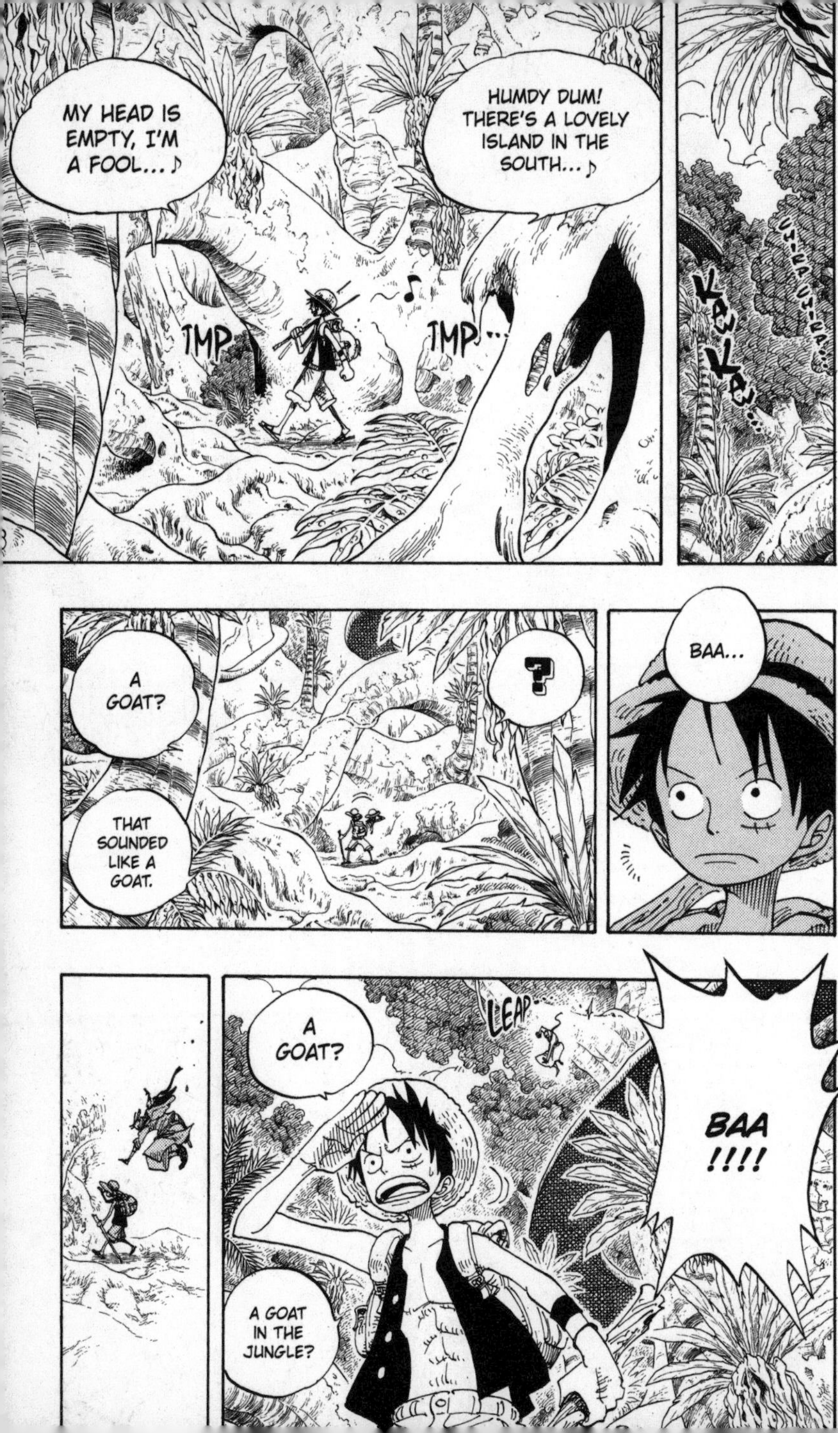
CHIRP CHIRP...
KEW KEW...
HUMDY DUM! THERE'S A LOVELY ISLAND IN THE SOUTH...♪
MY HEAD IS EMPTY, I'M A FOOL...♪
TMP...
TMP
BAA...
?
A GOAT?
THAT SOUNDED LIKE A GOAT.
BAA !!!!
LEAP
A GOAT?
A GOAT IN THE JUNGLE?

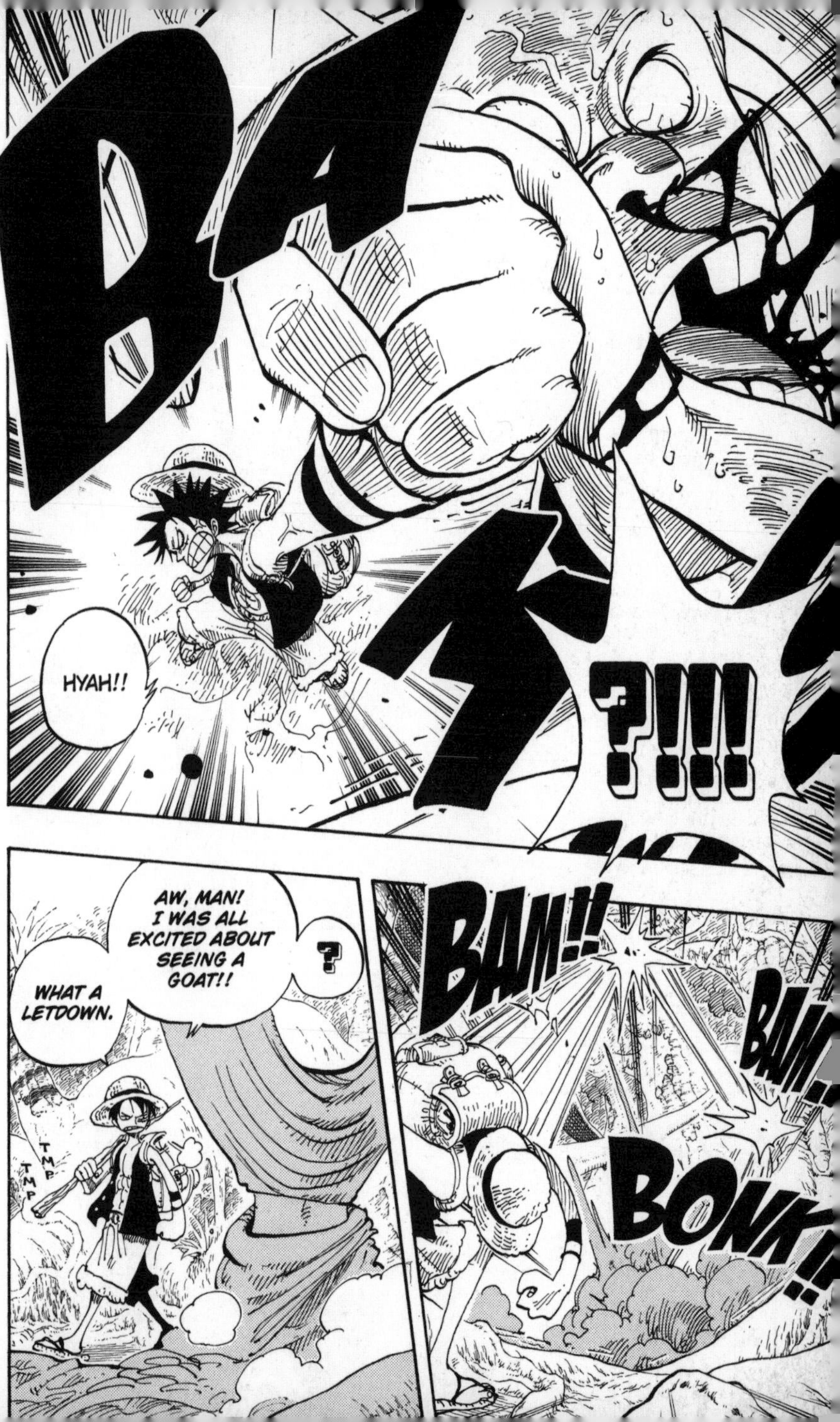
?!!!
HYAH!!
BAM!!
BAM!!
BONK!!
?
AW, MAN! I WAS ALL EXCITED ABOUT SEEING A GOAT!!
WHAT A LETDOWN.
TMP
TMP

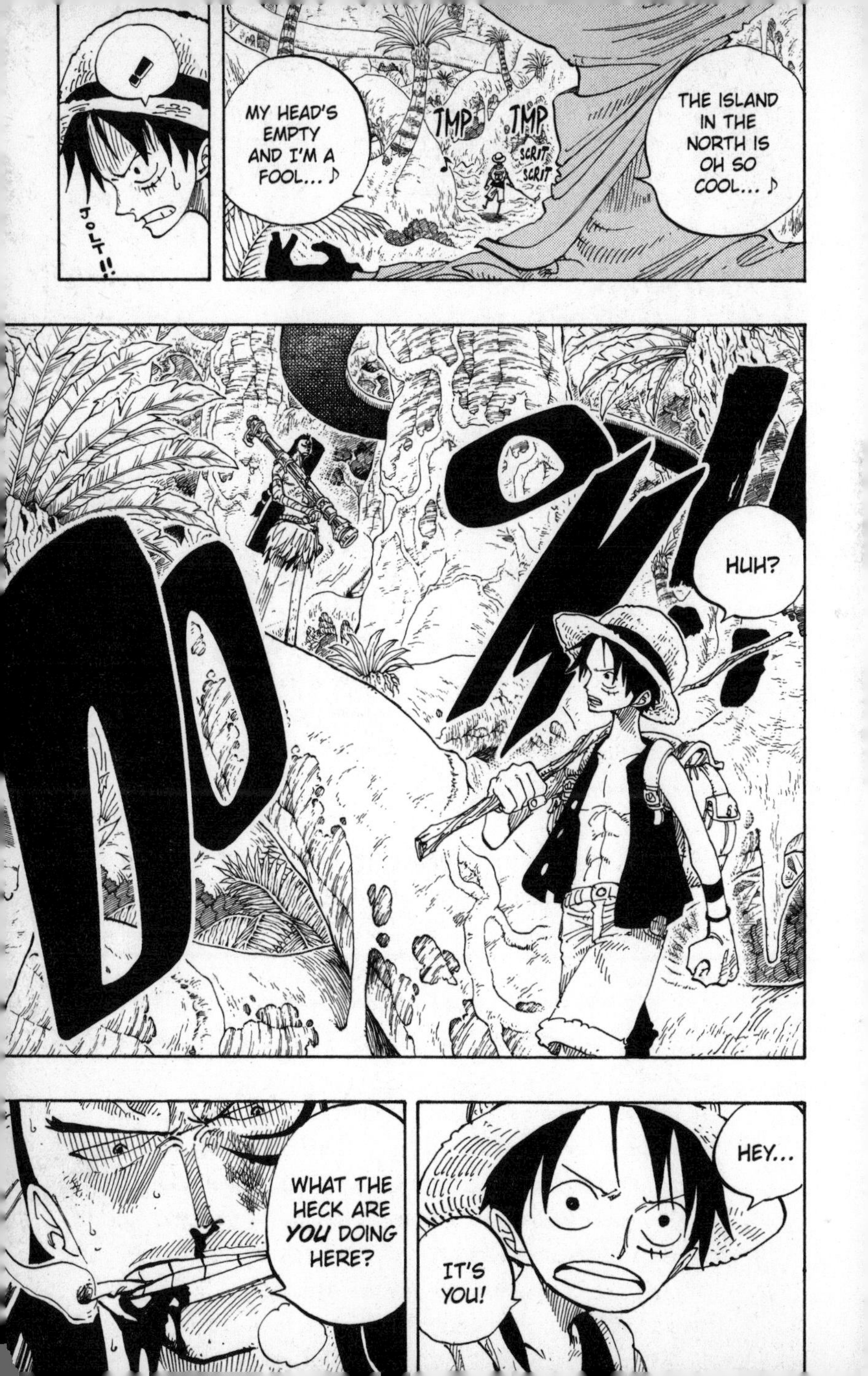
THE ISLAND IN THE NORTH IS OH SO COOL... ♪
TMP TMP
SCRIT SCRIT
MY HEAD'S EMPTY AND I'M A FOOL... ♪
!
JOLT!!
DOON!
HUH?
HEY...
IT'S YOU!
WHAT THE HECK ARE *YOU* DOING HERE?

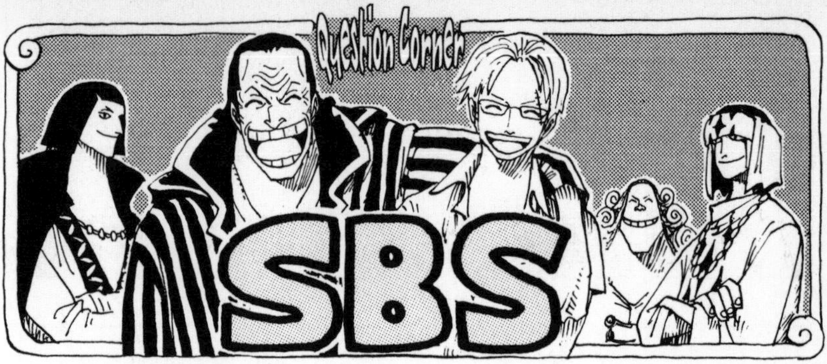
Question Corner
SBS

Q: Hello! Oda Sensei! In volume 25, you said that "manga is about people's dreams." Your words really made an impression on me. However, there's one strange thing. In my dreams, Nami only appears in bikinis, but in the manga, she's usually fully dressed. Why is that?

A: A super-skimpy Nami, eh? Well, if you'll remember, we did see her in the bath. That's even more skimpy than a bikini! And come to think of it, Vivi was shown in nothing but a towel. How skimpy do you want her to be?! I'll try harder next time.

Q: If Nico Robin were to spout limbs all over her body, how many would that be? 200 Flower-Flower?

-- Tomoya

A: Hmm... Yes. About that.

Q: Oda Sensei!!! Recently, my father said, "*One Piece* is a really weird manga." I almost ended up correcting him by saying, "Wrong!! *One Piece* is a really **great** manga!!" (seriously).

A: Oh, so you only thought it?! Say it out loud! Let's say it all together now!! "One Piece is a really weird manga!!" Yahoo! It's springtime.

Q: Oda Sensei, in *One Piece*, the characters often talk about "will." I never hear "will" used that way outside of manga. What does it mean? Do your other readers know what it means? Please tell me!

A: "Will," like "willpower," means having a strong heart. When a person has an intense desire, his will is strong. Strong-willed people are quite fascinating, don't you think?

Chapter 258:
THE MANY SOUTHS

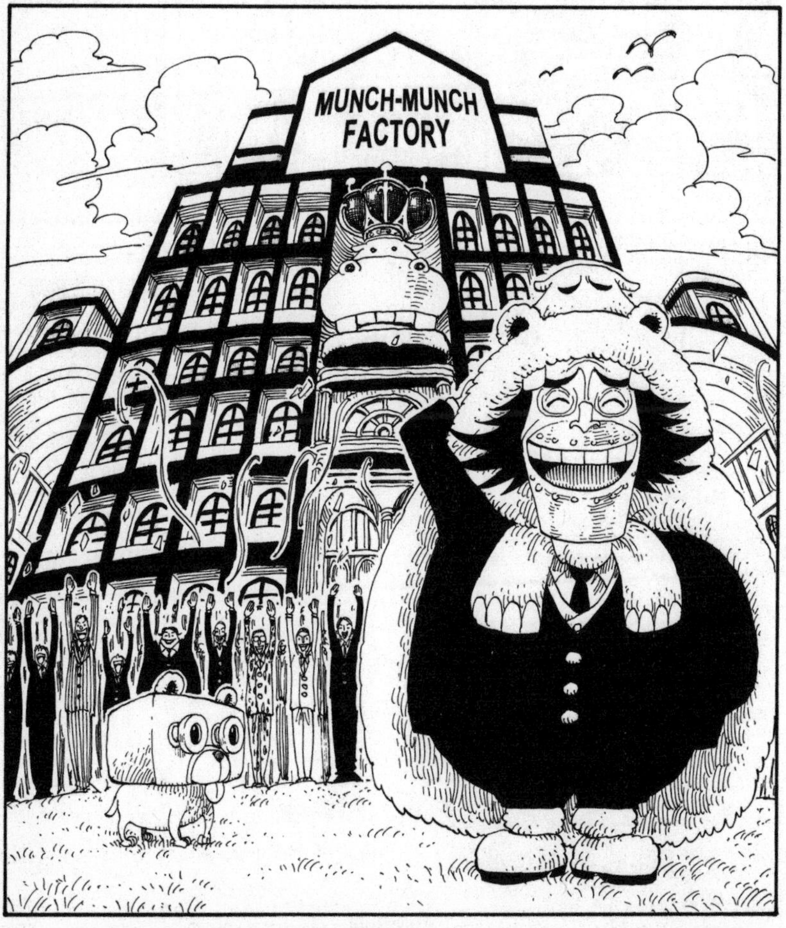
MUNCH-MUNCH
FACTORY

WAPOL'S OMNIVOROUS RAMPAGE, VOL. 20: "A TITAN OF INDUSTRY--THE MUNCH-MUNCH FACTORY IS BORN"

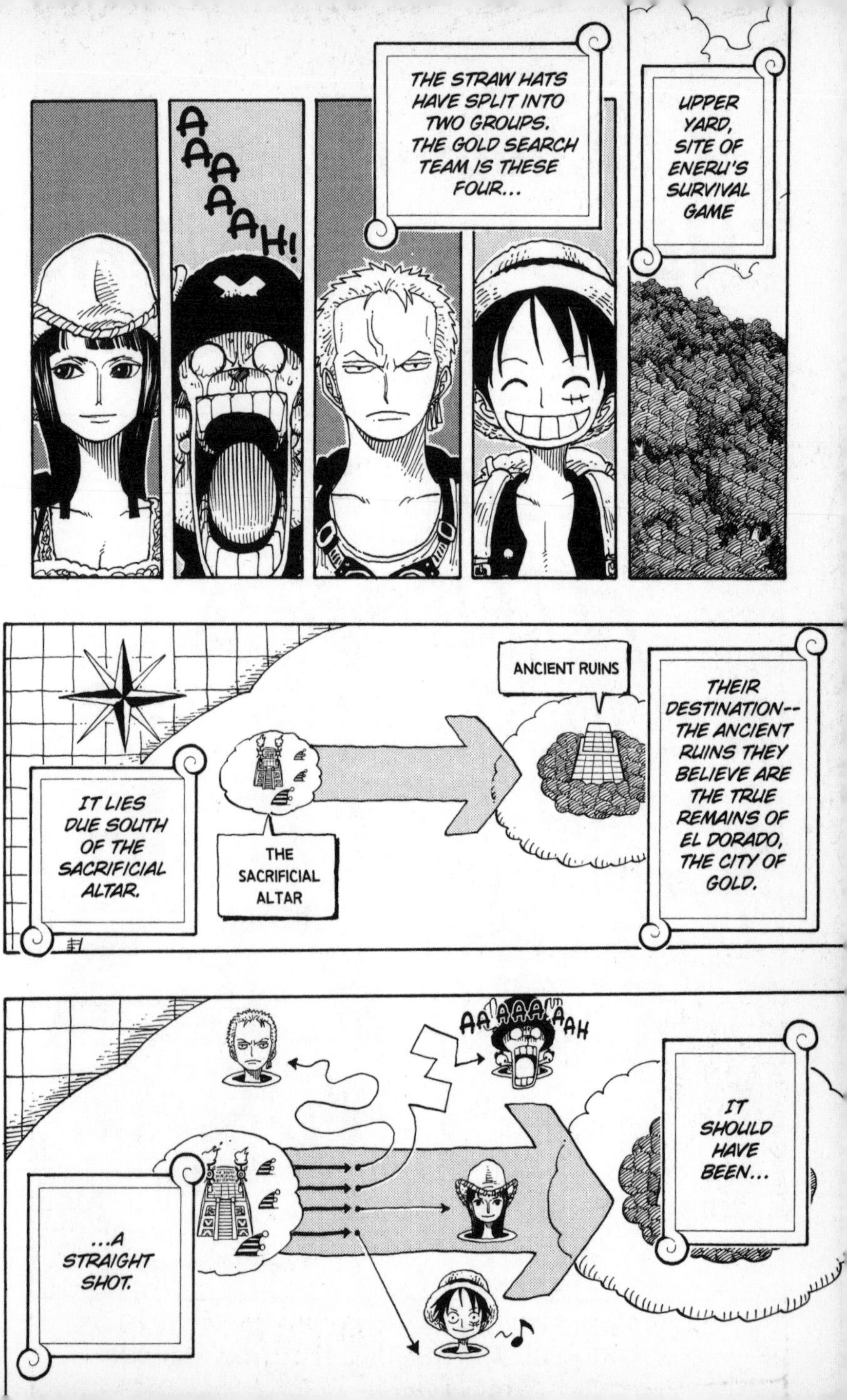
UPPER YARD, SITE OF ENERU'S SURVIVAL GAME
THE STRAW HATS HAVE SPLIT INTO TWO GROUPS. THE GOLD SEARCH TEAM IS THESE FOUR...
AAAAAH!
THEIR DESTINATION-- THE ANCIENT RUINS THEY BELIEVE ARE THE TRUE REMAINS OF EL DORADO, THE CITY OF GOLD.
ANCIENT RUINS
IT LIES DUE SOUTH OF THE SACRIFICIAL ALTAR.
THE SACRIFICIAL ALTAR
IT SHOULD HAVE BEEN...
AAAAAAAAH
...A STRAIGHT SHOT.

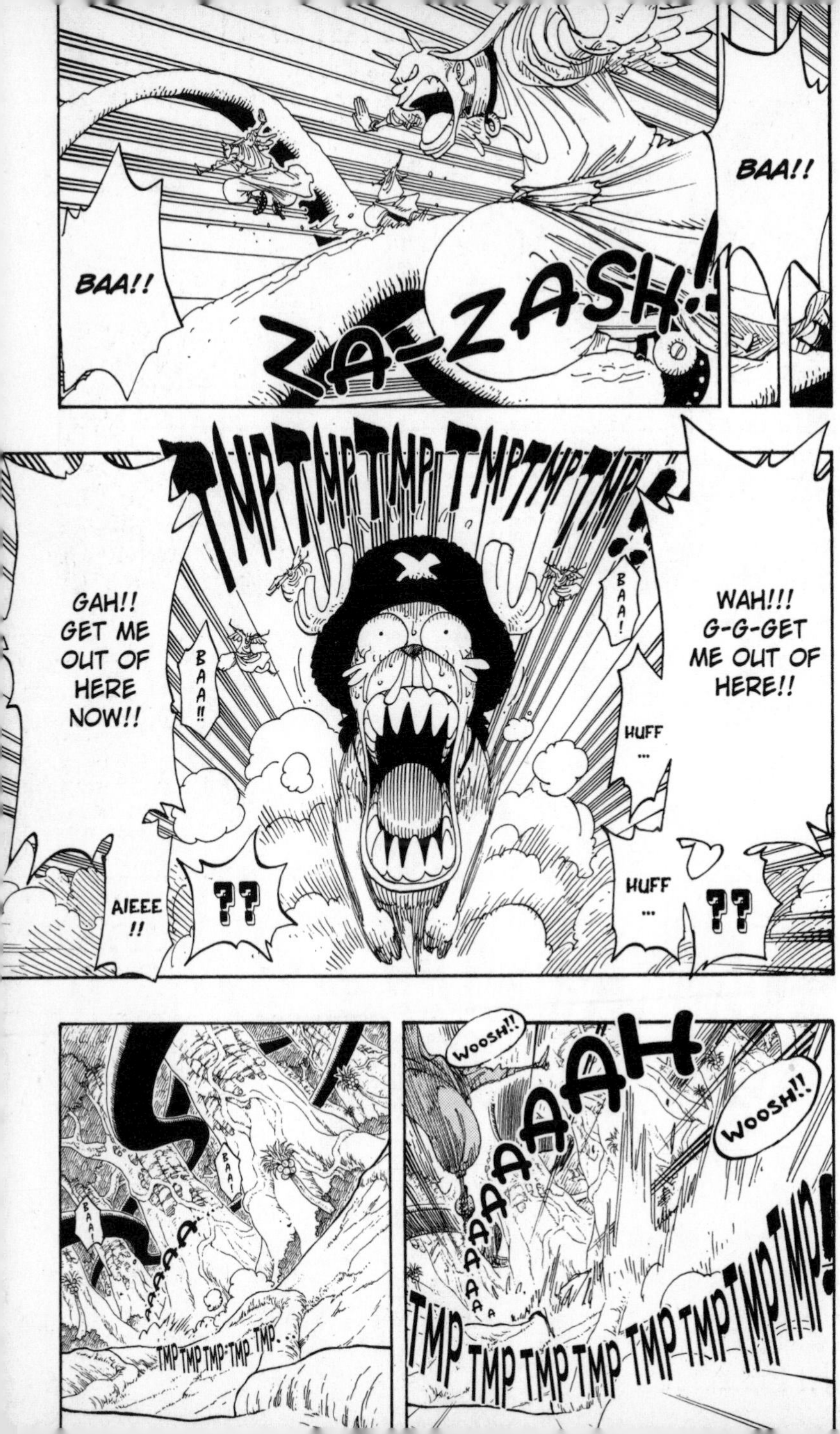
BAA!!
ZA-ZASH!!
BAA!!
TMP TMP TMP TMP TMP TMP!!
WAH!!! G-G-GET ME OUT OF HERE!!
BAA!
HUFF ...
HUFF ...
??
GAH!! GET ME OUT OF HERE NOW!!
BAAA!!
??
AIEEE !!
WOOSH!!
WOOSH!!
AAAAAAH
AAAAAA
TMP TMP TMP TMP TMP TMP TMP TMP!
BAA!
BAA!
AAAAA
TMP TMP TMP TMP TMP...

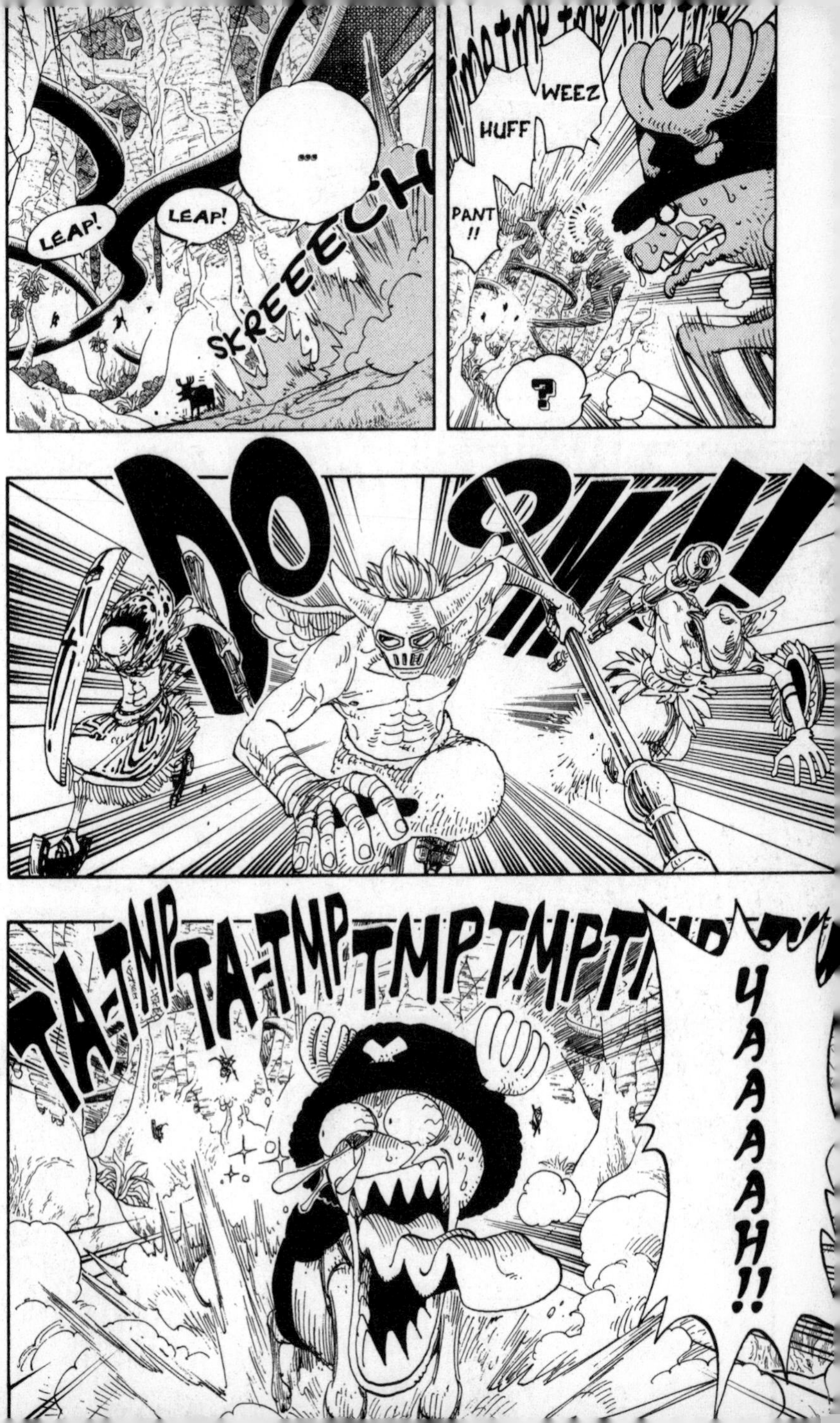
WEEZ
HUFF
PANT !!
?
...
LEAP!
LEAP!
SKREEECH
TA-TMP TA-TMP TMPTMPT
YAAAAAH!!

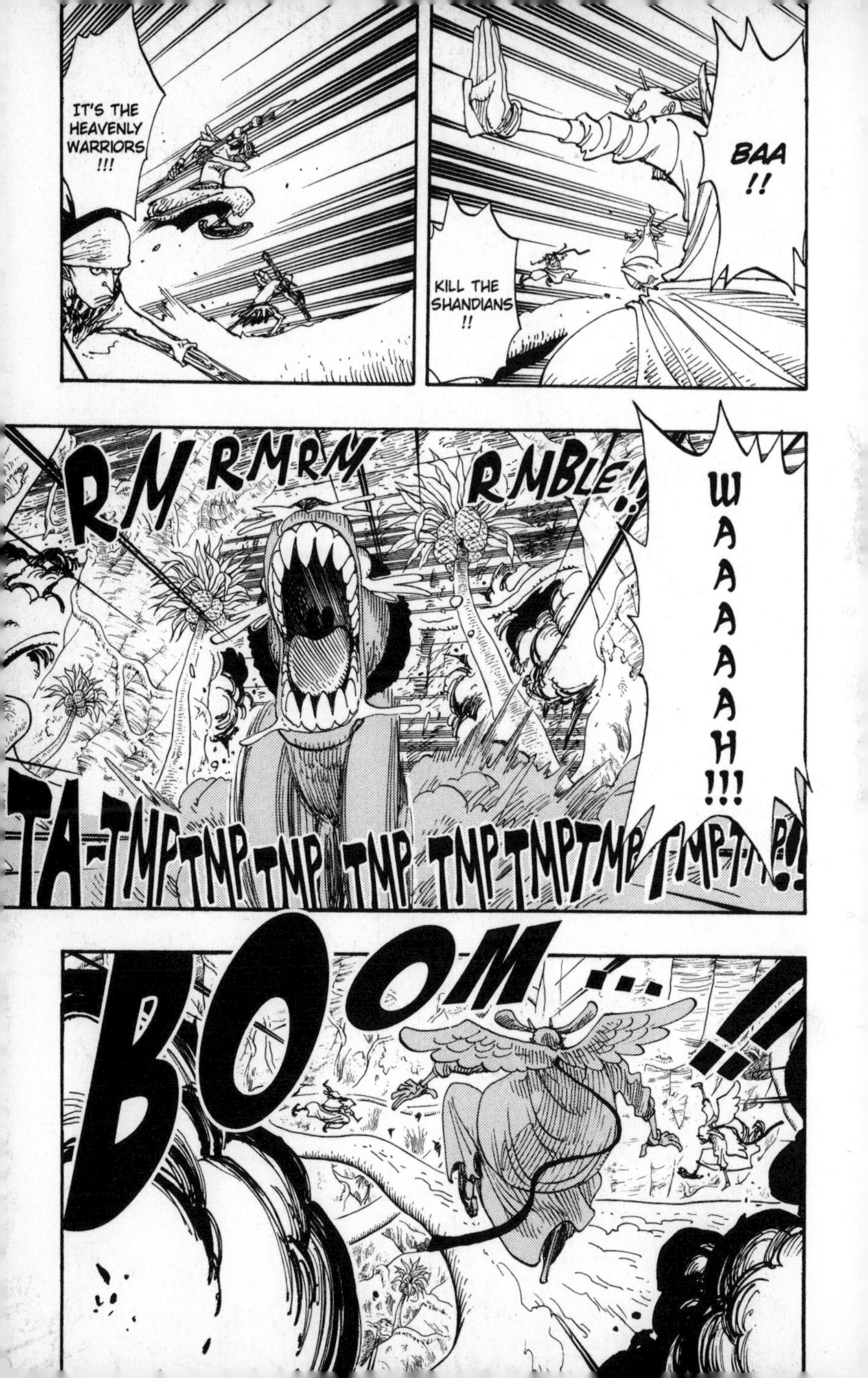
BAA !!
KILL THE SHANDIANS !!
IT'S THE HEAVENLY WARRIORS !!!
WAAAAAAH !!!
RM RMRM RMBLE!!
TA-TMP TMP TMP TMP TMP TMP TMP
BOOM...!!

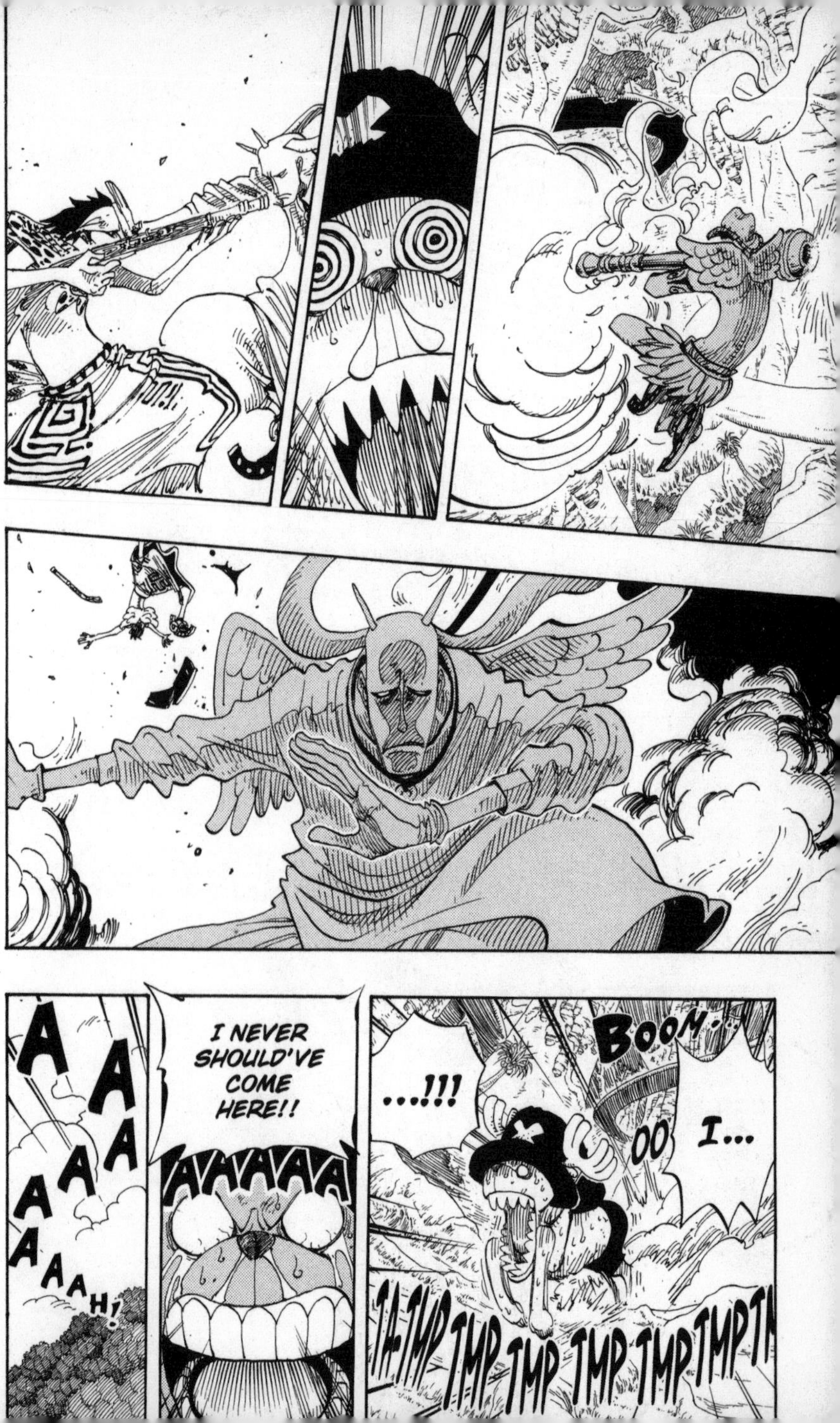
BOOM..
OO I...
...!!!
TA-TMP TMP TMP TMP TMP TMP
I NEVER SHOULD'VE COME HERE!!
AAAAAAA
AAAAAAAAH!

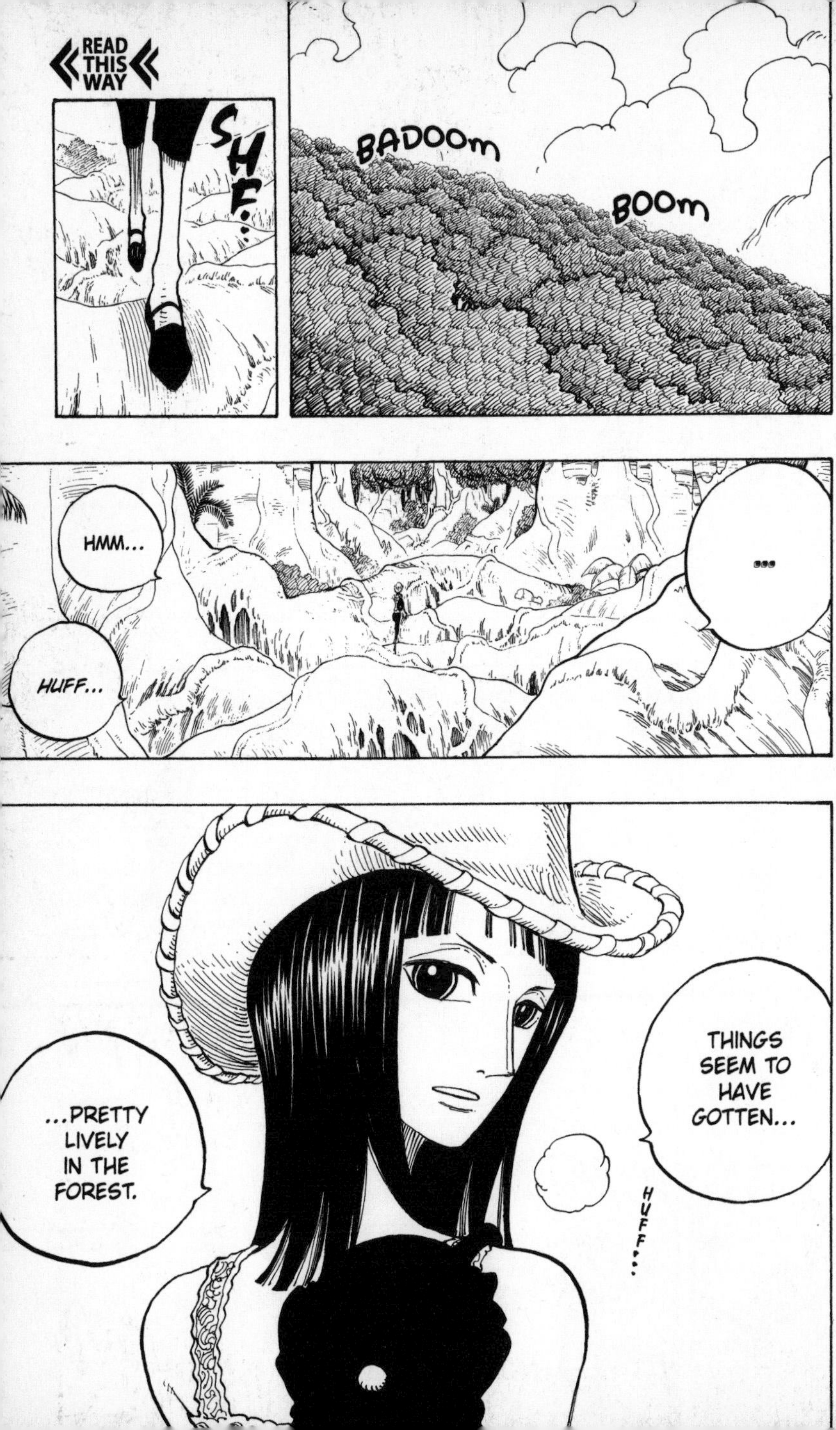
READ THIS WAY
BADOOM
BOOM
SHF...
...
HMM...
HUFF...
THINGS SEEM TO HAVE GOTTEN...
HUFF...
...PRETTY LIVELY IN THE FOREST.

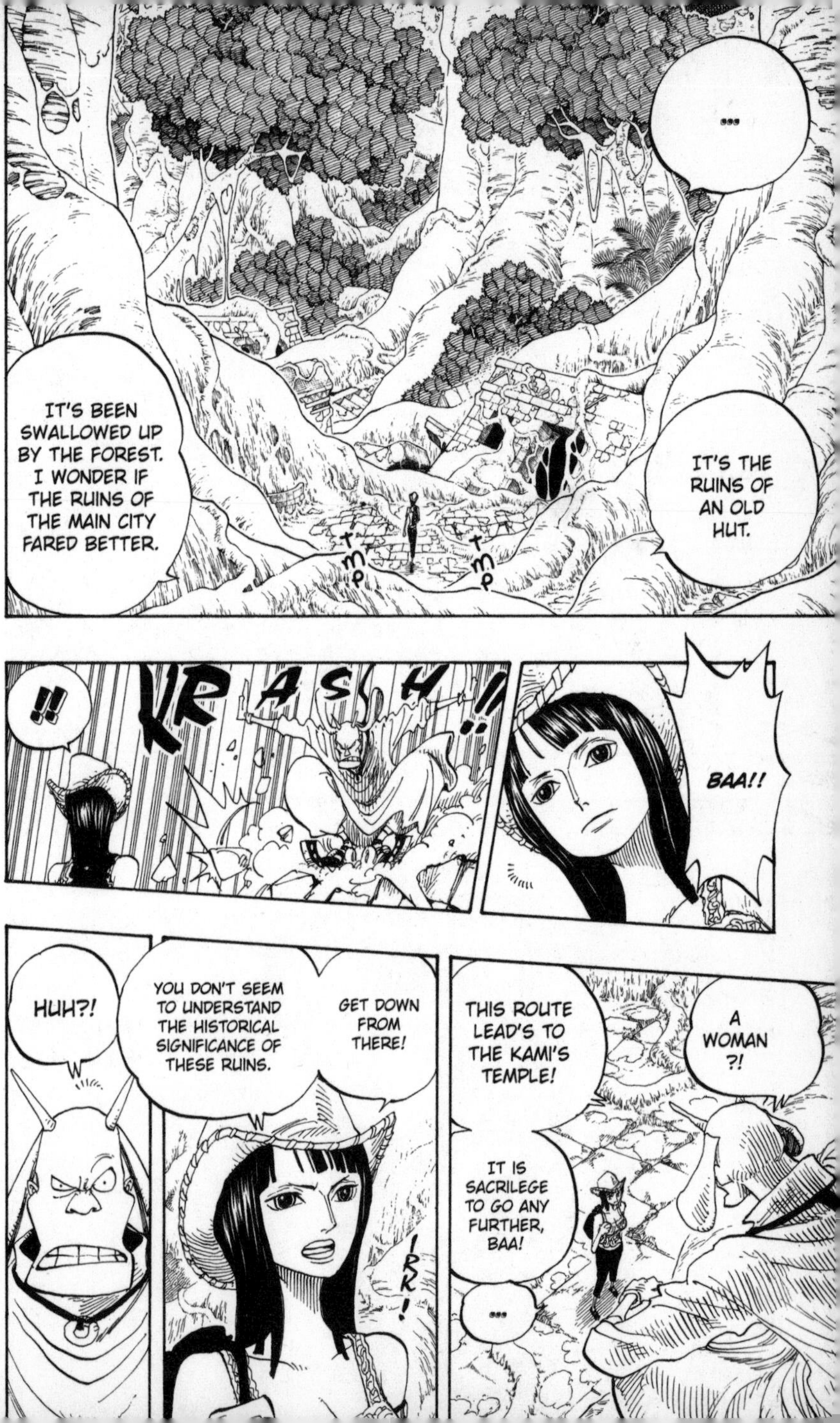
...
IT'S THE RUINS OF AN OLD HUT.
IT'S BEEN SWALLOWED UP BY THE FOREST. I WONDER IF THE RUINS OF THE MAIN CITY FARED BETTER.
TMP
TMP
BAA!!
!!
KRASH!!
A WOMAN?!
THIS ROUTE LEAD'S TO THE KAMI'S TEMPLE!
IT IS SACRILEGE TO GO ANY FURTHER, BAA!
...
GET DOWN FROM THERE!
YOU DON'T SEEM TO UNDERSTAND THE HISTORICAL SIGNIFICANCE OF THESE RUINS.
IRK!
HUH?!

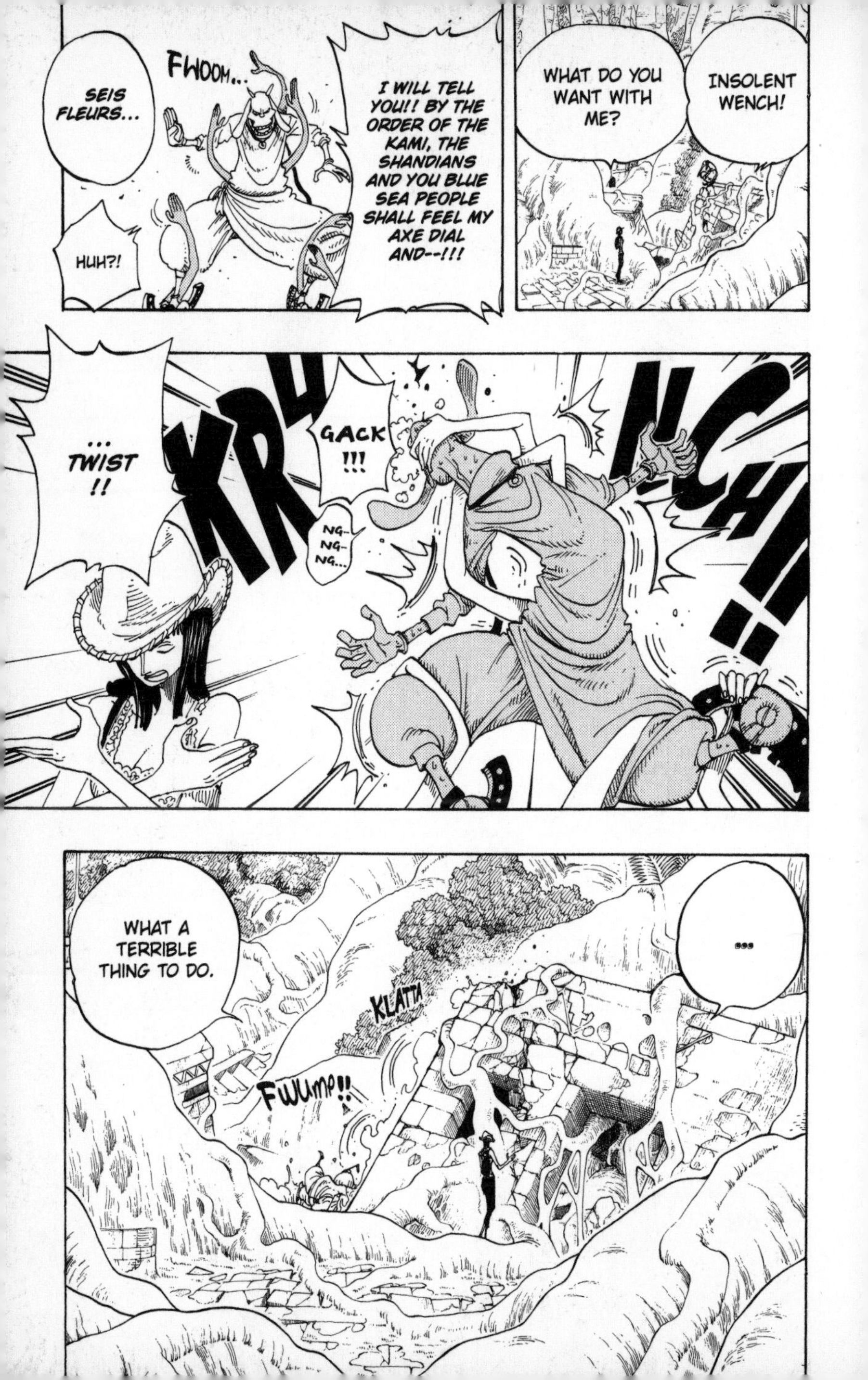
INSOLENT WENCH!
WHAT DO YOU WANT WITH ME?
I WILL TELL YOU!! BY THE ORDER OF THE KAMI, THE SHANDIANS AND YOU BLUE SEA PEOPLE SHALL FEEL MY AXE DIAL AND--!!!
FWOOM...
SEIS FLEURS...
HUH?!
KRUNCH!!
GACK!!!
NG-NG-NG...
... TWIST!!
...
KLATTA
WHAT A TERRIBLE THING TO DO.
FWUMP!!

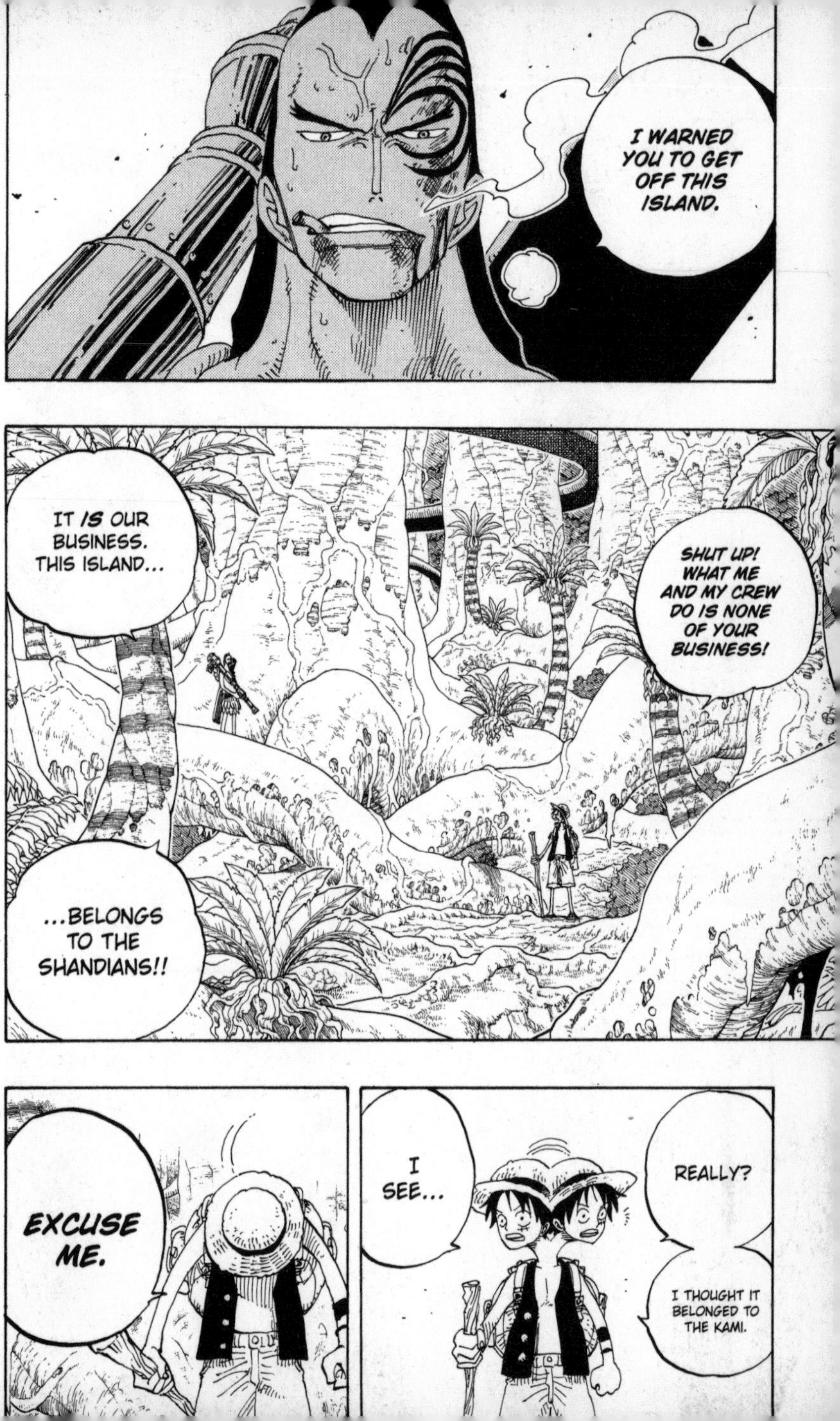
I WARNED YOU TO GET OFF THIS ISLAND.
SHUT UP! WHAT ME AND MY CREW DO IS NONE OF YOUR BUSINESS!
IT *IS* OUR BUSINESS. THIS ISLAND...
...BELONGS TO THE SHANDIANS!!
REALLY?
I SEE...
I THOUGHT IT BELONGED TO THE KAMI.
EXCUSE ME.

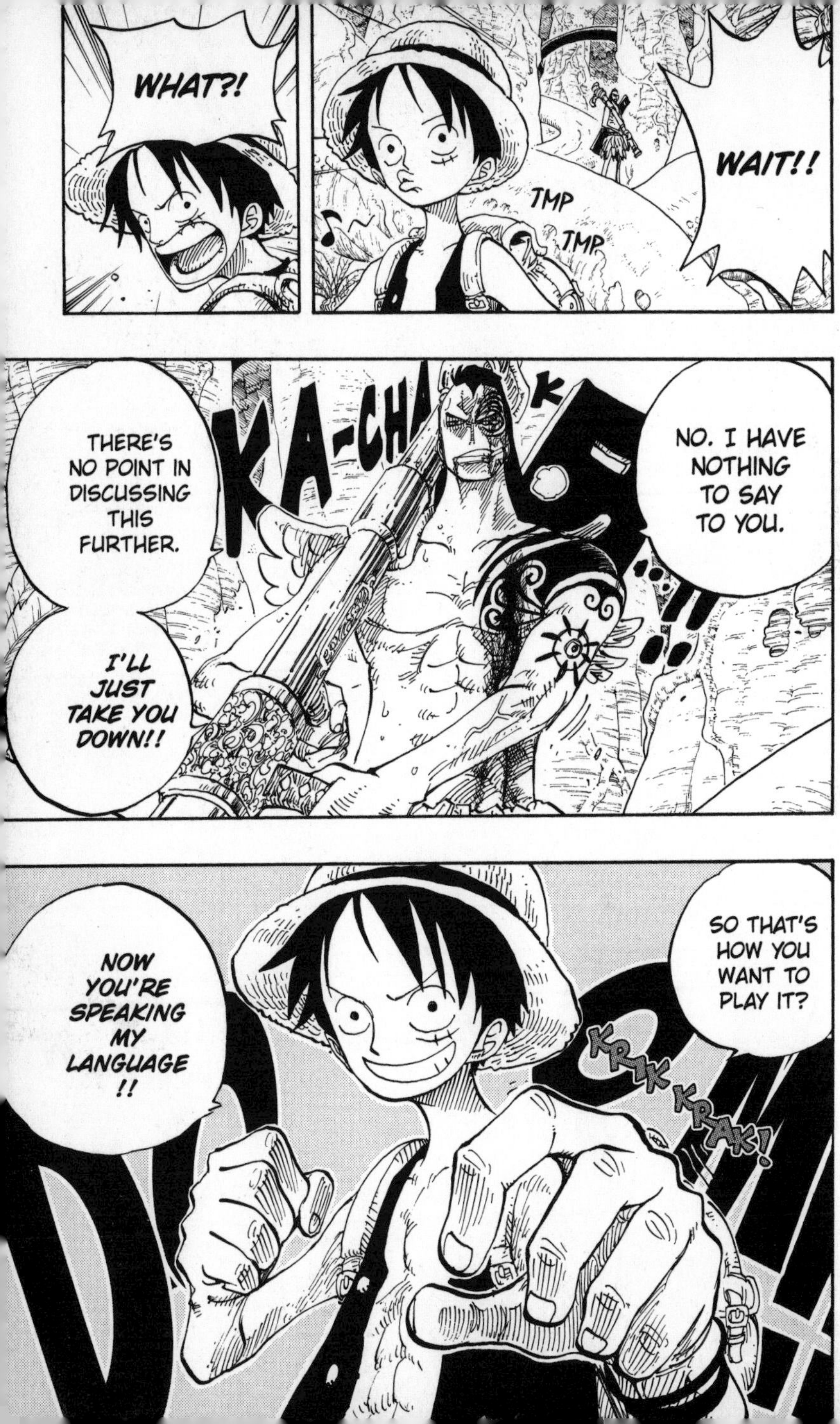
WAIT!!
TMP
TMP
WHAT?!
NO. I HAVE NOTHING TO SAY TO YOU.
KA-CHAK
THERE'S NO POINT IN DISCUSSING THIS FURTHER.
I'LL JUST TAKE YOU DOWN!!
SO THAT'S HOW YOU WANT TO PLAY IT?
KRAK KRAK!
NOW YOU'RE SPEAKING MY LANGUAGE!!

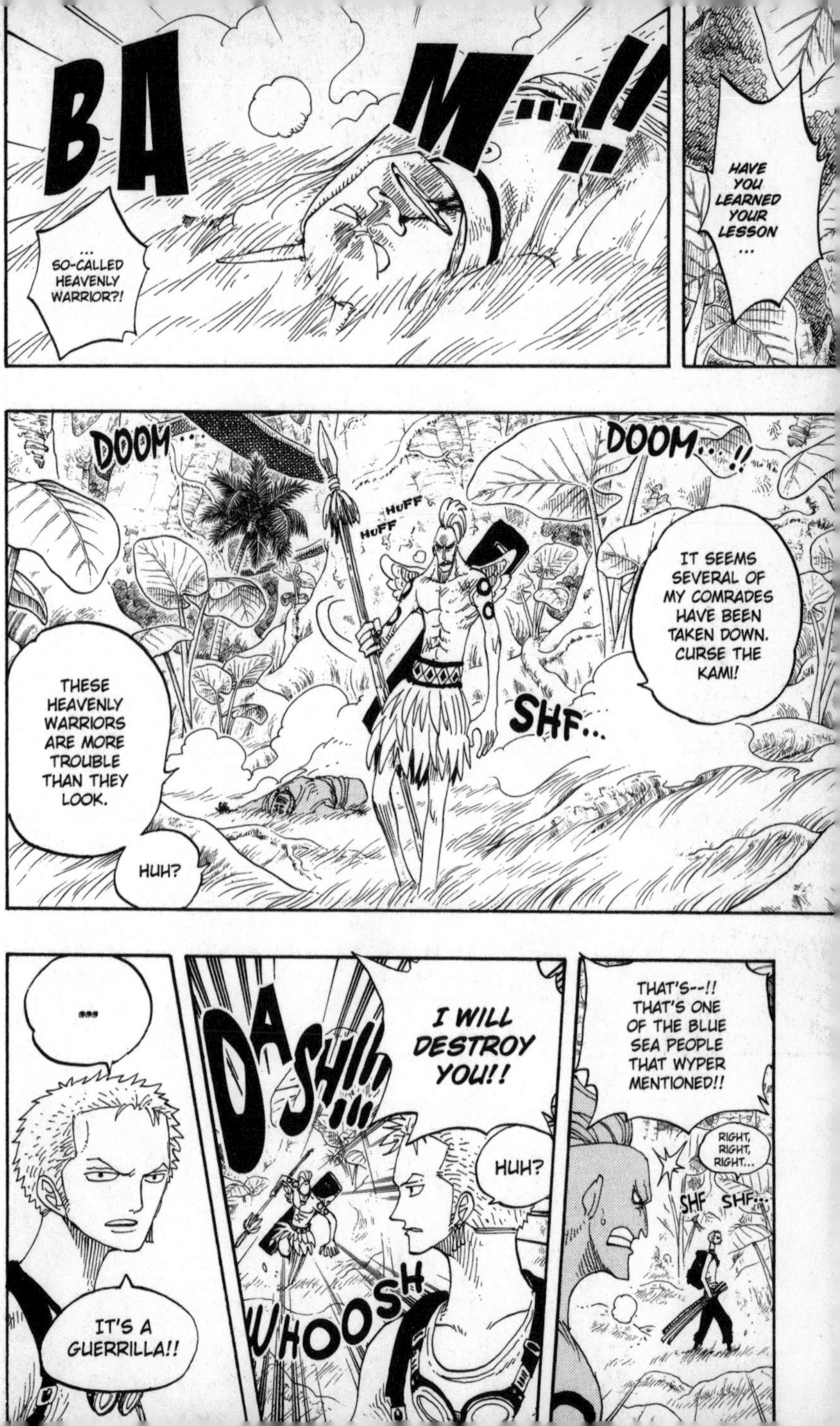
HAVE YOU LEARNED YOUR LESSON ...
BAM...!!
... SO-CALLED HEAVENLY WARRIOR?!
DOOM...!!
IT SEEMS SEVERAL OF MY COMRADES HAVE BEEN TAKEN DOWN. CURSE THE KAMI!
HUFF
HUFF
SHF...
DOOM...
THESE HEAVENLY WARRIORS ARE MORE TROUBLE THAN THEY LOOK.
HUH?
THAT'S--!! THAT'S ONE OF THE BLUE SEA PEOPLE THAT WYPER MENTIONED!!
RIGHT, RIGHT, RIGHT...
SHF SHF...
I WILL DESTROY YOU!!
DASH!!!
HUH?
WHOOSH
...
IT'S A GUERRILLA!!

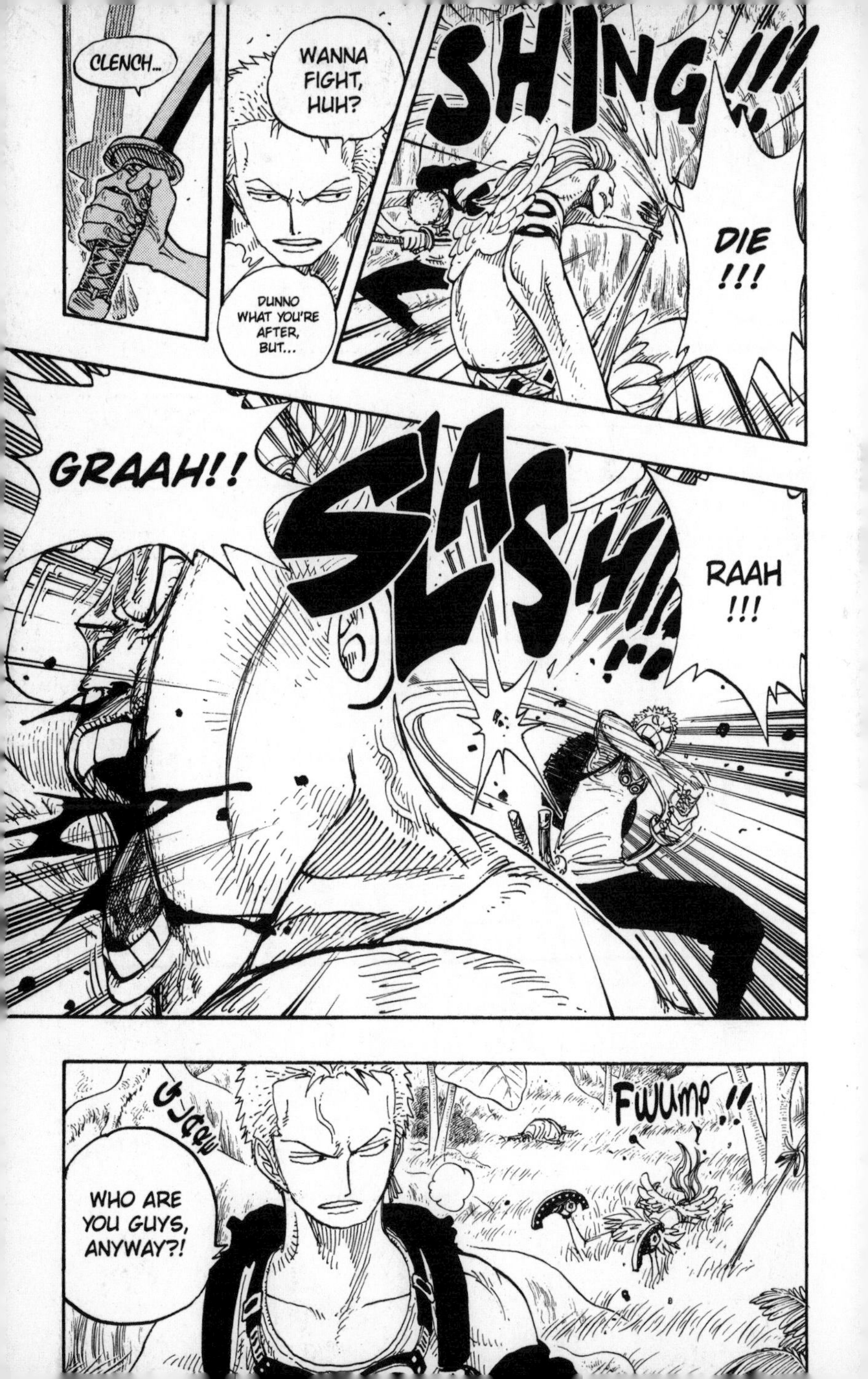
SHING!!!
DIE!!!
WANNA FIGHT, HUH?
DUNNO WHAT YOU'RE AFTER, BUT...
CLENCH...
RAAH!!!
SLASH!!
GRAAH!!
FWUMP!!
WHO ARE YOU GUYS, ANYWAY?!

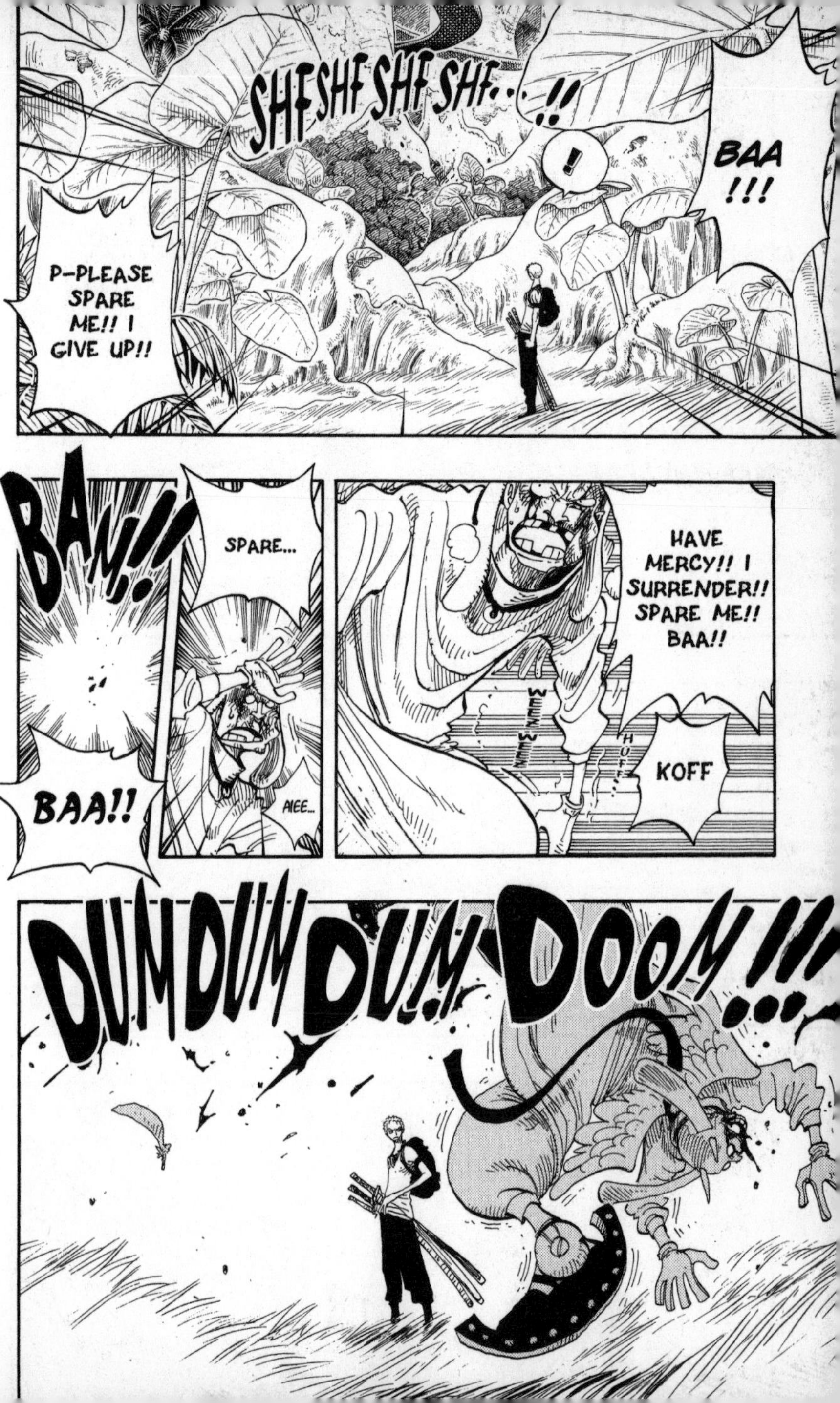
SHF SHF SHF SHF...!!
BAA!!!
!
P-PLEASE SPARE ME!! I GIVE UP!!
HAVE MERCY!! I SURRENDER!! SPARE ME!! BAA!!
WEEZ WEEZ
HUFF...
KOFF
SPARE...
AIEE...
BAN!!
BAA!!
DUM DUM DUM DOOM...!!!

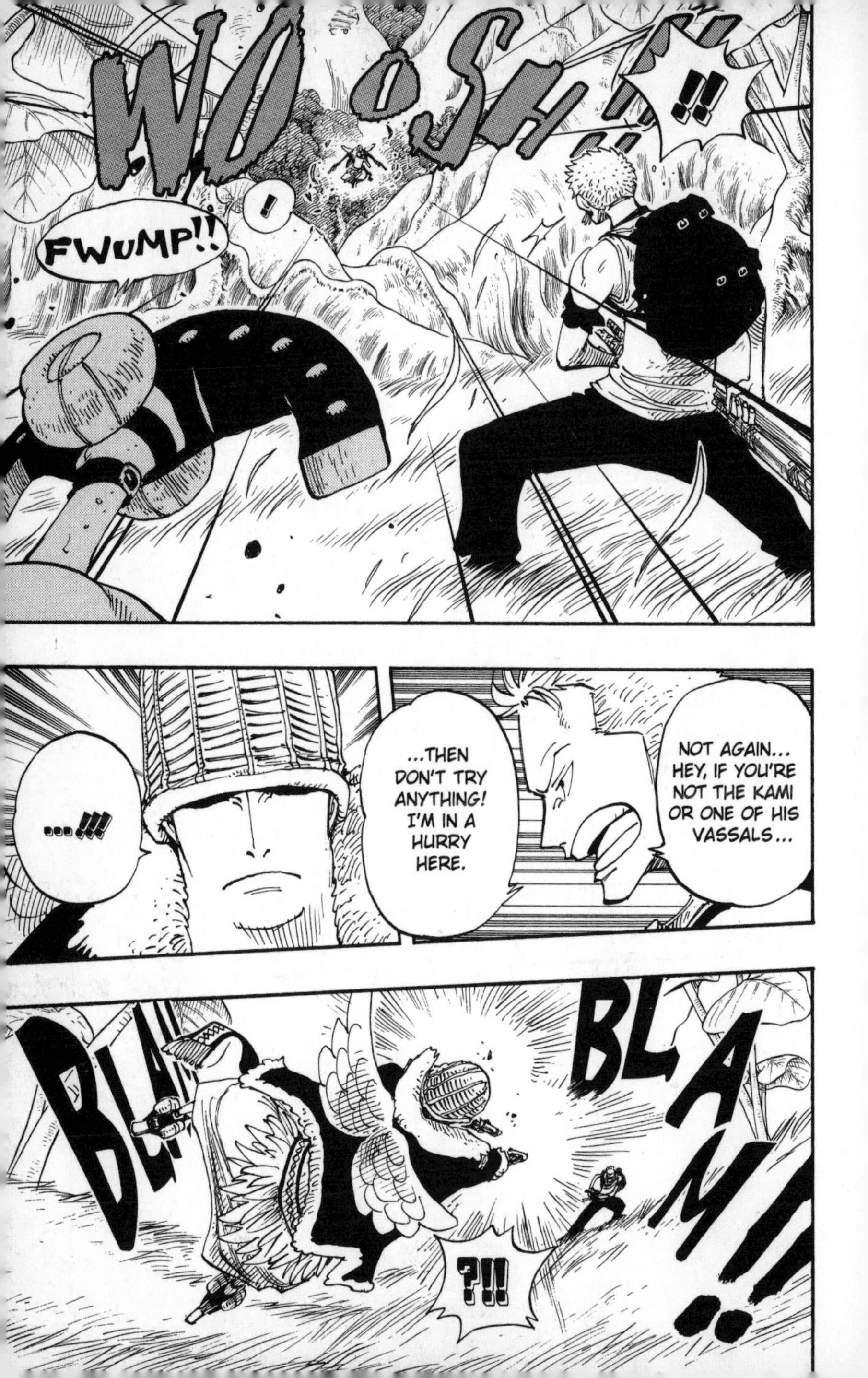
WOOSH!!
!
FWUMP!!
NOT AGAIN... HEY, IF YOU'RE NOT THE KAMI OR ONE OF HIS VASSALS...
...THEN DON'T TRY ANYTHING! I'M IN A HURRY HERE.
...!!!
BLAM!!
BLA
?!!

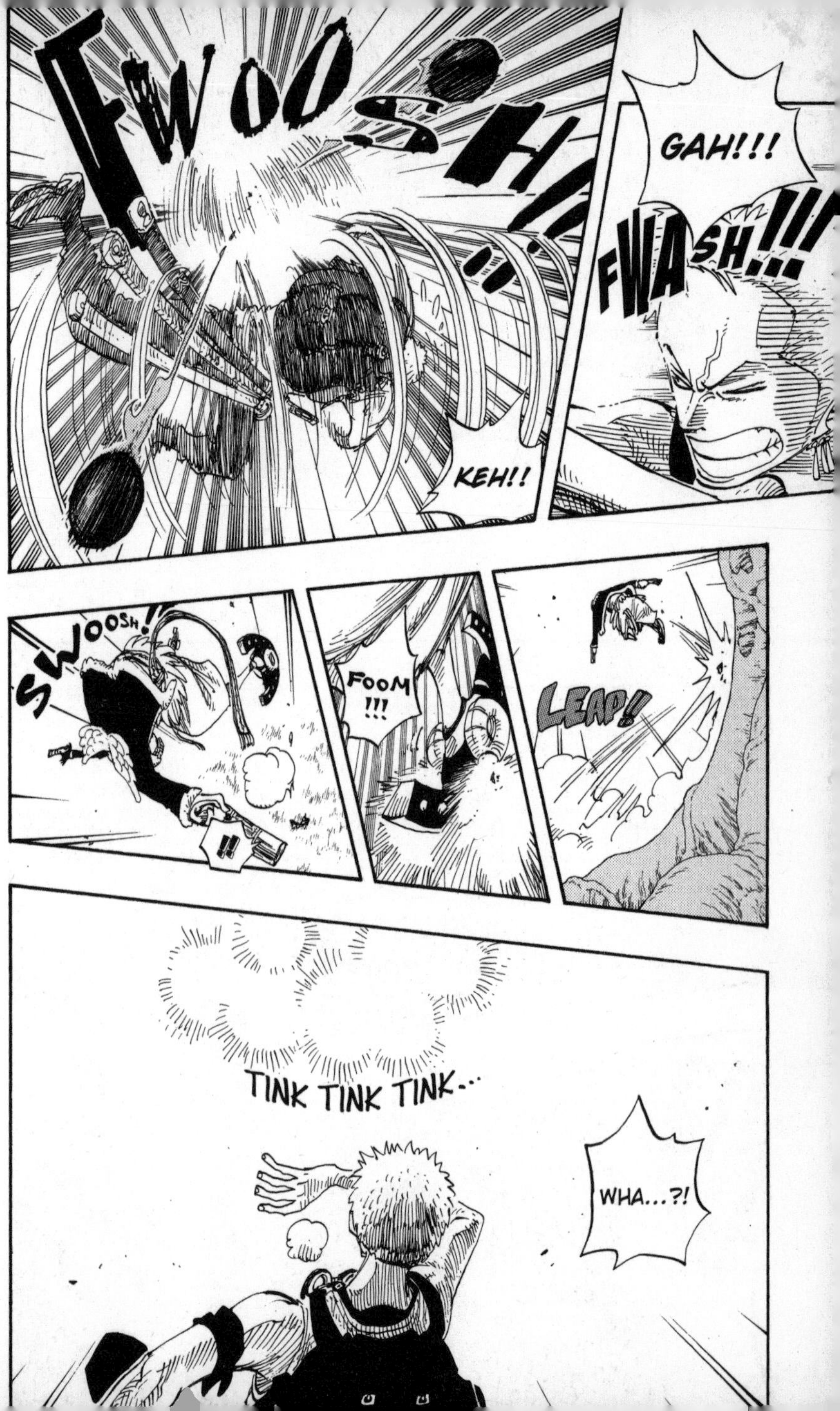
GAH!!!
FWASH!!!
FWOOSH!!
KEH!!
LEAP!!
FOOM!!!
SWOOSH!!
!!
TINK TINK TINK...
WHA...?!

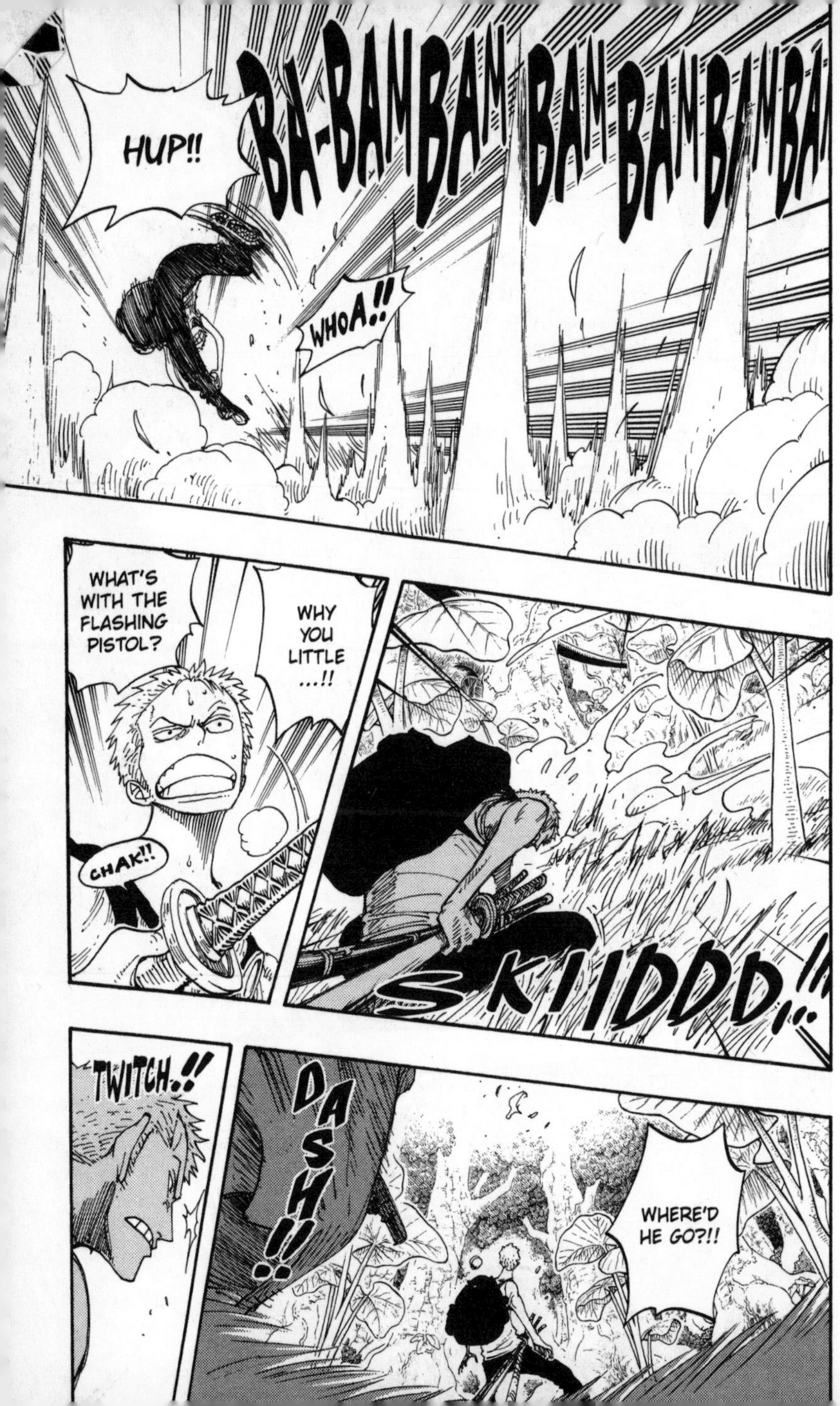
BA-BAMBAM BAM BAMBAMBA
HUP!!
WHOA!!
SKIIDDD!!
WHY YOU LITTLE ...!!
WHAT'S WITH THE FLASHING PISTOL?
CHAK!!
WHERE'D HE GO?!!
DASH!!
TWITCH..!!

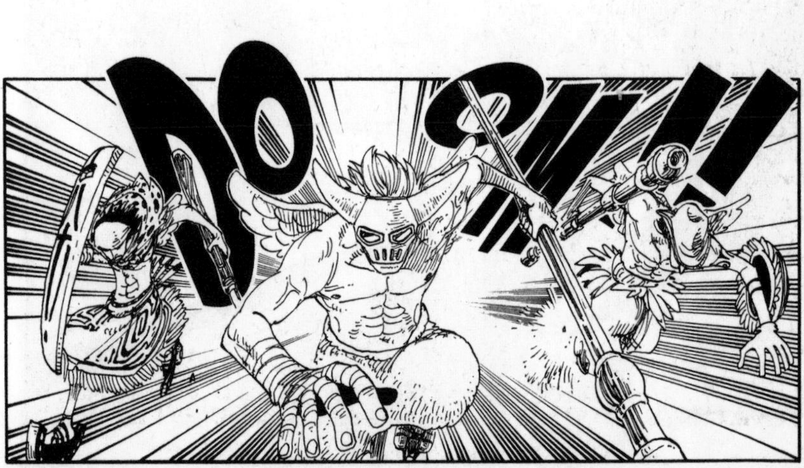
DOSH!!

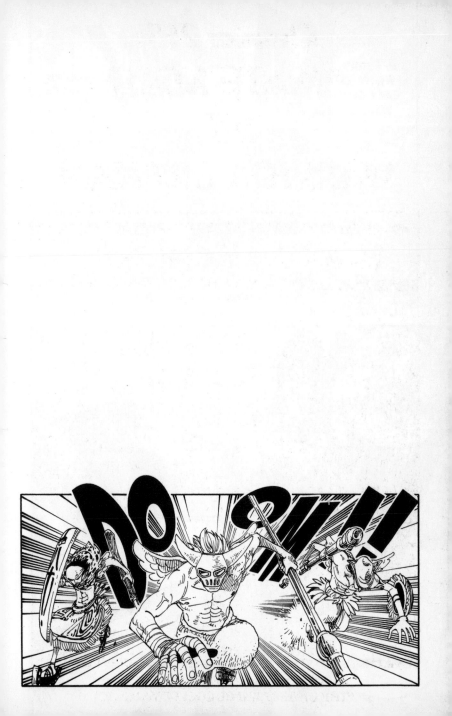

Chapter 259:
PIRATE ZOLO
VS.
WARRIOR BRAHAM

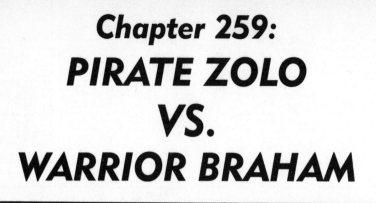

**WAPOL'S OMNIVOROUS RAMPAGE, VOL. 21:
"THE UPSTART WAPOL GOES CORPORATE!"**

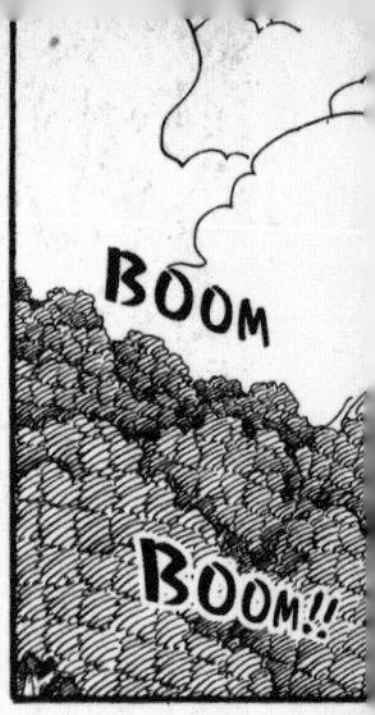
BOOM
BOOM!!
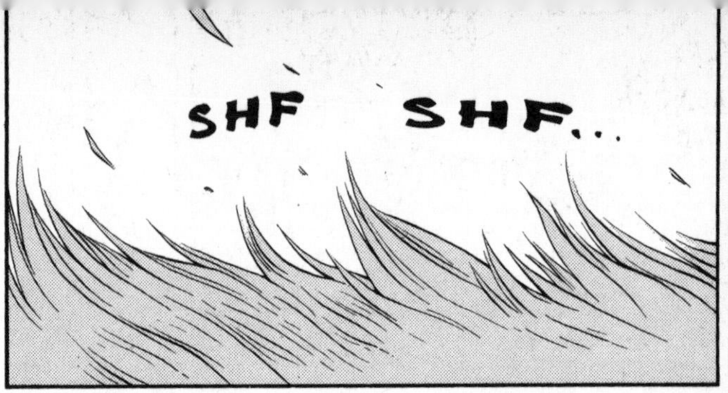
SHF SHF...
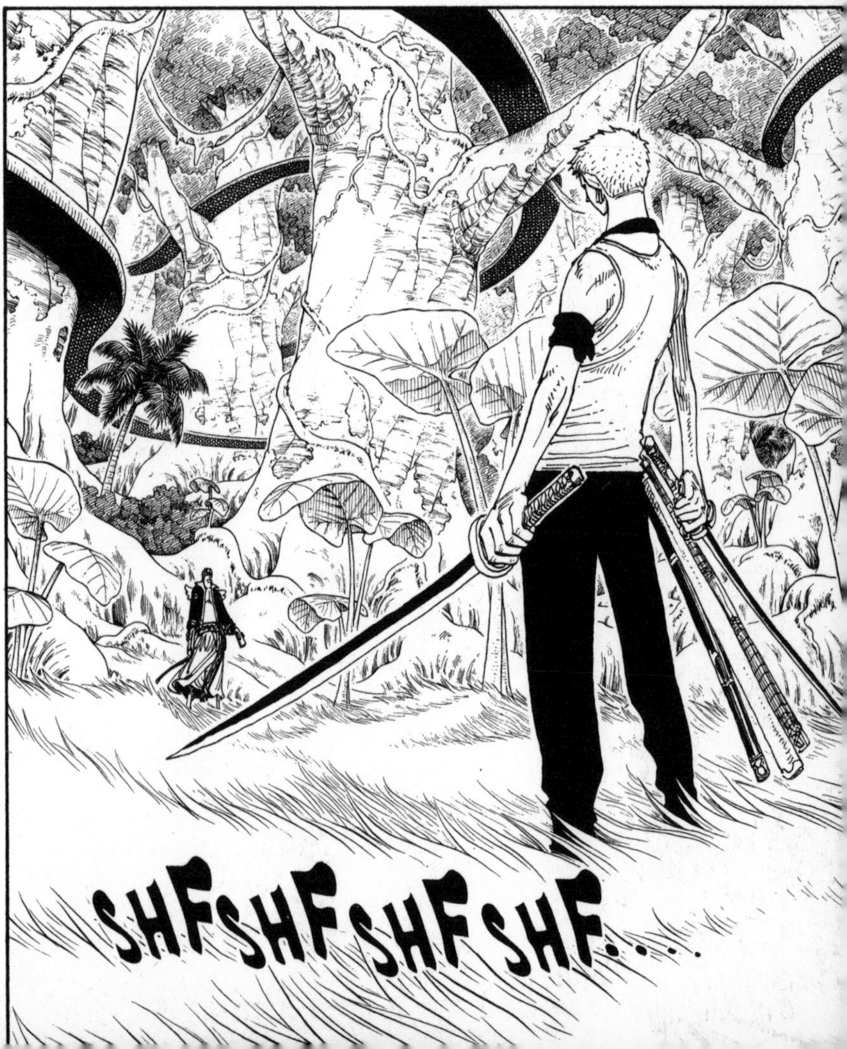
SHFSHFSHFSHF...

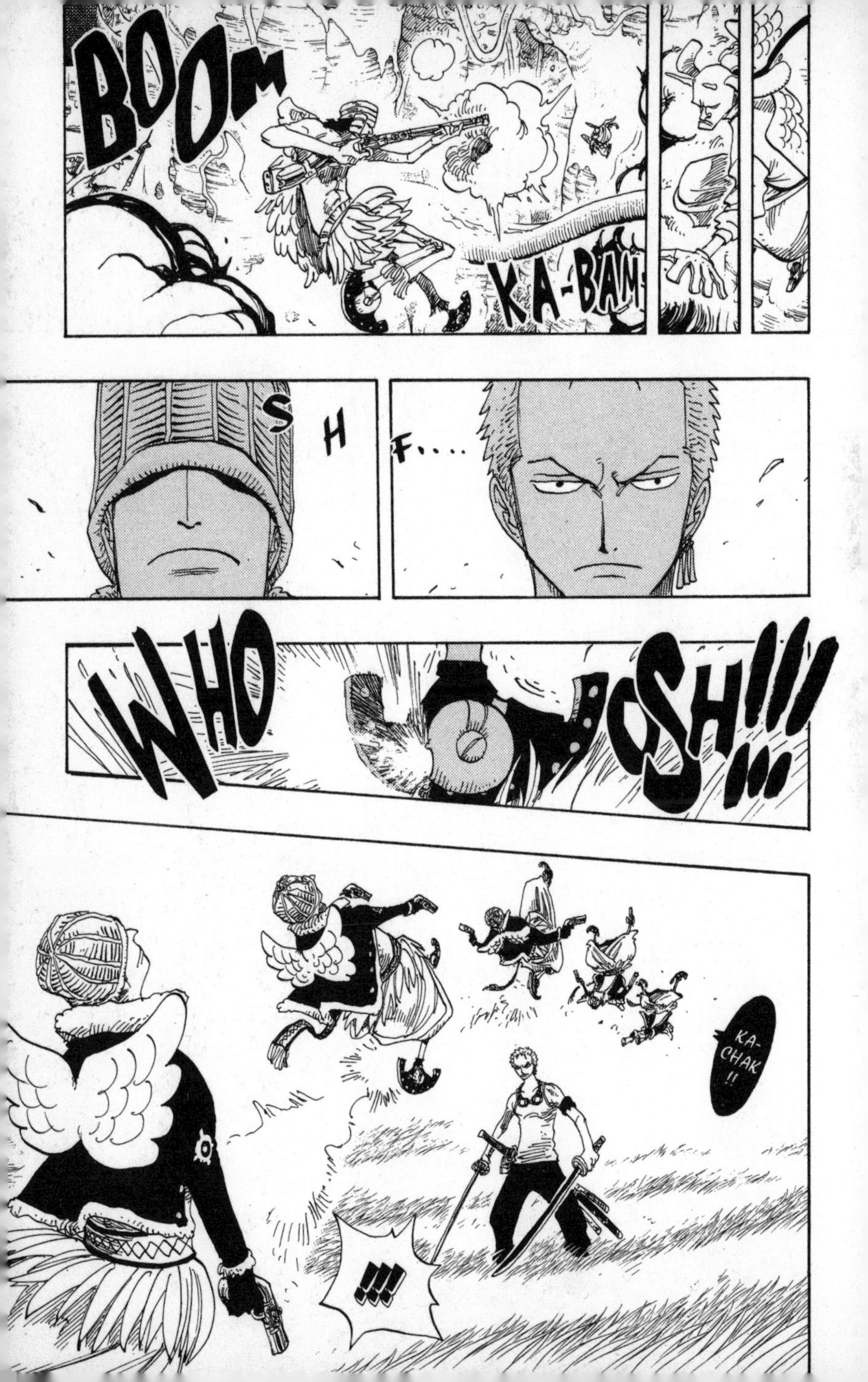
BOOM
KA-BAM
SHF....
WHOOSH!!!
KA-CHAK!!
!!!

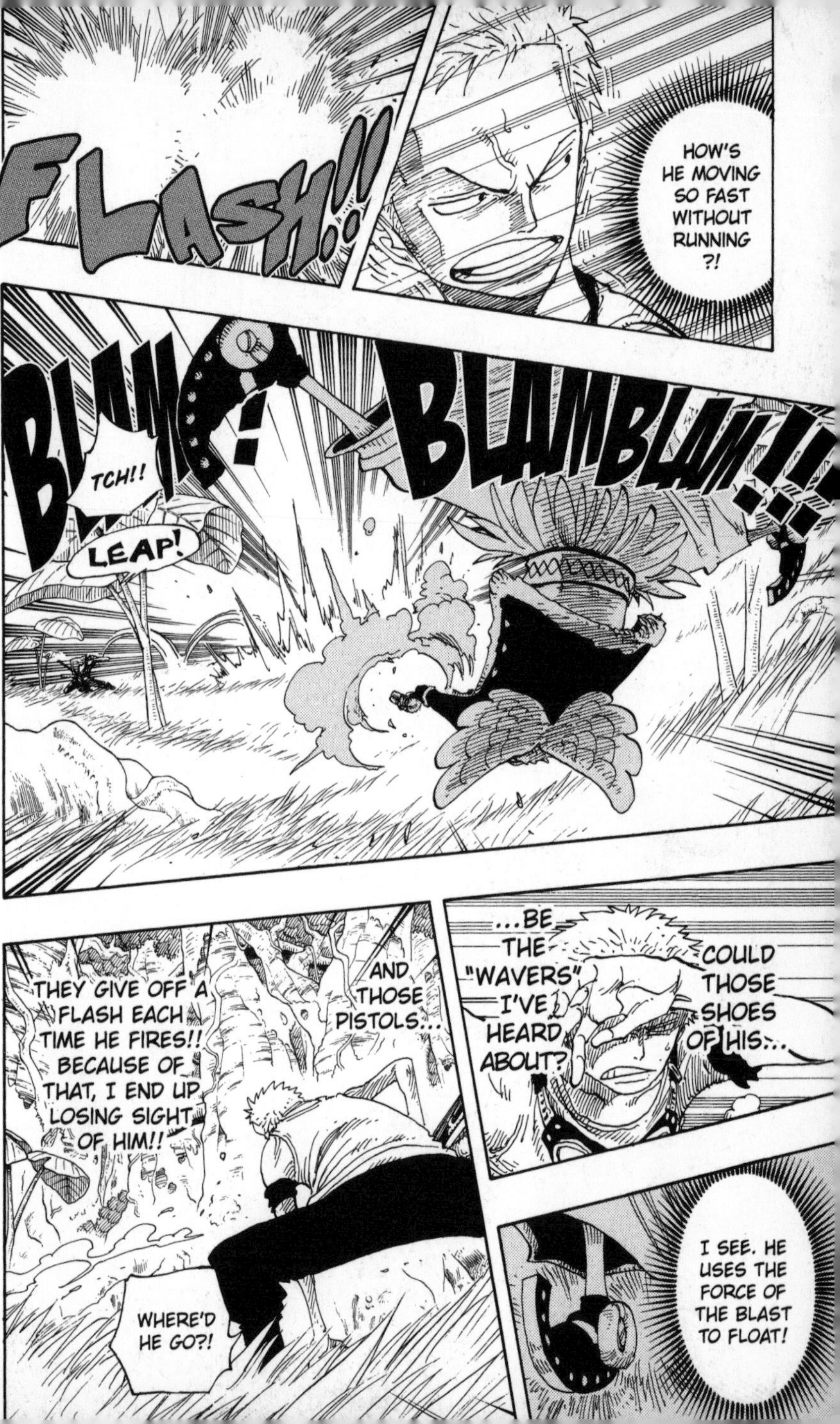
HOW'S HE MOVING SO FAST WITHOUT RUNNING ?!
FLASH!!
BLAMBLAM!!!
BLAM!
TCH!!
LEAP!
COULD THOSE SHOES OF HIS...
...BE THE "WAVERS" I'VE HEARD ABOUT?
I SEE. HE USES THE FORCE OF THE BLAST TO FLOAT!
AND THOSE PISTOLS...
THEY GIVE OFF A FLASH EACH TIME HE FIRES!! BECAUSE OF THAT, I END UP LOSING SIGHT OF HIM!!
WHERE'D HE GO?!

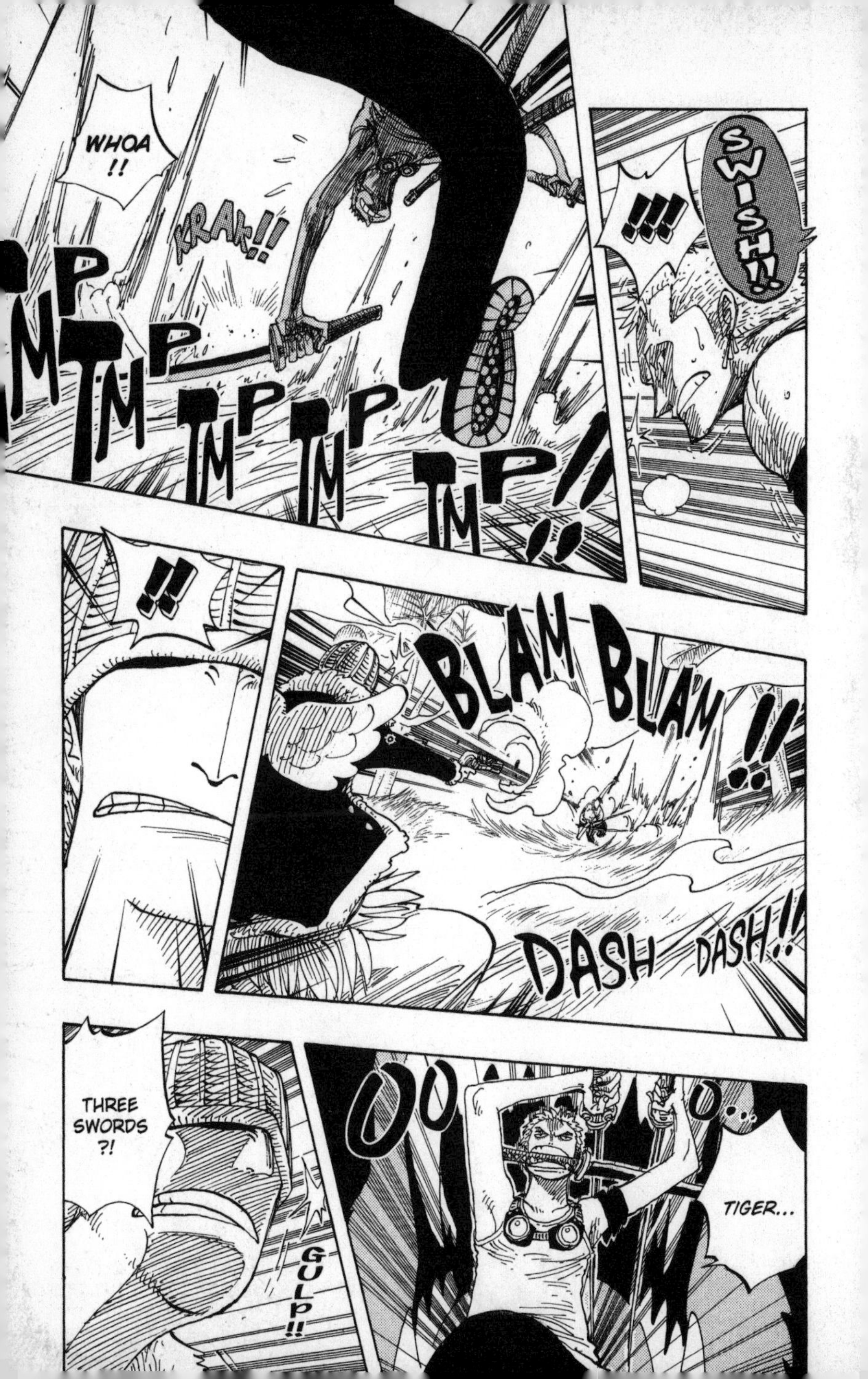

SWISH!!
!!!
WHOA!!
KRAK!!
TMP TMP TMP TMP TMP!!
BLAM BLAM!!
DASH DASH!!
!!
OOO...
TIGER...
THREE SWORDS?!
GULP!!

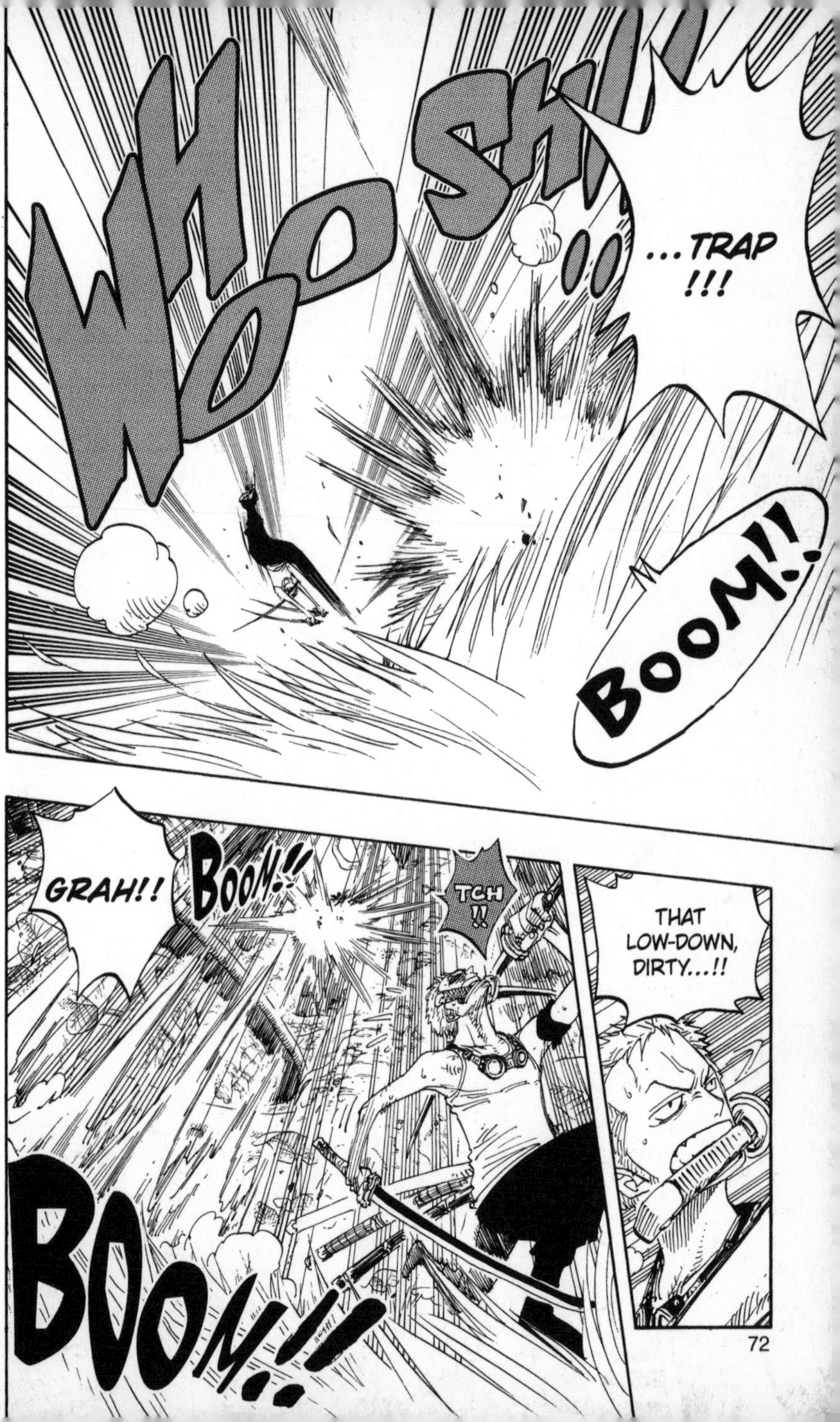
...TRAP!!!
WHOOSH!!
BOOM!!
THAT LOW-DOWN, DIRTY...!!
TCH!!
BOOM!!
GRAH!!
BOOM!!

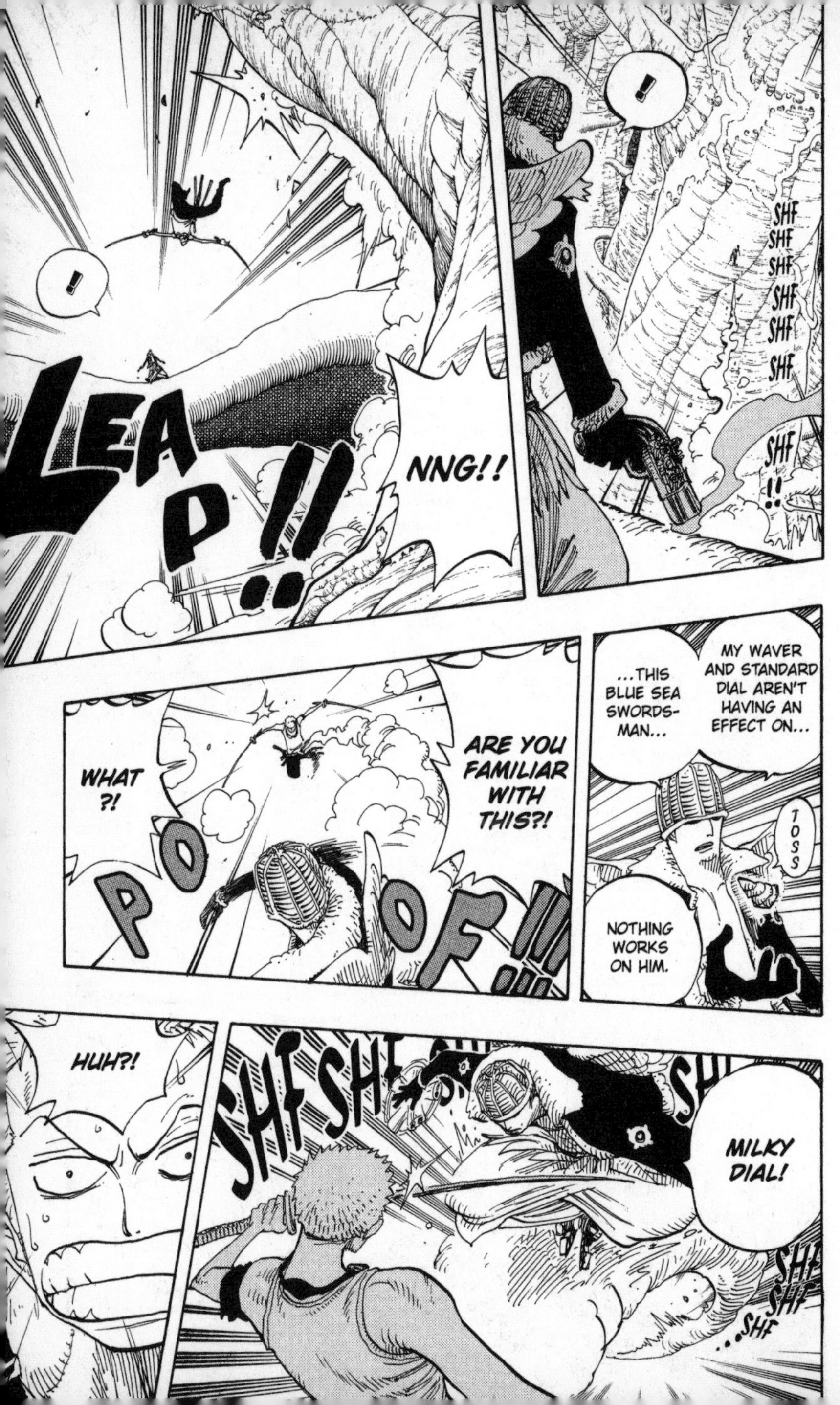
!
SHF SHF SHF SHF SHF SHF
SHF!!
!
NNG!!
LEAP!!
MY WAVER AND STANDARD DIAL AREN'T HAVING AN EFFECT ON...
...THIS BLUE SEA SWORDSMAN...
TOSS
NOTHING WORKS ON HIM.
ARE YOU FAMILIAR WITH THIS?!
WHAT?!
POOF!!
MILKY DIAL!
SHFSHF
SHF
SHF SHF ...SHF
HUH?!

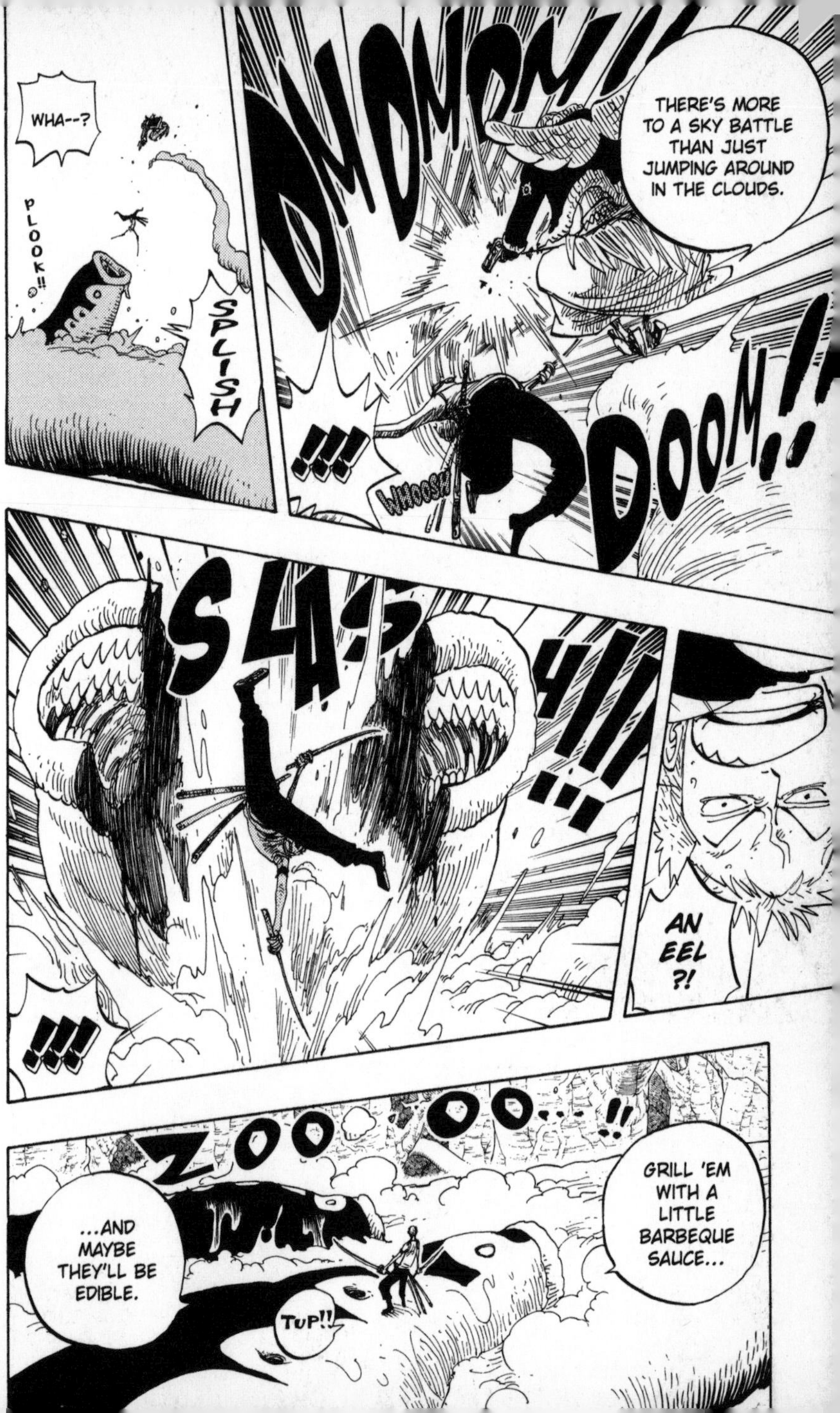
THERE'S MORE TO A SKY BATTLE THAN JUST JUMPING AROUND IN THE CLOUDS.
DMDMDM!!
DOOM!!
WHOOSH
!!!
WHA--?
PLOOK!!
SPLISH
AN EEL ?!
SLASH!!!
!!!
ZOOOO!!
GRILL 'EM WITH A LITTLE BARBEQUE SAUCE...
...AND MAYBE THEY'LL BE EDIBLE.
TUP!!

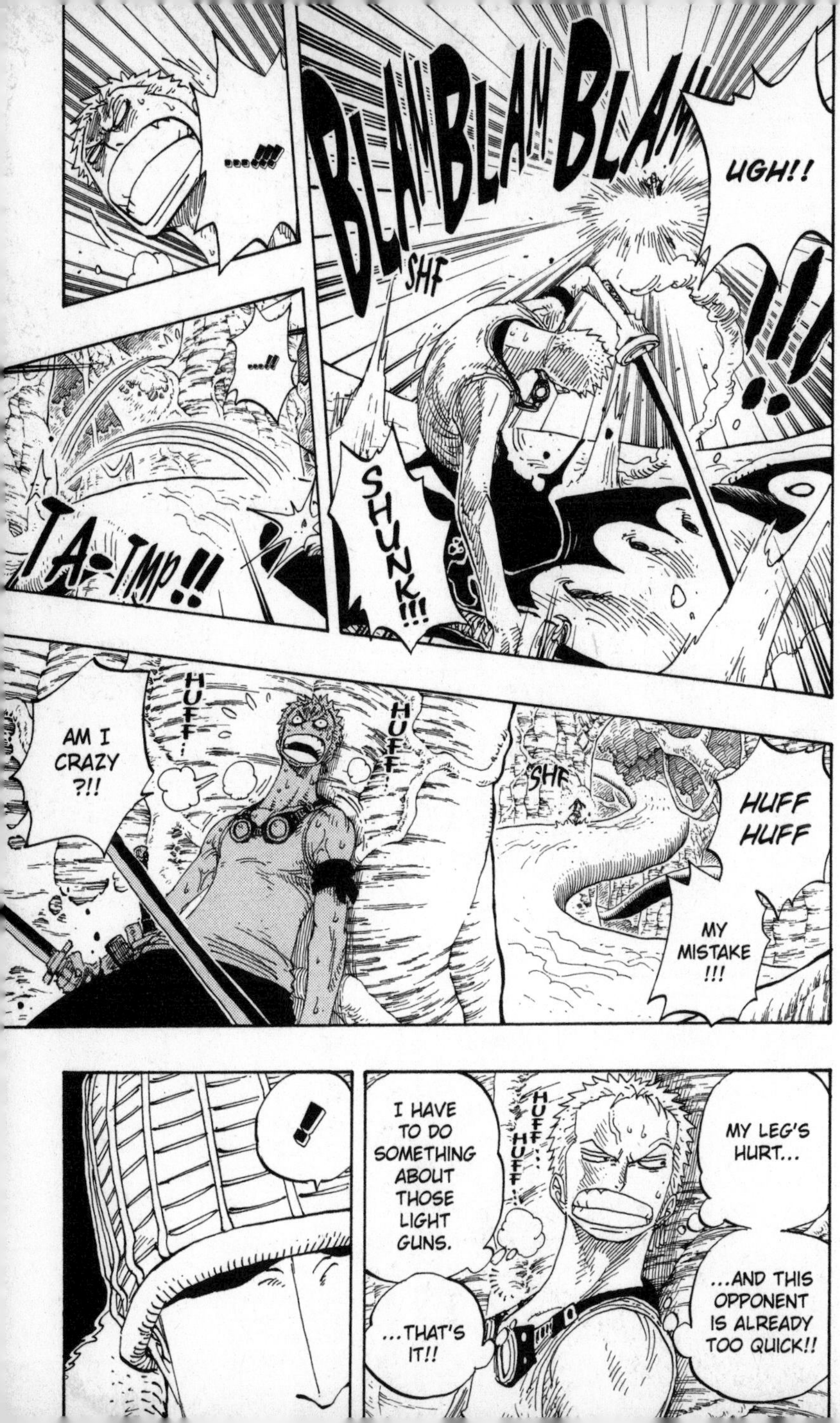
BLAM BLAM BLAM
UGH!!
!!
...!!!
SHF
SHUNK!!!
...!!
TA-TMP!!
SHF
HUFF HUFF
MY MISTAKE!!!
HUFF...
HUFF...
AM I CRAZY?!!
MY LEG'S HURT...
...AND THIS OPPONENT IS ALREADY TOO QUICK!!
HUFF...
HUFF...
I HAVE TO DO SOMETHING ABOUT THOSE LIGHT GUNS.
...THAT'S IT!!
!

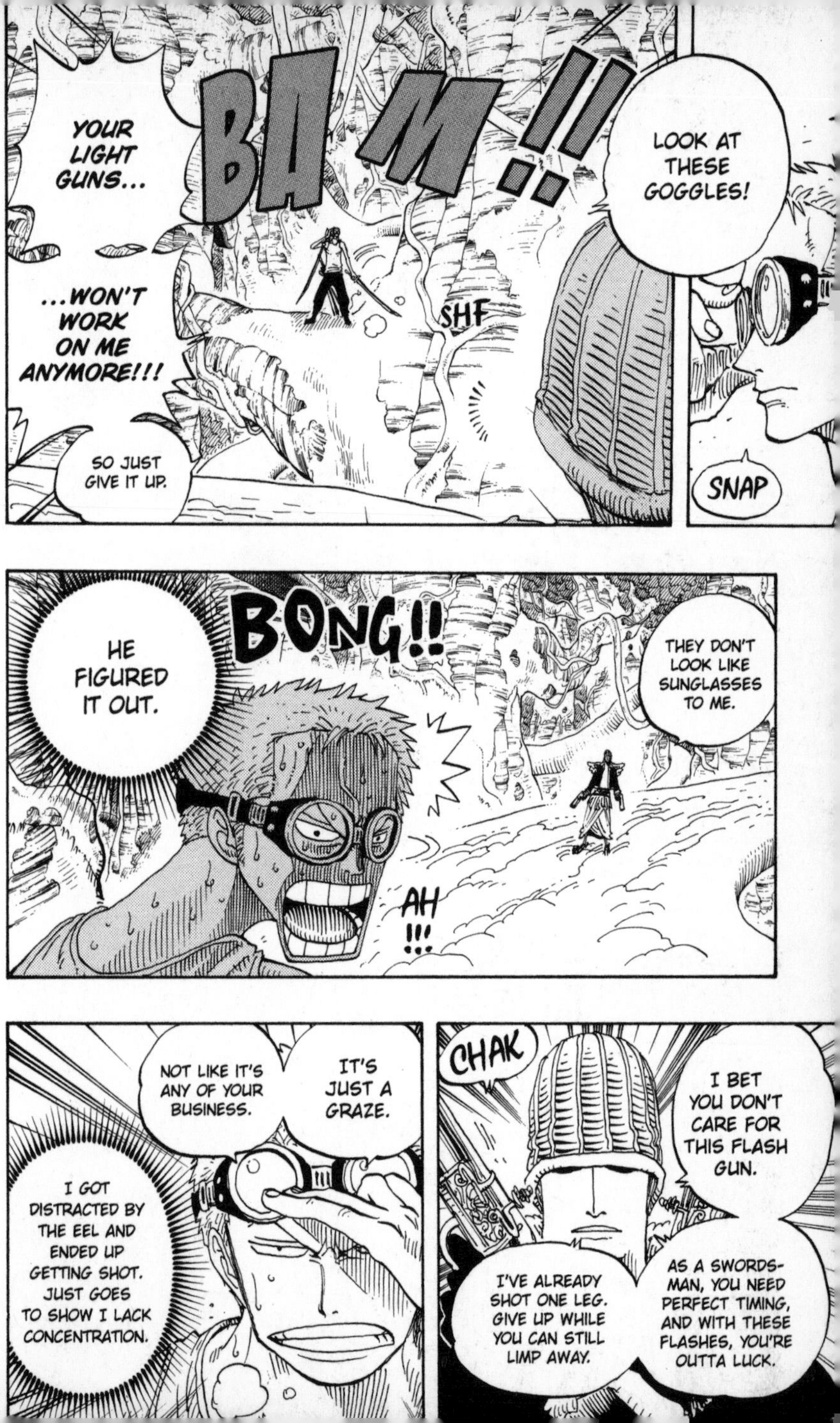
LOOK AT THESE GOGGLES!
SNAP
BAM!!
YOUR LIGHT GUNS...
...WON'T WORK ON ME ANYMORE!!!
SHF
SO JUST GIVE IT UP.
THEY DON'T LOOK LIKE SUNGLASSES TO ME.
BONG!!
HE FIGURED IT OUT.
AH!!!
I BET YOU DON'T CARE FOR THIS FLASH GUN.
CHAK
AS A SWORDS-MAN, YOU NEED PERFECT TIMING, AND WITH THESE FLASHES, YOU'RE OUTTA LUCK.
I'VE ALREADY SHOT ONE LEG. GIVE UP WHILE YOU CAN STILL LIMP AWAY.
IT'S JUST A GRAZE.
NOT LIKE IT'S ANY OF YOUR BUSINESS.
I GOT DISTRACTED BY THE EEL AND ENDED UP GETTING SHOT. JUST GOES TO SHOW I LACK CONCENTRATION.

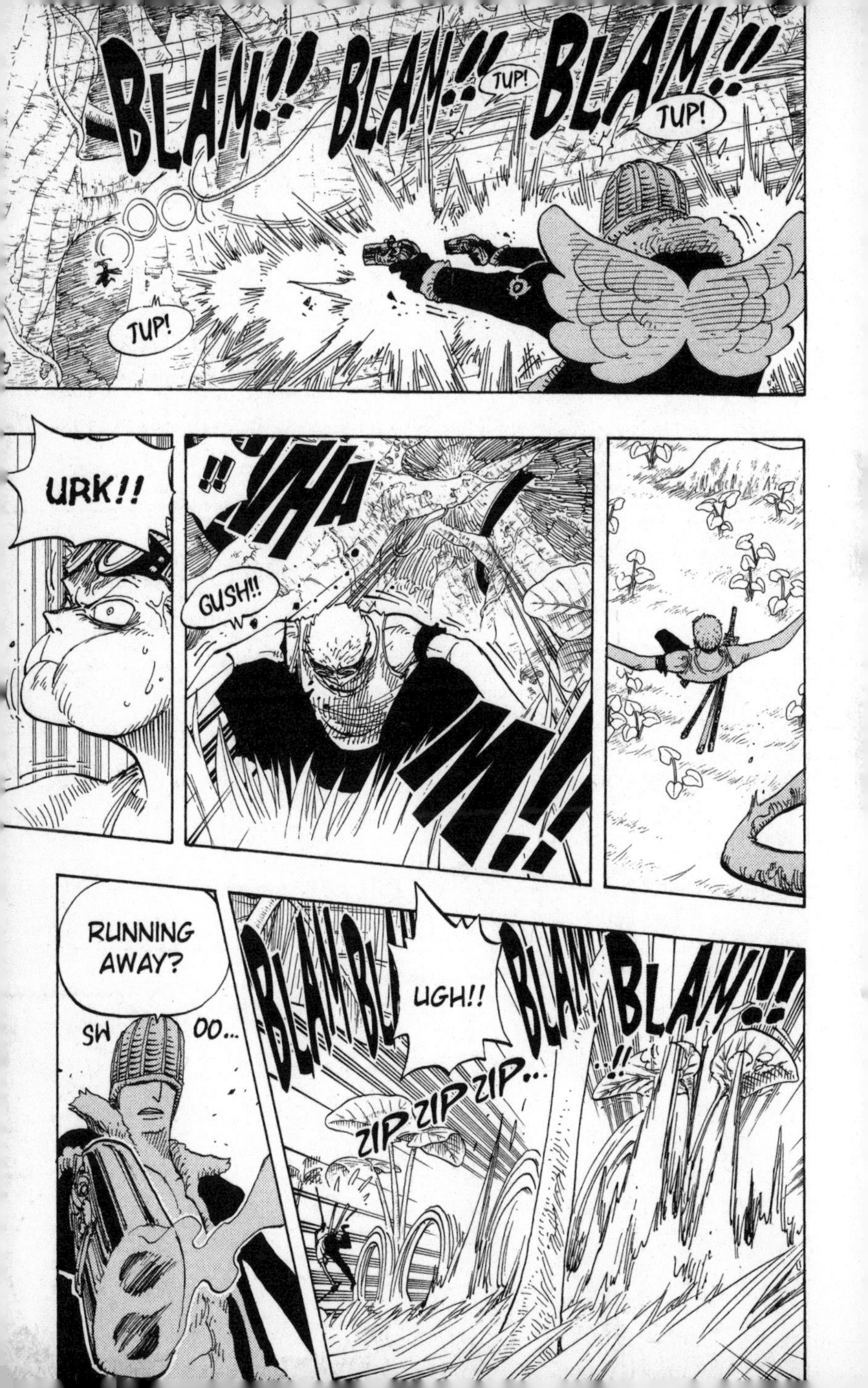
BLAM!!
TUP!
BLAM!!
TUP!
BLAM!!
TUP!
GUSH!!
URK!!
BLAM!!
BLAM
UGH!!
BLAM BL
ZIP ZIP ZIP...
RUNNING AWAY?
SWOO...

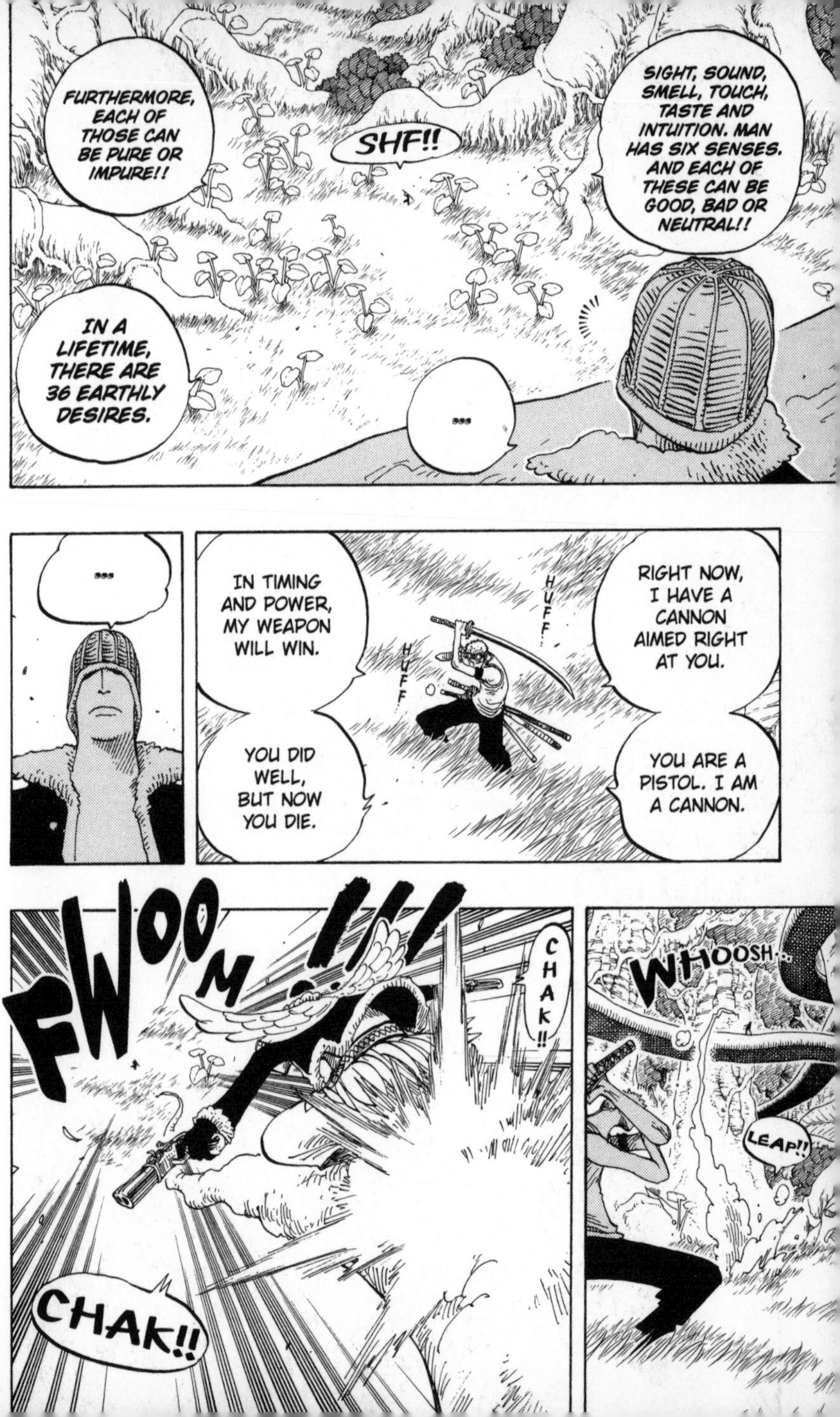

SIGHT, SOUND, SMELL, TOUCH, TASTE AND INTUITION. MAN HAS SIX SENSES. AND EACH OF THESE CAN BE GOOD, BAD OR NEUTRAL!!
SHF!!
FURTHERMORE, EACH OF THOSE CAN BE PURE OR IMPURE!!
IN A LIFETIME, THERE ARE 36 EARTHLY DESIRES.
...
RIGHT NOW, I HAVE A CANNON AIMED RIGHT AT YOU.
YOU ARE A PISTOL. I AM A CANNON.
HUFF
HUFF...
IN TIMING AND POWER, MY WEAPON WILL WIN.
YOU DID WELL, BUT NOW YOU DIE.
...
WHOOSH...
LEAP!!
CHAK!!
FWOOM!!!
CHAK!!

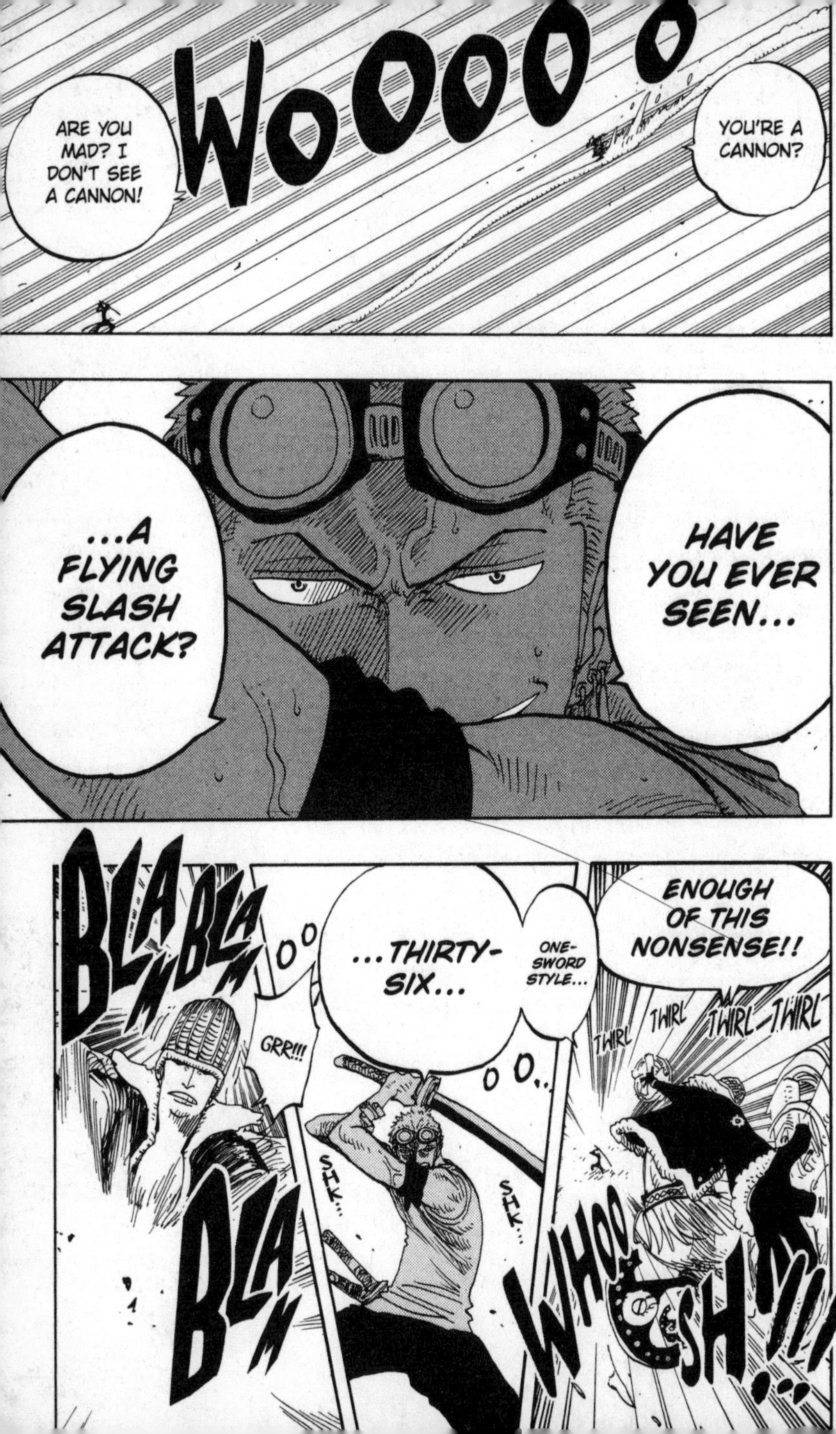
YOU'RE A CANNON?
WOOOO O
ARE YOU MAD? I DON'T SEE A CANNON!
HAVE YOU EVER SEEN...
...A FLYING SLASH ATTACK?
ENOUGH OF THIS NONSENSE!!
TWIRL TWIRL TWIRL TWIRL
WHOOSH!!!
ONE-SWORD STYLE...
...THIRTY-SIX...
OO...
SHK...
SHK...
GRR!!!
BLAM BLAM
BLAM

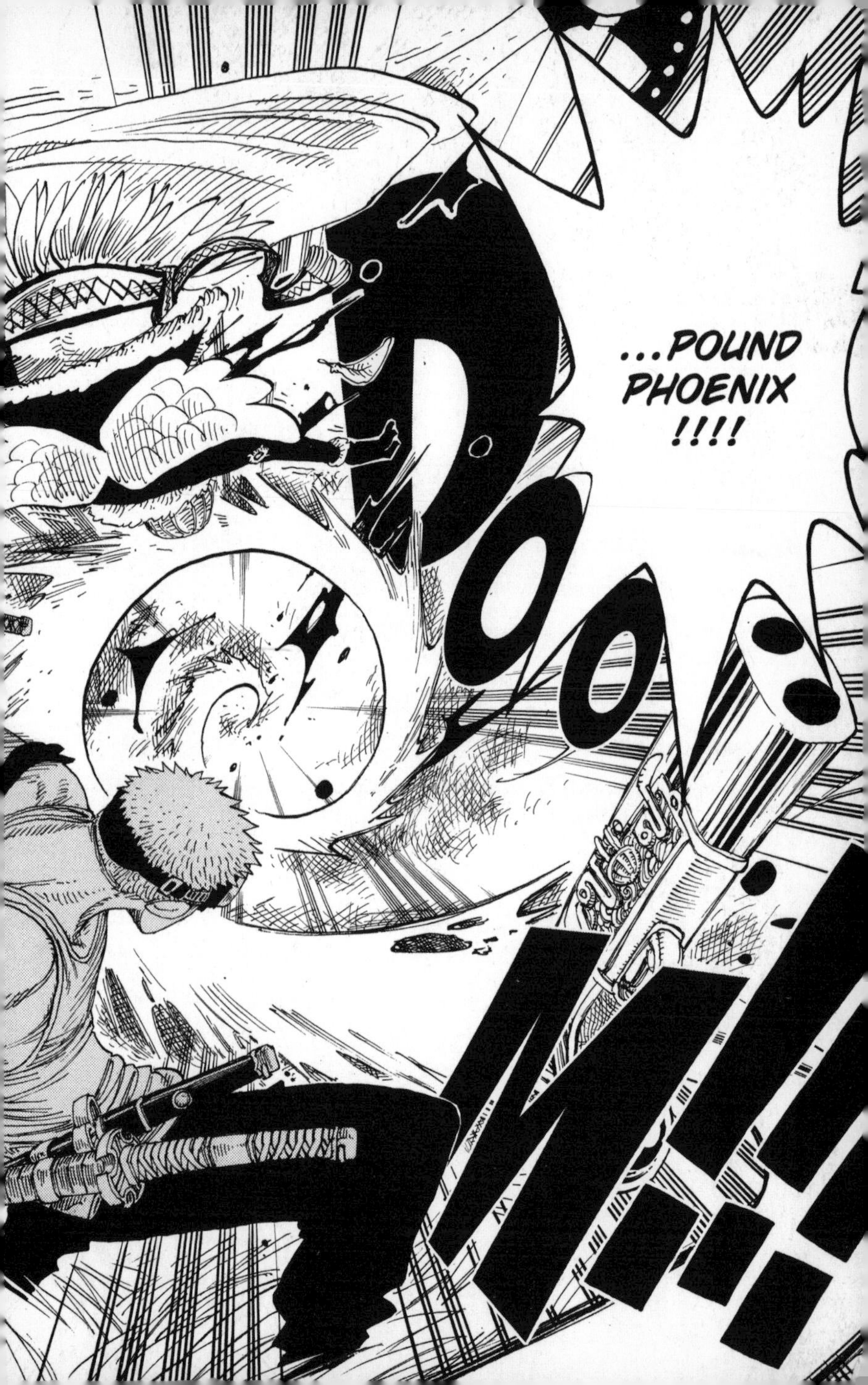
...POUND PHOENIX !!!!

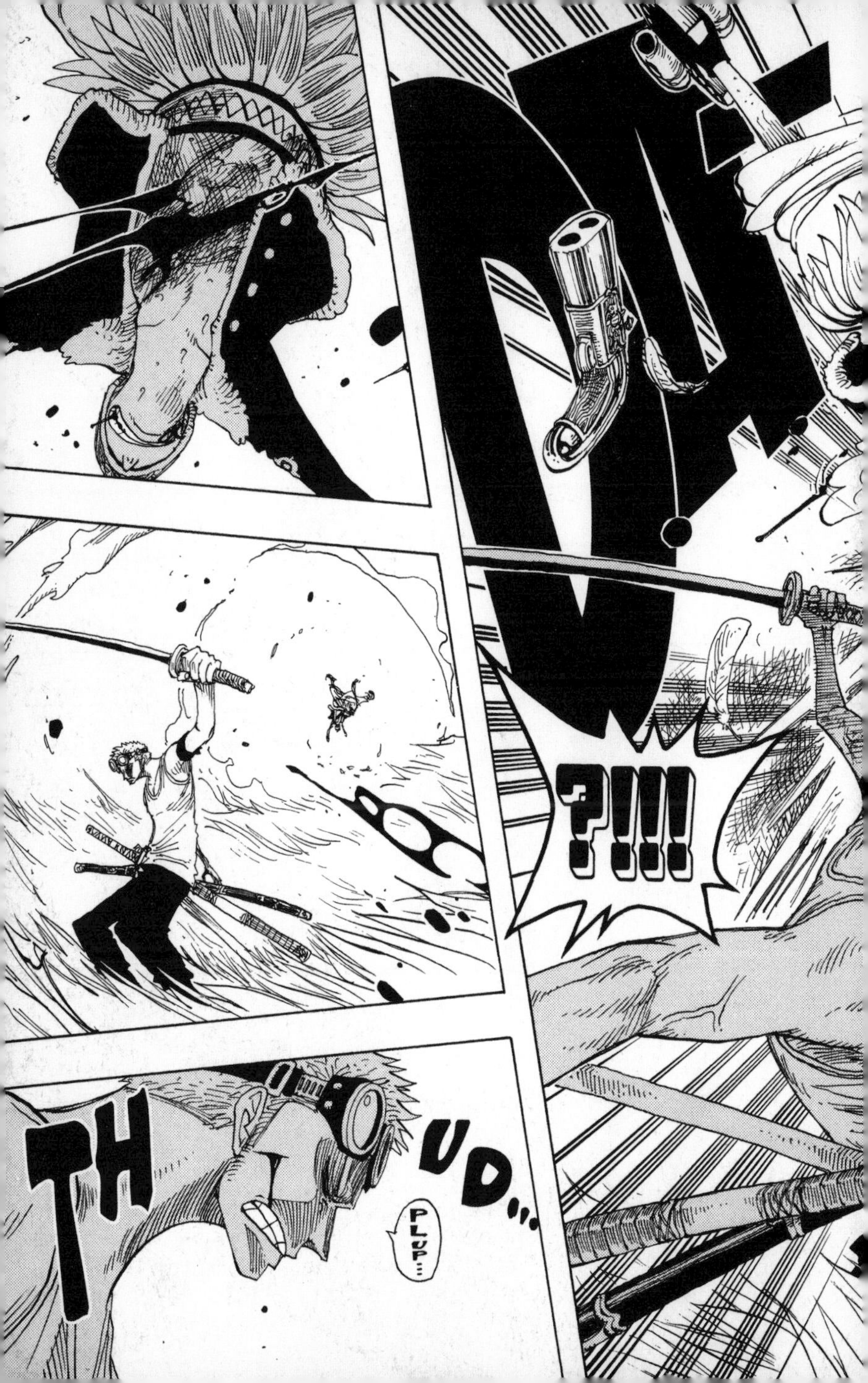
?!!!
THUD...
PLUP..

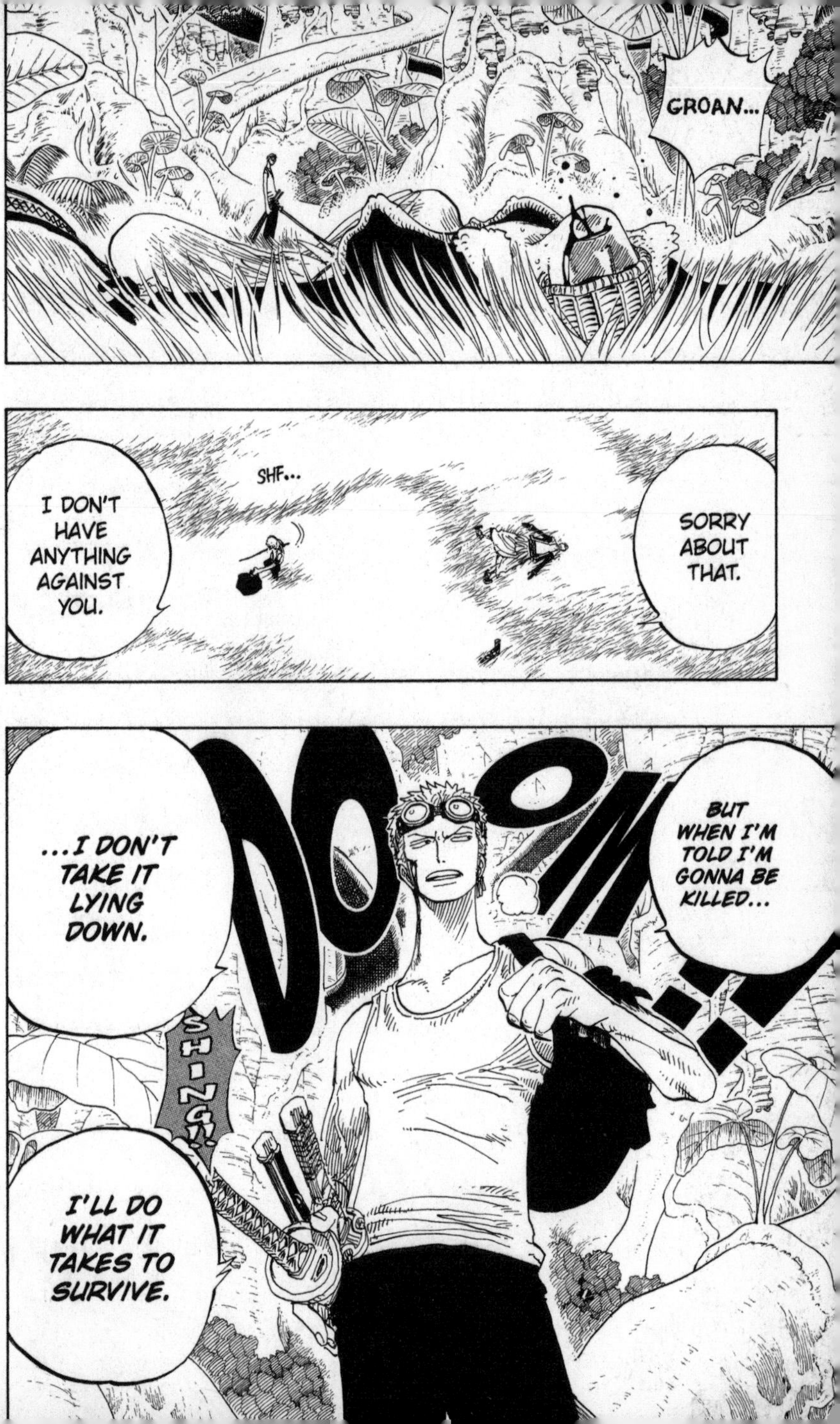
GROAN...
SORRY ABOUT THAT.
SHF...
I DON'T HAVE ANYTHING AGAINST YOU.
BUT WHEN I'M TOLD I'M GONNA BE KILLED...
DOOM..!!
...I DON'T TAKE IT LYING DOWN.
SHING!!
I'LL DO WHAT IT TAKES TO SURVIVE.

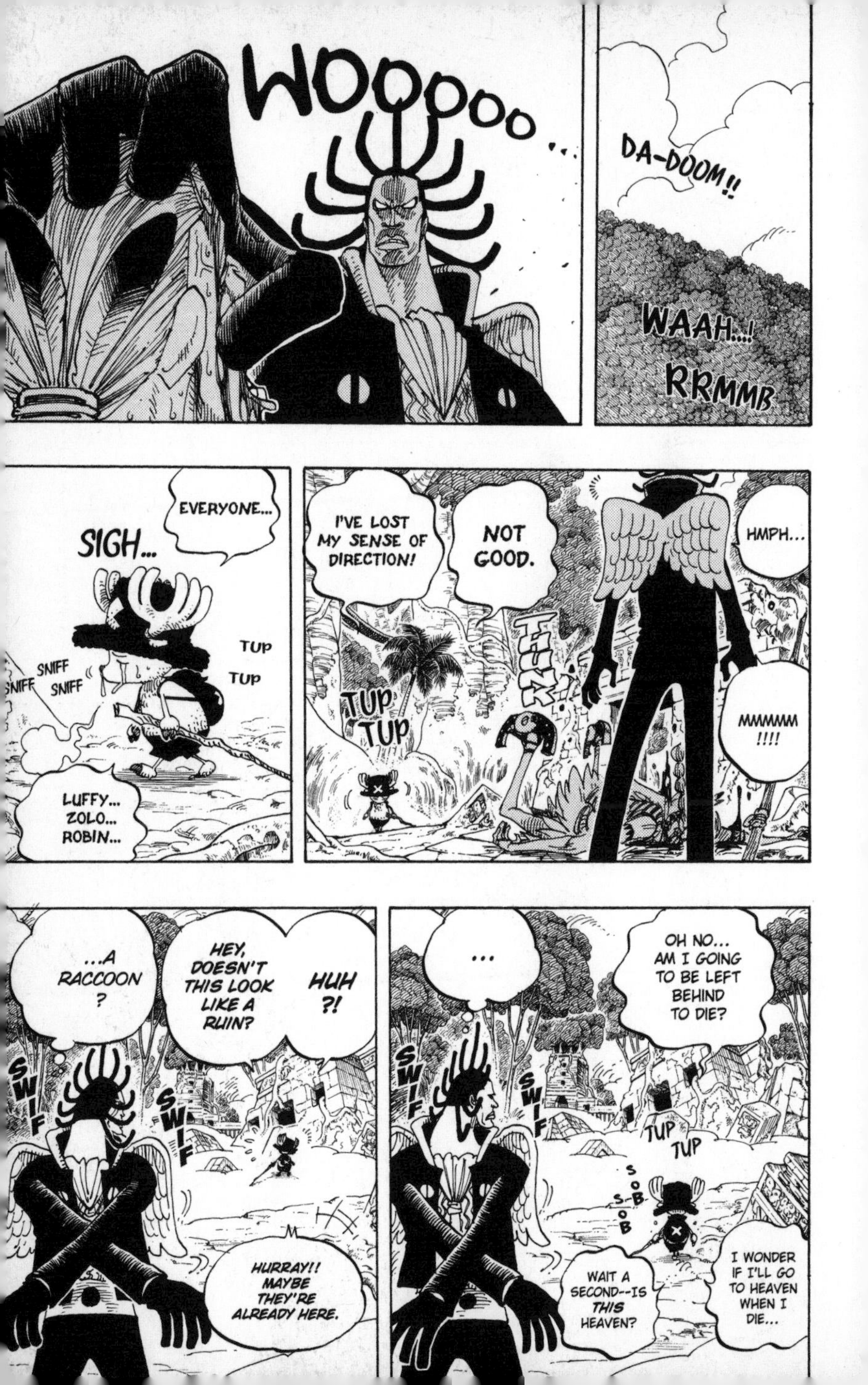
DA-DOOM!!
WAAH...!
RRMMB
WOOOOO...
HMPH...
MMMMM !!!!
NOT GOOD.
I'VE LOST MY SENSE OF DIRECTION!
THUNK
TUP TUP
EVERYONE...
SIGH...
TUP
TUP
SNIFF
SNIFF SNIFF
LUFFY... ZOLO... ROBIN...
OH NO... AM I GOING TO BE LEFT BEHIND TO DIE?
...
SWIF
TUP TUP
SOB SOB
I WONDER IF I'LL GO TO HEAVEN WHEN I DIE...
WAIT A SECOND--IS THIS HEAVEN?
HUH ?!
HEY, DOESN'T THIS LOOK LIKE A RUIN?
...A RACCOON ?
SWIF
SWIF
HURRAY!! MAYBE THEY'RE ALREADY HERE.

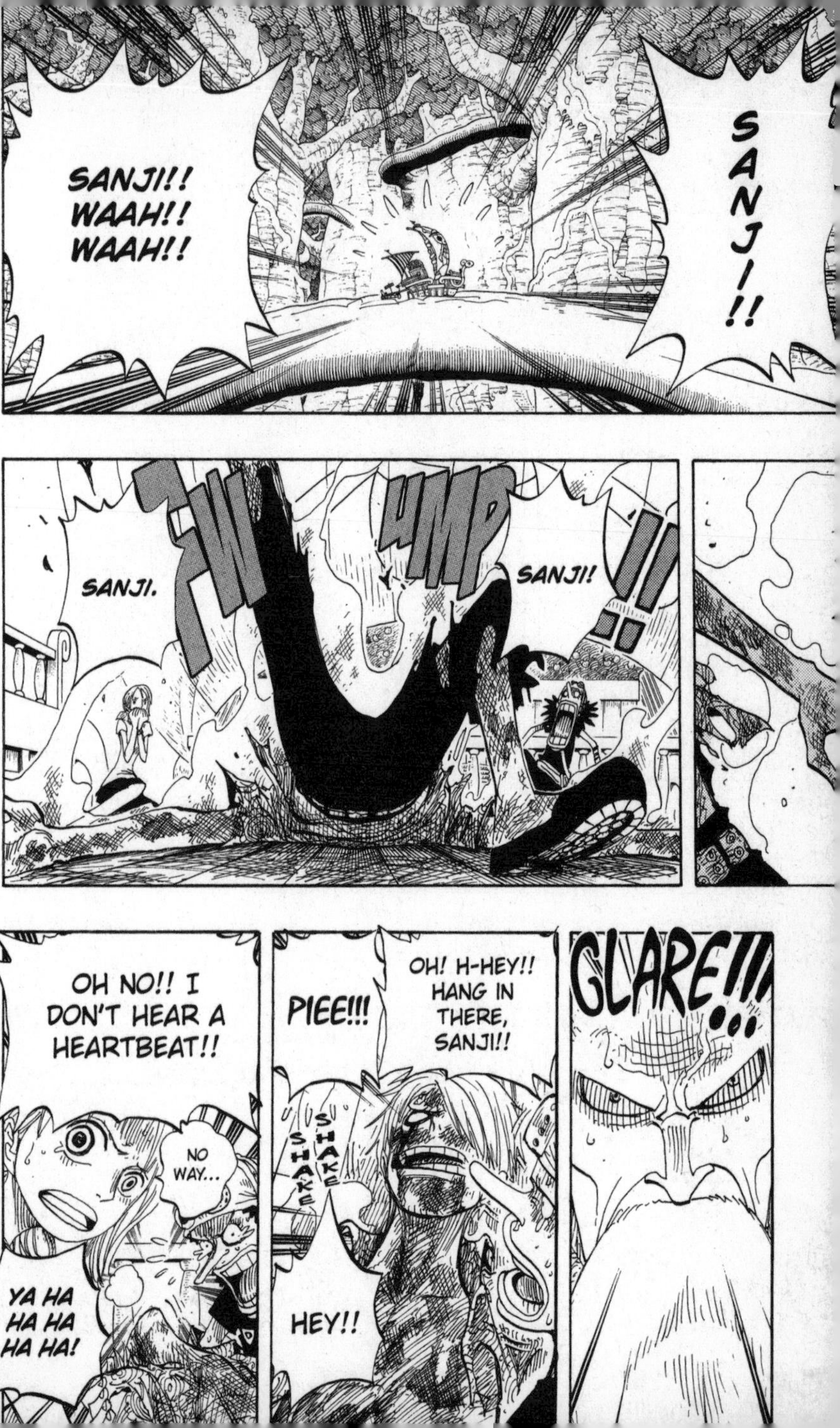
SANJI!!
SANJI!! WAAH!! WAAH!!
SANJI!
SANJI.
GLARE!!!
OH! H-HEY!! HANG IN THERE, SANJI!!
PIEE!!!
SHAKE SHAKE
SHAKE
HEY!!
OH NO!! I DON'T HEAR A HEARTBEAT!!
NO WAY...
YA HA HA HA HA HA!

Chapter 260: PIRATE LUFFY

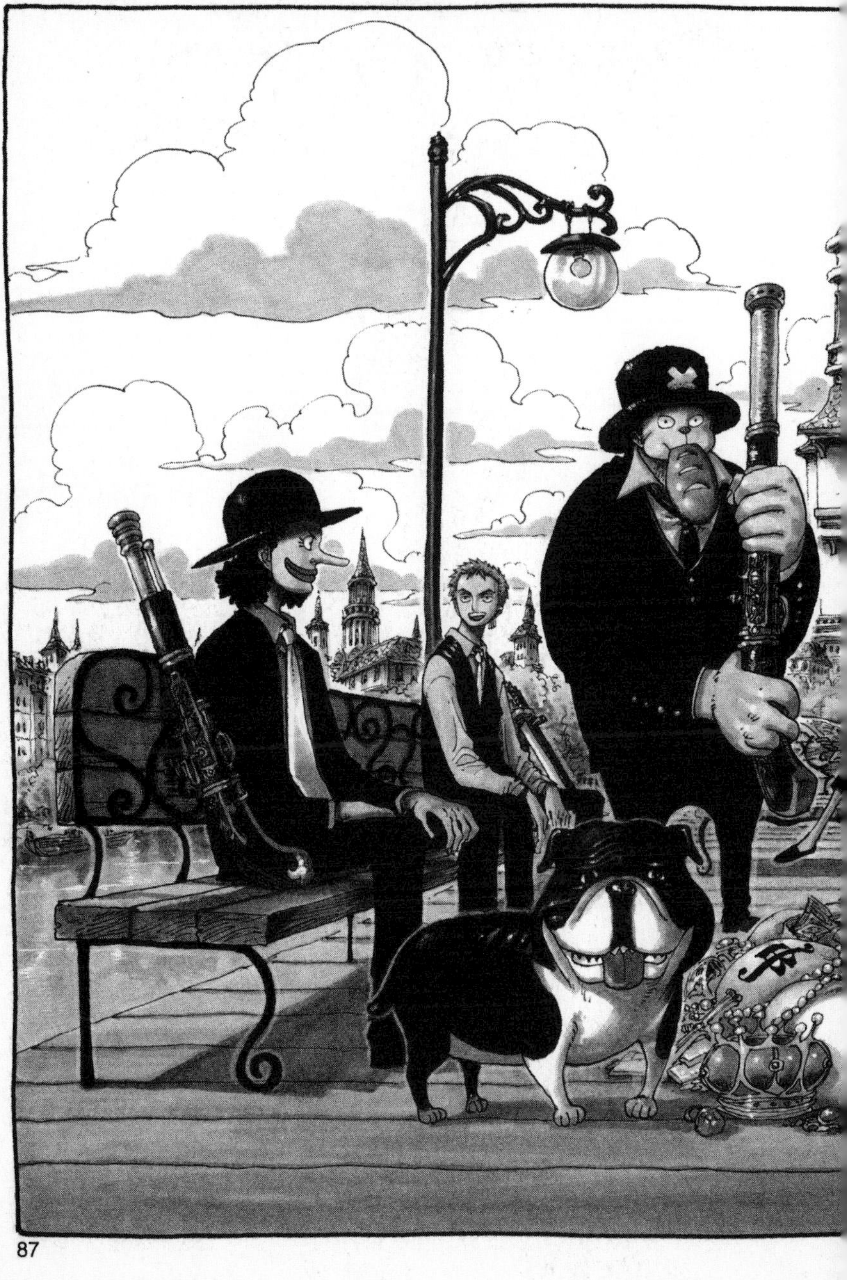

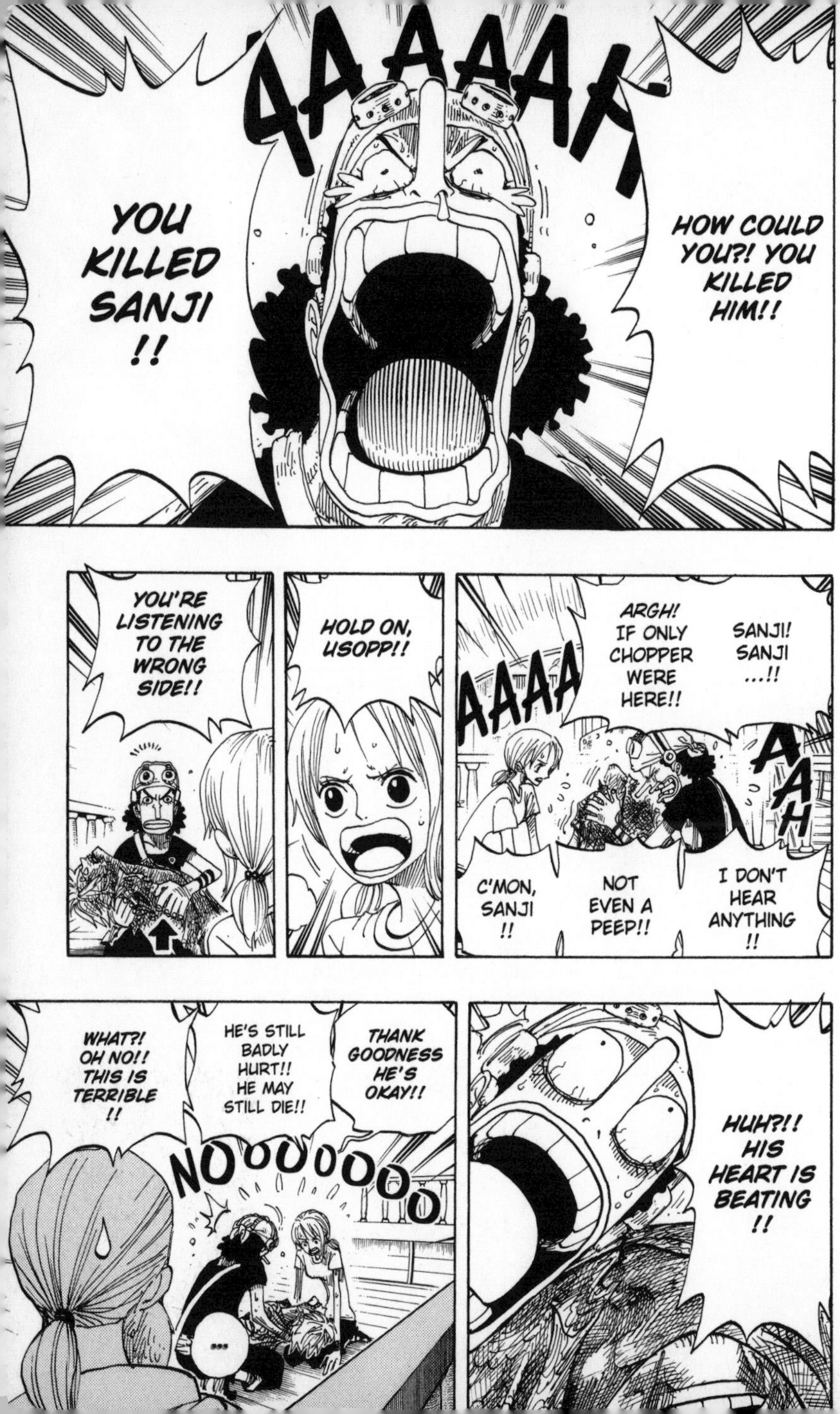
AAAAAH
HOW COULD YOU?! YOU KILLED HIM!!
YOU KILLED SANJI !!
SANJI! SANJI ...!!
ARGH! IF ONLY CHOPPER WERE HERE!!
AAAA
AAH
I DON'T HEAR ANYTHING !!
NOT EVEN A PEEP!!
C'MON, SANJI !!
HOLD ON, USOPP!!
YOU'RE LISTENING TO THE WRONG SIDE!!
HUH?!! HIS HEART IS BEATING !!
THANK GOODNESS HE'S OKAY!!
HE'S STILL BADLY HURT!! HE MAY STILL DIE!!
WHAT?! OH NO!! THIS IS TERRIBLE !!
NOOOOOOOOO

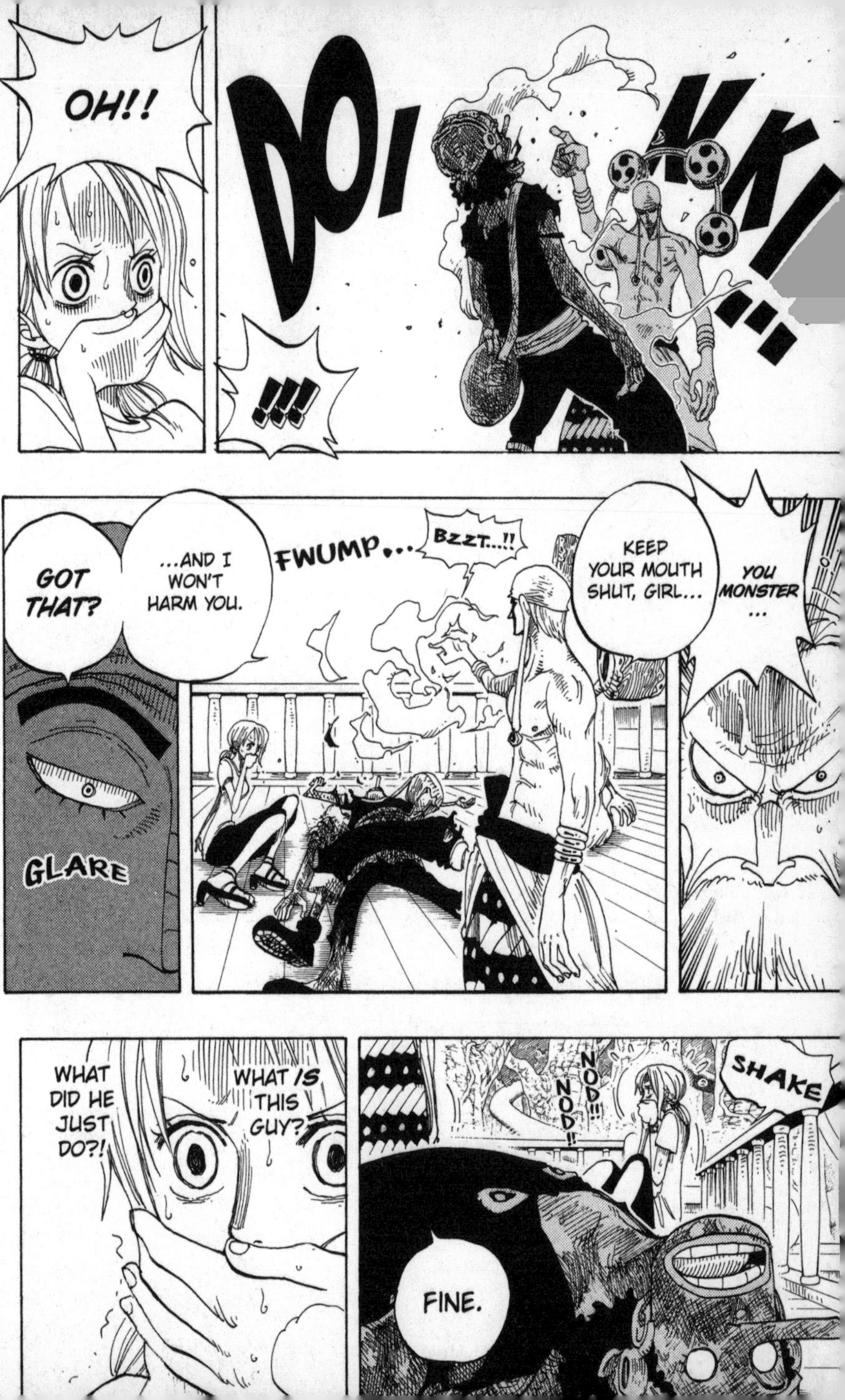
DOINK!!
!!!
OH!!
YOU MONSTER...
KEEP YOUR MOUTH SHUT, GIRL...
BZZT...!!
FWUMP...
...AND I WON'T HARM YOU.
GOT THAT?
GLARE
SHAKE
NOD!!
NOD!!
FINE.
WHAT IS THIS GUY?
WHAT DID HE JUST DO?!

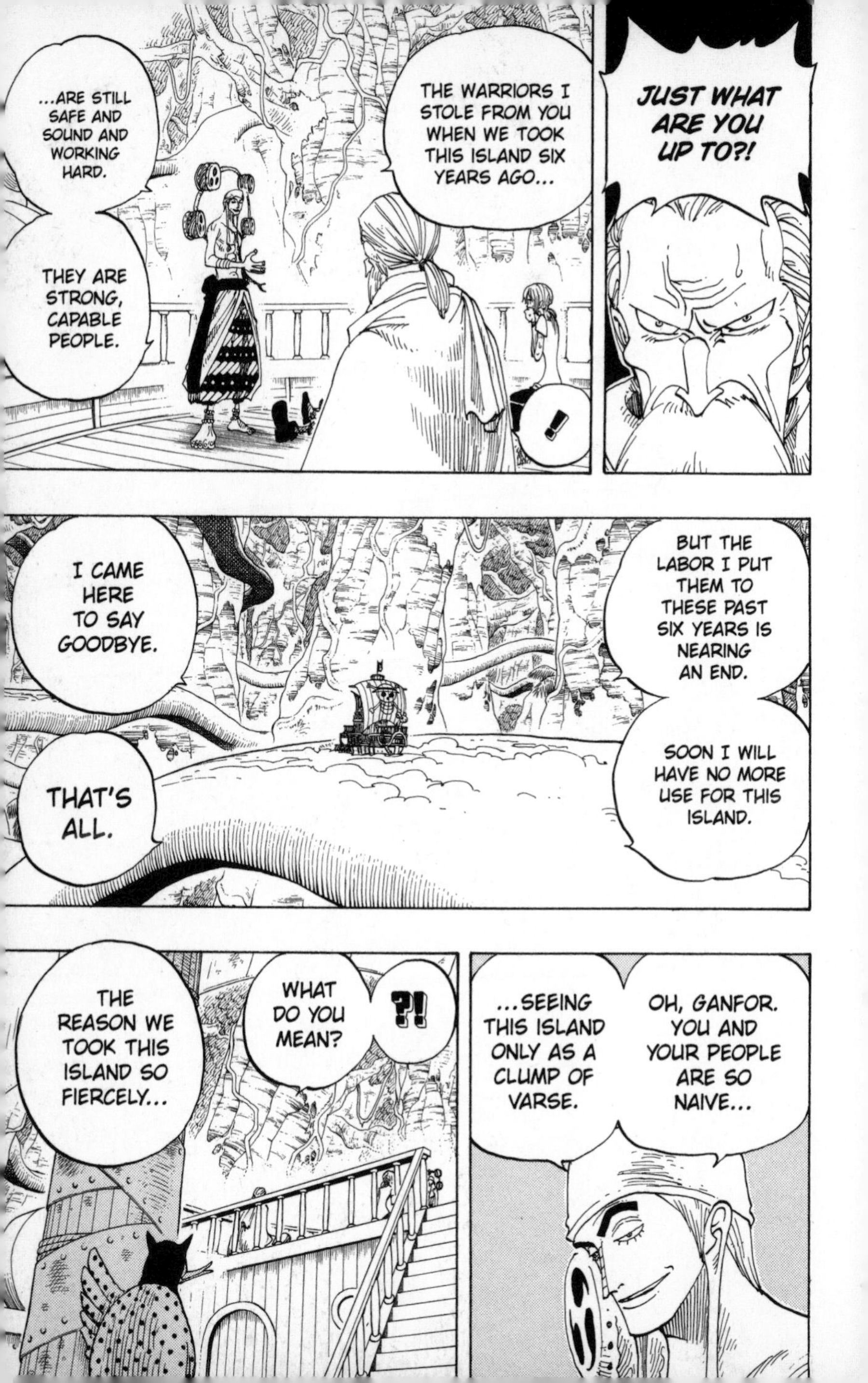
JUST WHAT ARE YOU UP TO?!
!
THE WARRIORS I STOLE FROM YOU WHEN WE TOOK THIS ISLAND SIX YEARS AGO...
...ARE STILL SAFE AND SOUND AND WORKING HARD.
THEY ARE STRONG, CAPABLE PEOPLE.
BUT THE LABOR I PUT THEM TO THESE PAST SIX YEARS IS NEARING AN END.
SOON I WILL HAVE NO MORE USE FOR THIS ISLAND.
I CAME HERE TO SAY GOODBYE.
THAT'S ALL.
OH, GANFOR. YOU AND YOUR PEOPLE ARE SO NAIVE...
...SEEING THIS ISLAND ONLY AS A CLUMP OF VARSE.
?!
WHAT DO YOU MEAN?
THE REASON WE TOOK THIS ISLAND SO FIERCELY...

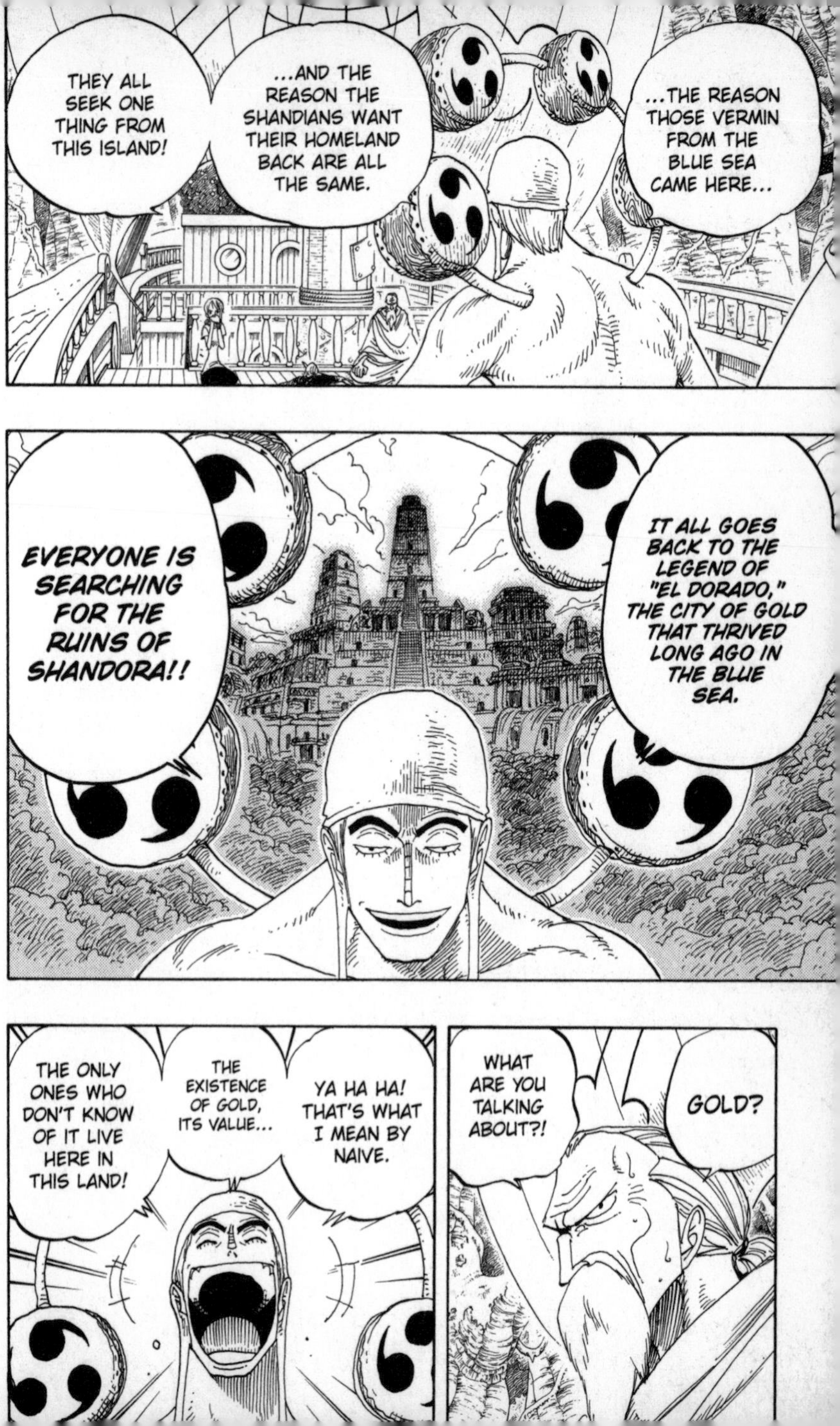
...THE REASON THOSE VERMIN FROM THE BLUE SEA CAME HERE...
...AND THE REASON THE SHANDIANS WANT THEIR HOMELAND BACK ARE ALL THE SAME.
THEY ALL SEEK ONE THING FROM THIS ISLAND!
IT ALL GOES BACK TO THE LEGEND OF "EL DORADO," THE CITY OF GOLD THAT THRIVED LONG AGO IN THE BLUE SEA.
EVERYONE IS SEARCHING FOR THE RUINS OF SHANDORA!!
GOLD?
WHAT ARE YOU TALKING ABOUT?!
YA HA HA! THAT'S WHAT I MEAN BY NAIVE.
THE EXISTENCE OF GOLD, ITS VALUE...
THE ONLY ONES WHO DON'T KNOW OF IT LIVE HERE IN THIS LAND!

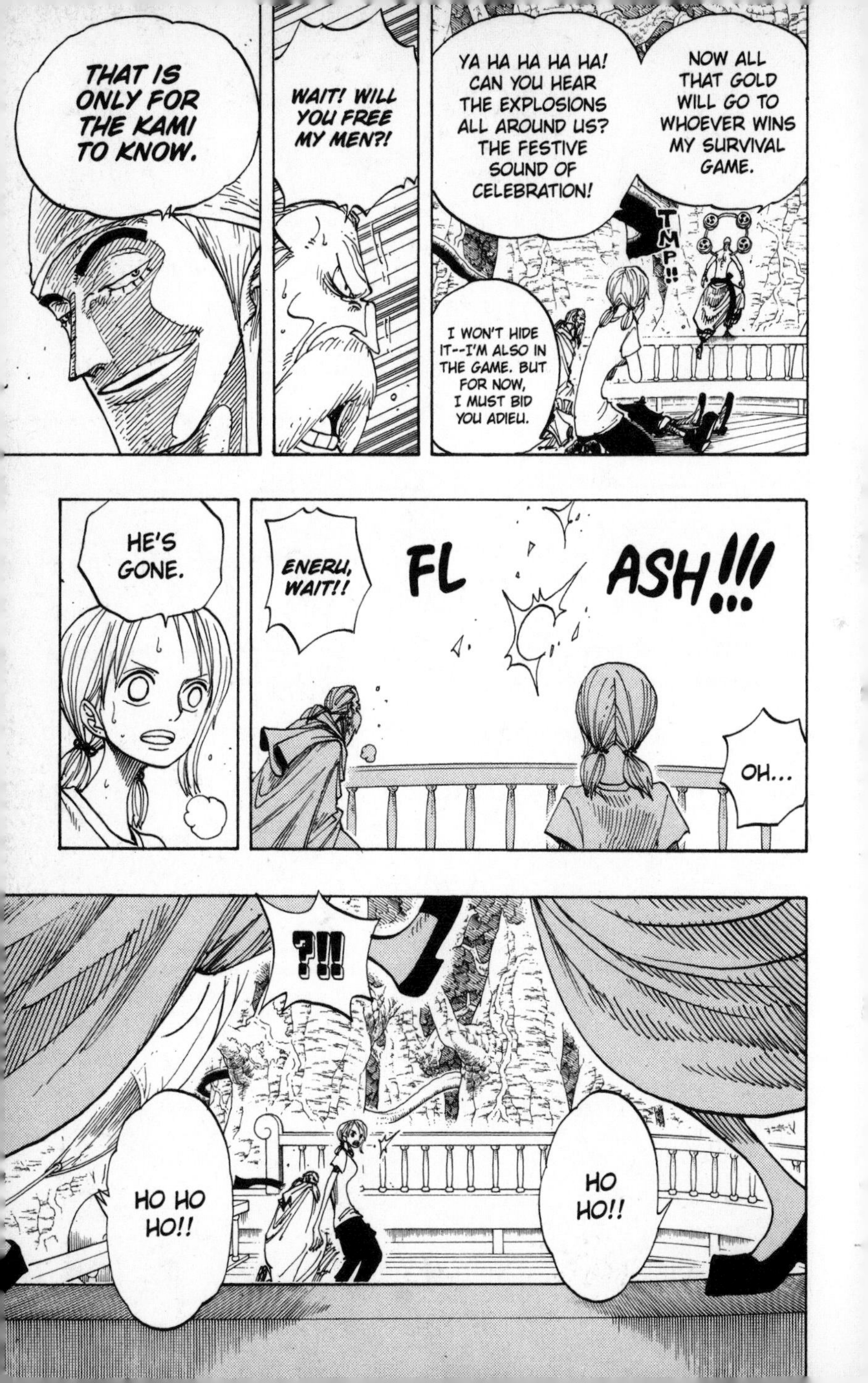
NOW ALL THAT GOLD WILL GO TO WHOEVER WINS MY SURVIVAL GAME.
YA HA HA HA HA! CAN YOU HEAR THE EXPLOSIONS ALL AROUND US? THE FESTIVE SOUND OF CELEBRATION!
TMP!!
I WON'T HIDE IT--I'M ALSO IN THE GAME. BUT FOR NOW, I MUST BID YOU ADIEU.
WAIT! WILL YOU FREE MY MEN?!
THAT IS ONLY FOR THE KAMI TO KNOW.
FL ASH!!!
ENERU, WAIT!!
OH...
HE'S GONE.
?!!
HO HO!!
HO HO HO!!

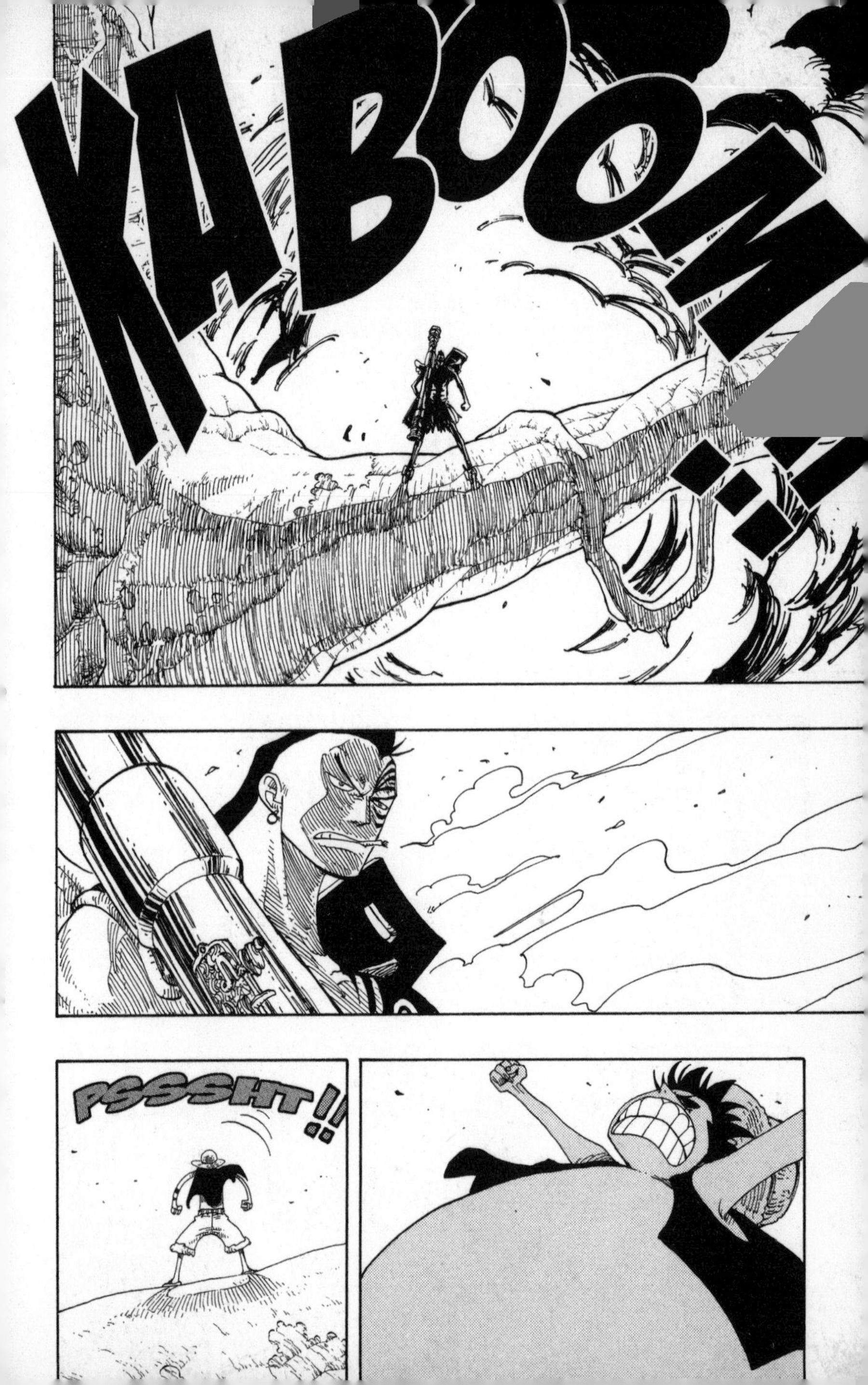
KABOOM!!
PSSSHT!!

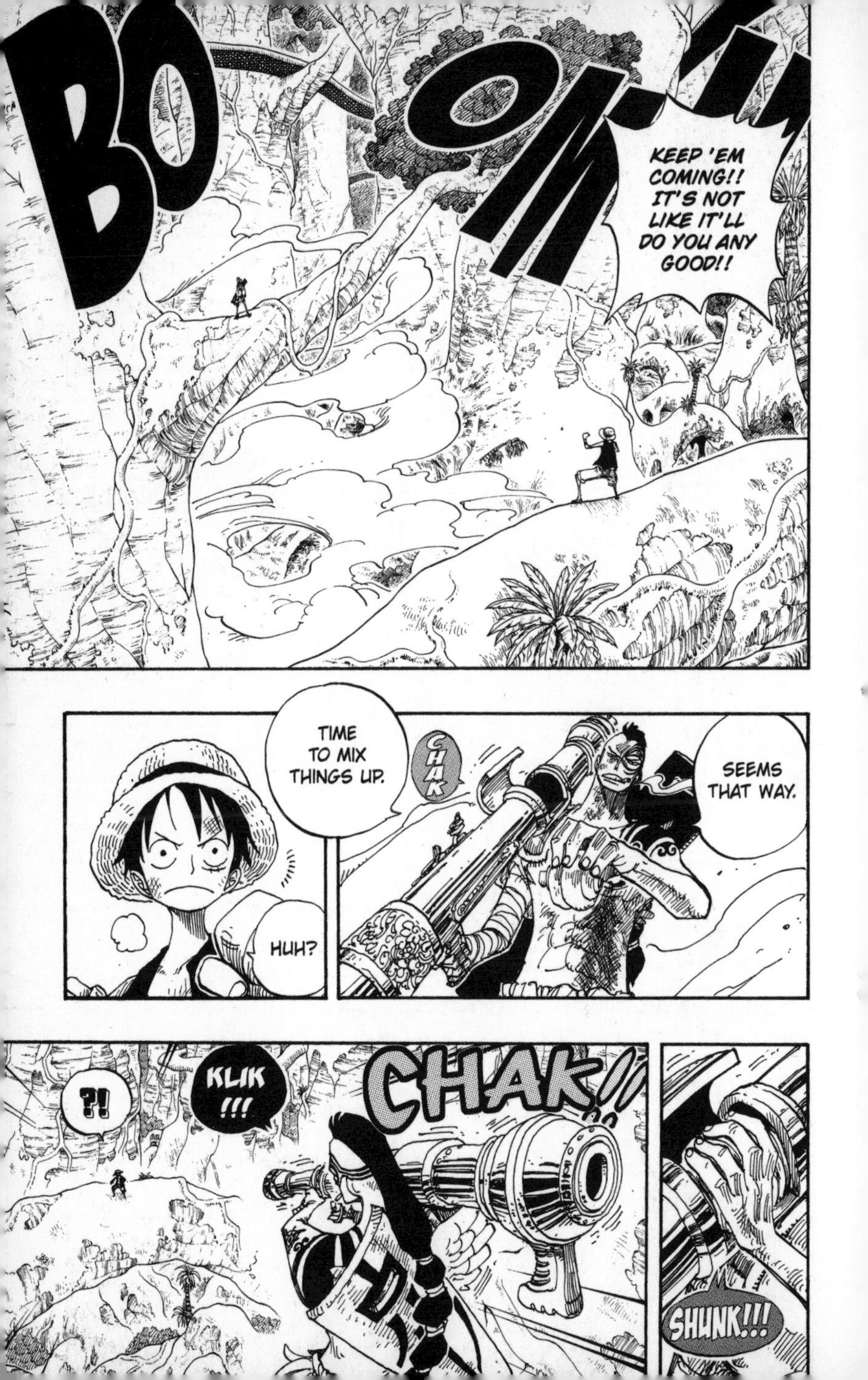
KEEP 'EM COMING!! IT'S NOT LIKE IT'LL DO YOU ANY GOOD!!
SEEMS THAT WAY.
CHAK
TIME TO MIX THINGS UP.
HUH?
SHUNK!!!
CHAK!!
KLIK !!!
?!

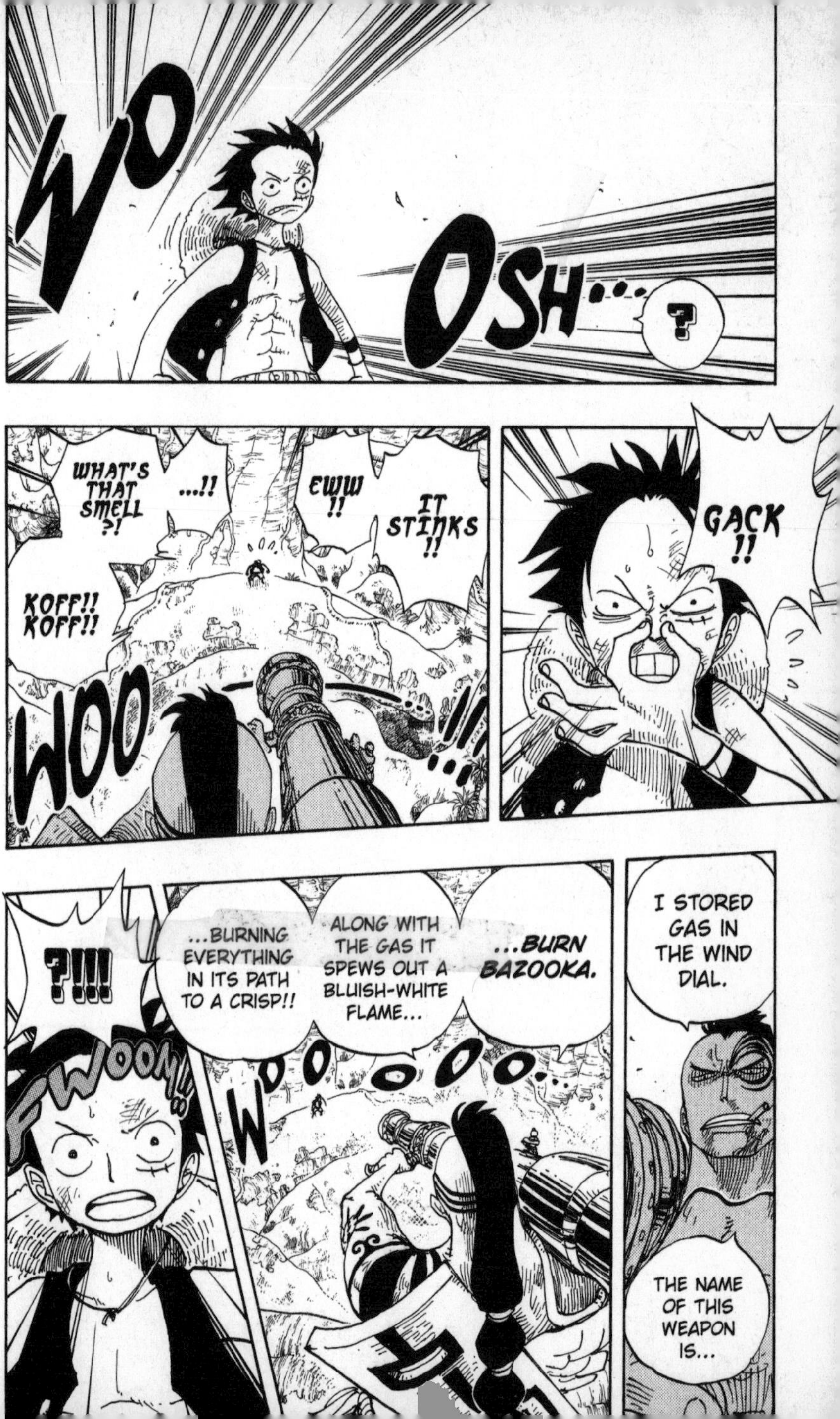
WOOSH...
?
GACK!!
IT STINKS!!
EWW!!
...!!
WHAT'S THAT SMELL?!
KOFF!! KOFF!!
WOO...!!!
I STORED GAS IN THE WIND DIAL.
THE NAME OF THIS WEAPON IS...
...BURN BAZOOKA.
ALONG WITH THE GAS IT SPEWS OUT A BLUISH-WHITE FLAME...
...BURNING EVERYTHING IN ITS PATH TO A CRISP!!
WOOOOOO...
?!!!
FWOOM!!

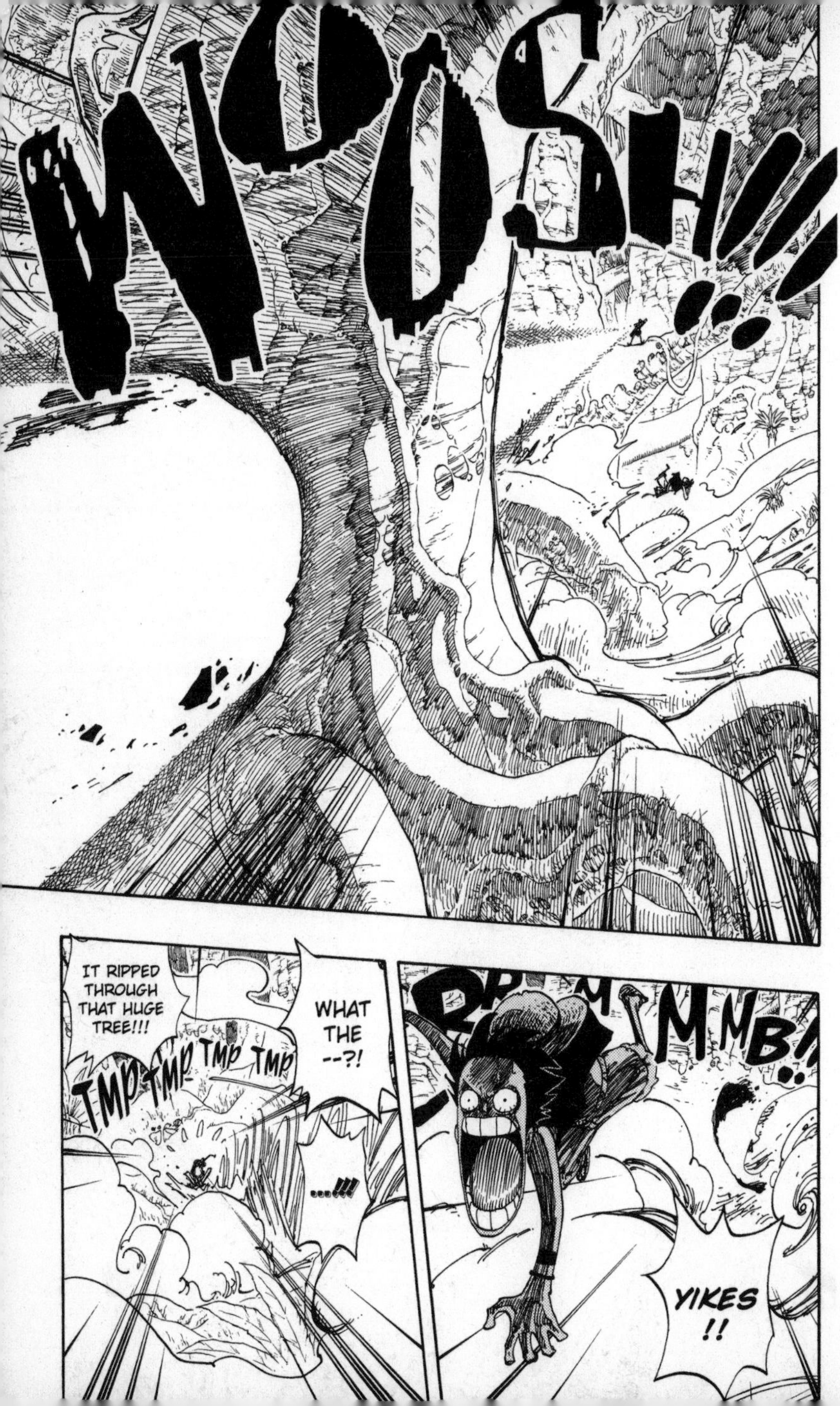
WOOSH!!!
MMB!!
YIKES !!
WHAT THE --?!
IT RIPPED THROUGH THAT HUGE TREE!!!
TMP TMP TMP TMP
...!!!

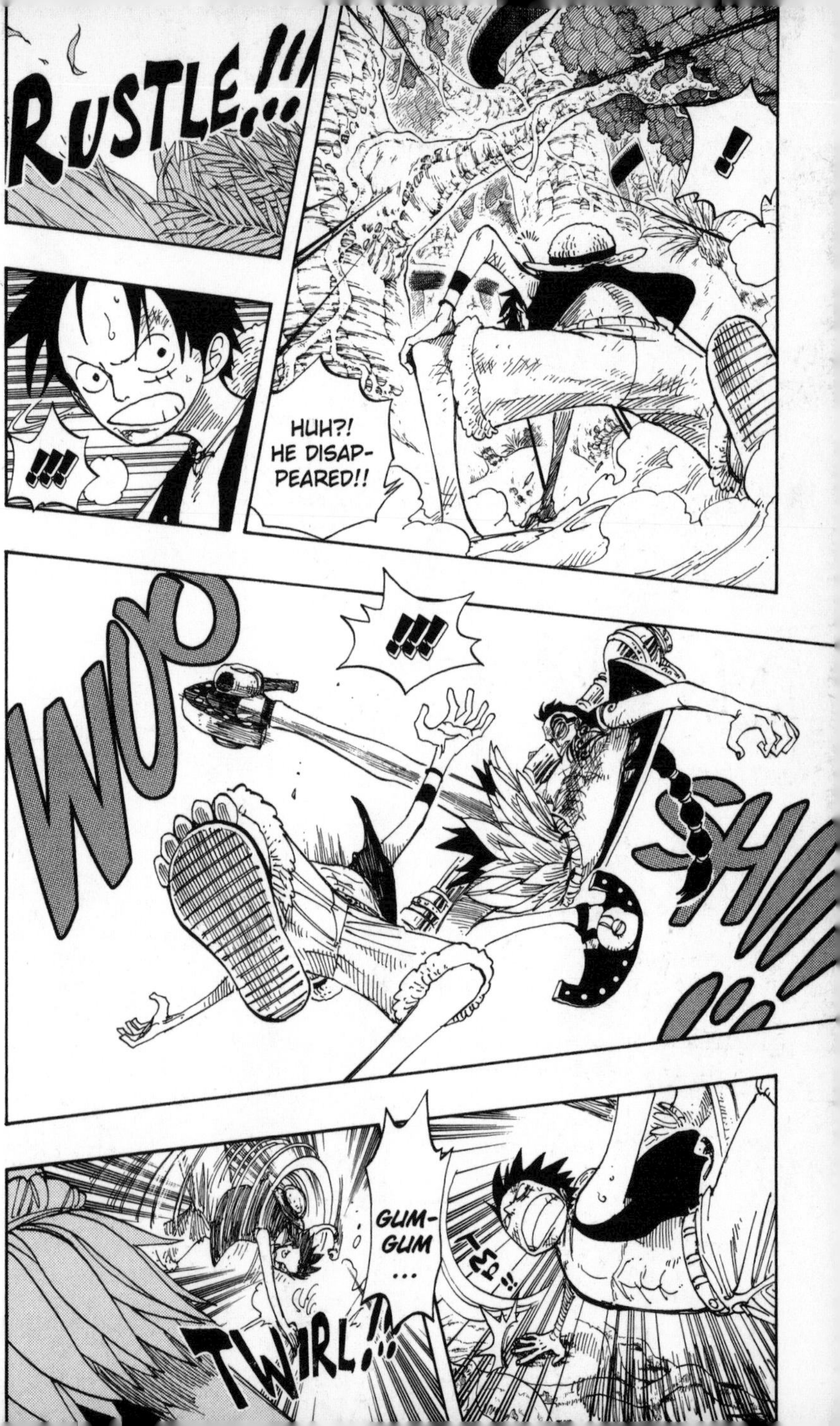
!
HUH?! HE DISAP-PEARED!!
RUSTLE!!!
!!!
SH!!
!!!
WOO
GUM-GUM ...
TWIRL!!

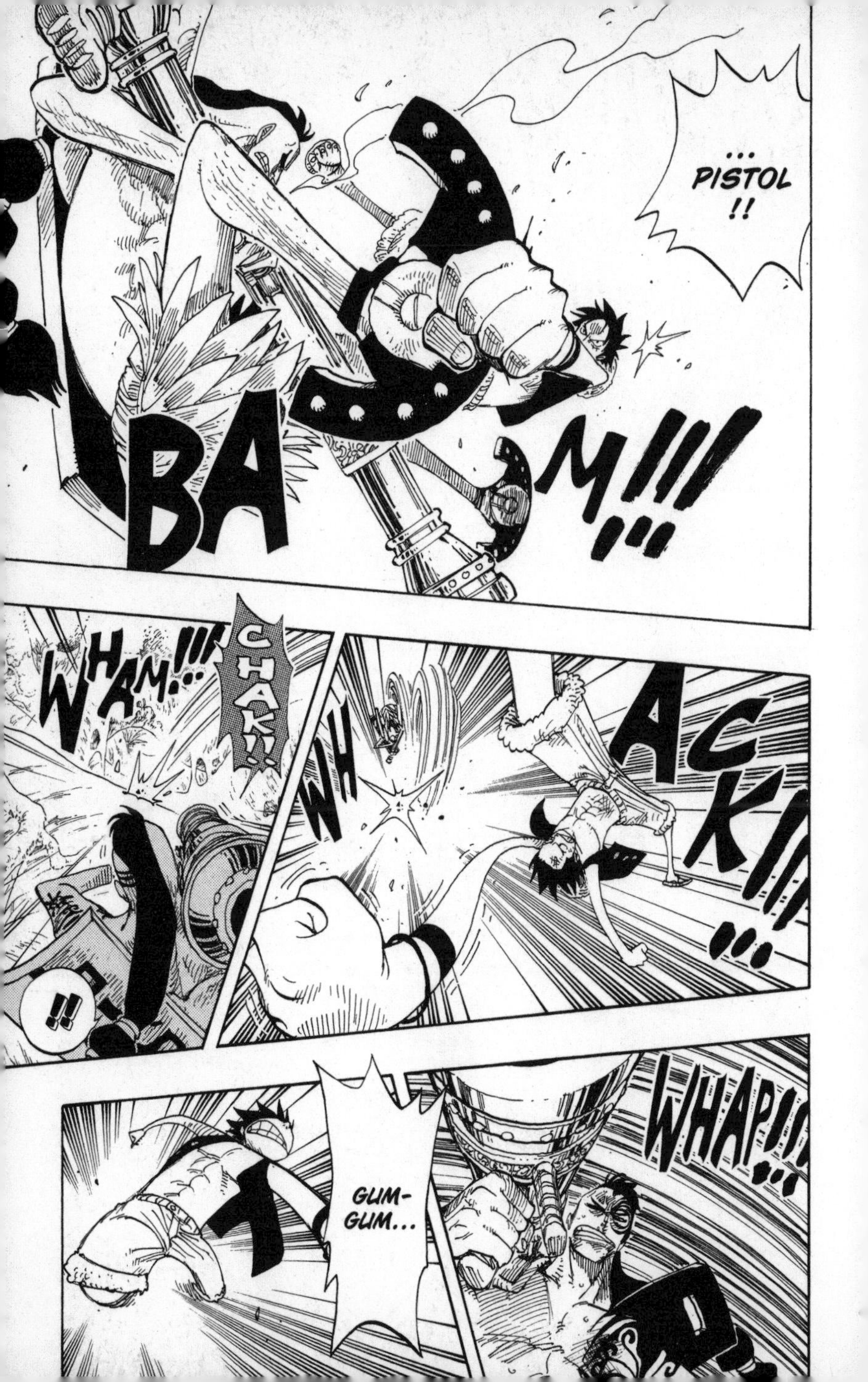
... PISTOL !!
BAM!!!
WHACK!!!
WHAM!!!
CHAK!!
!!
WHAP!!!
GUM-GUM...

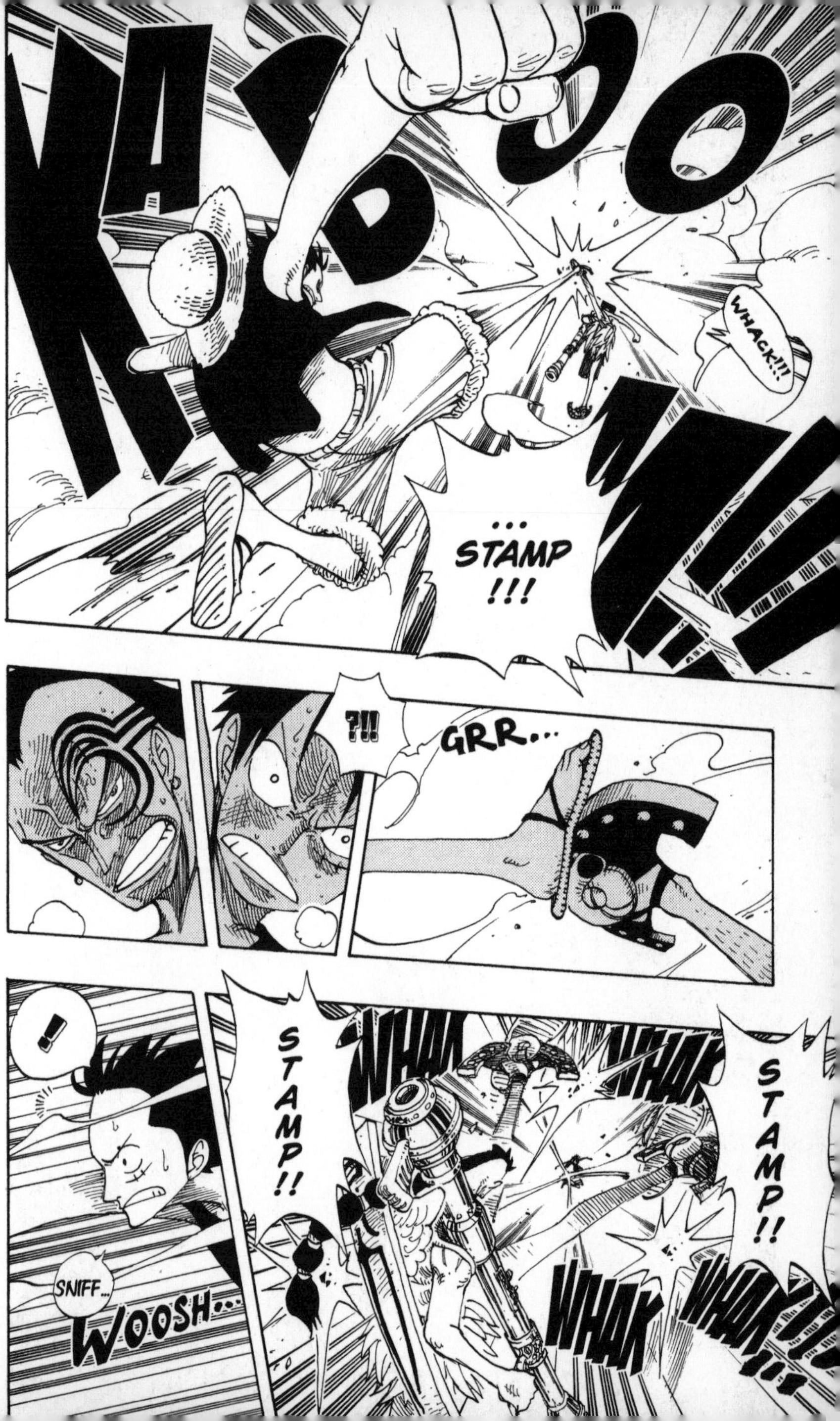
WHACK!!!
KADOOM!!
...STAMP!!!
GRR...
?!!
STAMP!!
WHAK
WHAK
STAMP!!
WHAK
WHAK!!!
!
SNIFF...
WOOSH...

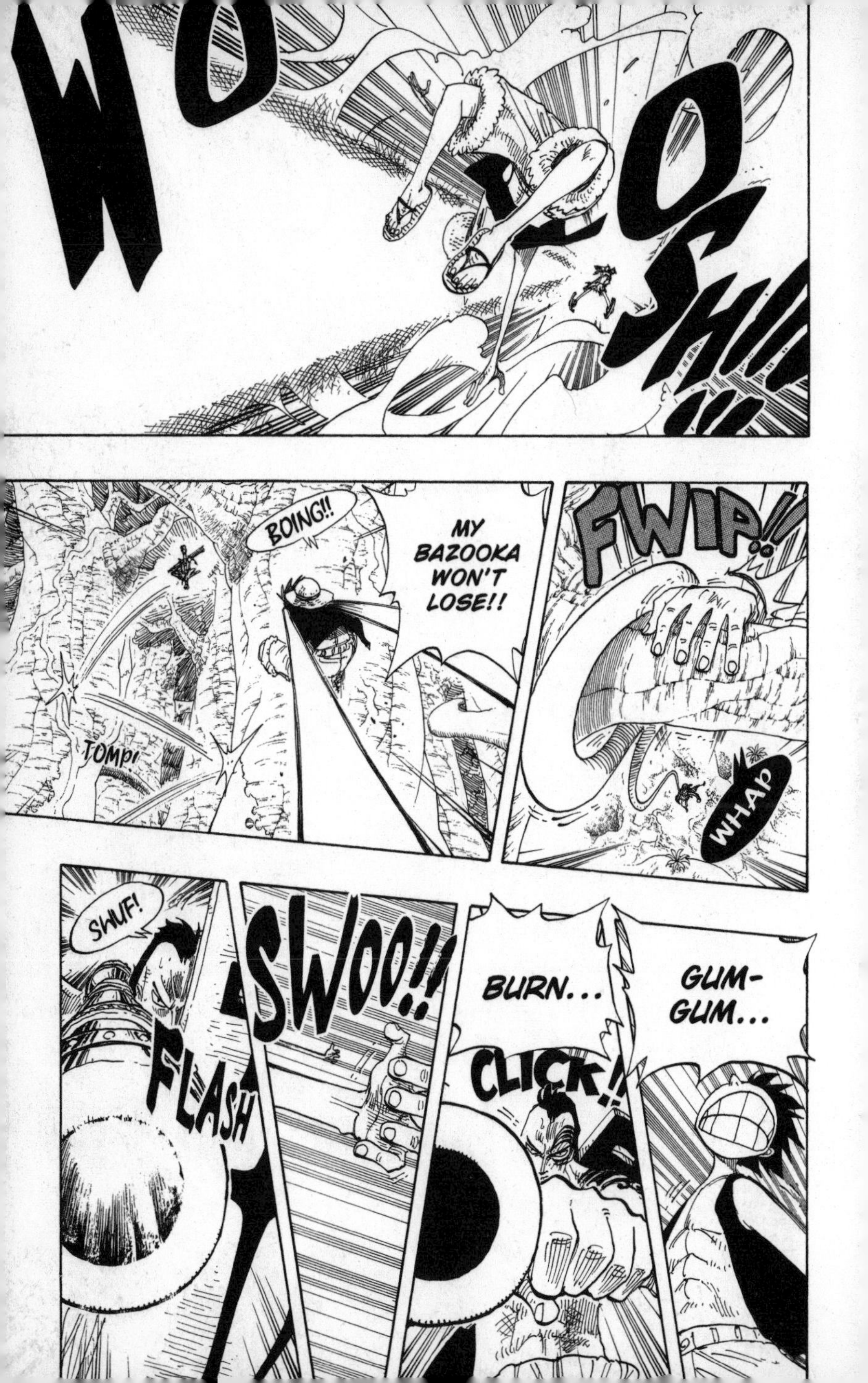
WOOSH!!!
FWIP!!
WHAP
MY BAZOOKA WON'T LOSE!!
BOING!!
TOMP!
GUM-GUM...
BURN...
CLICK!!
SWOO!!
SWUF!
FLASH

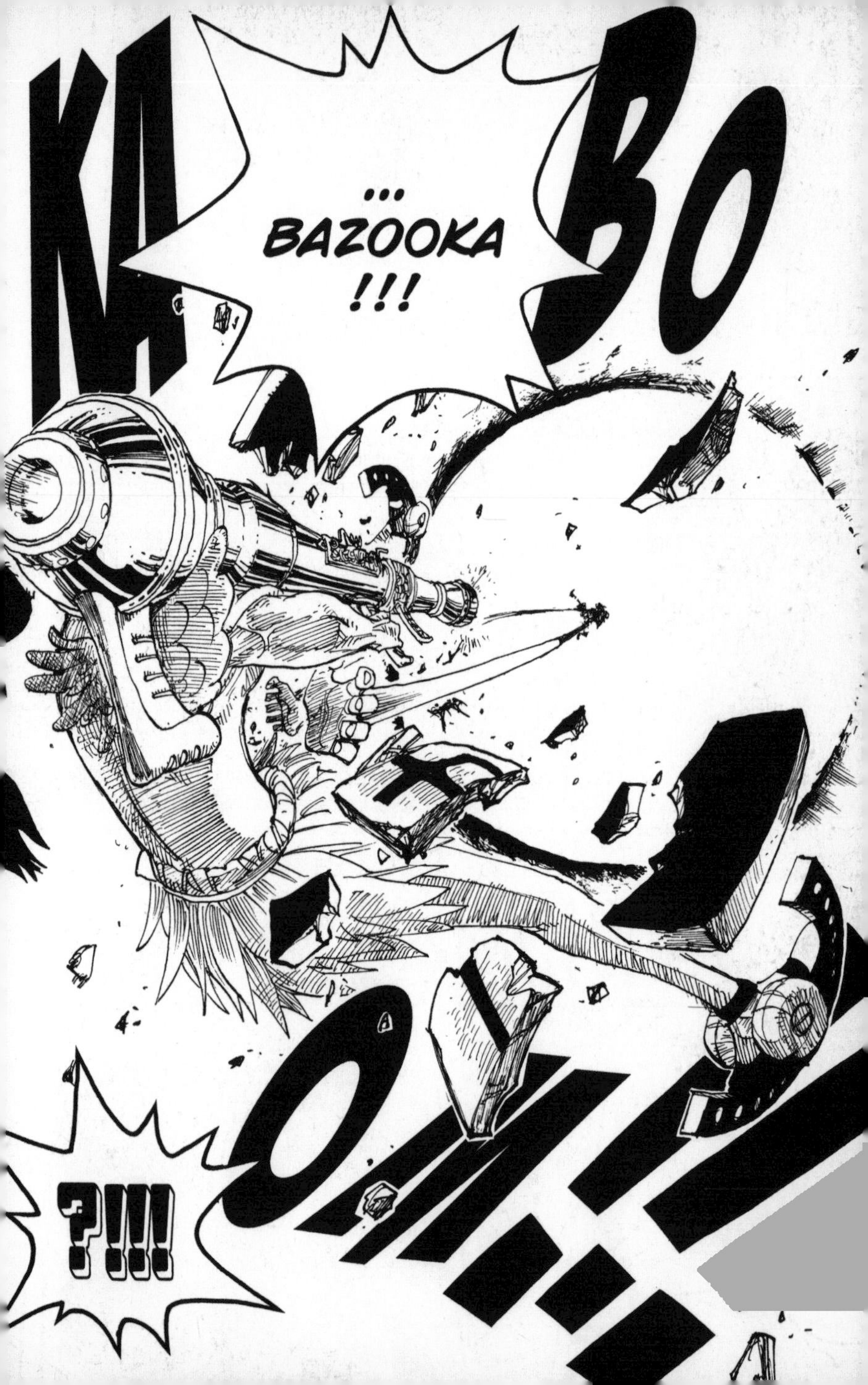
KABOOM
... BAZOOKA !!!
?!!!

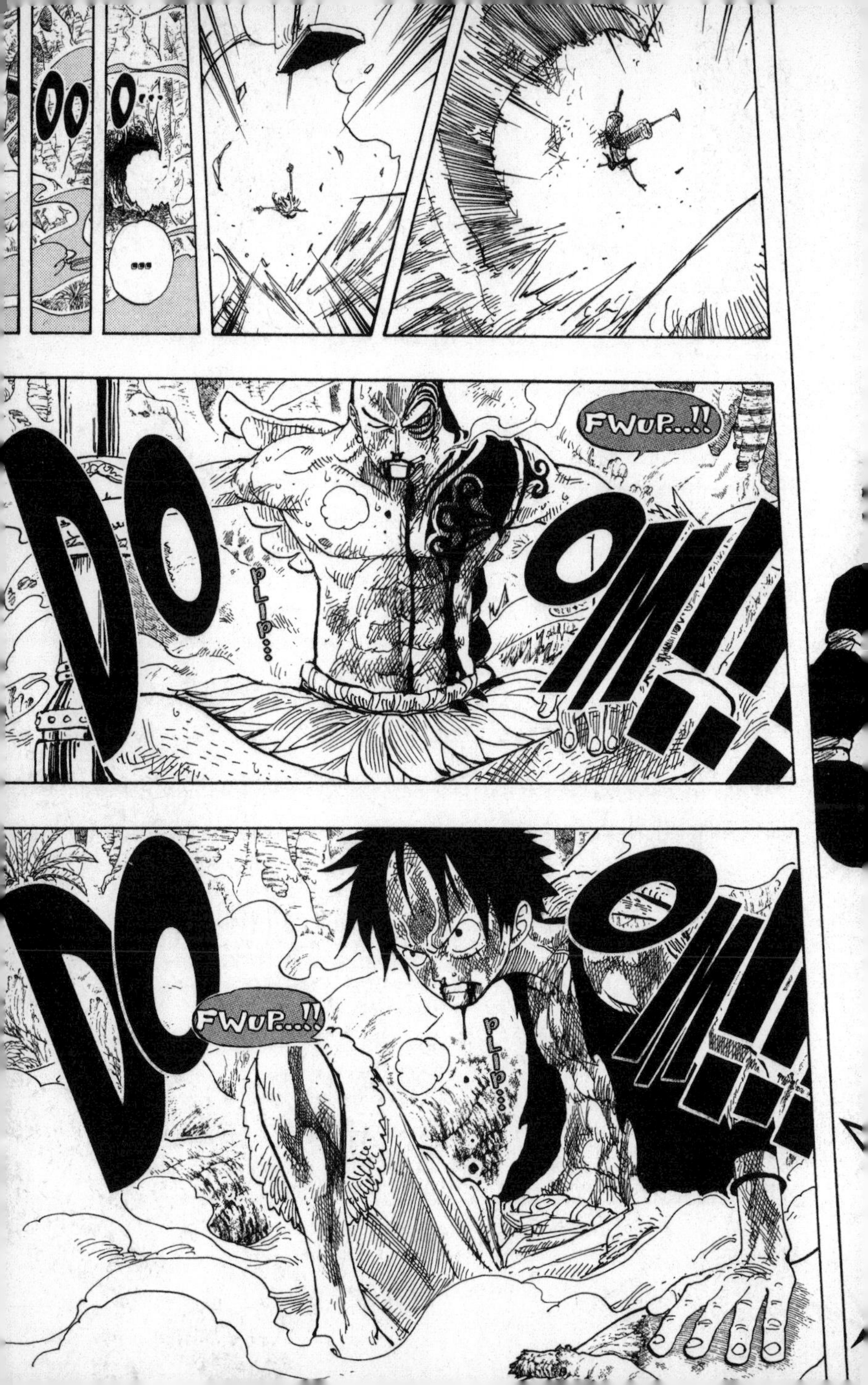
O...
...
OO
FWUP...!!
OM!!
DO
PLIP...
OM!!
DO
FWUP...!!
PLIP...

Q: Yo! Odacchi! I can't even do my homework when I think about this, so please hear me out! I don't remember in which volume's Question Corner, but you mentioned that as you draw *One Piece* your face makes the same expressions as the characters'. If that's true, Odacchi, then you must be able to pop your eyeballs out.

A: Yes, I am able to. I mean, of course. When I'm surprised, it's much more dramatic than my drawings. My personal best for eye-popping is 18 shockers. The world record is 84 shockers. Everyone, please do your best too.

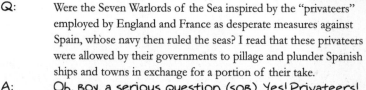

Q: Were the Seven Warlords of the Sea inspired by the "privateers" employed by England and France as desperate measures against Spain, whose navy then ruled the seas? I read that these privateers were allowed by their governments to pillage and plunder Spanish ships and towns in exchange for a portion of their take.

A: Oh, boy, a serious question (sob). Yes! Privateers! Simply put, they are pirates that were legalized by their nations.
Long ago, such people did exist. They were considered heroes in their own lands and vile plunderers by others.
If one looks at history, pirates were not always labeled as criminals. At times, they were considered useful. Now whether or not this is a good thing is another matter. Pirates are pirates, after all. Sometimes, even the most dastardly of crimes can sometimes be mistaken for justice.

Chapter 261:
WARRIOR GENBO VS. HEAVENLY WARRIORS COMMANDER YAMA

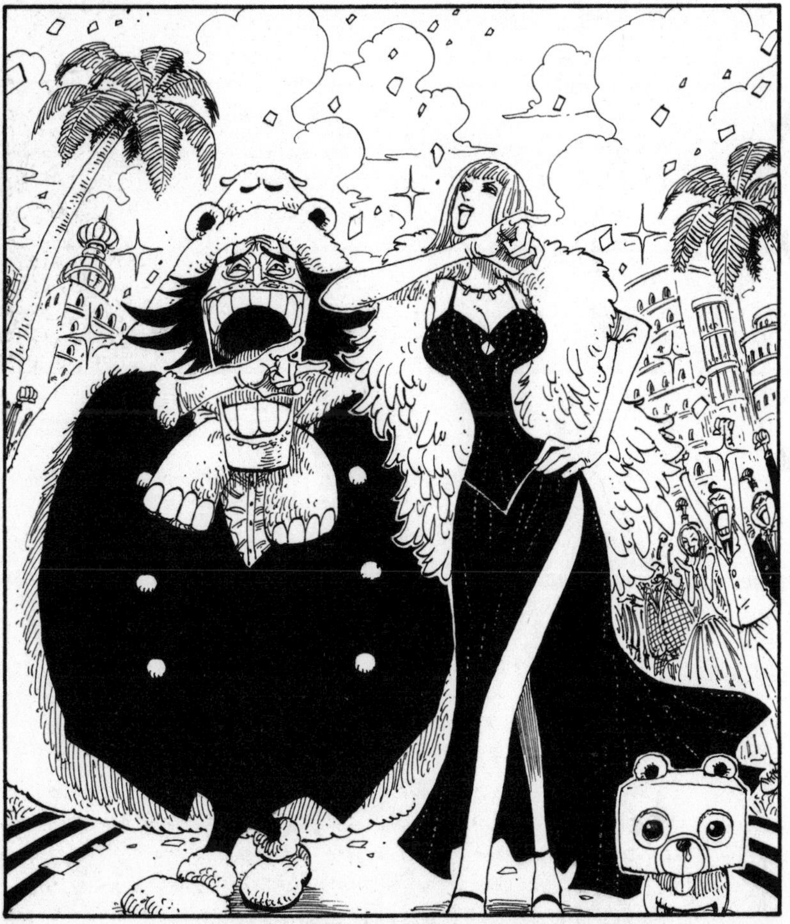

WAPOL'S OMNIVOROUS RAMPAGE, VOL. 22:
"I MARRIED MISS UNIVERSE"

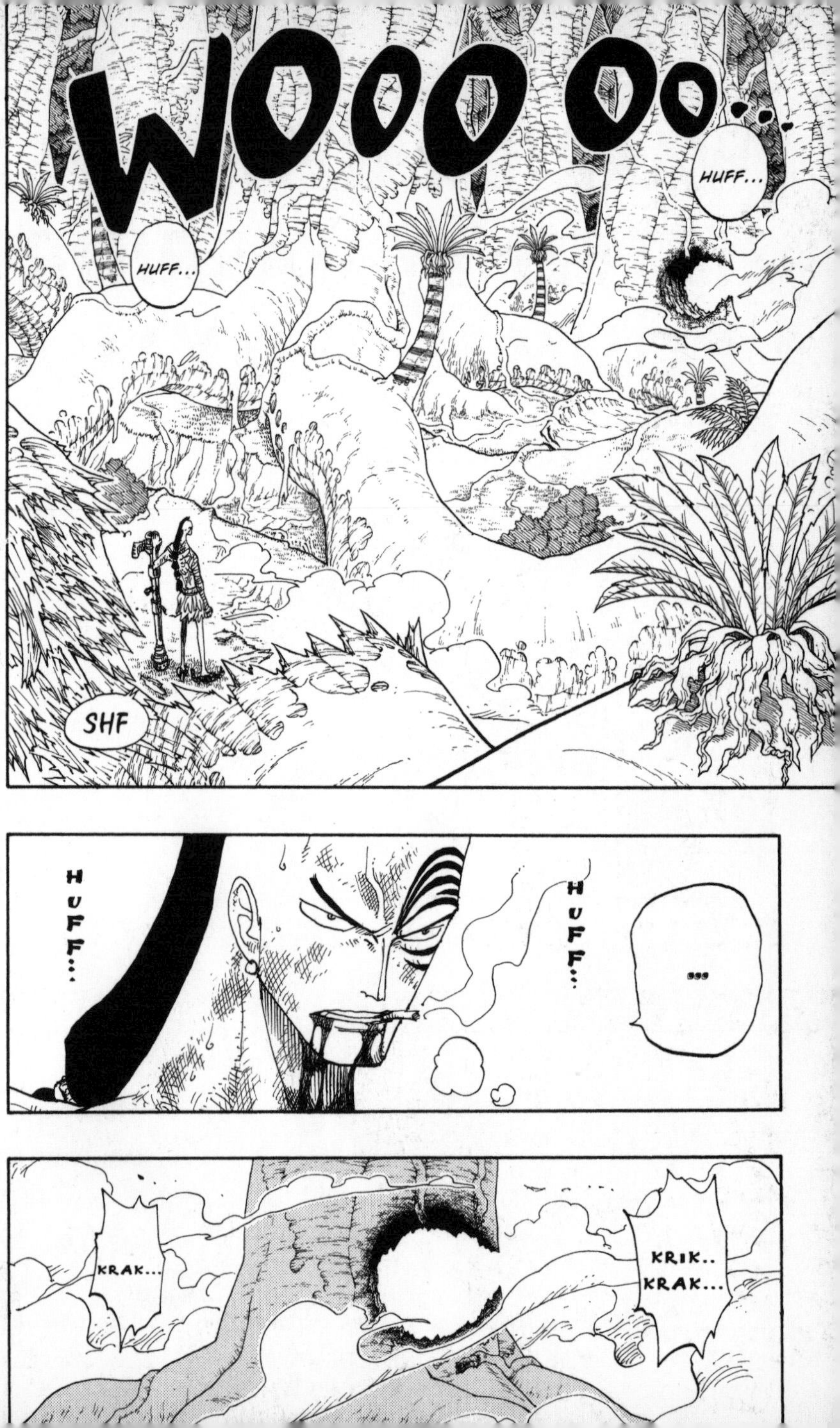
WOOOOO..
HUFF...
HUFF...
SHF
...
HUFF...
HUFF...
KRIK..
KRAK...
KRAK...

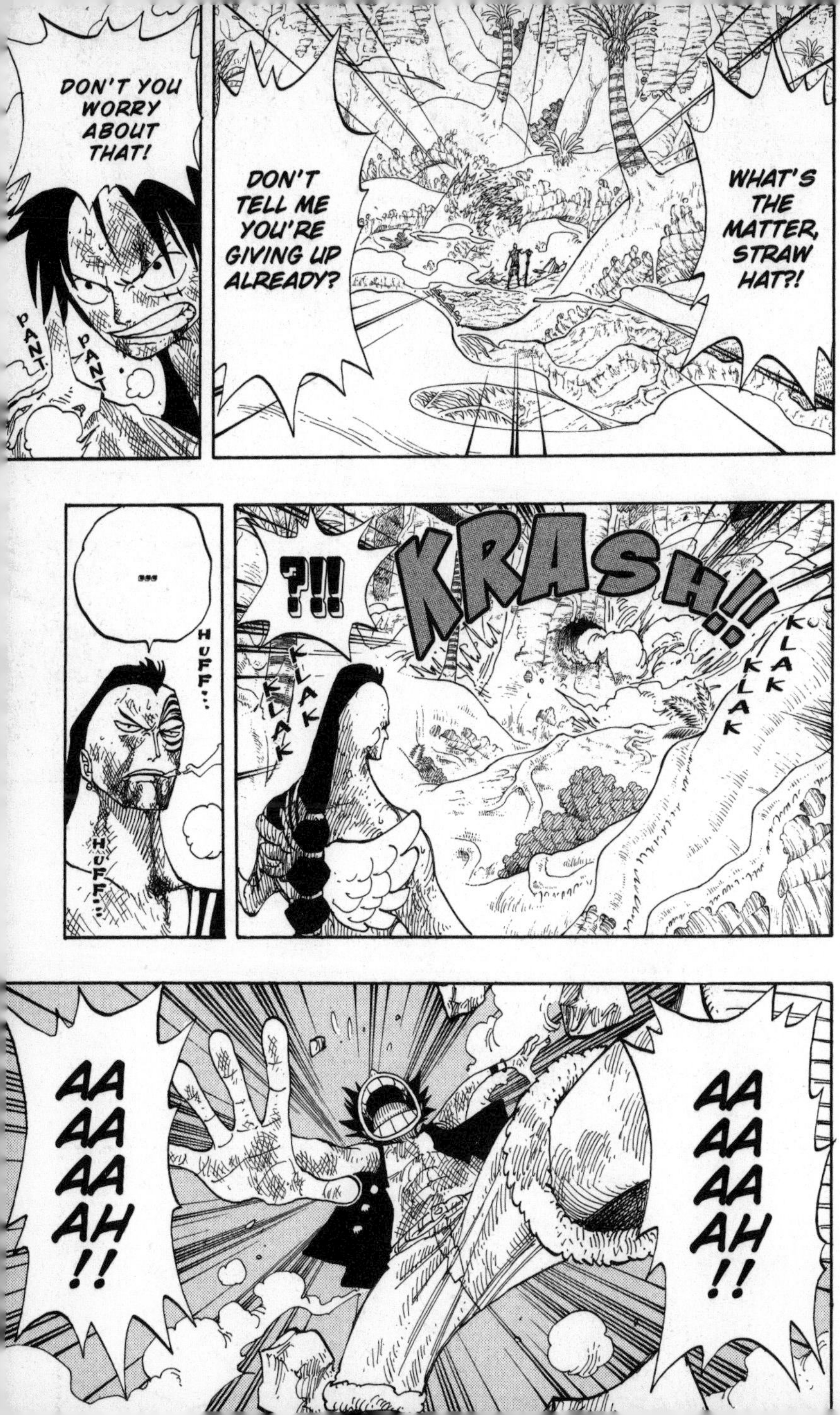
WHAT'S THE MATTER, STRAW HAT?!
DON'T TELL ME YOU'RE GIVING UP ALREADY?
DON'T YOU WORRY ABOUT THAT!
PANT
PANT
KRASH!!
KLAK KLAK
?!!
KLAK KLAK
...
HUFF...
HUFF...
AAAAAAAH!!
AAAAAAAH!!

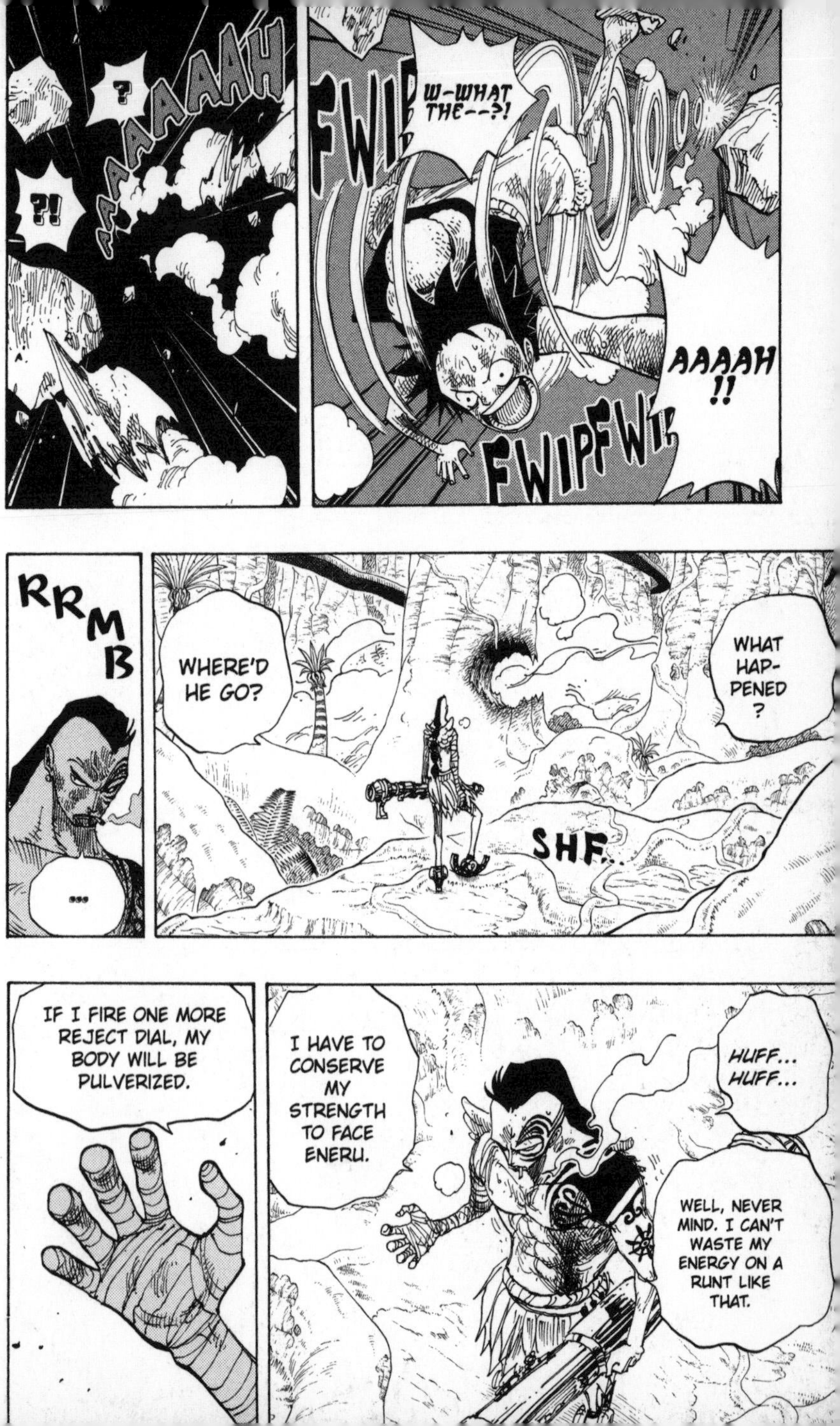

FWIP
W-WHAT THE--?!
AAAAH !!
FWIPFWIP
?
?!
...AAAAAAH
WHAT HAP-PENED ?
WHERE'D HE GO?
SHF...
RRMB
...
HUFF... HUFF...
WELL, NEVER MIND. I CAN'T WASTE MY ENERGY ON A RUNT LIKE THAT.
I HAVE TO CONSERVE MY STRENGTH TO FACE ENERU.
IF I FIRE ONE MORE REJECT DIAL, MY BODY WILL BE PULVERIZED.

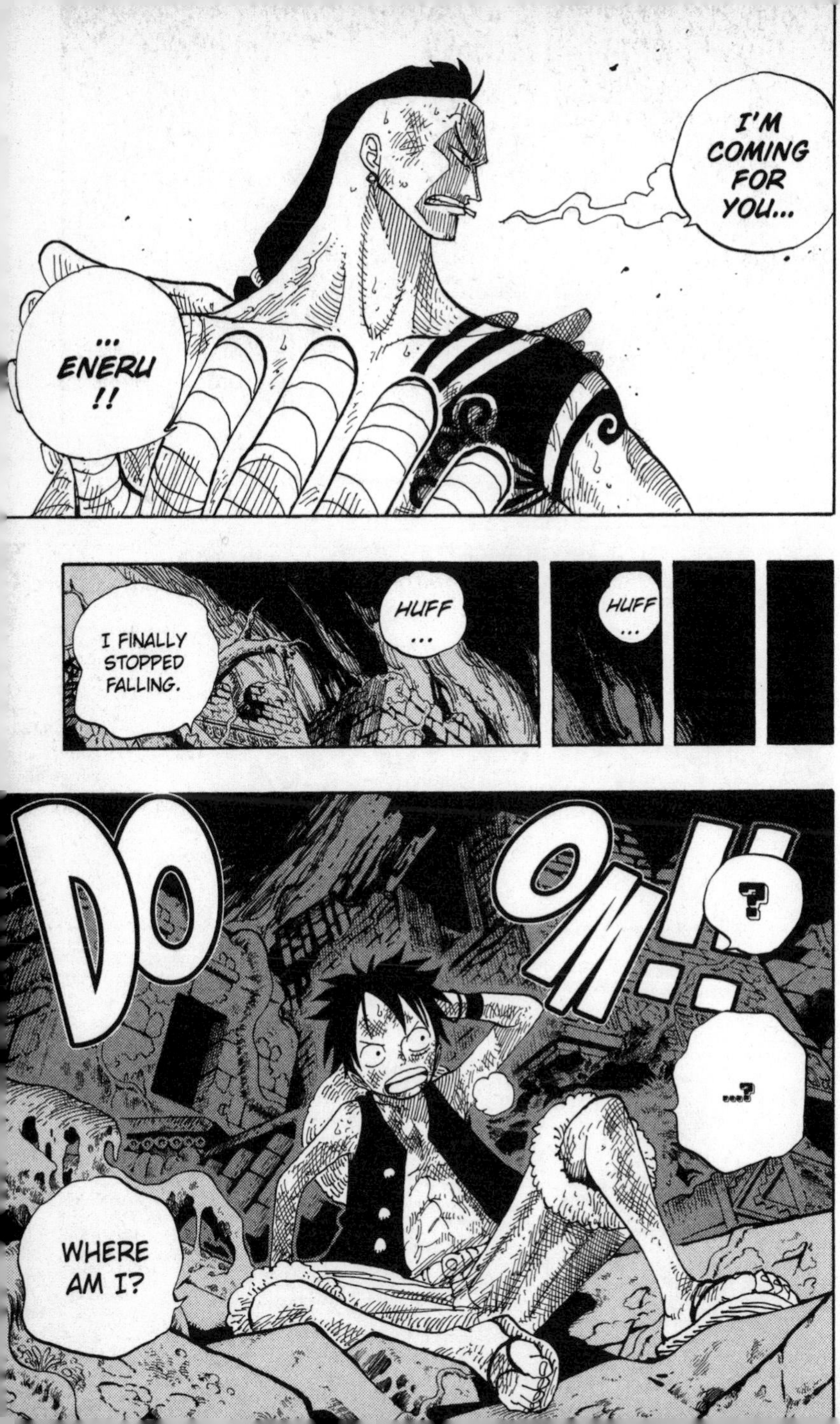
I'M COMING FOR YOU...
... ENERU !!
HUFF ...
HUFF ...
I FINALLY STOPPED FALLING.
DOON!!
?
...?
WHERE AM I?

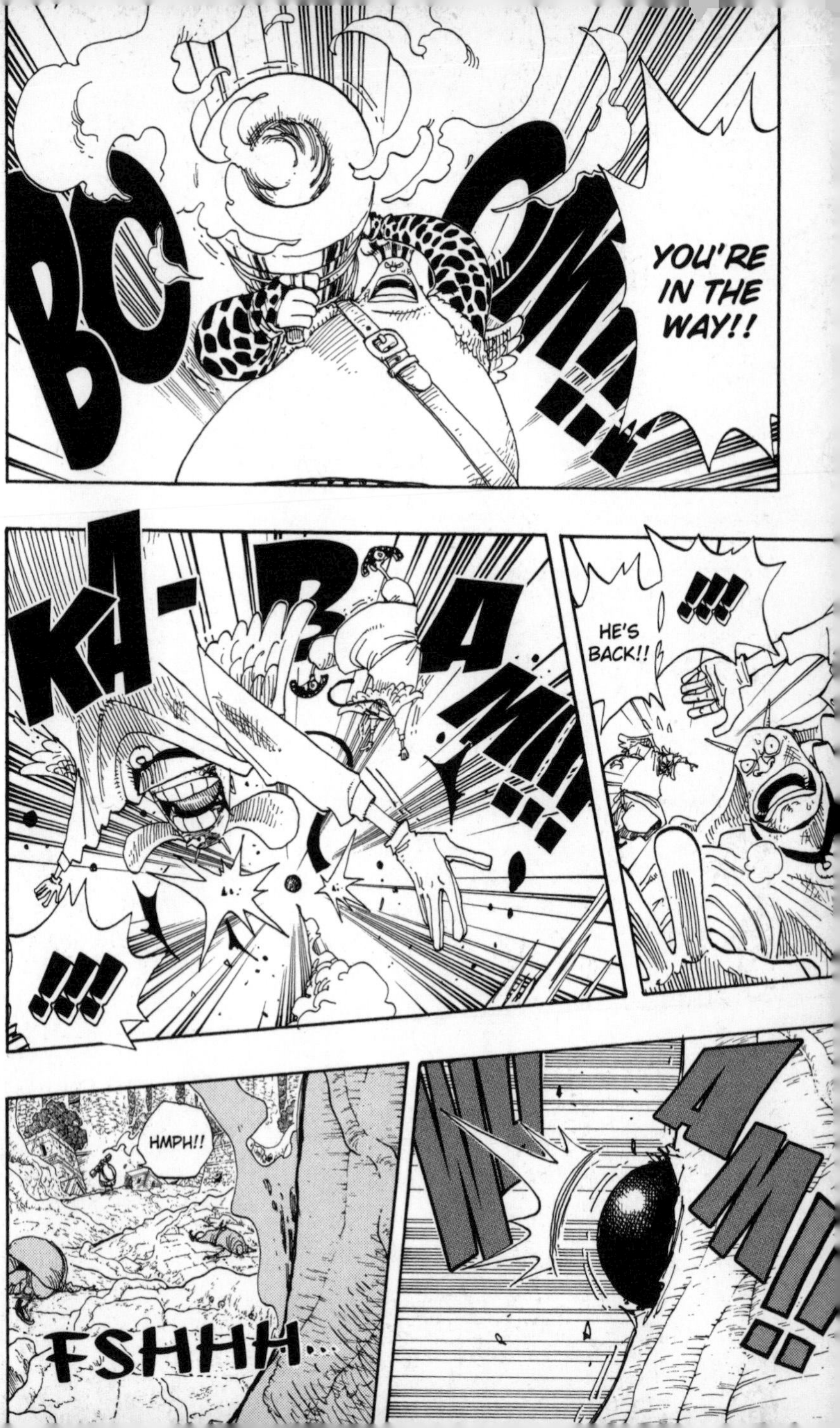
YOU'RE IN THE WAY!!
BOOM!!
!!!
HE'S BACK!!
KA-BAM!!
!!!
WHAM!!
HMPH!!
FSHHH...

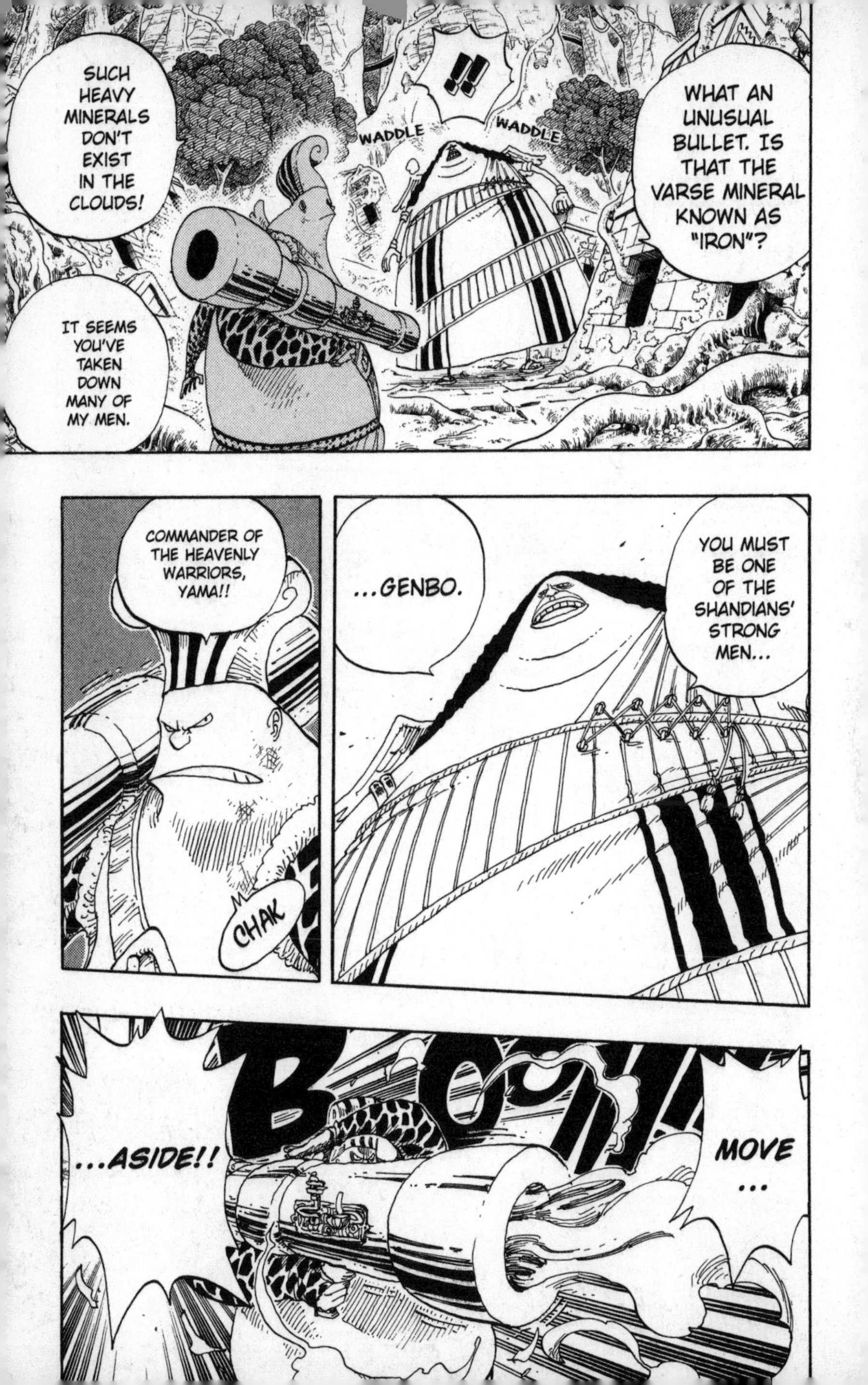
!!
WADDLE
WADDLE
WHAT AN UNUSUAL BULLET. IS THAT THE VARSE MINERAL KNOWN AS "IRON"?
SUCH HEAVY MINERALS DON'T EXIST IN THE CLOUDS!
IT SEEMS YOU'VE TAKEN DOWN MANY OF MY MEN.
YOU MUST BE ONE OF THE SHANDIANS' STRONG MEN...
...GENBO.
COMMANDER OF THE HEAVENLY WARRIORS, YAMA!!
CHAK
MOVE ...
BOOM
...ASIDE!!

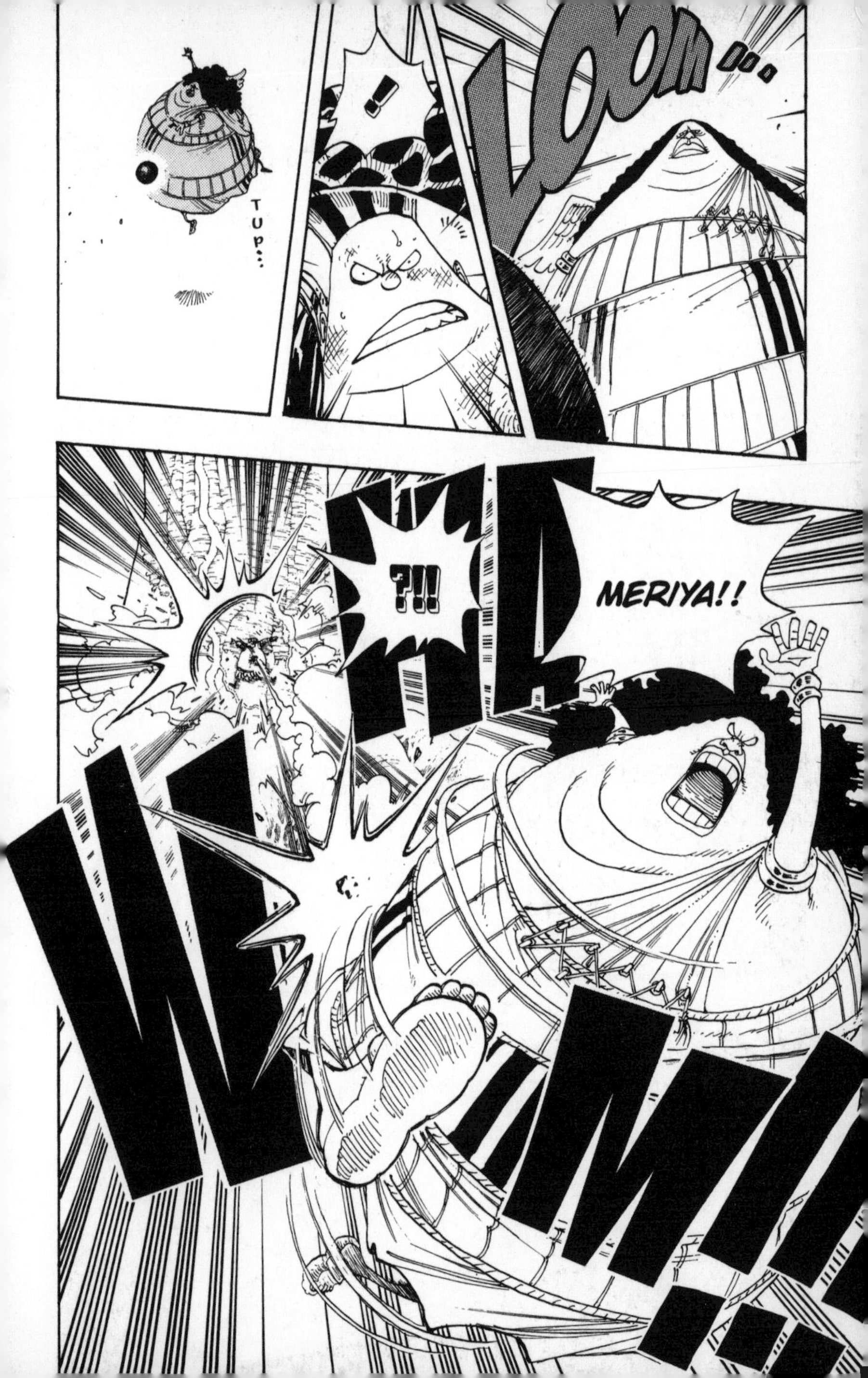
VOOM...
!
TUP...
?!!
MERIYA!!

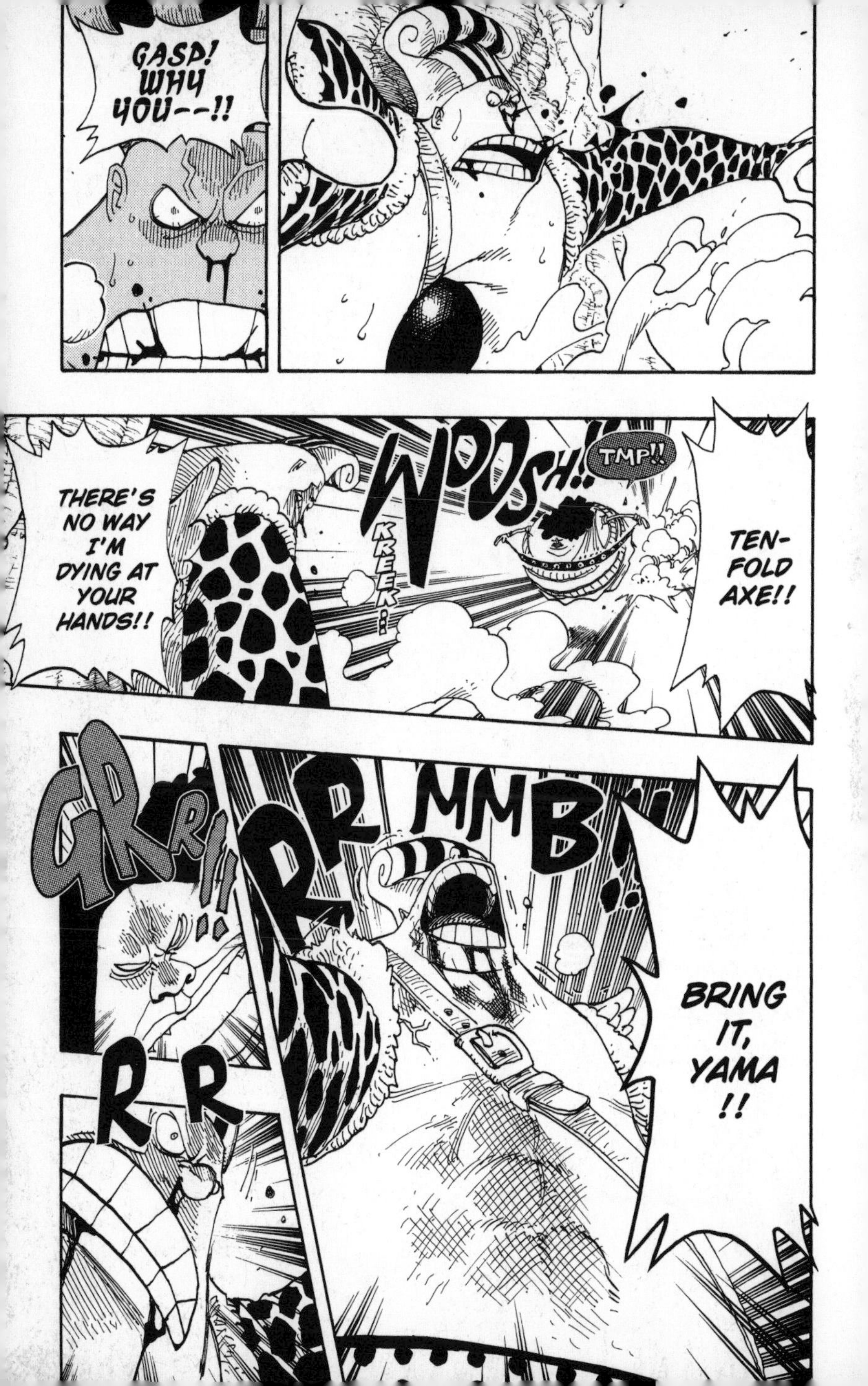
GASP! WHY YOU--!!
TEN-FOLD AXE!!
WOOSH!!
TMP!!
KREEK!!
THERE'S NO WAY I'M DYING AT YOUR HANDS!!
BRING IT, YAMA!!
RRMMB!!
GRR!!
R R

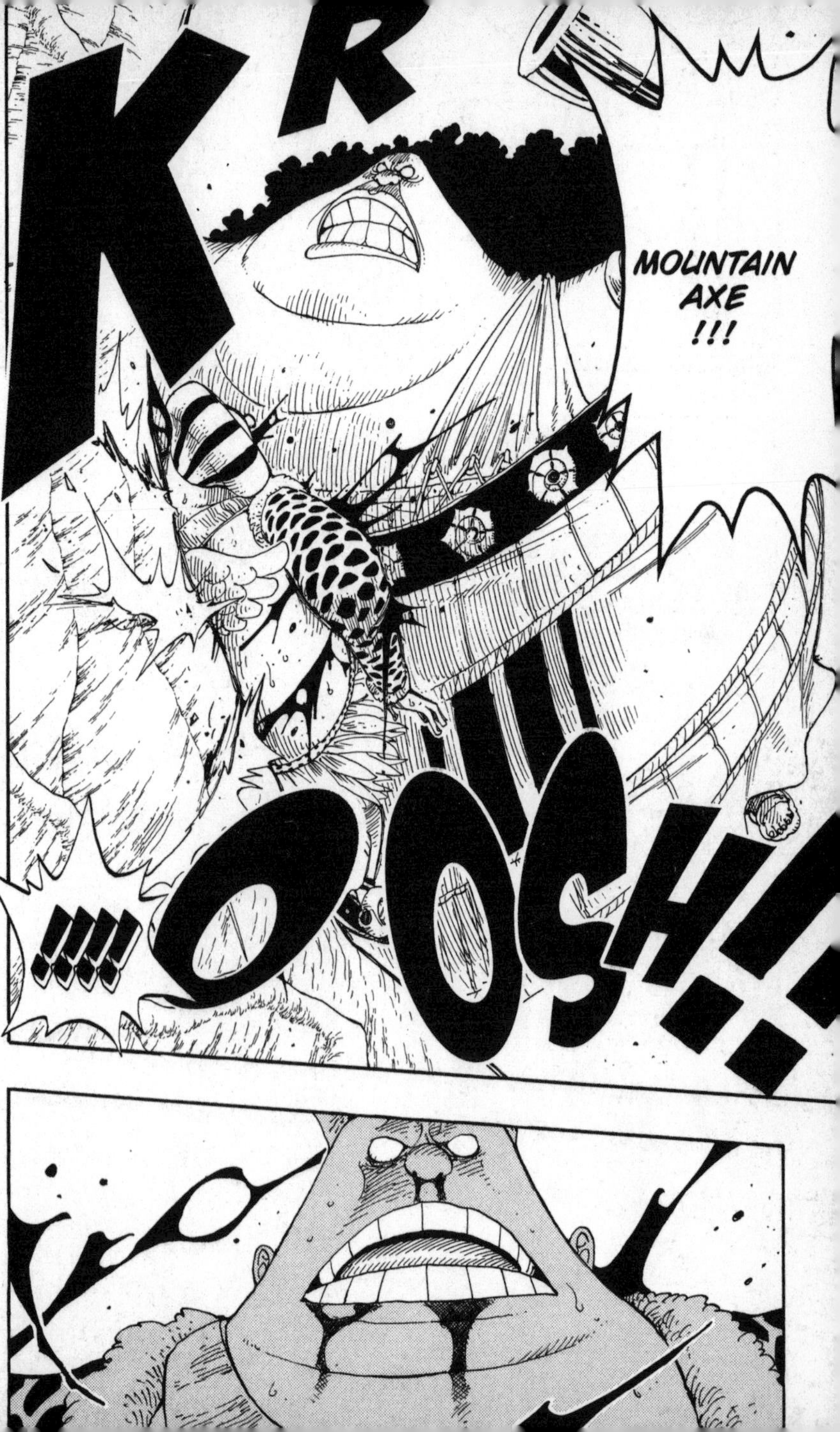

KR
MOUNTAIN AXE !!!
OOSH!!
!!!!

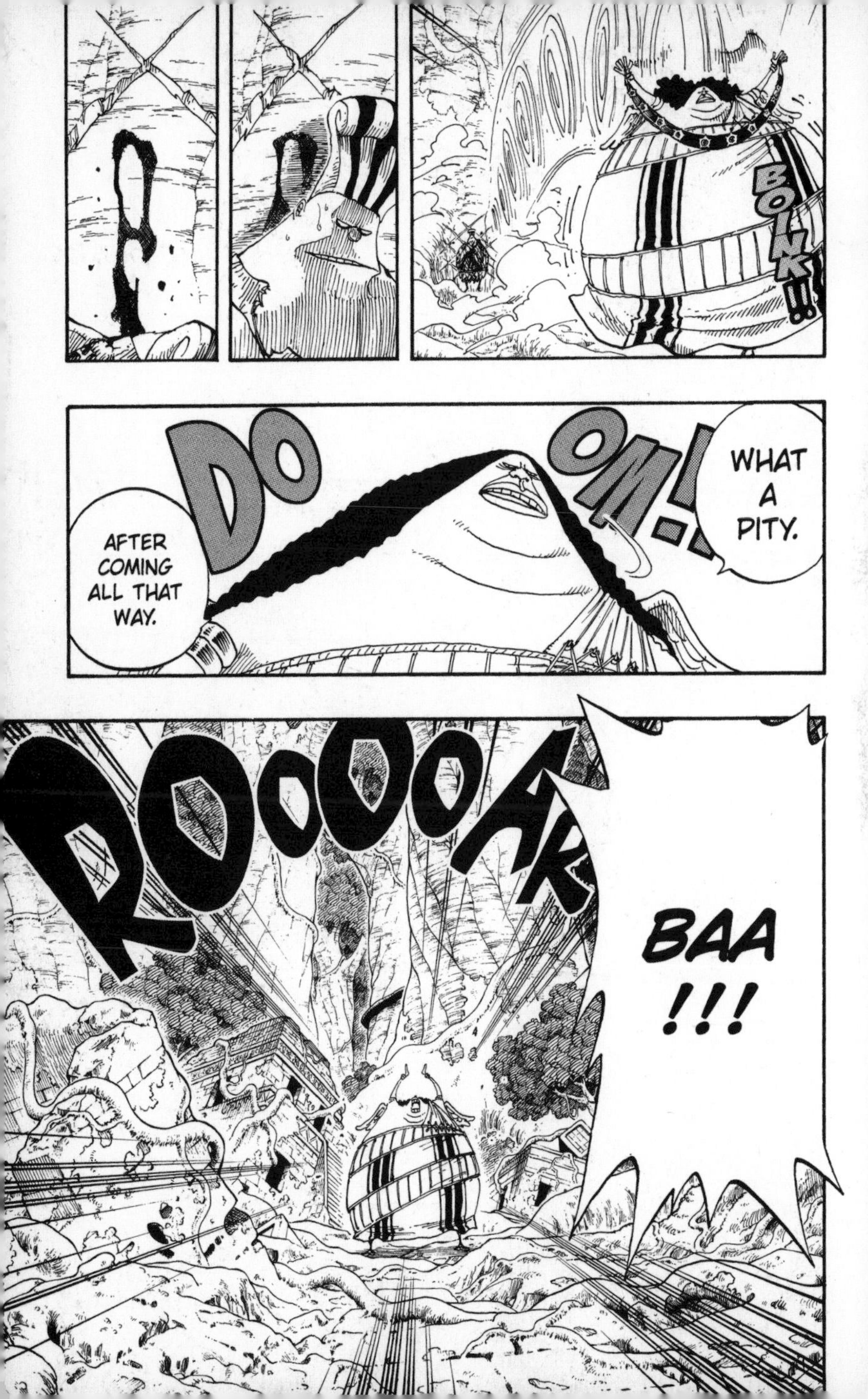
BOINK!!
WHAT A PITY.
DOOM..!!
AFTER COMING ALL THAT WAY.
BAA!!!
ROOOOAR

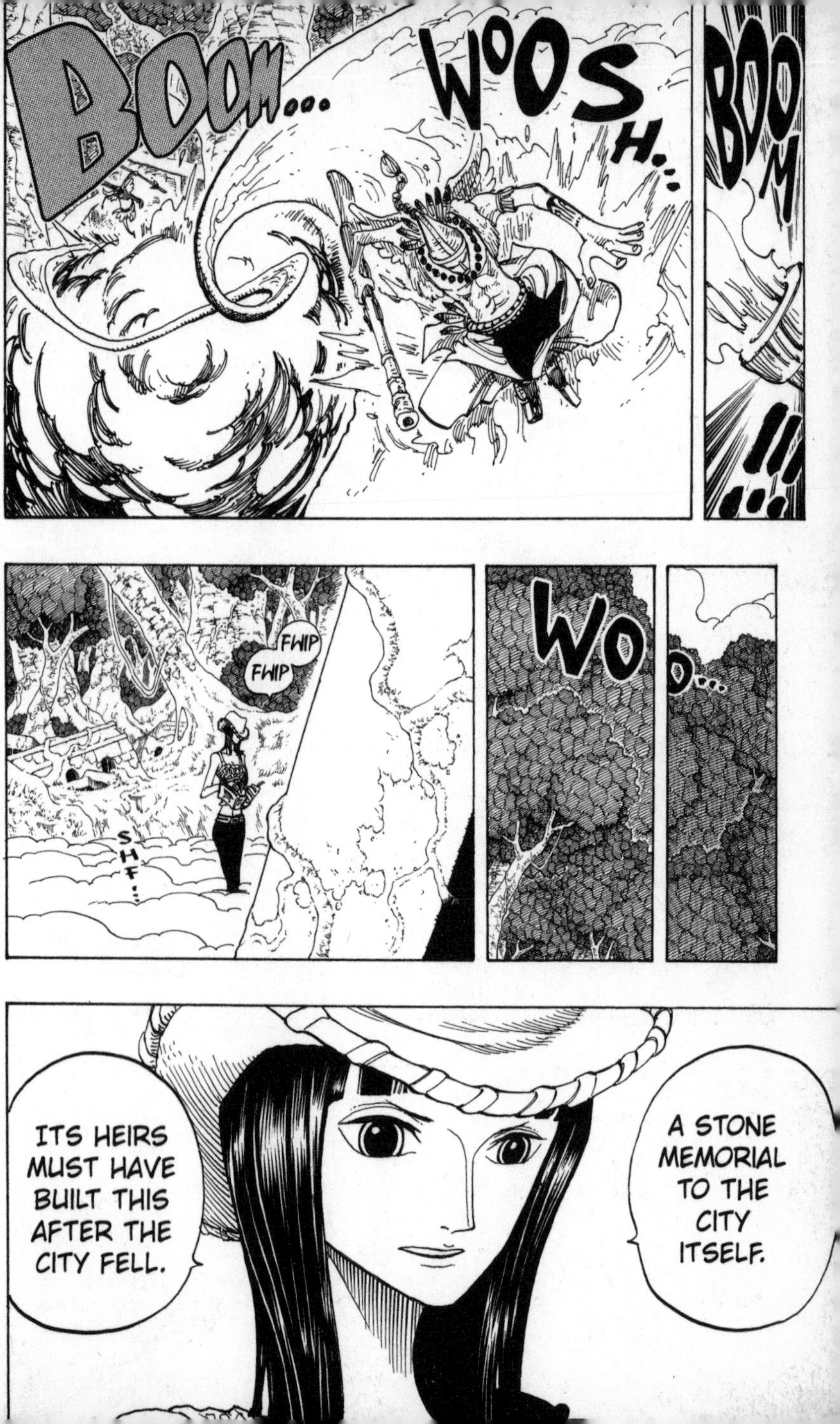
BOOM
!!...!!
WOOSH...
BOOM...
WO
O...
FWIP
FWIP
SHF...
A STONE MEMORIAL TO THE CITY ITSELF.
ITS HEIRS MUST HAVE BUILT THIS AFTER THE CITY FELL.

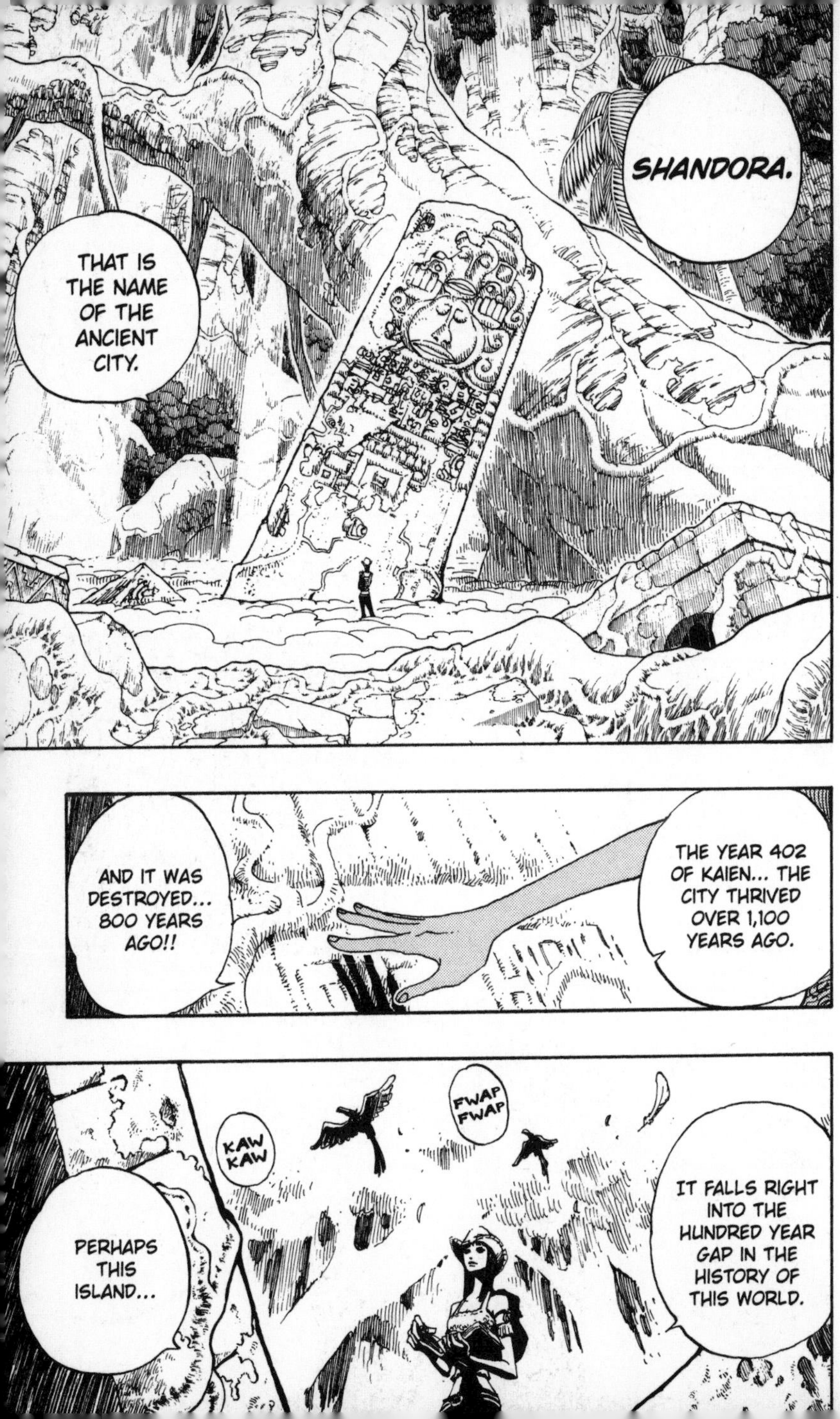
SHANDORA.
THAT IS THE NAME OF THE ANCIENT CITY.
THE YEAR 402 OF KAIEN... THE CITY THRIVED OVER 1,100 YEARS AGO.
AND IT WAS DESTROYED... 800 YEARS AGO!!
IT FALLS RIGHT INTO THE HUNDRED YEAR GAP IN THE HISTORY OF THIS WORLD.
FWAP FWAP
KAW KAW
PERHAPS THIS ISLAND...

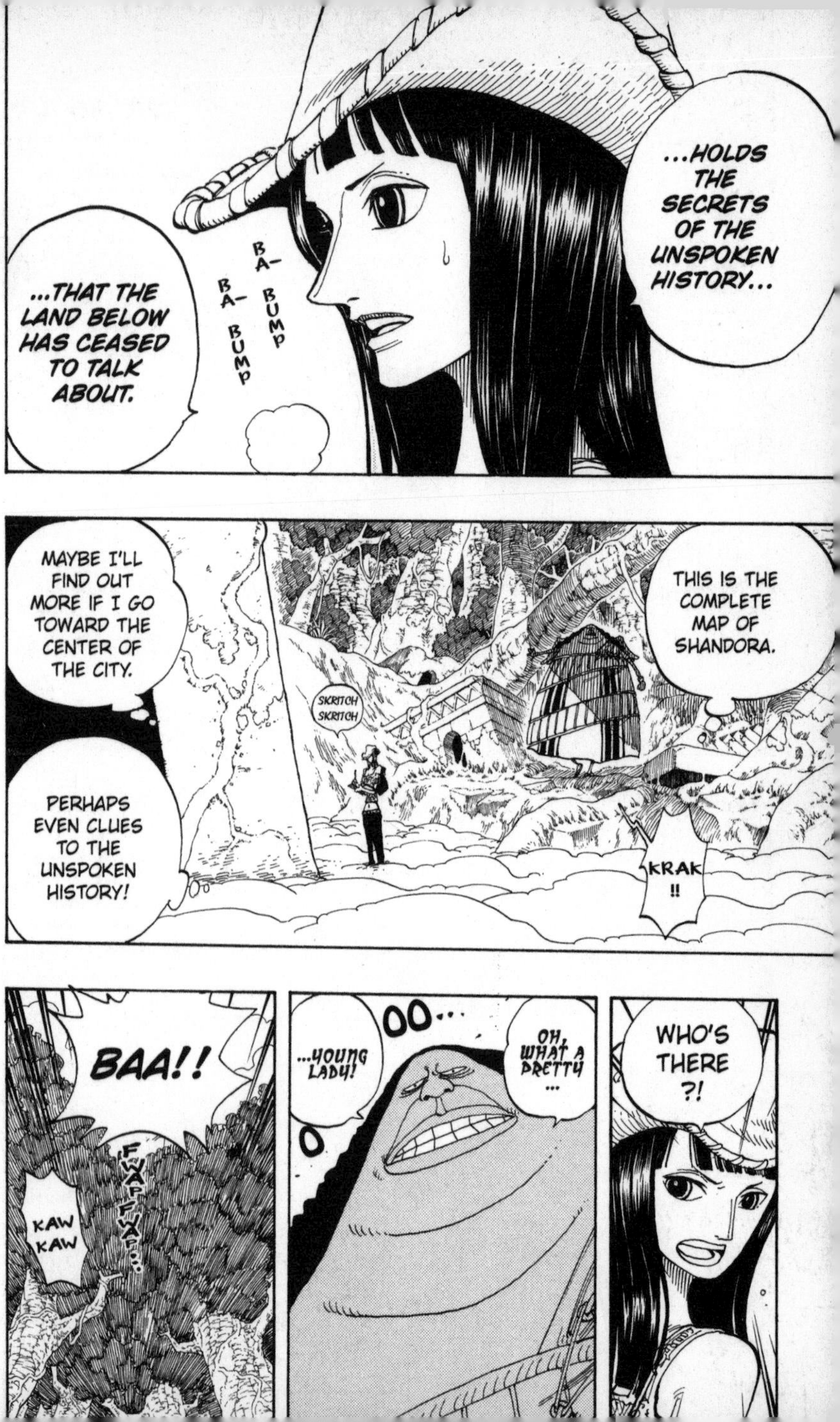
...HOLDS THE SECRETS OF THE UNSPOKEN HISTORY...
BA- BUMP
BA- BUMP
...THAT THE LAND BELOW HAS CEASED TO TALK ABOUT.
THIS IS THE COMPLETE MAP OF SHANDORA.
KRAK!!
SKRITCH SKRITCH
MAYBE I'LL FIND OUT MORE IF I GO TOWARD THE CENTER OF THE CITY.
PERHAPS EVEN CLUES TO THE UNSPOKEN HISTORY!
WHO'S THERE?!
OH, WHAT A PRETTY...
OO...
...YOUNG LADY!
BAA!!
FWAP FWAP...
KAW KAW

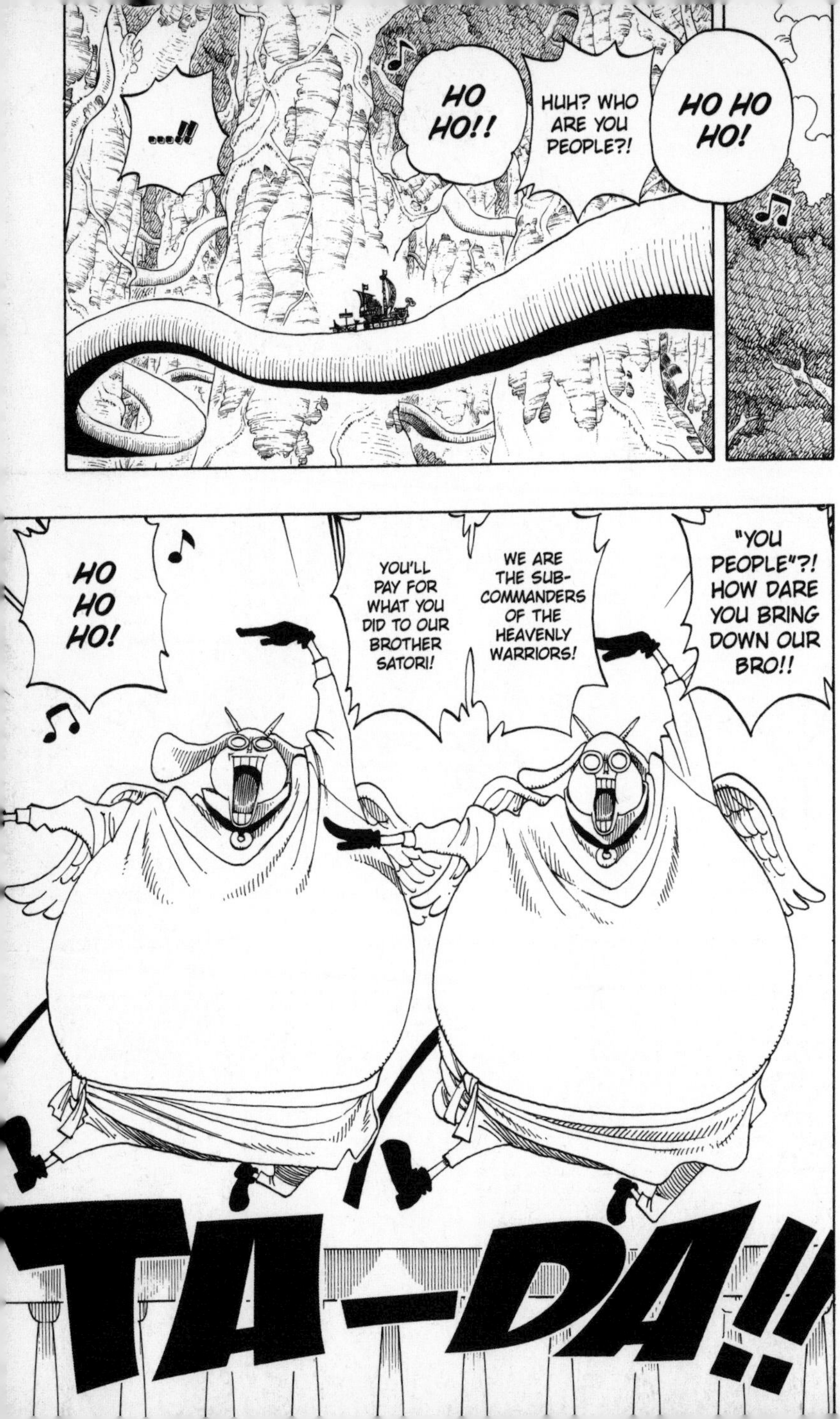
HO HO HO!
HUH? WHO ARE YOU PEOPLE?!
HO HO!!
...!!
"YOU PEOPLE"?! HOW DARE YOU BRING DOWN OUR BRO!!
WE ARE THE SUB-COMMANDERS OF THE HEAVENLY WARRIORS!
YOU'LL PAY FOR WHAT YOU DID TO OUR BROTHER SATORI!
HO HO HO!
TA-DA!!

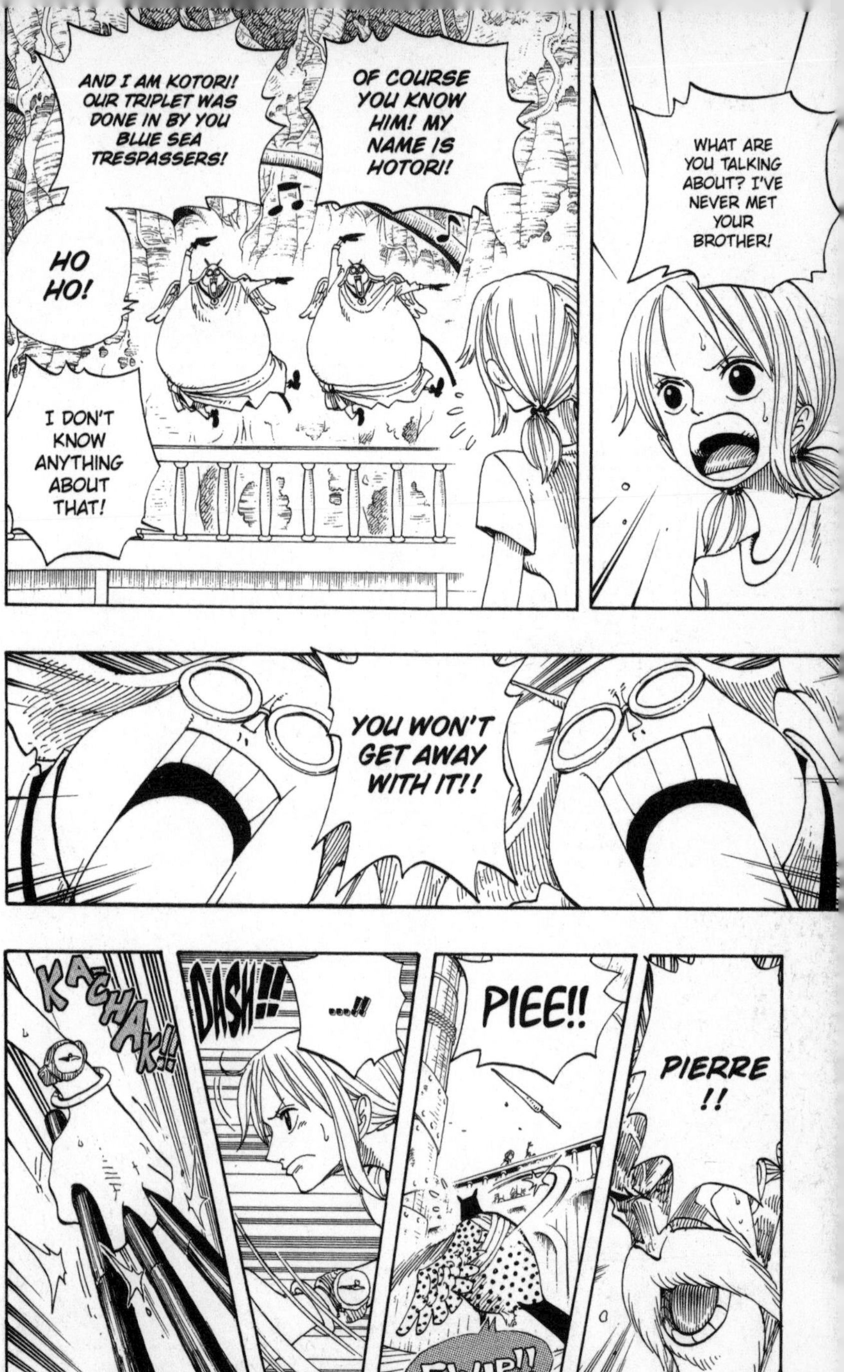
WHAT ARE YOU TALKING ABOUT? I'VE NEVER MET YOUR BROTHER!
OF COURSE YOU KNOW HIM! MY NAME IS HOTORI!
AND I AM KOTORI! OUR TRIPLET WAS DONE IN BY YOU BLUE SEA TRESPASSERS!
HO HO!
I DON'T KNOW ANYTHING ABOUT THAT!
YOU WON'T GET AWAY WITH IT!!
PIERRE !!
PIEE!!
FWIP!!
...!!
DASH!!
KACHAK!!

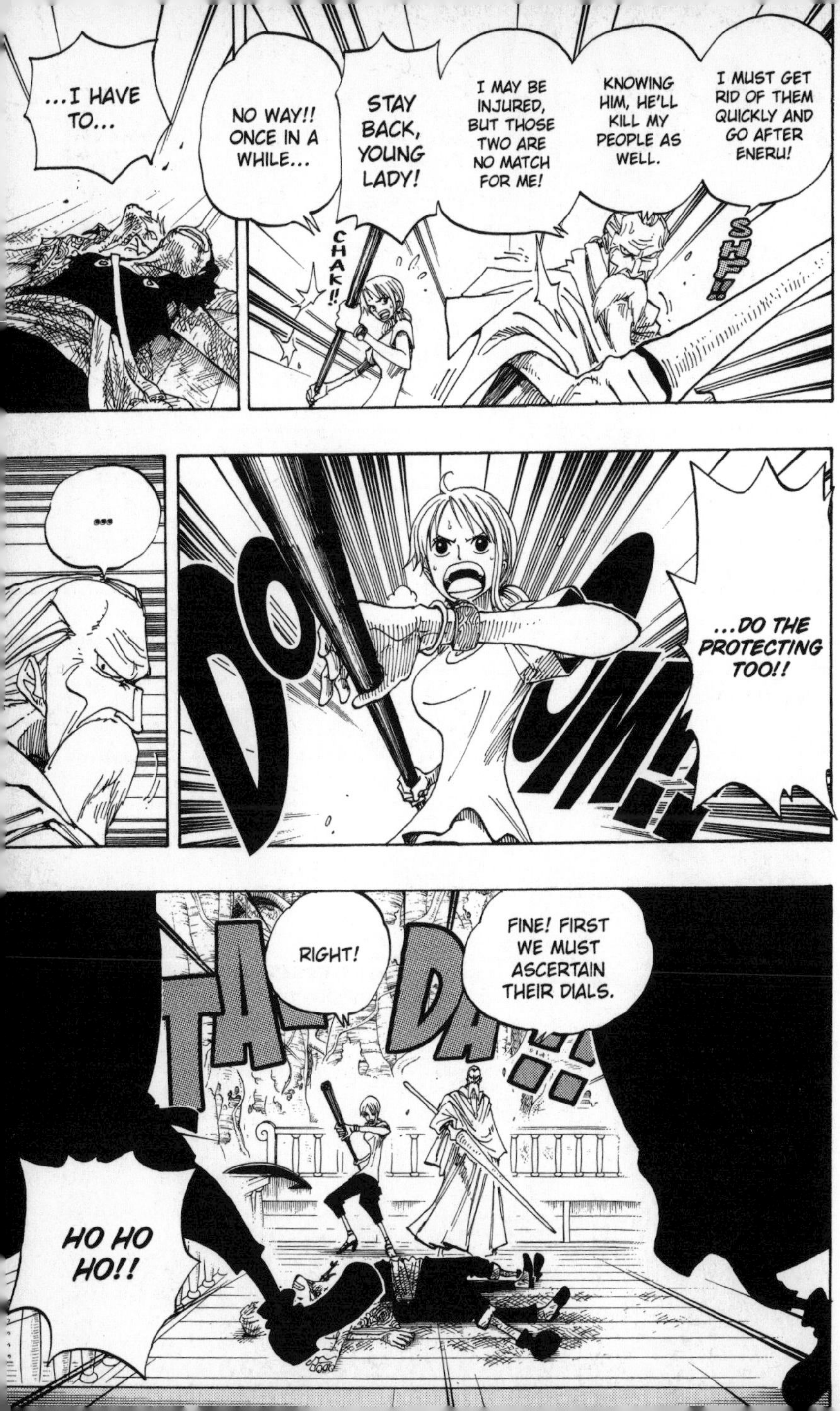
I MUST GET RID OF THEM QUICKLY AND GO AFTER ENERU!
SHF!!
KNOWING HIM, HE'LL KILL MY PEOPLE AS WELL.
I MAY BE INJURED, BUT THOSE TWO ARE NO MATCH FOR ME!
STAY BACK, YOUNG LADY!
CHAK!!
NO WAY!! ONCE IN A WHILE...
...I HAVE TO...
...DO THE PROTECTING TOO!!
...
FINE! FIRST WE MUST ASCERTAIN THEIR DIALS.
RIGHT!
HO HO HO!!

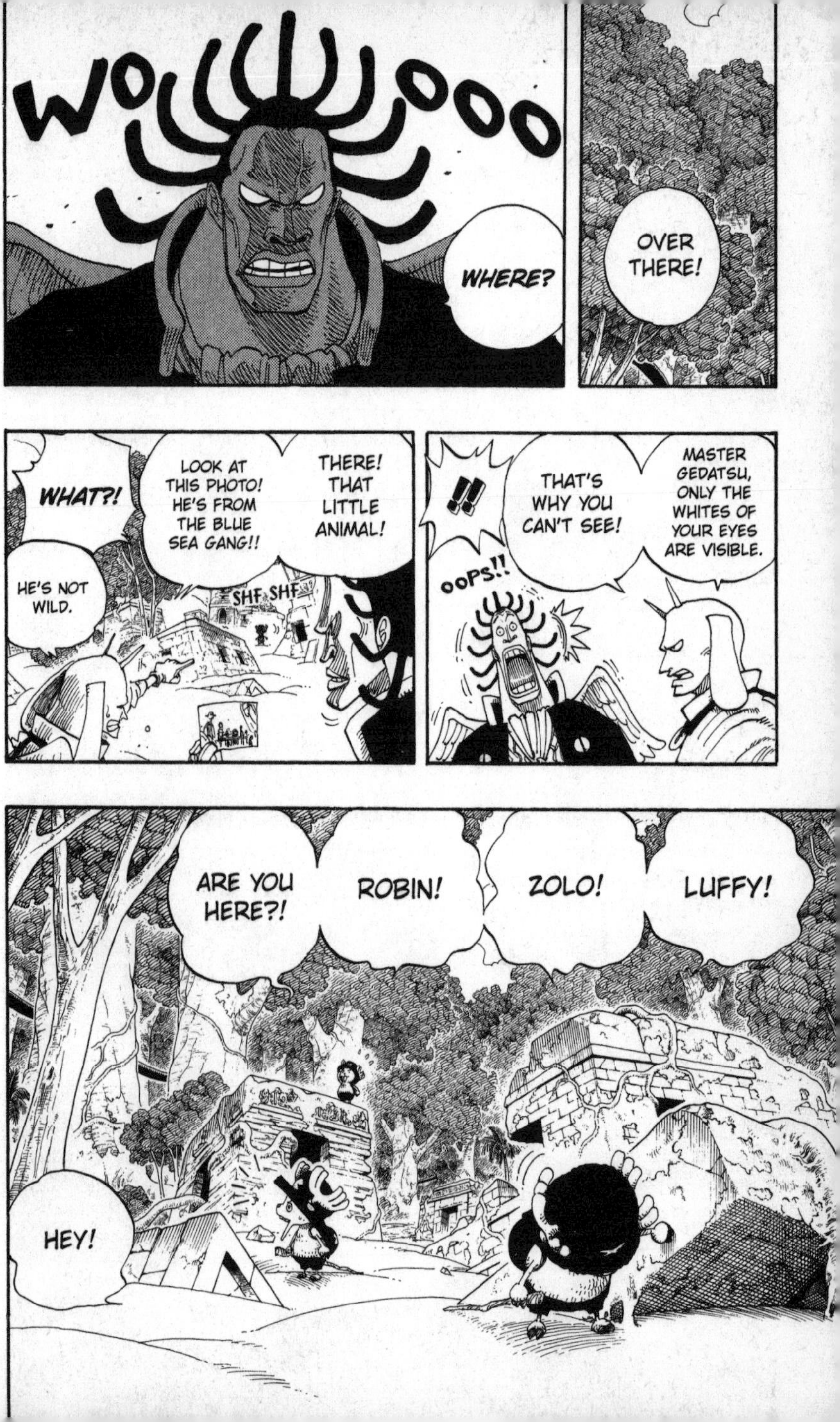
OVER THERE!
WOOOO
WHERE?
MASTER GEDATSU, ONLY THE WHITES OF YOUR EYES ARE VISIBLE.
THAT'S WHY YOU CAN'T SEE!
!!
OOPS!!
THERE! THAT LITTLE ANIMAL!
LOOK AT THIS PHOTO! HE'S FROM THE BLUE SEA GANG!!
WHAT?!
SHF SHF
HE'S NOT WILD.
LUFFY!
ZOLO!
ROBIN!
ARE YOU HERE?!
HEY!

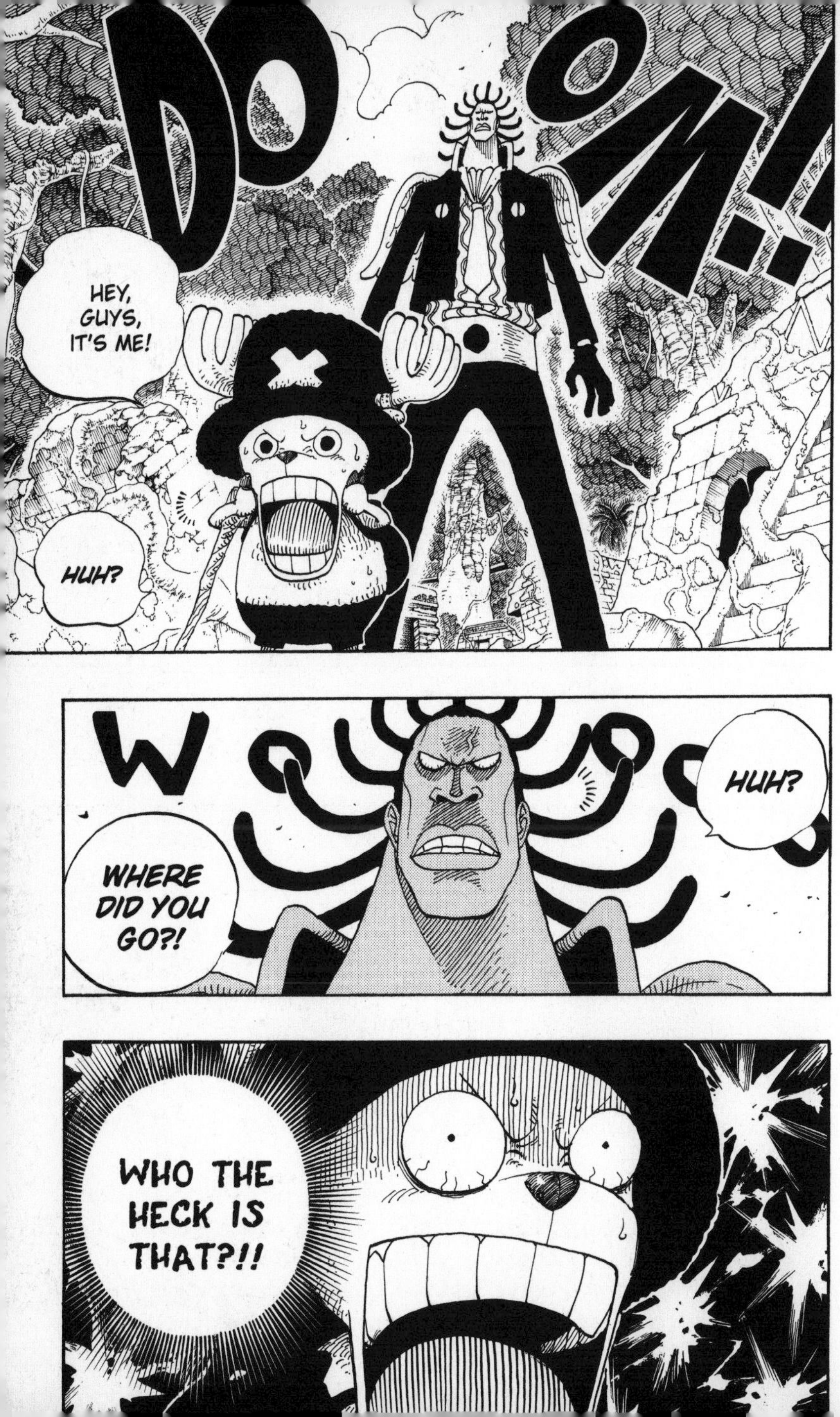
DOOM!!
HEY, GUYS, IT'S ME!
HUH?
HUH?
W
WHERE DID YOU GO?!
WHO THE HECK IS THAT?!!

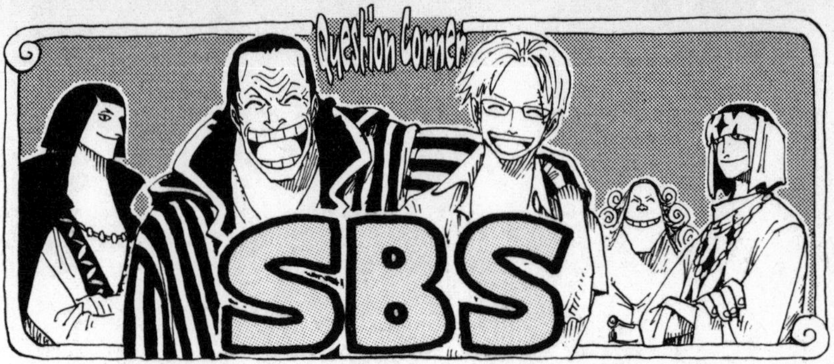
Question Corner
SBS

Q: Hello, Mr. Oda! I have something I'd like to ask you. In volume 25, there's a scene with Whitebeard on pages 158–159. What I'd like to ask is why are all the nurses around him wearing leopard print tights? Was it just coincidence? Or is it that the world's strongest man, the great pirate "Whitebeard" Edward Newgate, likes leopards prints?♡
Please tell me the secret, Mr. Oda!
Leopard prints! ♡

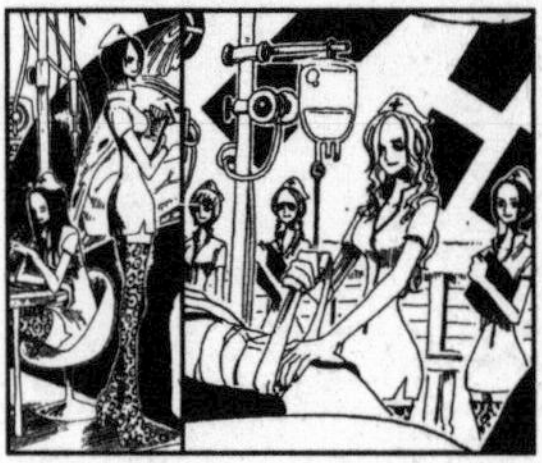

A: Leopard prints have the feel of...wildness, y' know? They're great. Speaking of which, it seems there's an increase in nurses wearing pants at hospitals lately. Isn't that sad? Makes me wanna cry. I mean, that's what Whitebeard said. Yeah, Whitebeard! "I highly recommended that all nurses wear such uniforms!" said Whitebeard. Whitebeard. That selfish old fart!

Q: Hello, Oda Sensei! I want to become a manga artist, and I'm thinking of submitting my work to *Weekly Shonen Jump* magazine, but there's something I don't quite understand. Does the manga that I submit need to have special features like screen tones? Also, where would I get such things? I'm serious, so please tell me!

-- A passionate, amateur manga-making guy

A: Sure thing. I receive LOTS of questions along these lines. Maybe sometime soon, I'll do a page that explains the basics of drawing manga. For manga-drawing materials, you can't just go to any old stationary shop. Go to an art store. The shop clerks there can help you out.

Chapter 262:

PIRATE CHOPPER VS. VASSAL GEDATSU

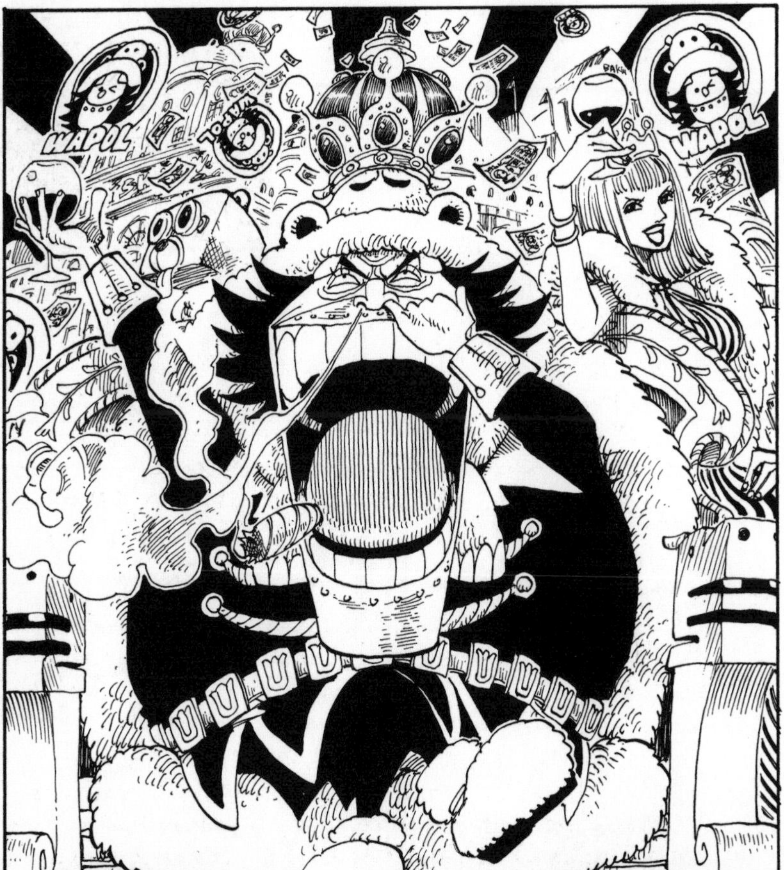
WAPOL
WAPOL
WAPOL
WAPOL

WAPOL'S OMNIVOROUS RAMPAGE, THE FINAL CHAPTER:
"THE BIG EVIL IS BACK! WAPOL SETS HIS SIGHTS ON THE WORLD"

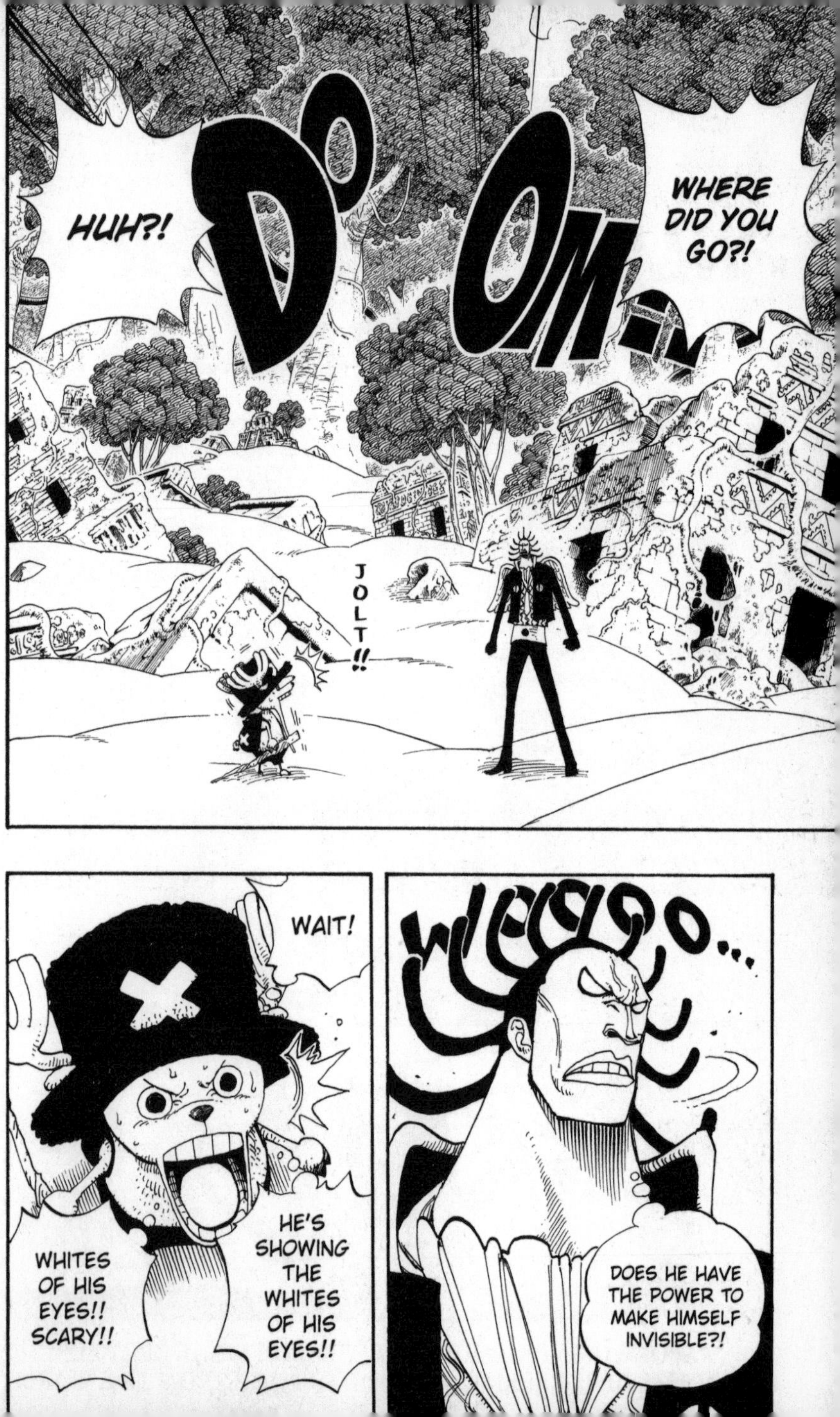
WHERE DID YOU GO?!
DOOM...
HUH?!
JOLT!!
WOOOO...
DOES HE HAVE THE POWER TO MAKE HIMSELF INVISIBLE?!
WAIT!
HE'S SHOWING THE WHITES OF HIS EYES!!
WHITES OF HIS EYES!! SCARY!!

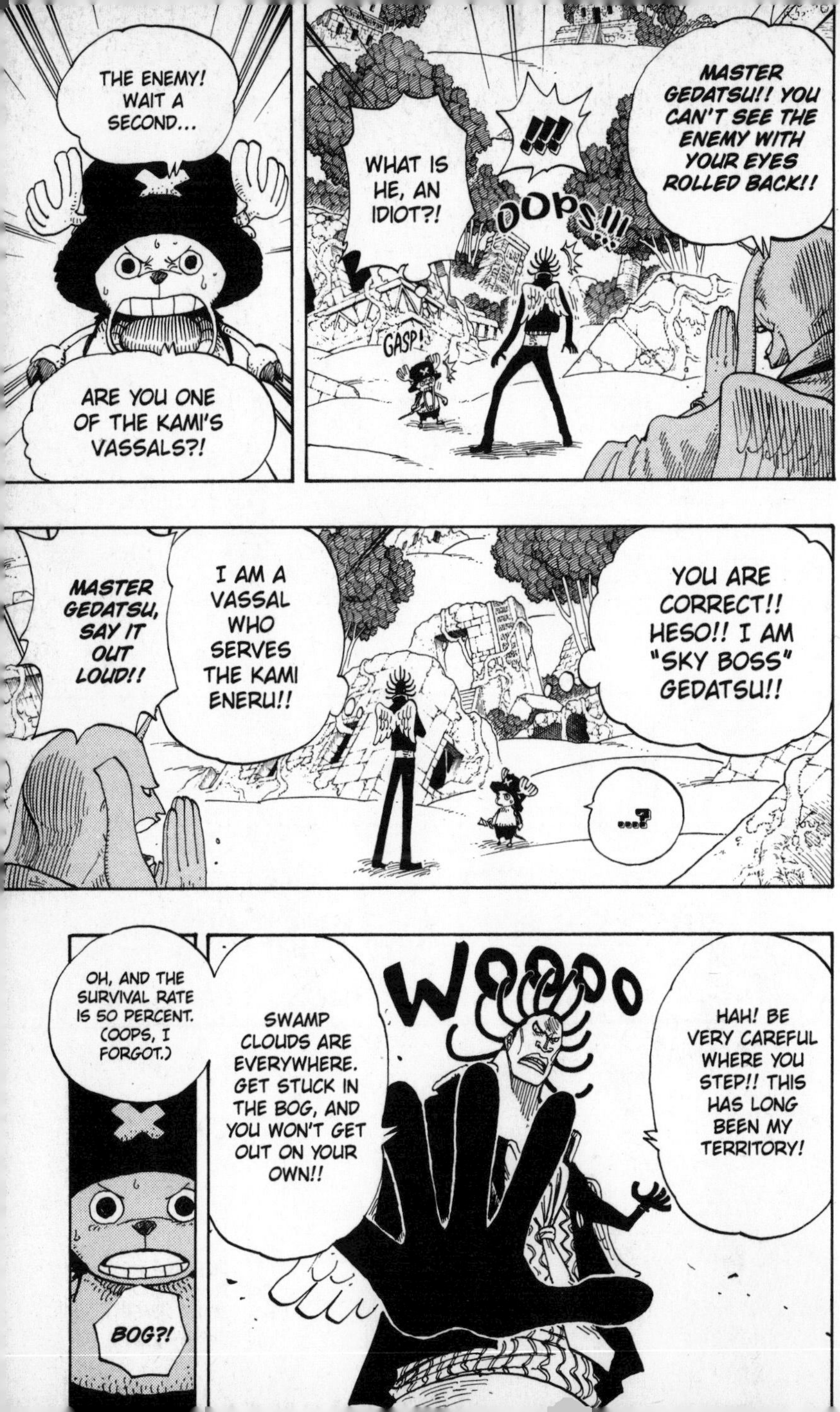
MASTER GEDATSU!! YOU CAN'T SEE THE ENEMY WITH YOUR EYES ROLLED BACK!!
!!!
OOPS!!!
WHAT IS HE, AN IDIOT?!
GASP!
THE ENEMY! WAIT A SECOND...
ARE YOU ONE OF THE KAMI'S VASSALS?!
YOU ARE CORRECT!! HESO!! I AM "SKY BOSS" GEDATSU!!
...?
I AM A VASSAL WHO SERVES THE KAMI ENERU!!
MASTER GEDATSU, SAY IT OUT LOUD!!
WOOOO
HAH! BE VERY CAREFUL WHERE YOU STEP!! THIS HAS LONG BEEN MY TERRITORY!
SWAMP CLOUDS ARE EVERYWHERE. GET STUCK IN THE BOG, AND YOU WON'T GET OUT ON YOUR OWN!!
OH, AND THE SURVIVAL RATE IS 50 PERCENT. (OOPS, I FORGOT.)
BOG?!

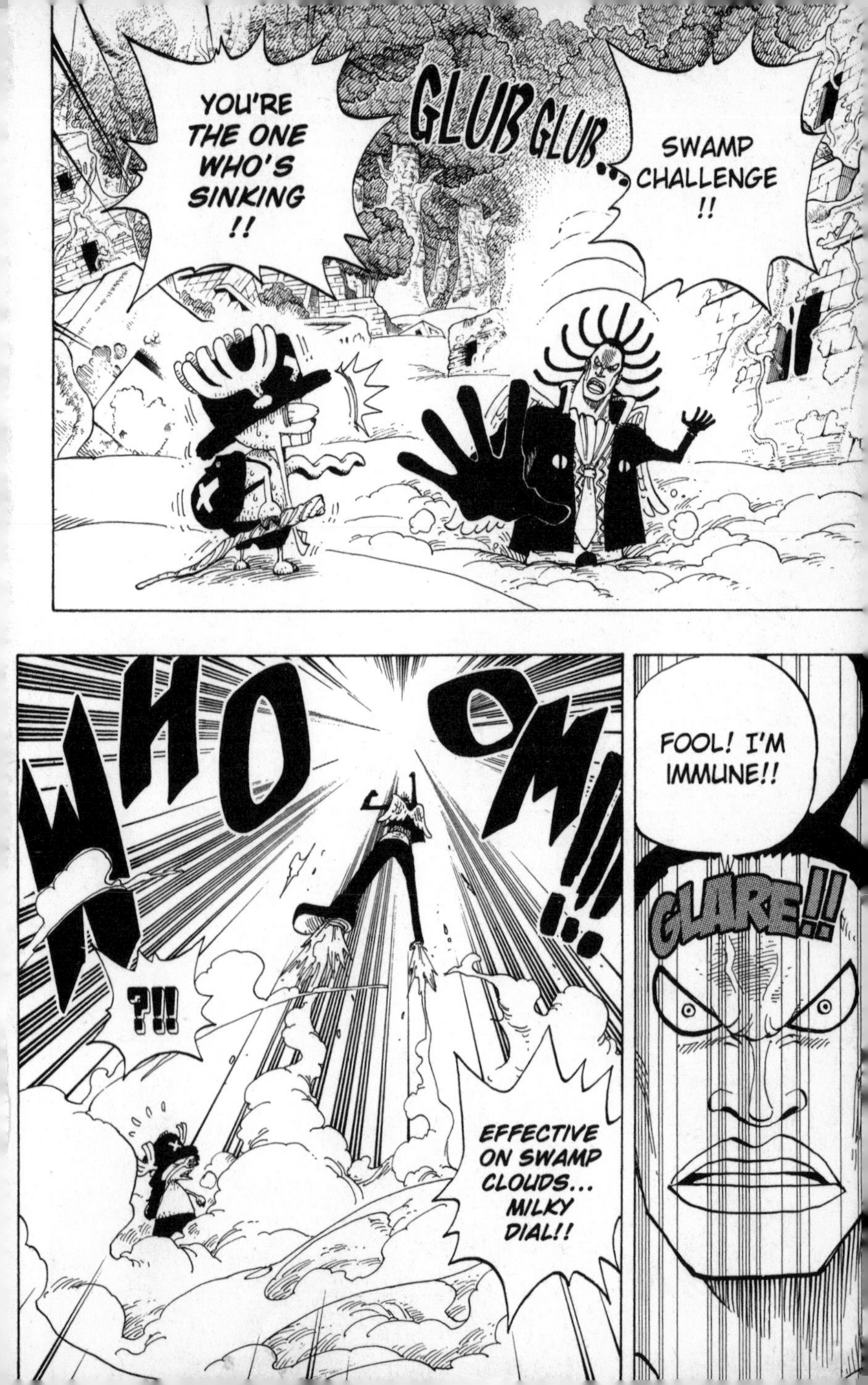
SWAMP CHALLENGE!!
GLUB GLUB...
YOU'RE THE ONE WHO'S SINKING!!
FOOL! I'M IMMUNE!!
GLARE!!
WHOOM!!
?!!
EFFECTIVE ON SWAMP CLOUDS... MILKY DIAL!!

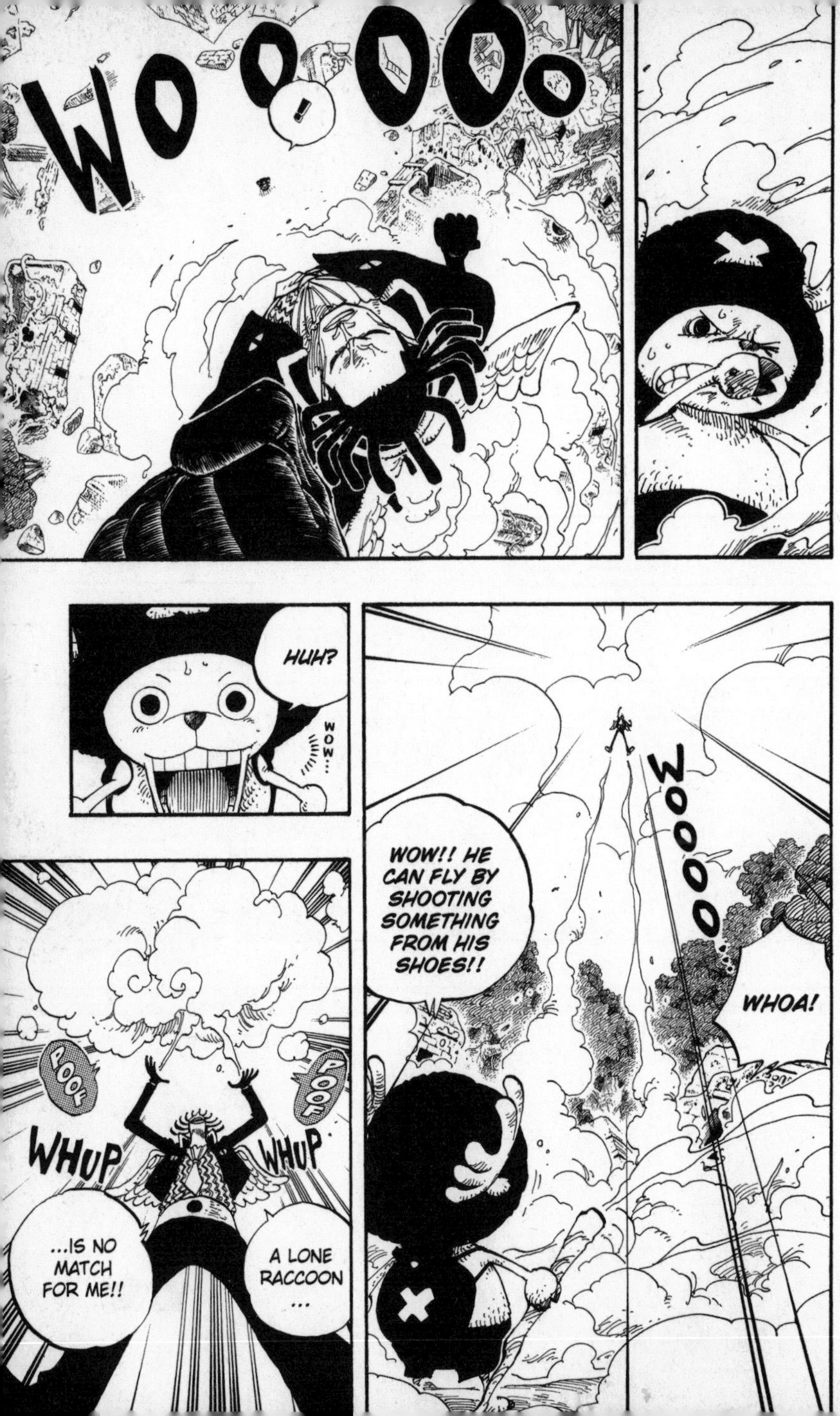
WOOOOO
!
WOOOOO
WOW!! HE CAN FLY BY SHOOTING SOMETHING FROM HIS SHOES!!
WHOA!
HUH?
WOW WOW...
POOF
POOF
WHUP
WHUP
A LONE RACCOON ...
...IS NO MATCH FOR ME!!

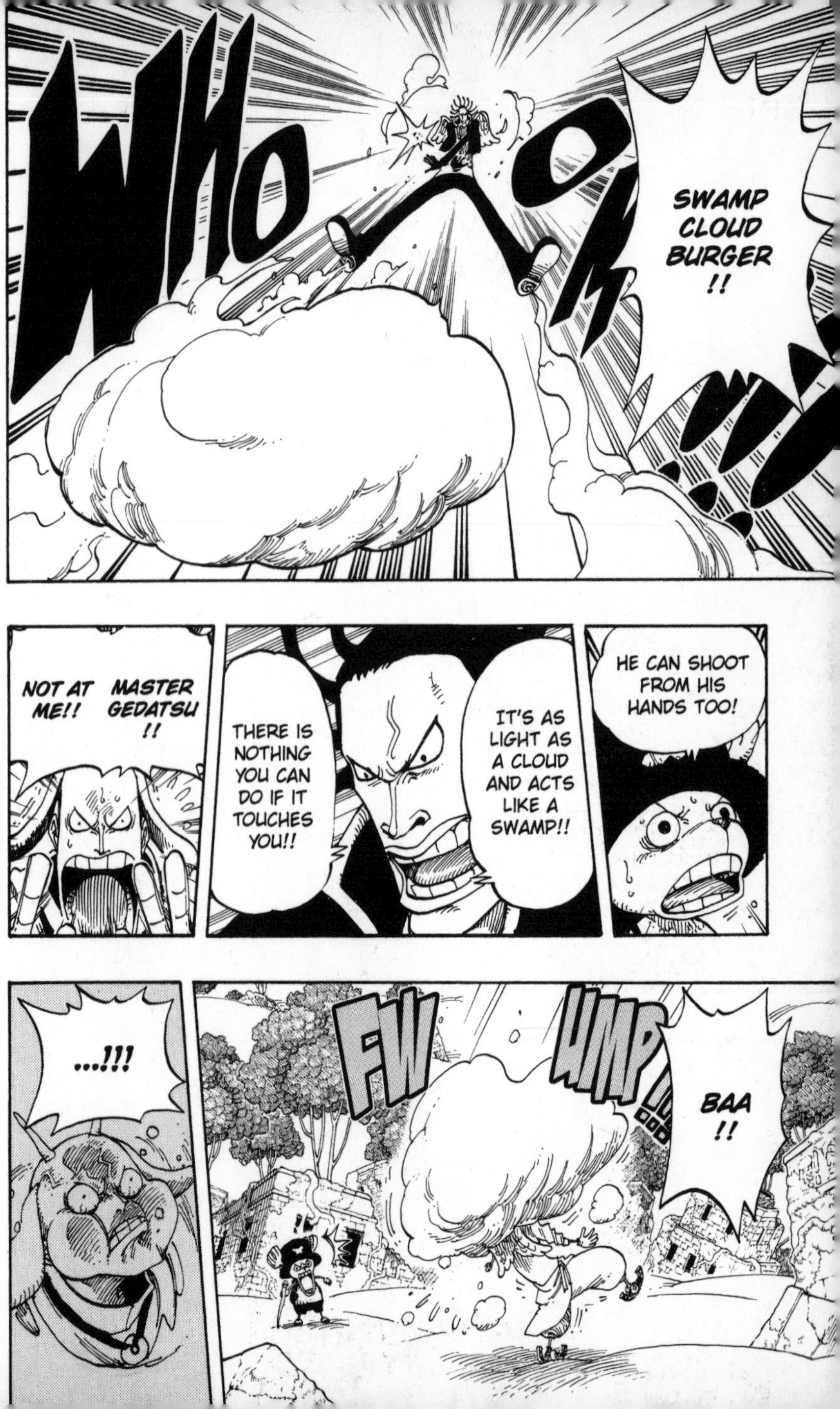
WHOOM
SWAMP CLOUD BURGER !!
HE CAN SHOOT FROM HIS HANDS TOO!
IT'S AS LIGHT AS A CLOUD AND ACTS LIKE A SWAMP!!
THERE IS NOTHING YOU CAN DO IF IT TOUCHES YOU!!
MASTER GEDATSU !!
NOT AT ME!!
BAA !!
FWUMP
...!!!

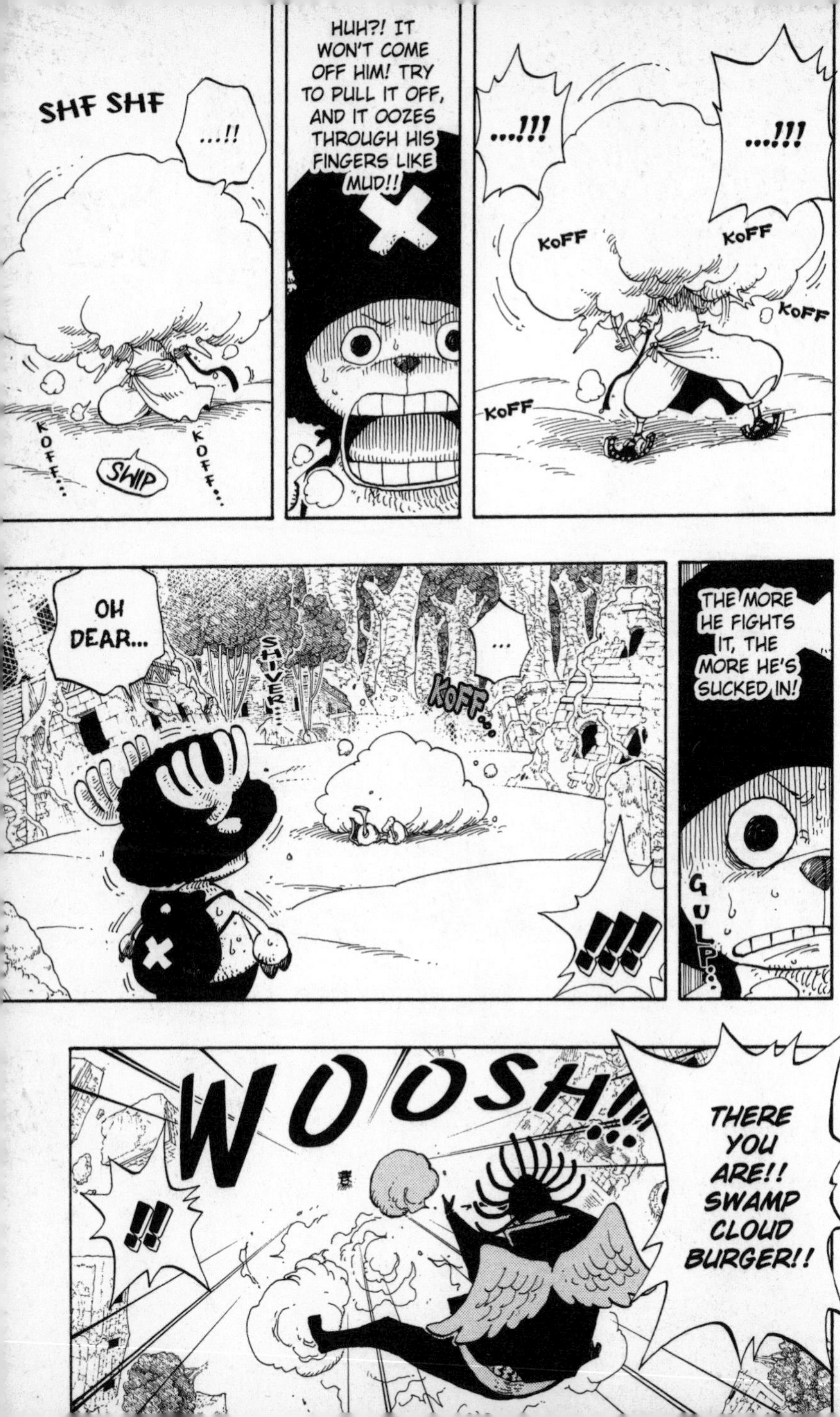
...!!!
...!!!
KOFF
KOFF
KOFF
KOFF
HUH?! IT WON'T COME OFF HIM! TRY TO PULL IT OFF, AND IT OOZES THROUGH HIS FINGERS LIKE MUD!!
SHF SHF
...!!
KOFF...
SWIP
KOFF...
THE MORE HE FIGHTS IT, THE MORE HE'S SUCKED IN!
GULP...
!!!
...
KOFF...
SHIVER...
OH DEAR...
THERE YOU ARE!! SWAMP CLOUD BURGER!!
WOOSH!!
!!

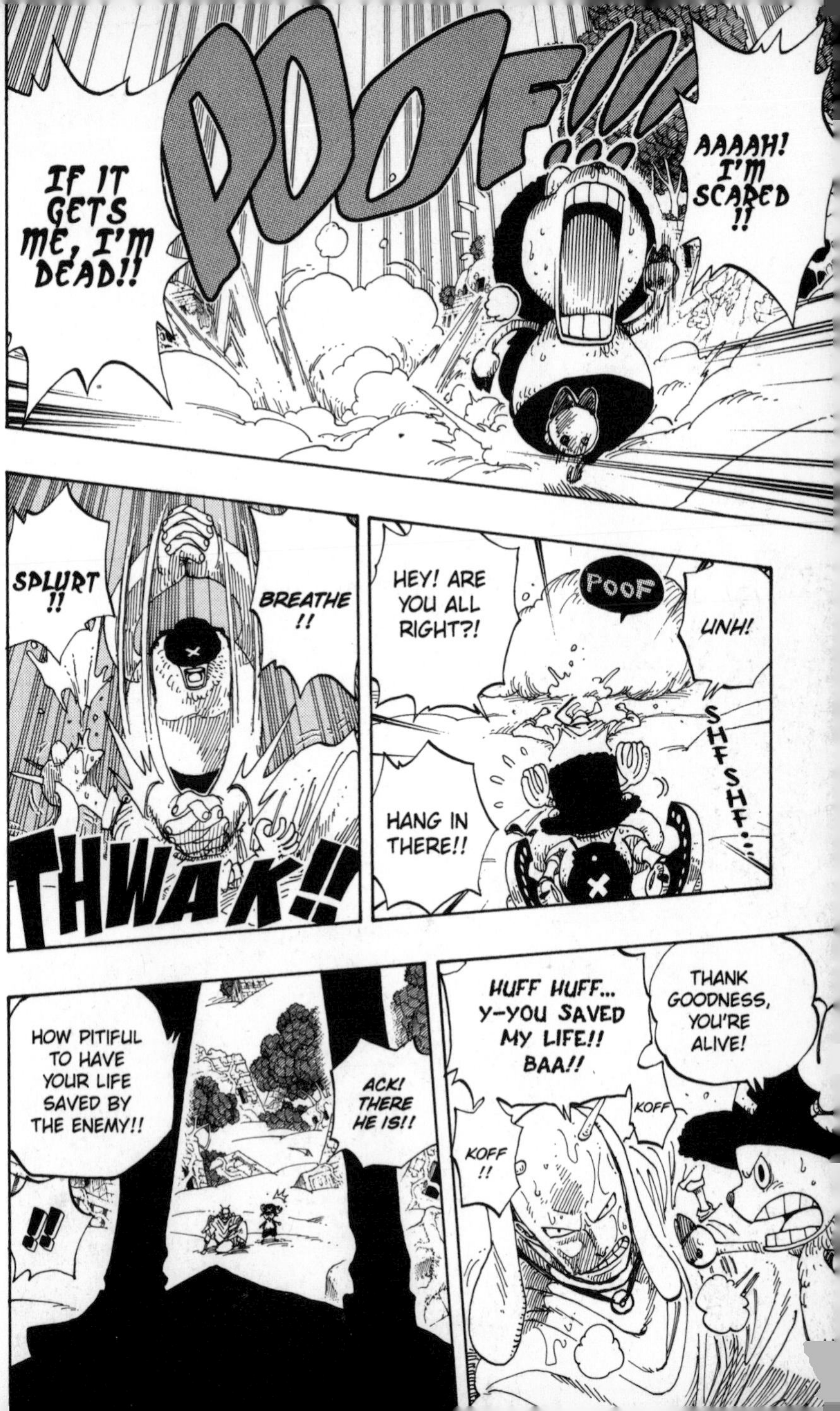
AAAAH! I'M SCARED!!
POOF!!
IF IT GETS ME, I'M DEAD!!
UNH!
SHF SHF...
POOF
HEY! ARE YOU ALL RIGHT?!
HANG IN THERE!!
BREATHE!!
SPLURT!!
THWAK!!
THANK GOODNESS, YOU'RE ALIVE!
HUFF HUFF... Y-YOU SAVED MY LIFE!! BAA!!
KOFF
KOFF!!
ACK! THERE HE IS!!
HOW PITIFUL TO HAVE YOUR LIFE SAVED BY THE ENEMY!!
!!

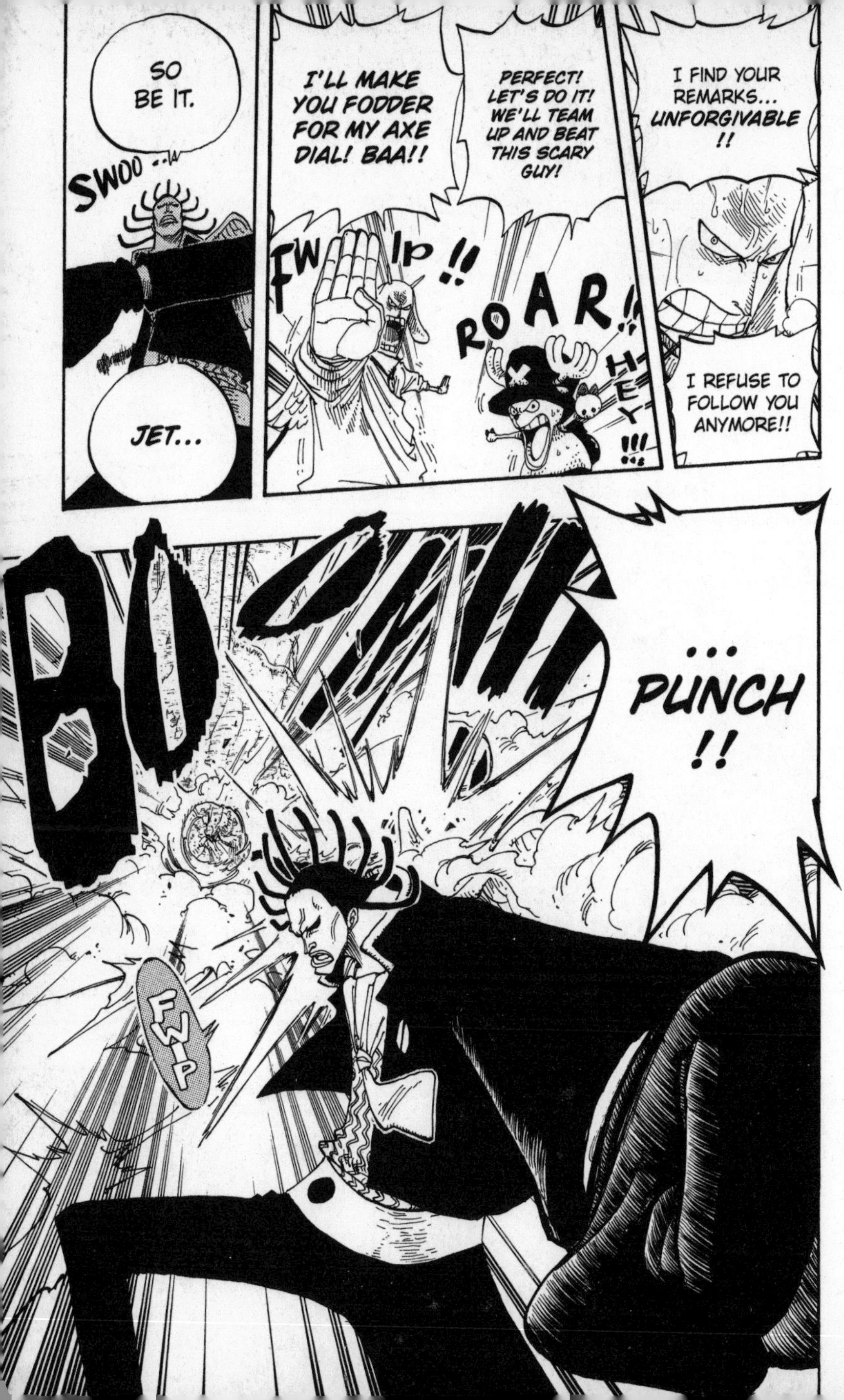
I FIND YOUR REMARKS... UNFORGIVABLE!!
I REFUSE TO FOLLOW YOU ANYMORE!!
PERFECT! LET'S DO IT! WE'LL TEAM UP AND BEAT THIS SCARY GUY!
I'LL MAKE YOU FODDER FOR MY AXE DIAL! BAA!!
FWIP!!
ROAR!!
HEY!!!
SO BE IT.
SWOO...
JET...
...PUNCH!!
BOOM
FWIP

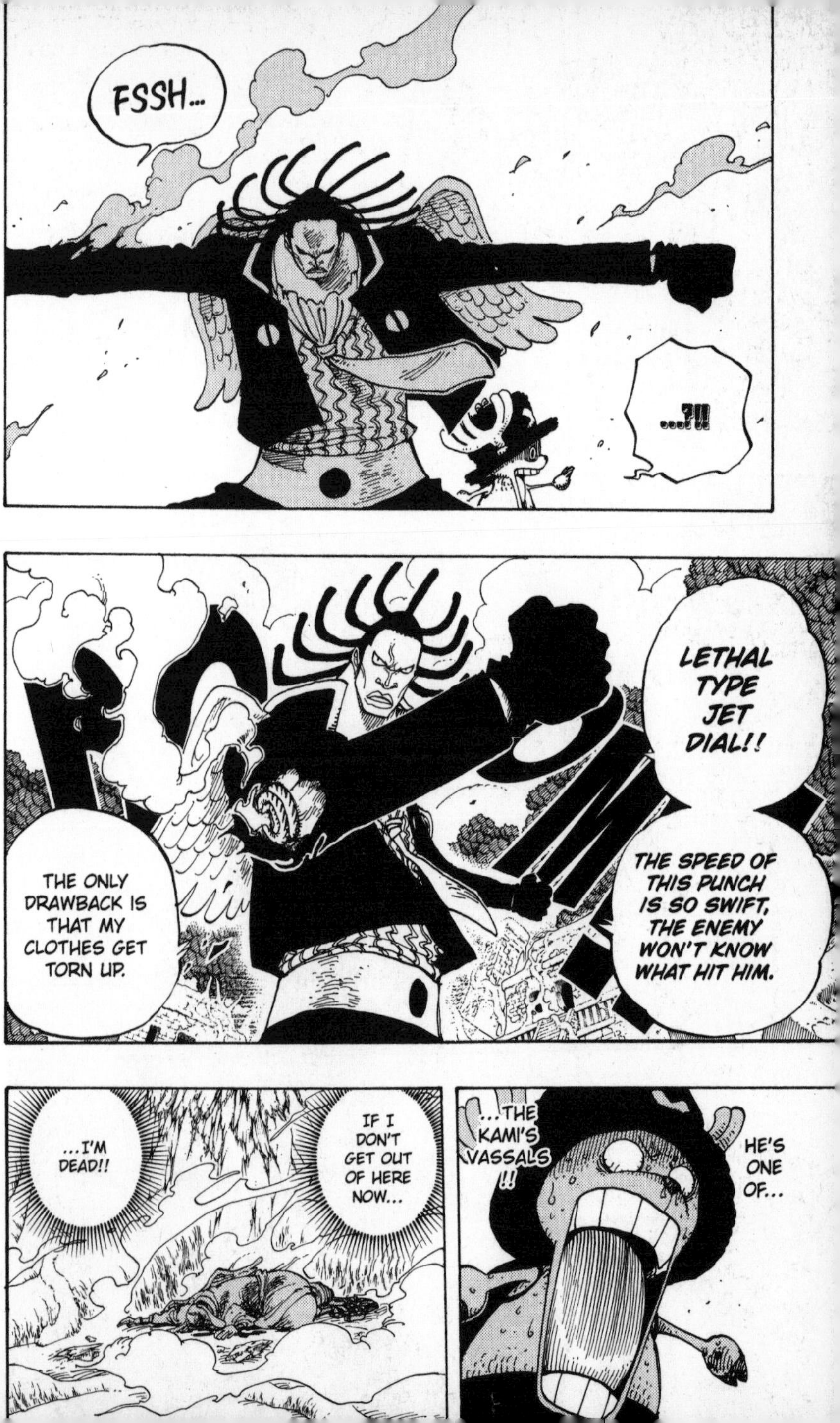
FSSH...
...?!!
LETHAL TYPE JET DIAL!!
THE SPEED OF THIS PUNCH IS SO SWIFT, THE ENEMY WON'T KNOW WHAT HIT HIM.
THE ONLY DRAWBACK IS THAT MY CLOTHES GET TORN UP.
HE'S ONE OF...
...THE KAMI'S VASSALS!!
IF I DON'T GET OUT OF HERE NOW...
...I'M DEAD!!

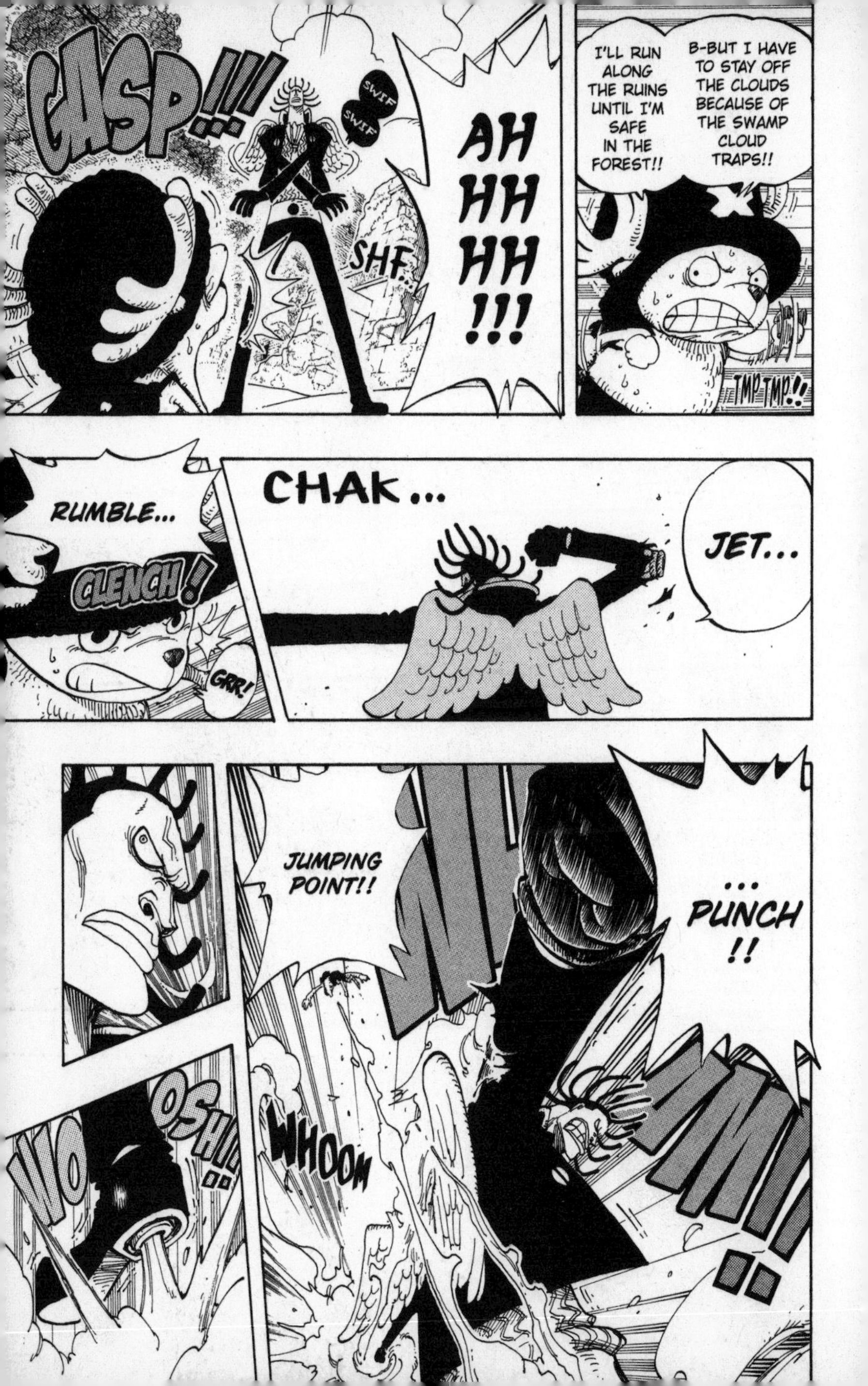
I'LL RUN ALONG THE RUINS UNTIL I'M SAFE IN THE FOREST!!
B-BUT I HAVE TO STAY OFF THE CLOUDS BECAUSE OF THE SWAMP CLOUD TRAPS!!
TMP TMP!!
AH HH HH HH !!!
SWIF
SWIF
SHF...
GASP!!!...
JET...
CHAK...
RUMBLE...
CLENCH!
GRR!
... PUNCH !!
JUMPING POINT!!
WHOOM
WOOSH!!..

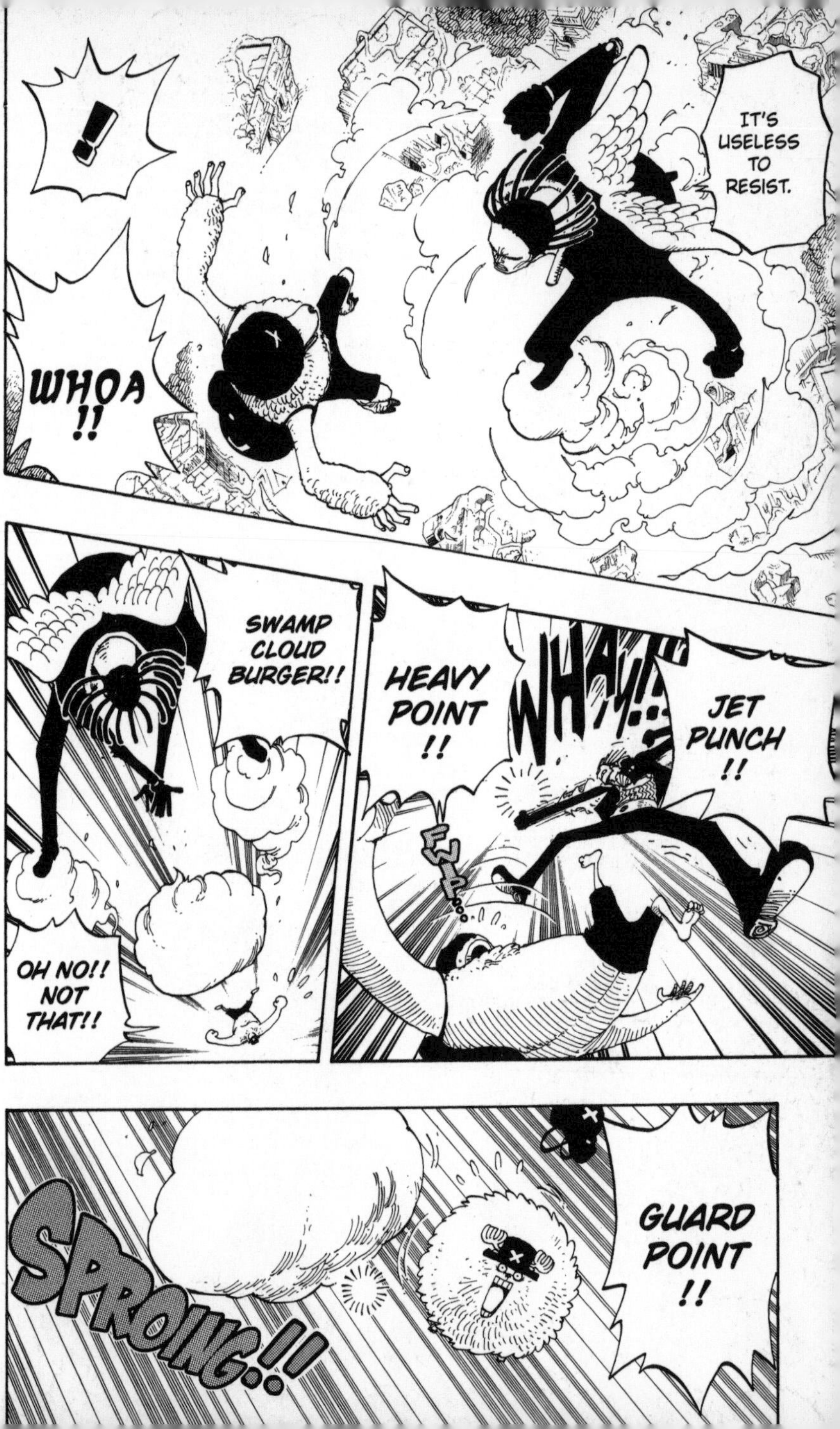
IT'S USELESS TO RESIST.
!
WHOA!!
JET PUNCH!!
HEAVY POINT!!
SWAMP CLOUD BURGER!!
OH NO!! NOT THAT!!
GUARD POINT!!
SPROING!!!

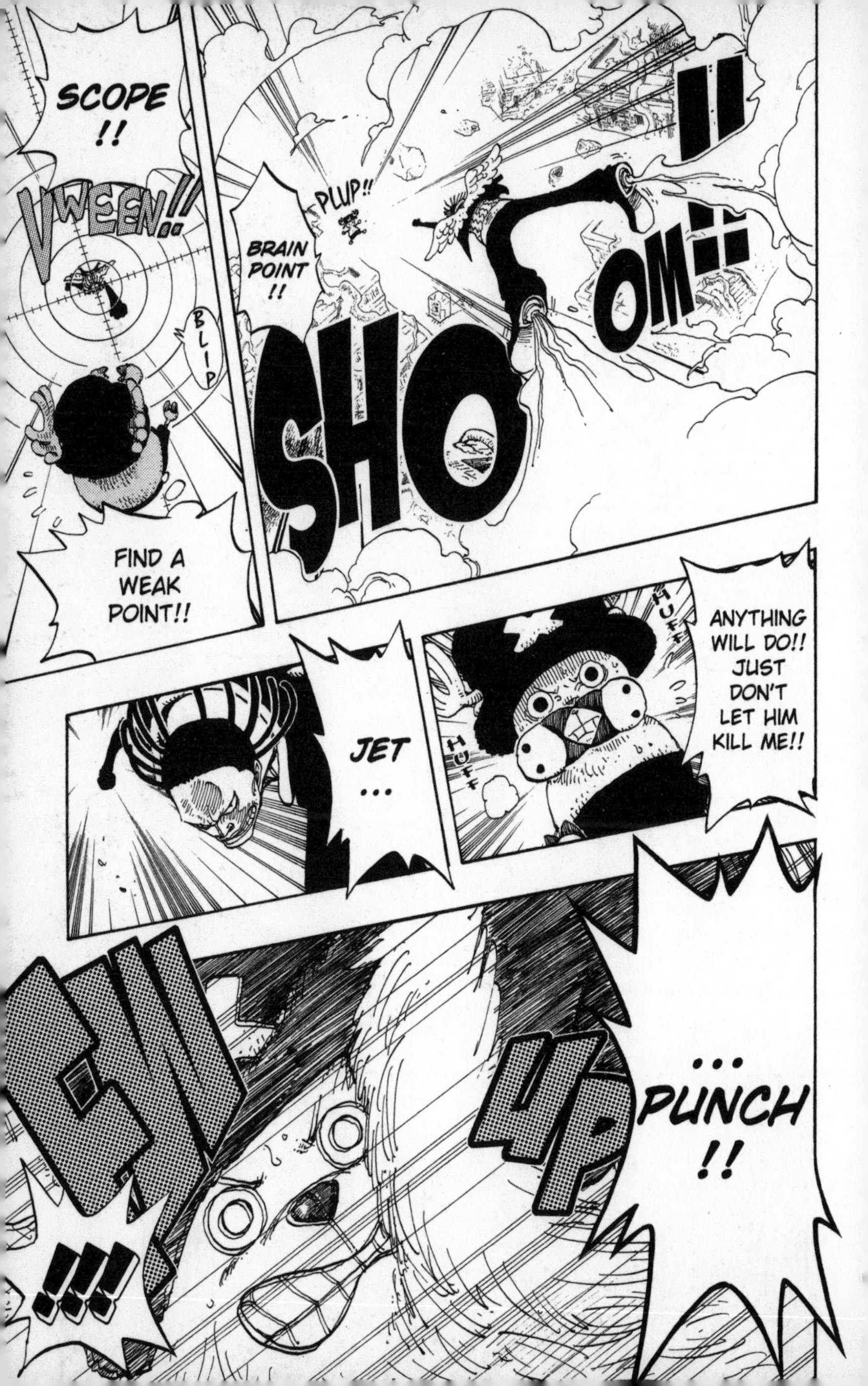
SHOOM!!
PLUP!!
BRAIN POINT !!
SCOPE !!
VWEEN!!
BLIP
FIND A WEAK POINT!!
ANYTHING WILL DO!! JUST DON'T LET HIM KILL ME!!
HUFF
HUFF
JET ...
... PUNCH !!

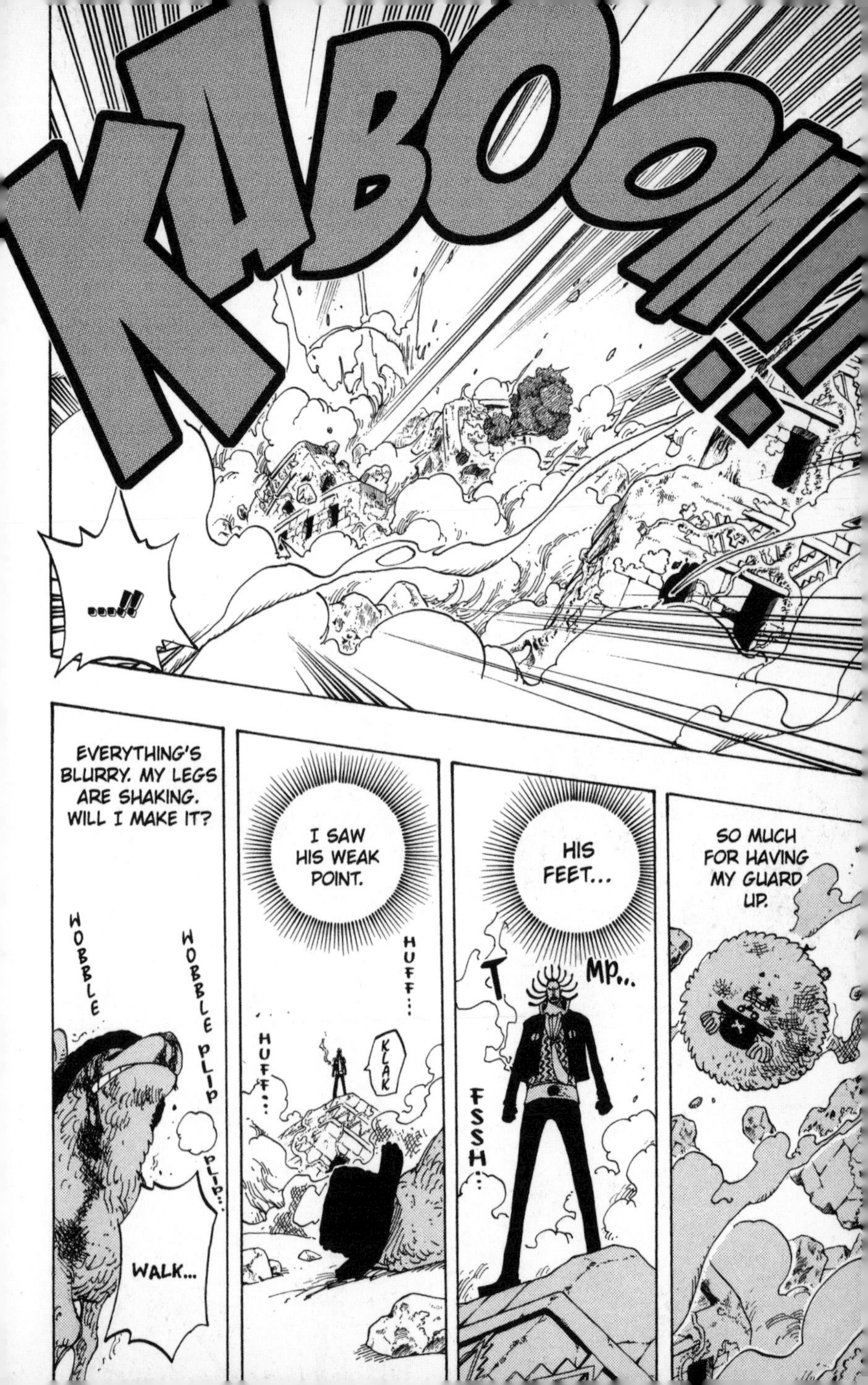
KABOOM!!
...!!
SO MUCH FOR HAVING MY GUARD UP.
HIS FEET...
MP...
T
FSSH...
I SAW HIS WEAK POINT.
HUFF...
KLAK
HUFF...
EVERYTHING'S BLURRY. MY LEGS ARE SHAKING. WILL I MAKE IT?
WOBBLE
WOBBLE
PLIP
PLIP...
WALK...

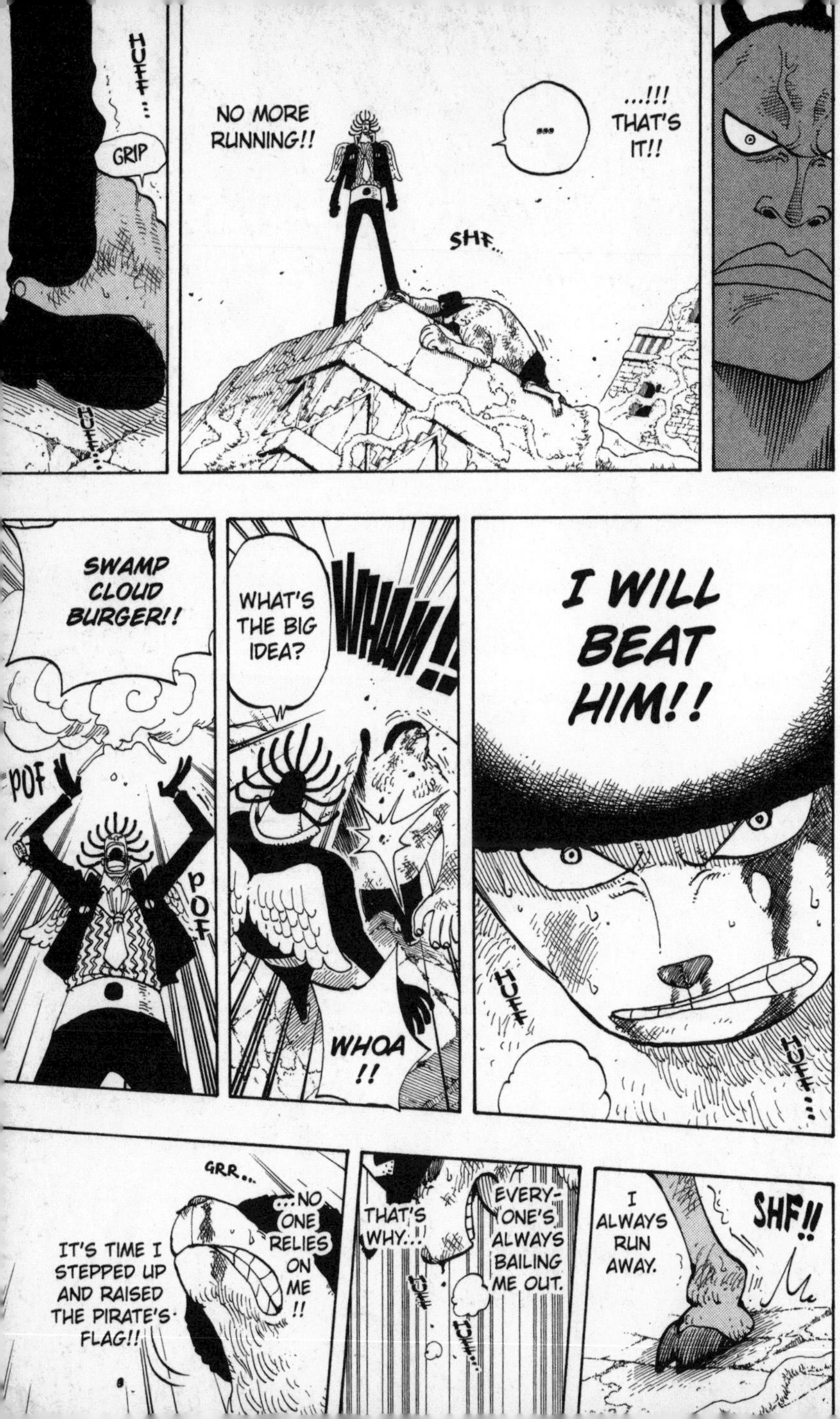
...!!! THAT'S IT!!
...
NO MORE RUNNING!!
SHF...
HUFF...
GRIP
HUFF...
I WILL BEAT HIM!!
HUFF
HUFF...
WHAM!!
WHAT'S THE BIG IDEA?
WHOA!!
SWAMP CLOUD BURGER!!
POF
POF
SHF!!
I ALWAYS RUN AWAY.
EVERYONE'S ALWAYS BAILING ME OUT.
THAT'S WHY...!
HUFF
HUFF...
GRR...
...NO ONE RELIES ON ME!!
IT'S TIME I STEPPED UP AND RAISED THE PIRATE'S FLAG!!

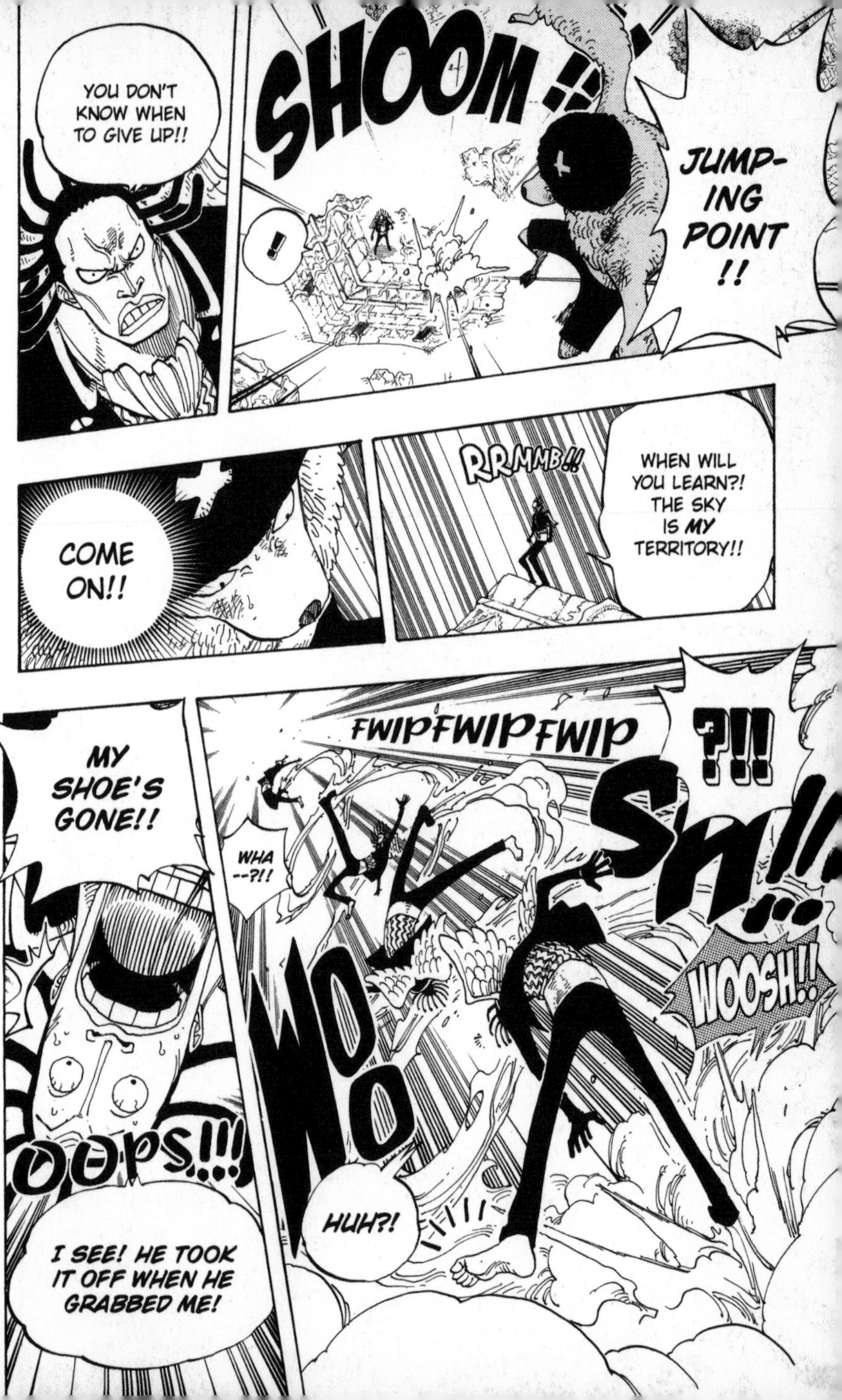
SHOOM!!
JUMPING POINT!!
!
YOU DON'T KNOW WHEN TO GIVE UP!!
RRMMB!!
WHEN WILL YOU LEARN?! THE SKY IS MY TERRITORY!!
COME ON!!
?!!
FWIPFWIPFWIP
Sh!!!
WOOSH!!
WHA--?!!
HUH?!
MY SHOE'S GONE!!
OOPS!!!
I SEE! HE TOOK IT OFF WHEN HE GRABBED ME!

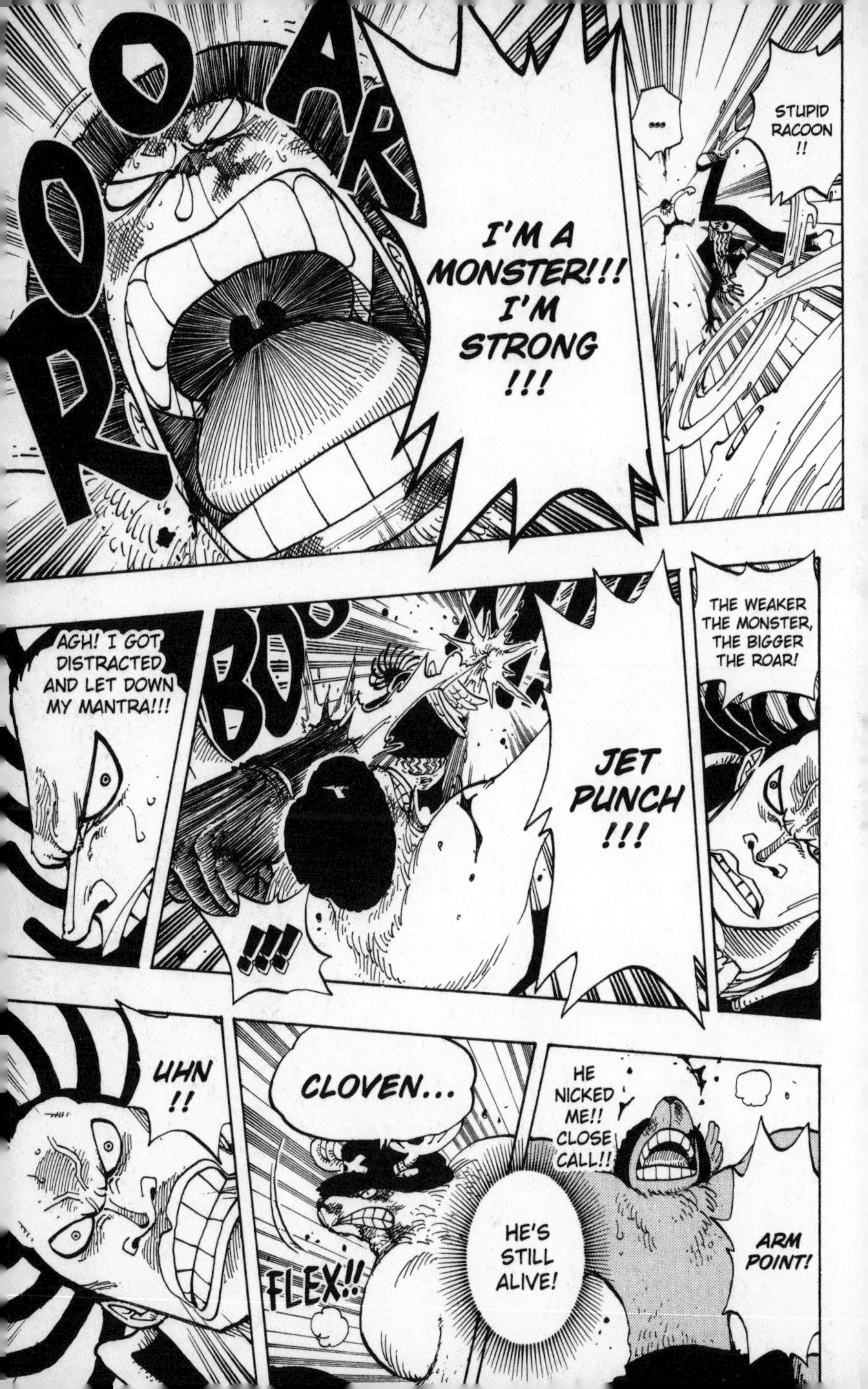
STUPID RACOON !!
...
I'M A MONSTER!!! I'M STRONG !!!
ROOAR
THE WEAKER THE MONSTER, THE BIGGER THE ROAR!
JET PUNCH !!!
BOOM
!!!
AGH! I GOT DISTRACTED AND LET DOWN MY MANTRA!!!
ARM POINT!
HE NICKED ME!! CLOSE CALL!!
HE'S STILL ALIVE!
CLOVEN...
FLEX!!
UHN !!

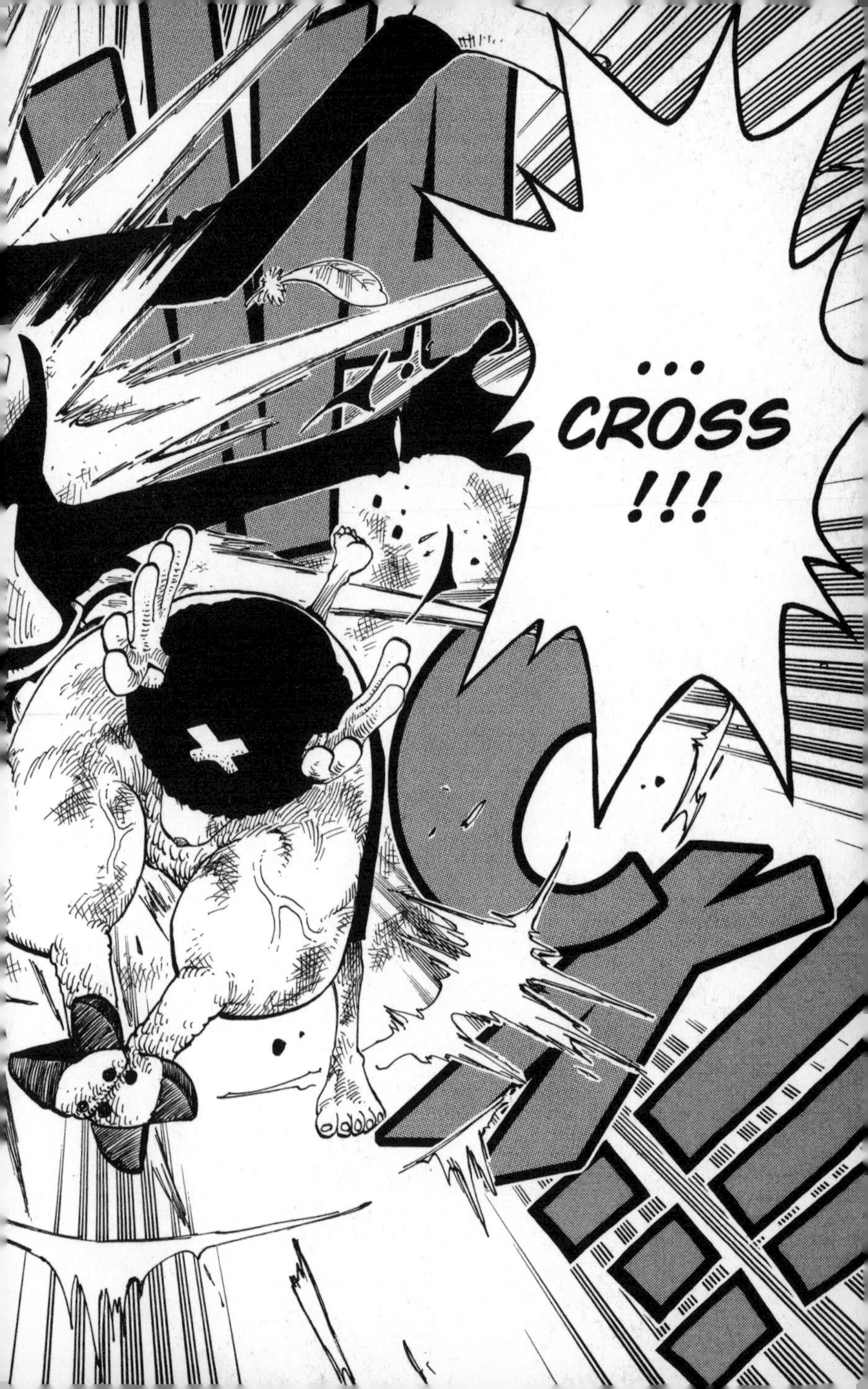
...CROSS!!!

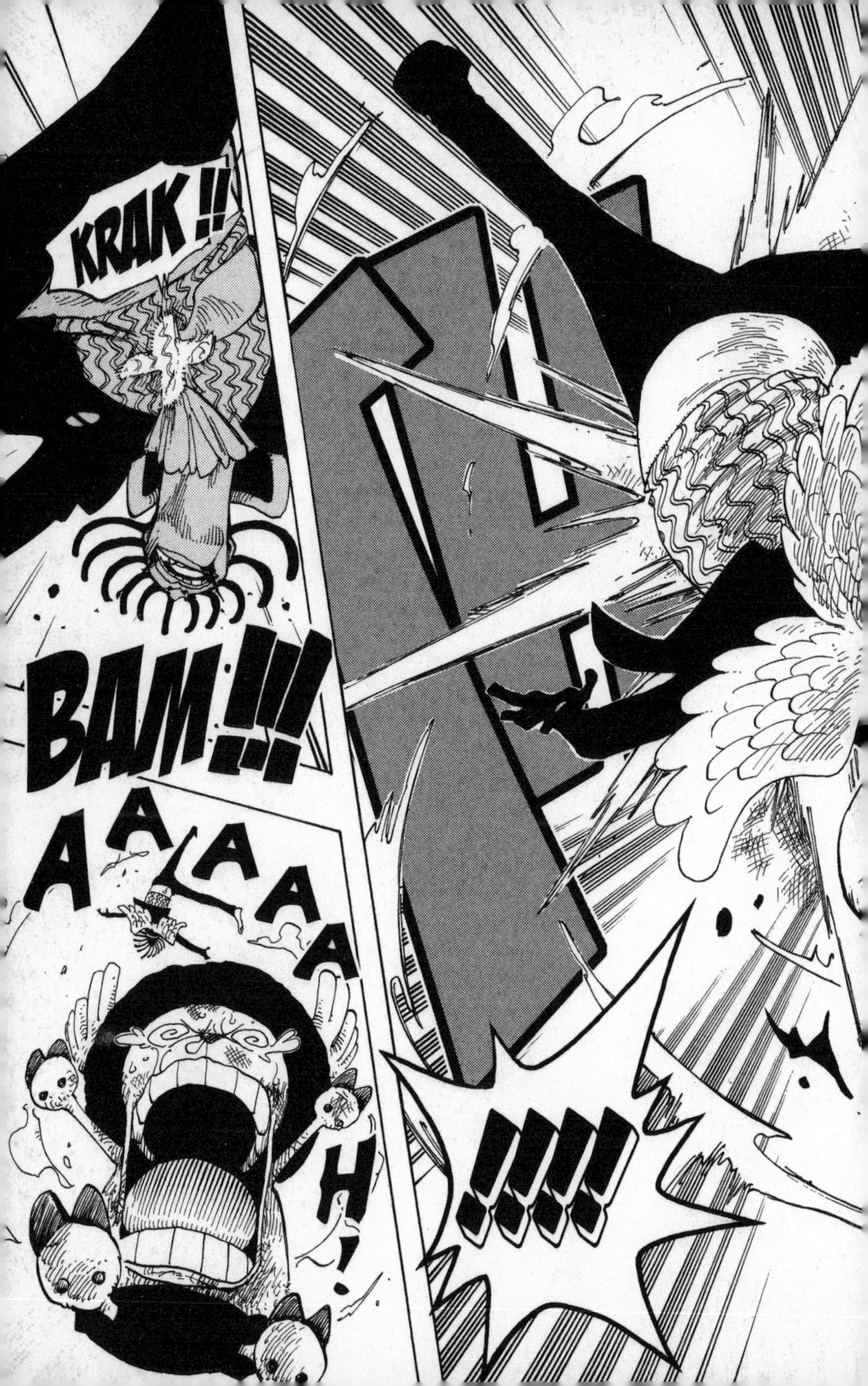
KRAK!!
BAM!!!
!!!!
AAAAAAAH!

COLORING PAGE!! (REQUESTED BY "WORLD CHAMPION MIKA" AND "CRICKET VISITS THE SHOP")

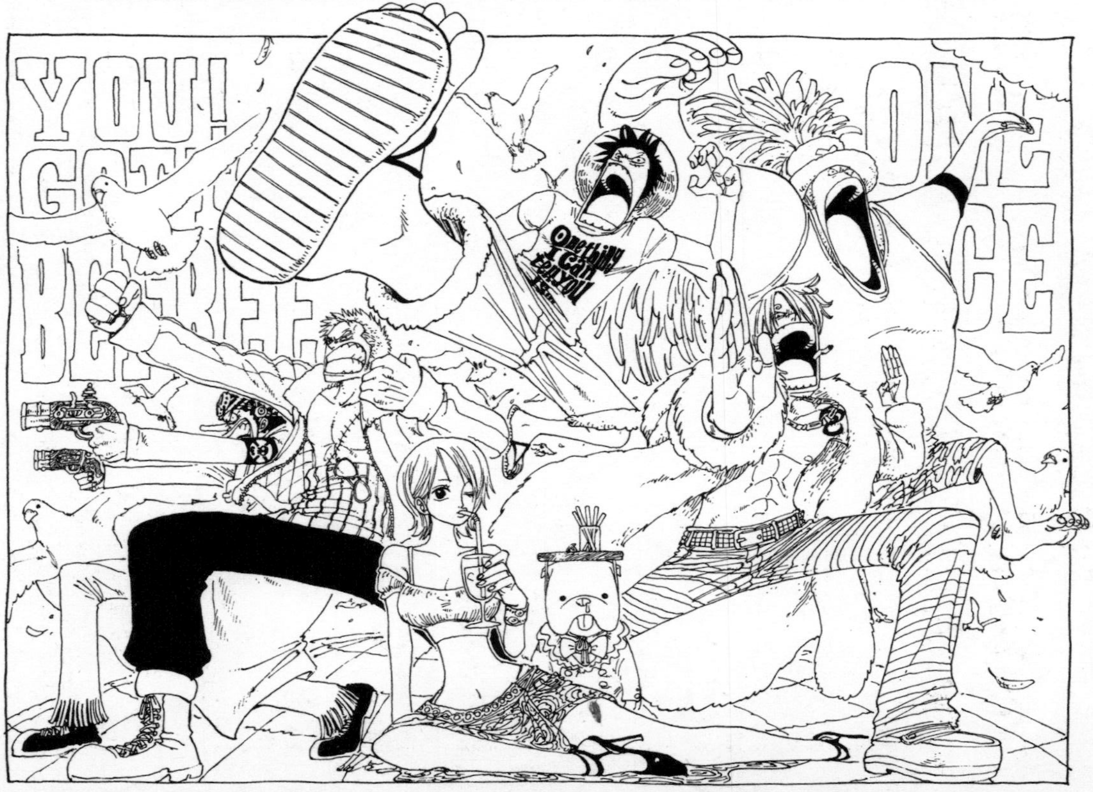
YOU!
Onething I can tell you is...

Chapter 263:
PIRATE NAMI AND THE WEIRD KNIGHT VS. HEAVENLY WARRIORS SUBCOMMANDERS HOTORI AND KOTORI

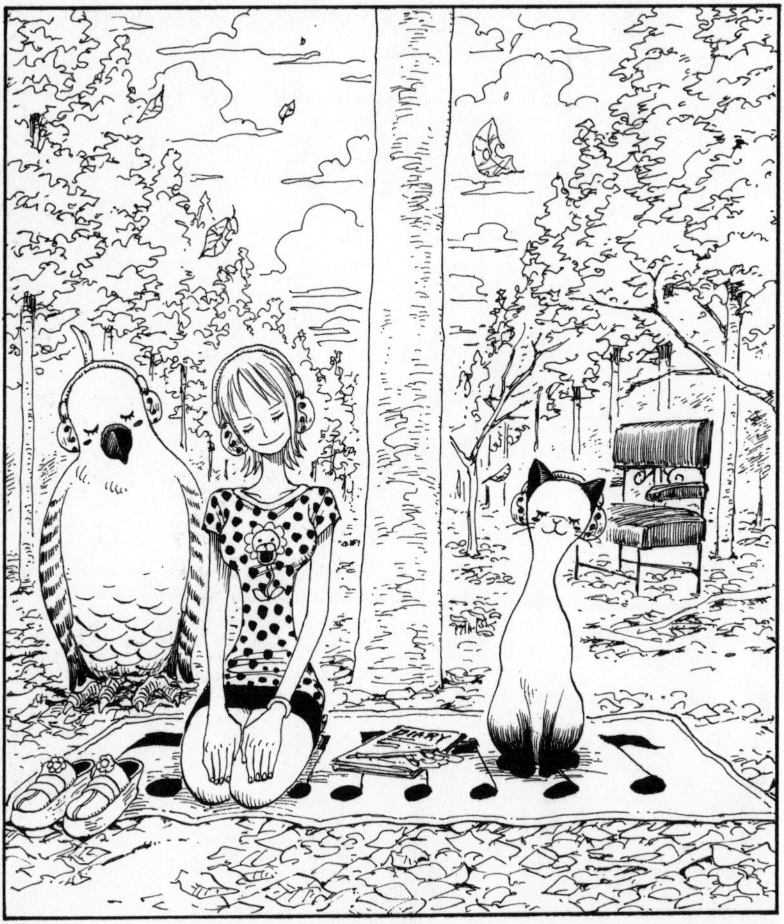
DIARY

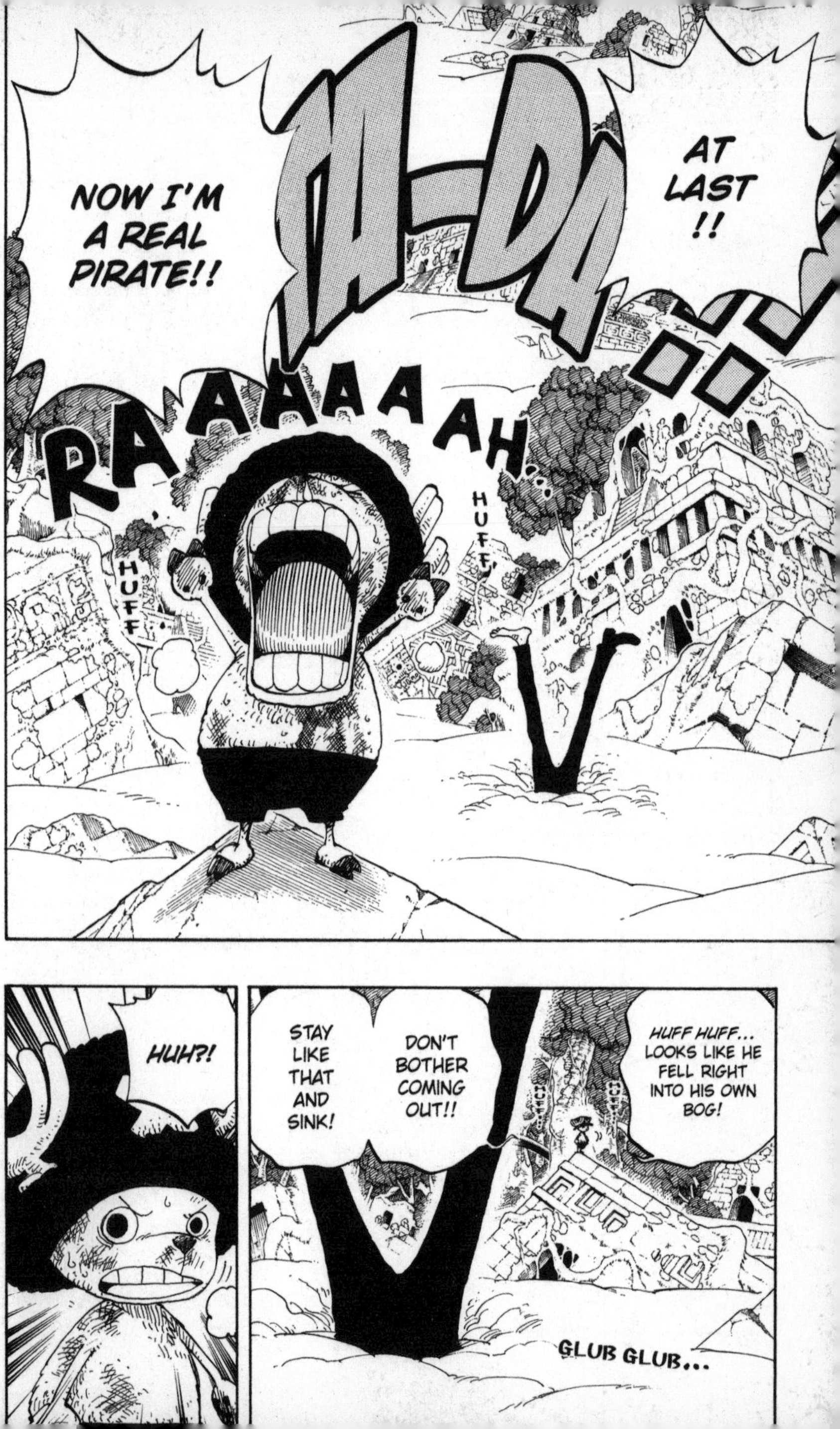
AT LAST!!
TA-DA
NOW I'M A REAL PIRATE!!
RAAAAAAH...
HUFF
HUFF
HUFF HUFF... LOOKS LIKE HE FELL RIGHT INTO HIS OWN BOG!
DON'T BOTHER COMING OUT!!
STAY LIKE THAT AND SINK!
GLUB GLUB...
HUH?!

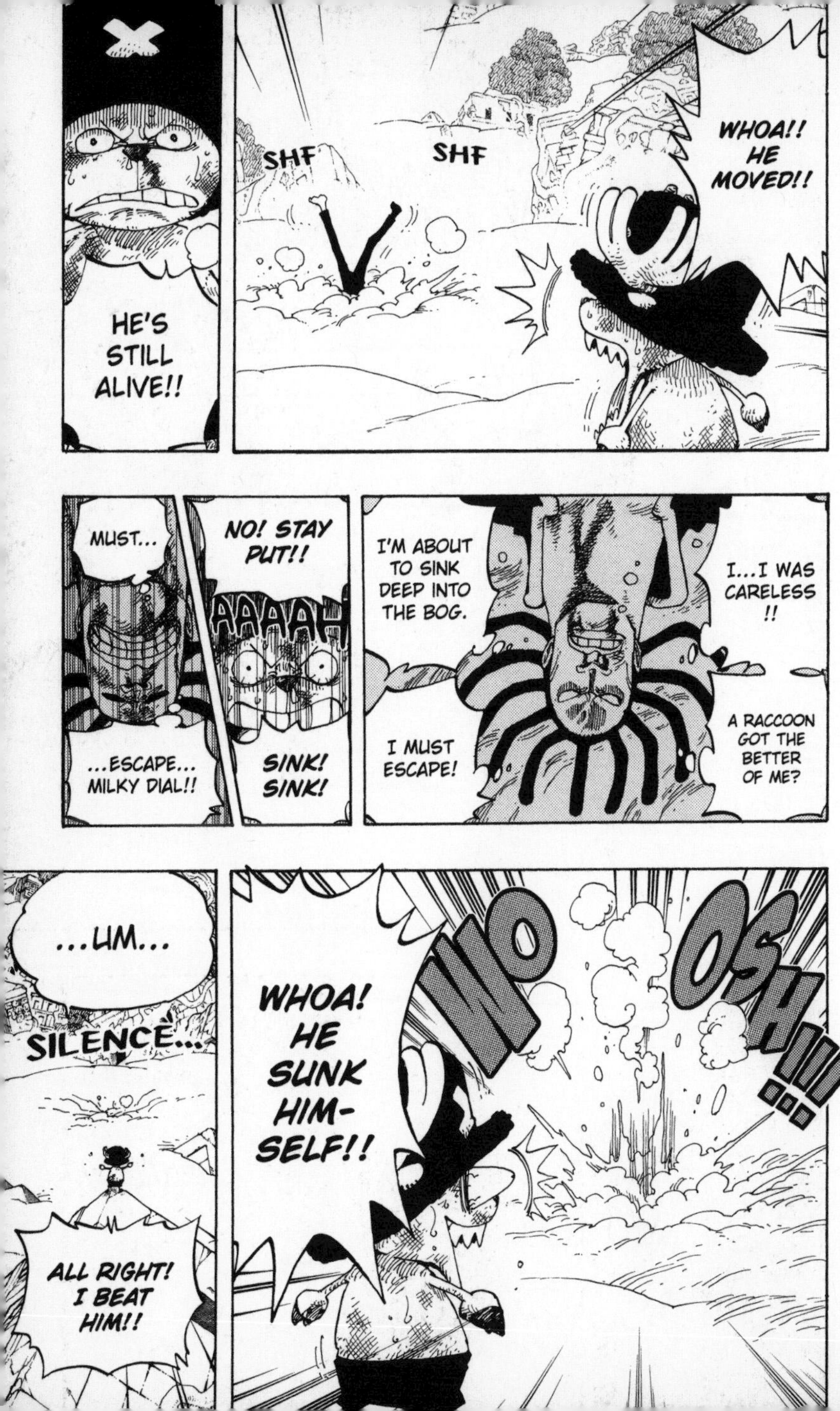
WHOA!! HE MOVED!!
SHF
SHF
HE'S STILL ALIVE!!
I...I WAS CARELESS!!
I'M ABOUT TO SINK DEEP INTO THE BOG.
A RACCOON GOT THE BETTER OF ME?
I MUST ESCAPE!
NO! STAY PUT!!
AAAAAH
SINK! SINK!
MUST...
...ESCAPE... MILKY DIAL!!
WHOOSH!!!
WHOA! HE SUNK HIM-SELF!!
...UM...
SILENCE...
ALL RIGHT! I BEAT HIM!!

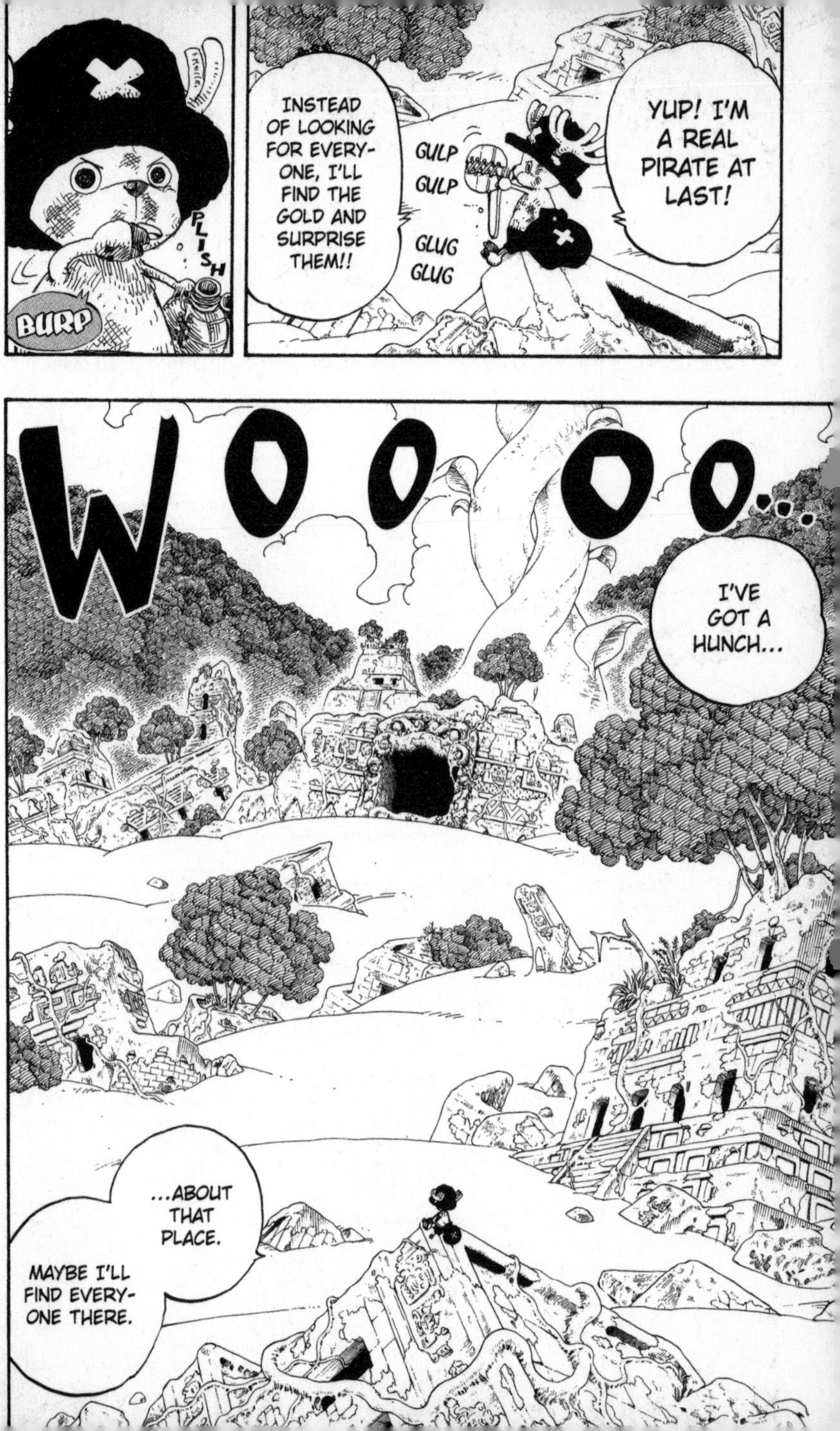
YUP! I'M A REAL PIRATE AT LAST!
GULP GULP
GLUG GLUG
INSTEAD OF LOOKING FOR EVERY-ONE, I'LL FIND THE GOLD AND SURPRISE THEM!!
PLISH
BURP
WOOOO...
I'VE GOT A HUNCH...
...ABOUT THAT PLACE.
MAYBE I'LL FIND EVERY-ONE THERE.

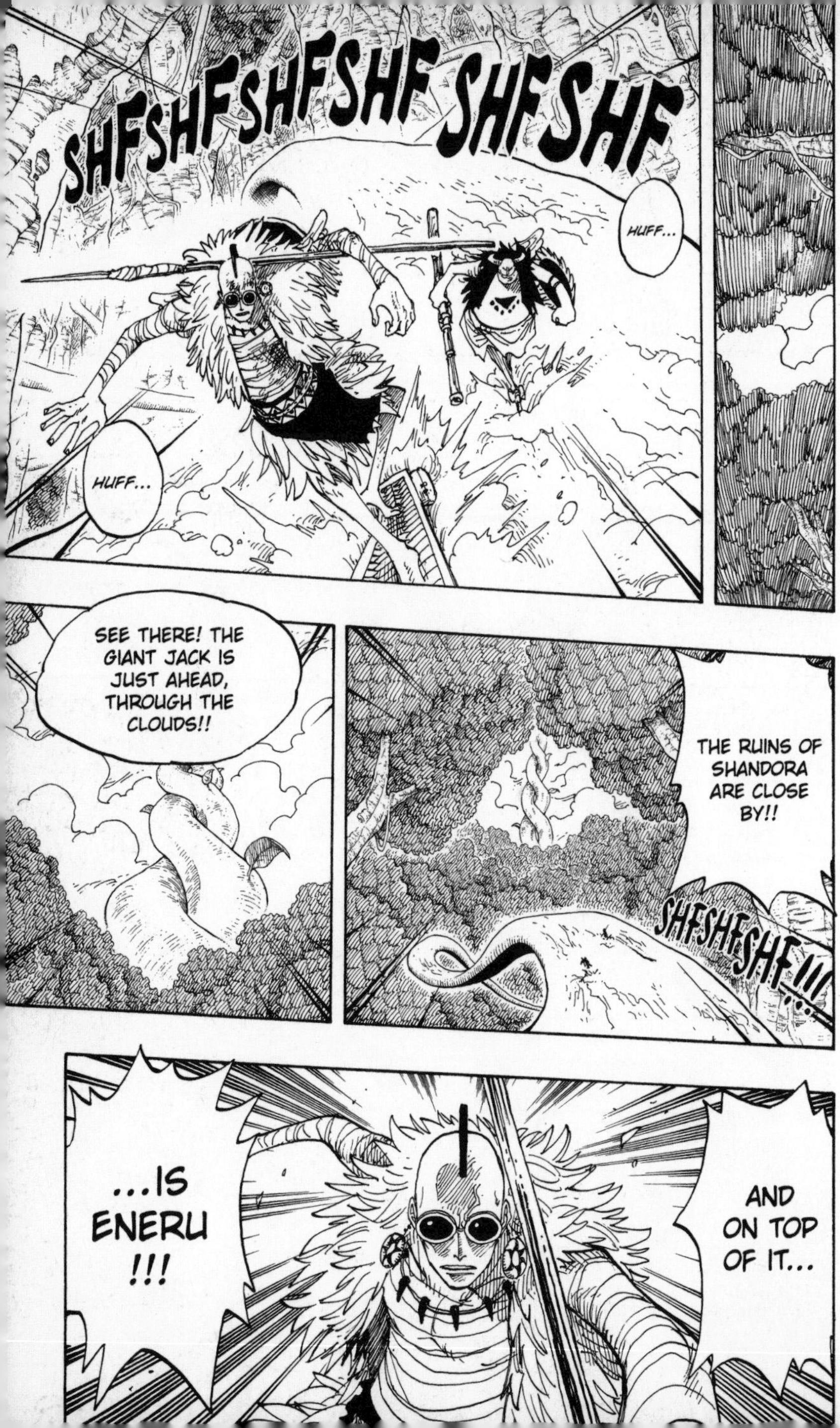
SHFSHFSHFSHF SHFSHF
HUFF...
HUFF...
THE RUINS OF SHANDORA ARE CLOSE BY!!
SHFSHFSHF!!!
SEE THERE! THE GIANT JACK IS JUST AHEAD, THROUGH THE CLOUDS!!
AND ON TOP OF IT...
...IS ENERU !!!

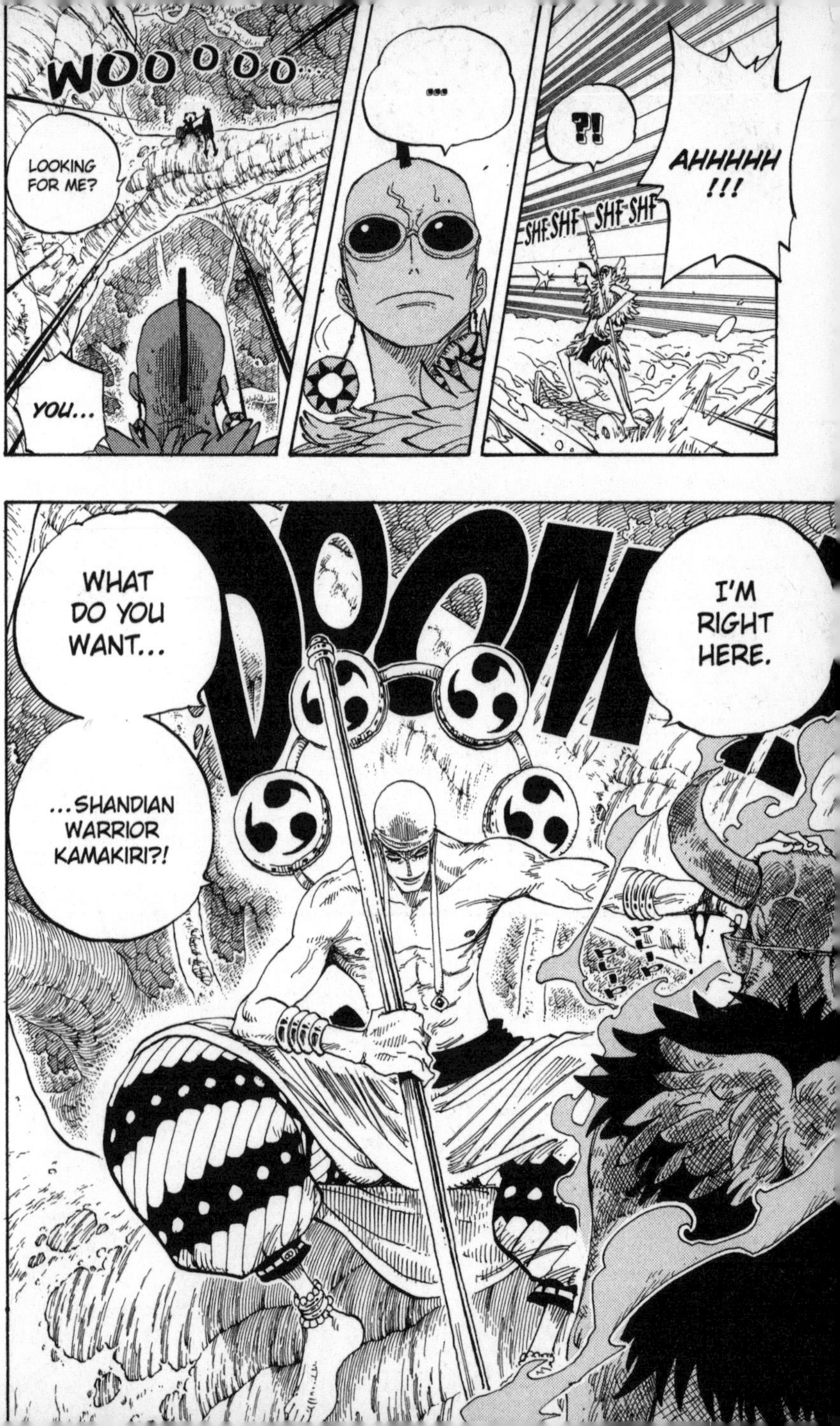
AHHHHH !!!
?!
SHF SHF SHF SHF
...
WOOOOO...
LOOKING FOR ME?
YOU...
I'M RIGHT HERE.
DOOM
WHAT DO YOU WANT...
...SHANDIAN WARRIOR KAMAKIRI?!

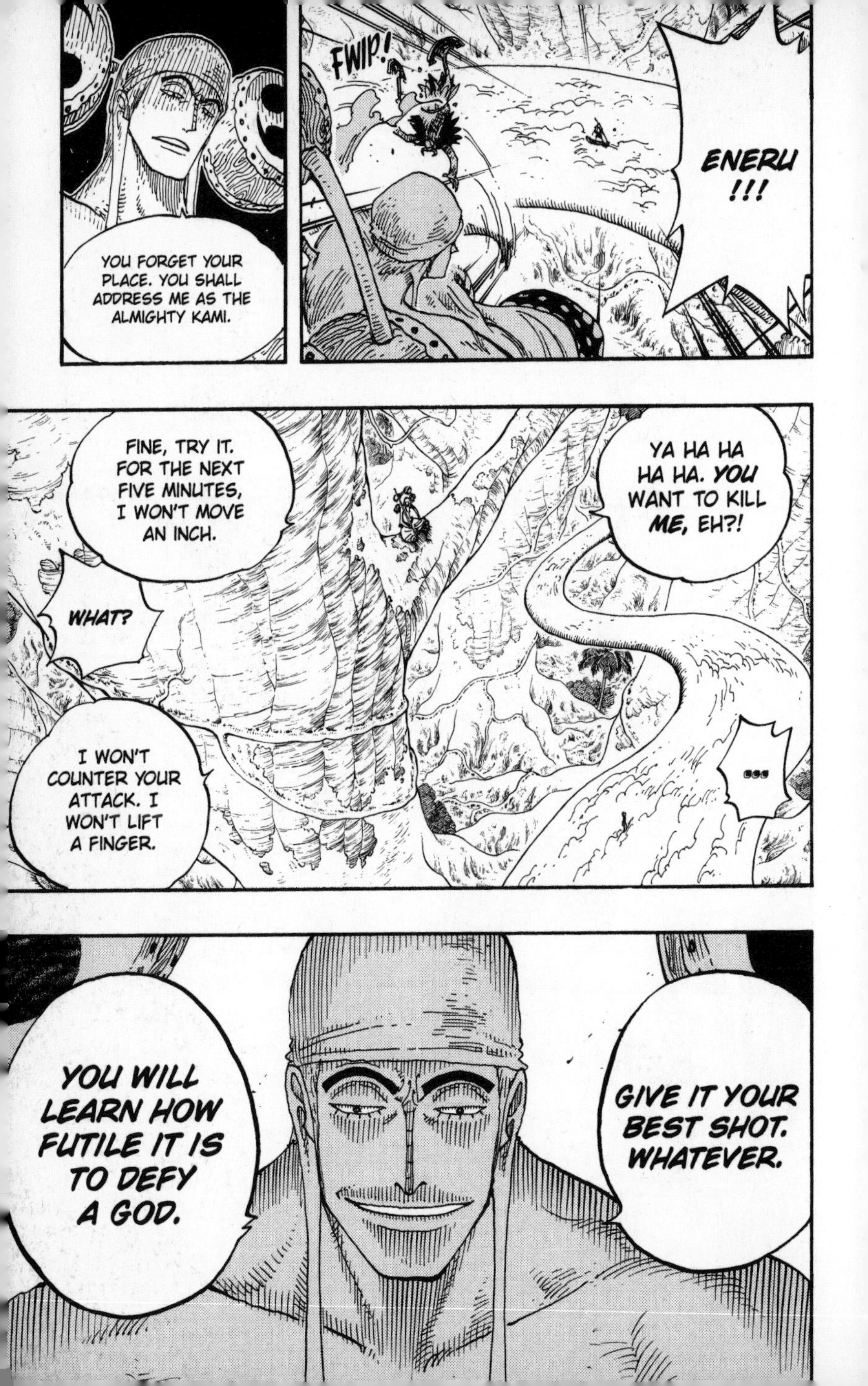
FWIP!
ENERU!!!
YOU FORGET YOUR PLACE. YOU SHALL ADDRESS ME AS THE ALMIGHTY KAMI.
YA HA HA HA HA. YOU WANT TO KILL ME, EH?!
FINE, TRY IT. FOR THE NEXT FIVE MINUTES, I WON'T MOVE AN INCH.
WHAT?
...
I WON'T COUNTER YOUR ATTACK. I WON'T LIFT A FINGER.
GIVE IT YOUR BEST SHOT. WHATEVER.
YOU WILL LEARN HOW FUTILE IT IS TO DEFY A GOD.

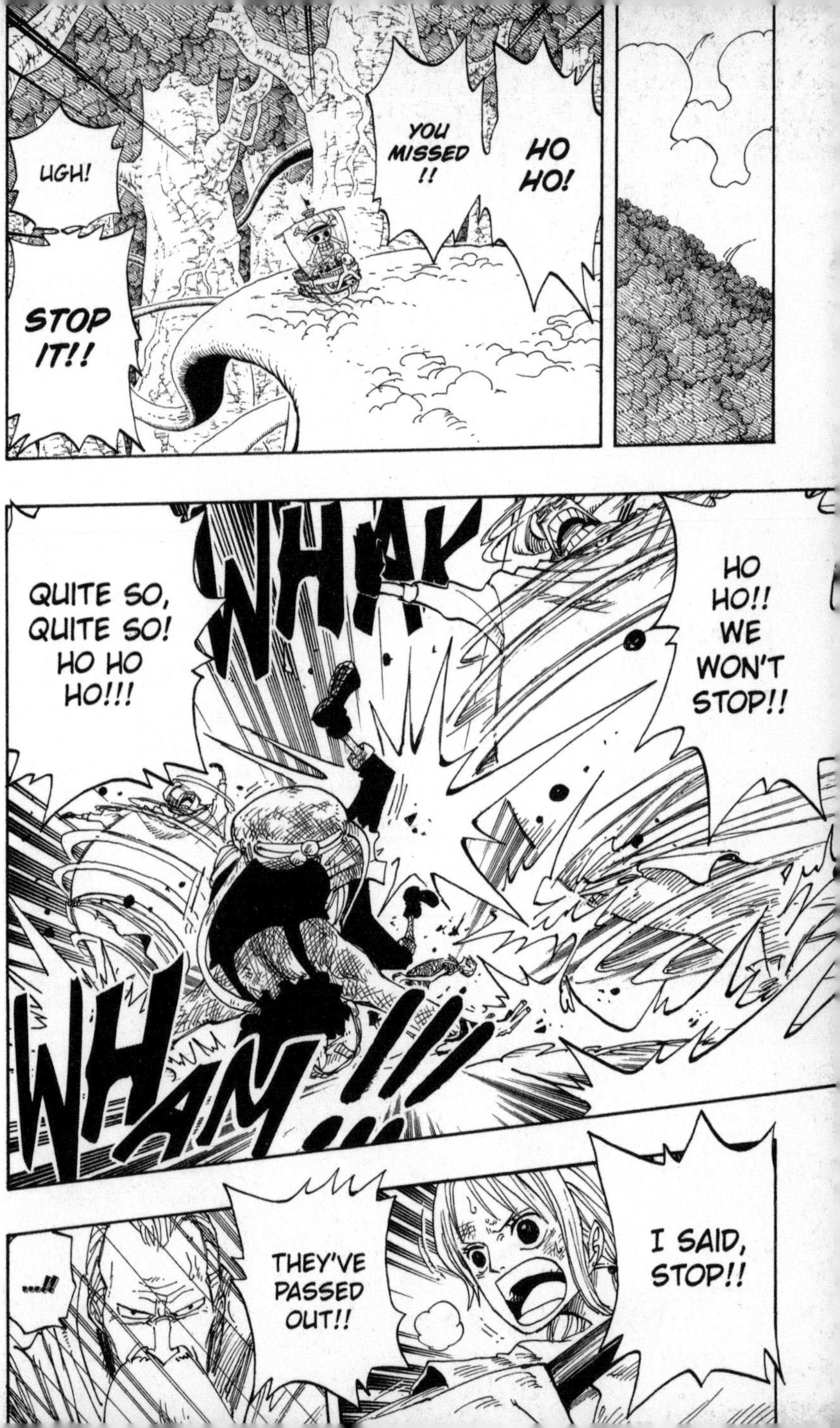

HO HO!
YOU MISSED !!
UGH!
STOP IT!!
HO HO!! WE WON'T STOP!!
QUITE SO, QUITE SO! HO HO HO!!!
WHAM!!!
I SAID, STOP!!
THEY'VE PASSED OUT!!
...!!

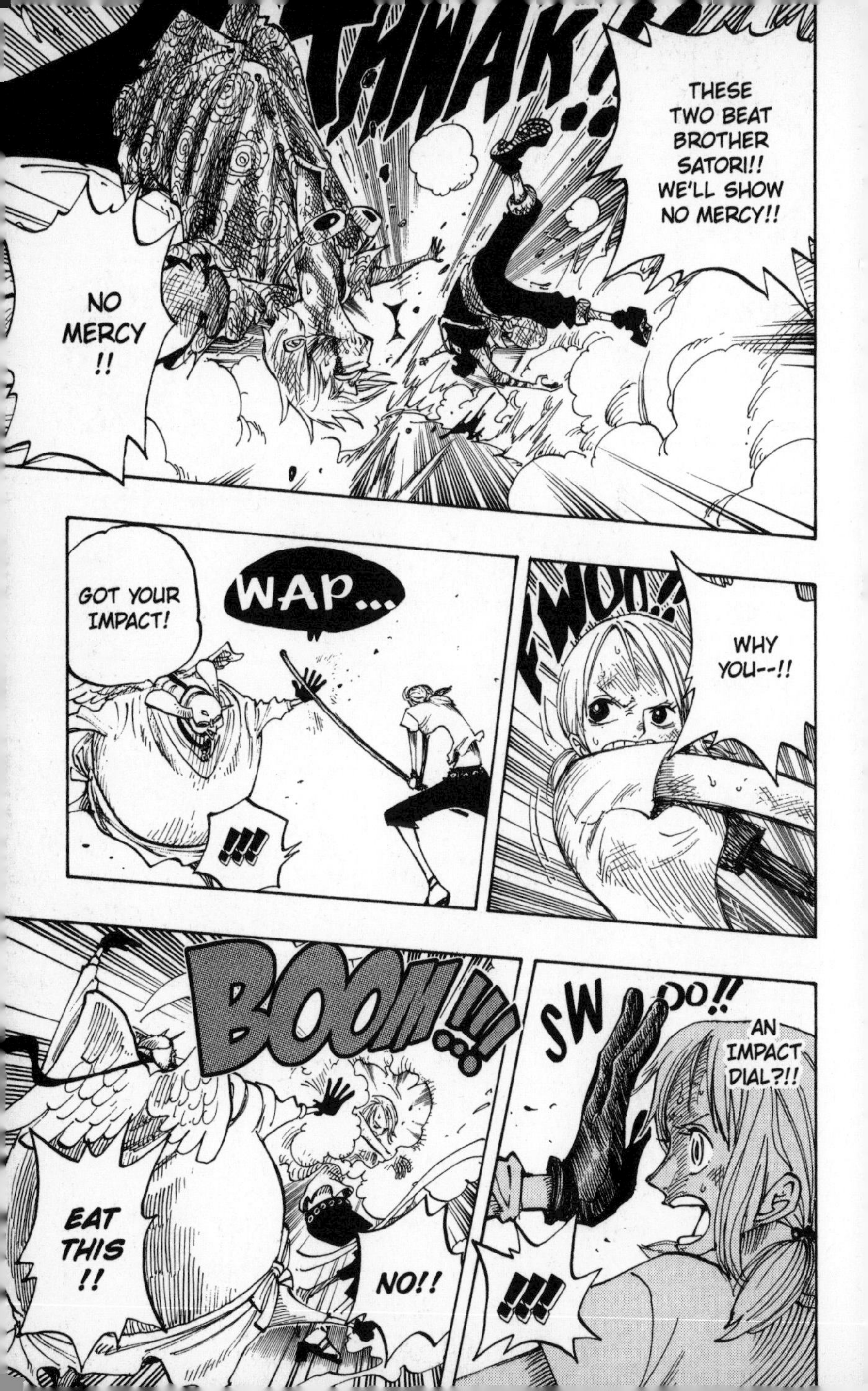

THESE TWO BEAT BROTHER SATORI!! WE'LL SHOW NO MERCY!!
NO MERCY !!
WHY YOU--!!
WAP...
GOT YOUR IMPACT!
!!!
AN IMPACT DIAL?!!
!!!
BOOM!!!
NO!!
EAT THIS !!

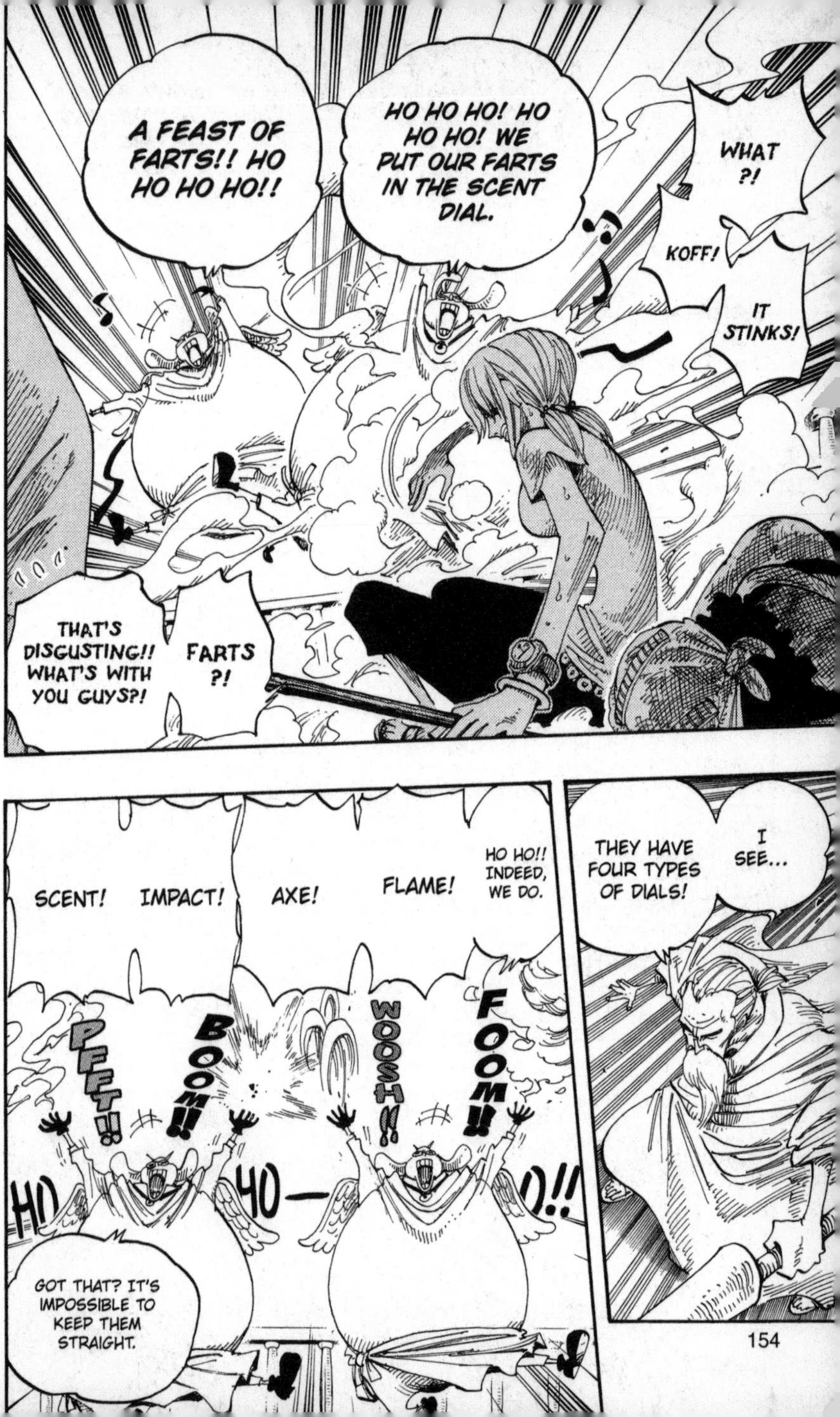
WHAT ?!
KOFF!
IT STINKS!
HO HO HO! HO HO HO! WE PUT OUR FARTS IN THE SCENT DIAL.
A FEAST OF FARTS!! HO HO HO HO!!
FARTS ?!
THAT'S DISGUSTING!! WHAT'S WITH YOU GUYS?!
I SEE...
THEY HAVE FOUR TYPES OF DIALS!
HO HO!! INDEED, WE DO.
FLAME!
AXE!
IMPACT!
SCENT!
FOOM!!
WOOSH!!
BOOM!!
PFFT!!
HO HO—O!!
GOT THAT? IT'S IMPOSSIBLE TO KEEP THEM STRAIGHT.

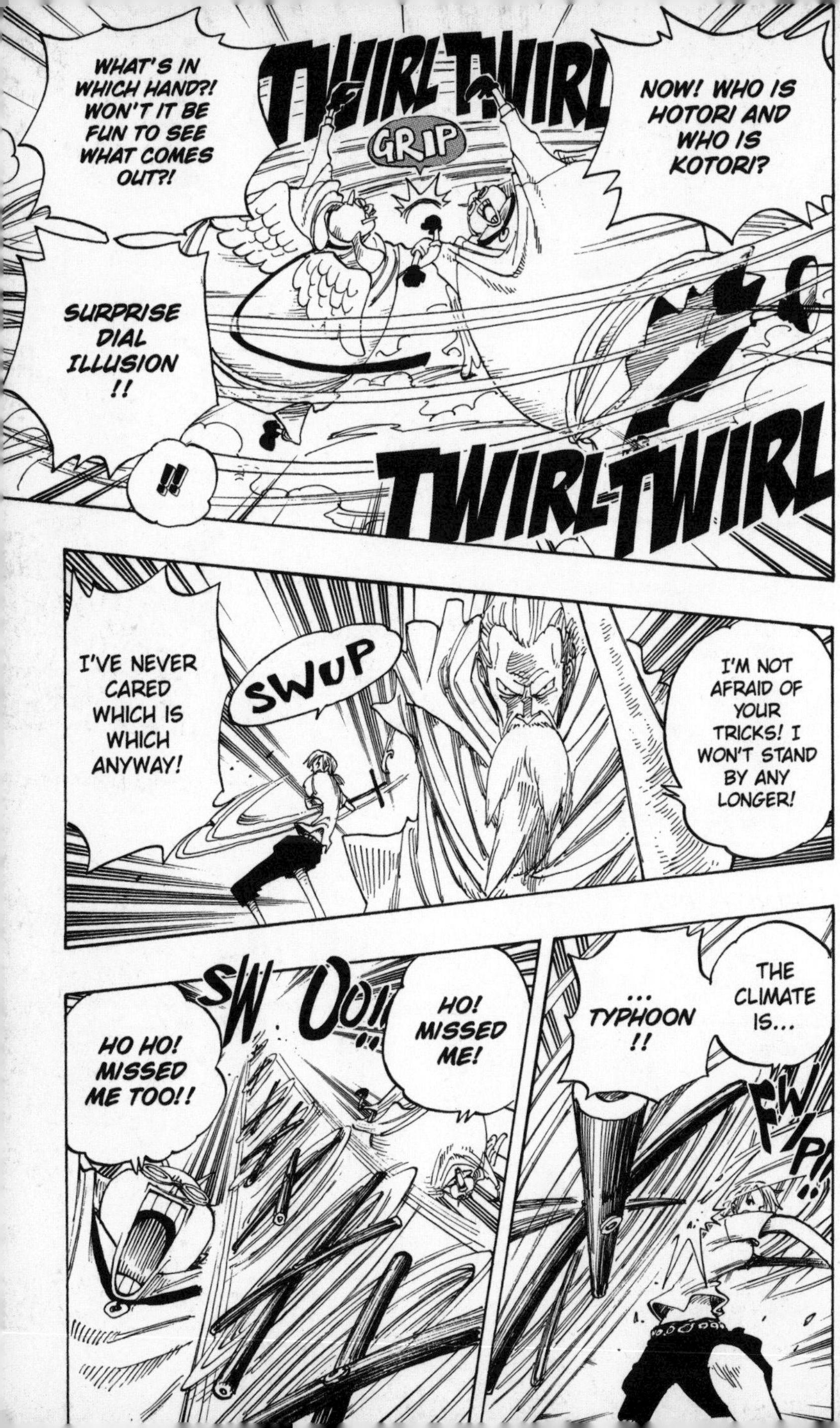

NOW! WHO IS HOTORI AND WHO IS KOTORI?
TWIRL TWIRL
GRIP
WHAT'S IN WHICH HAND?! WON'T IT BE FUN TO SEE WHAT COMES OUT?!
SURPRISE DIAL ILLUSION !!
TWIRL TWIRL
!!
I'M NOT AFRAID OF YOUR TRICKS! I WON'T STAND BY ANY LONGER!
SWUP
I'VE NEVER CARED WHICH IS WHICH ANYWAY!
THE CLIMATE IS...
... TYPHOON !!
FWIP!!
HO! MISSED ME!
HO HO! MISSED ME TOO!!

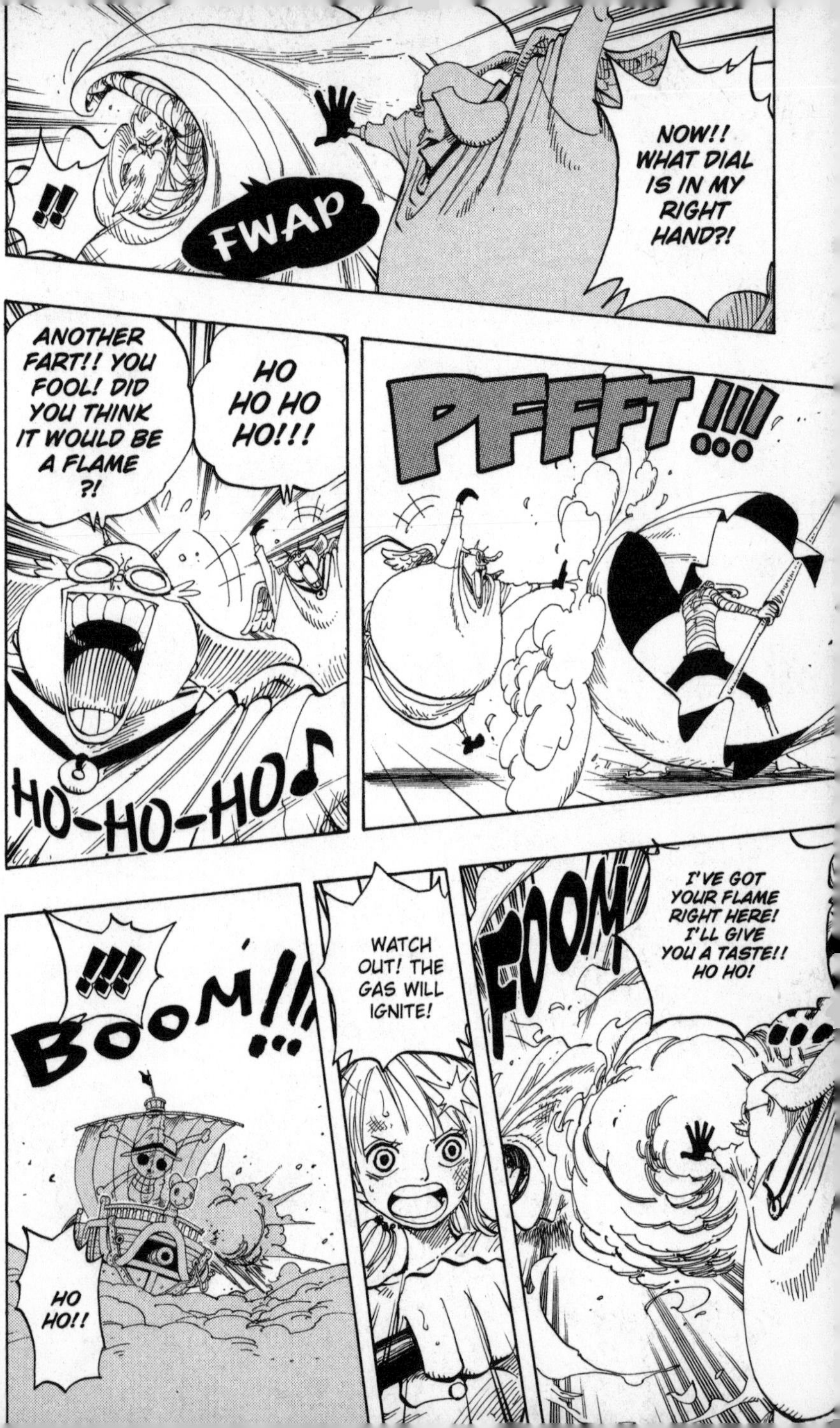
NOW!! WHAT DIAL IS IN MY RIGHT HAND?!
!!
FWAP
PFFFT!!!...
HO HO HO HO!!!
ANOTHER FART!! YOU FOOL! DID YOU THINK IT WOULD BE A FLAME ?!
HO-HO-HO♪
I'VE GOT YOUR FLAME RIGHT HERE! I'LL GIVE YOU A TASTE!! HO HO!
FOOM
...
WATCH OUT! THE GAS WILL IGNITE!
!!!
BOOM!!!...
HO HO!!

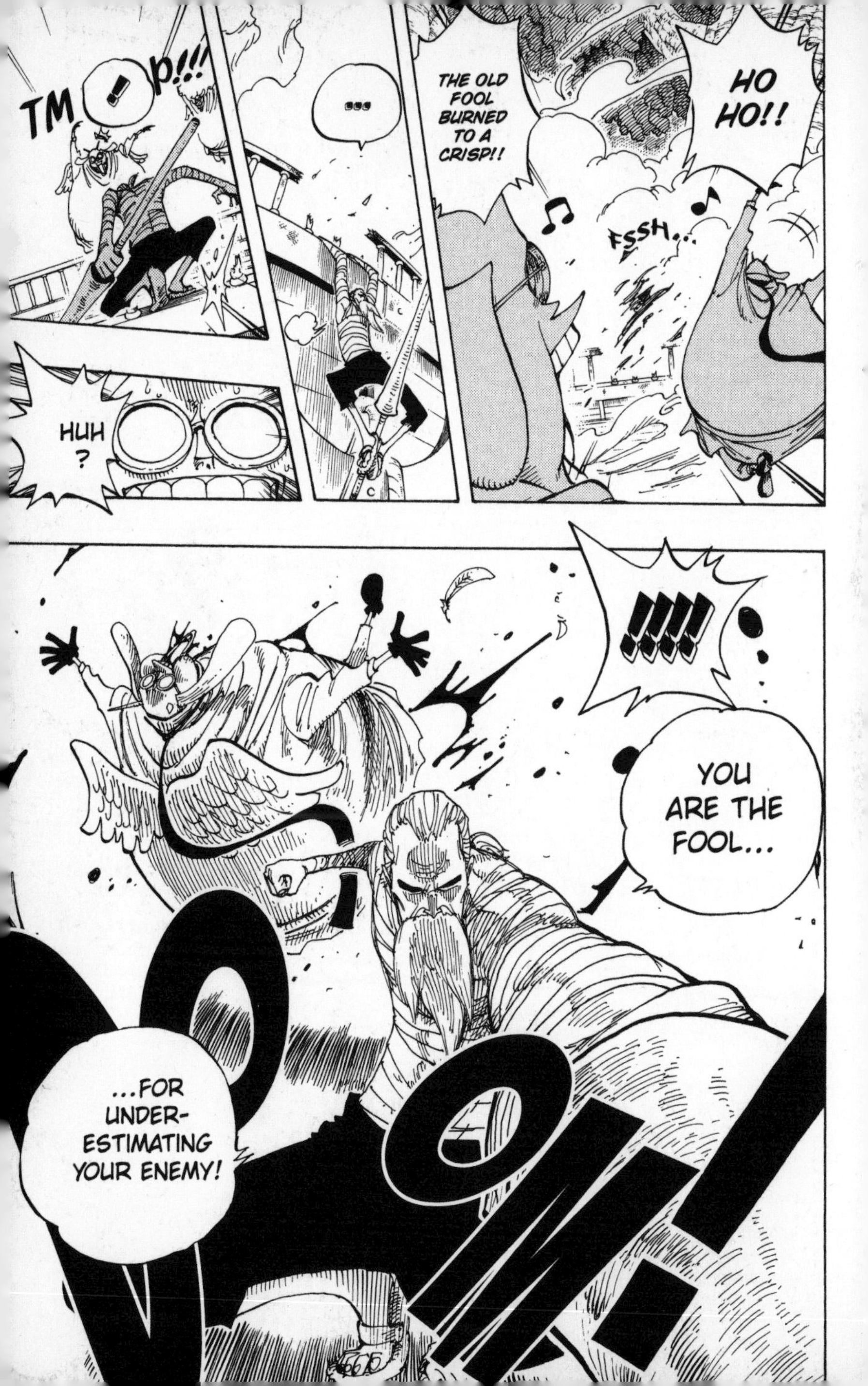
HO HO!!
THE OLD FOOL BURNED TO A CRISP!!
FSSH...
...
TMP!!!
!
HUH ?
!!!!
YOU ARE THE FOOL...
...FOR UNDER-ESTIMATING YOUR ENEMY!

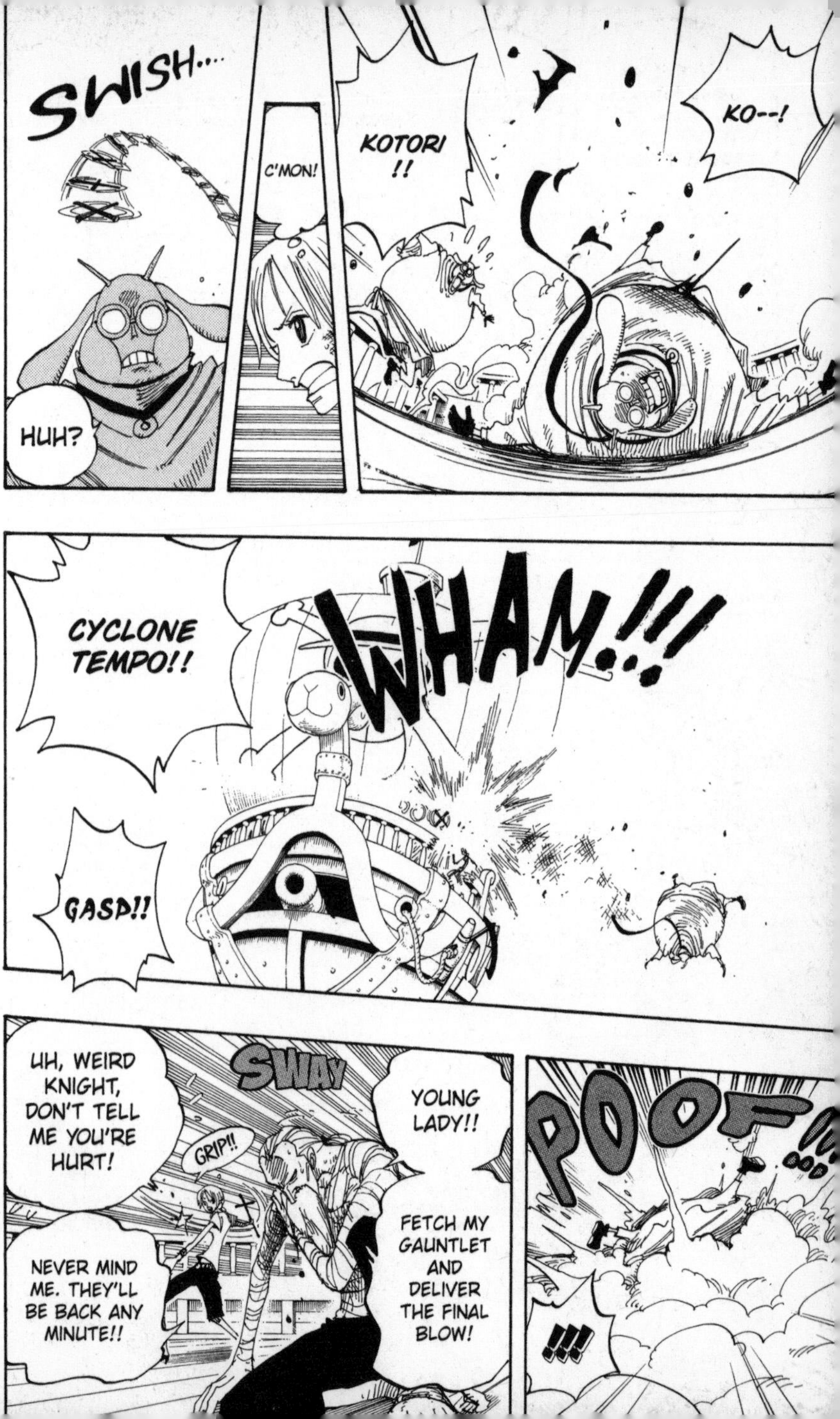
KO--!
KOTORI !!
C'MON!
SWISH....
HUH?
WHAM!!!
CYCLONE TEMPO!!
GASP!!
POOF!!
YOUNG LADY!!
SWAY
UH, WEIRD KNIGHT, DON'T TELL ME YOU'RE HURT!
GRIP!!
FETCH MY GAUNTLET AND DELIVER THE FINAL BLOW!
NEVER MIND ME. THEY'LL BE BACK ANY MINUTE!!
!!!

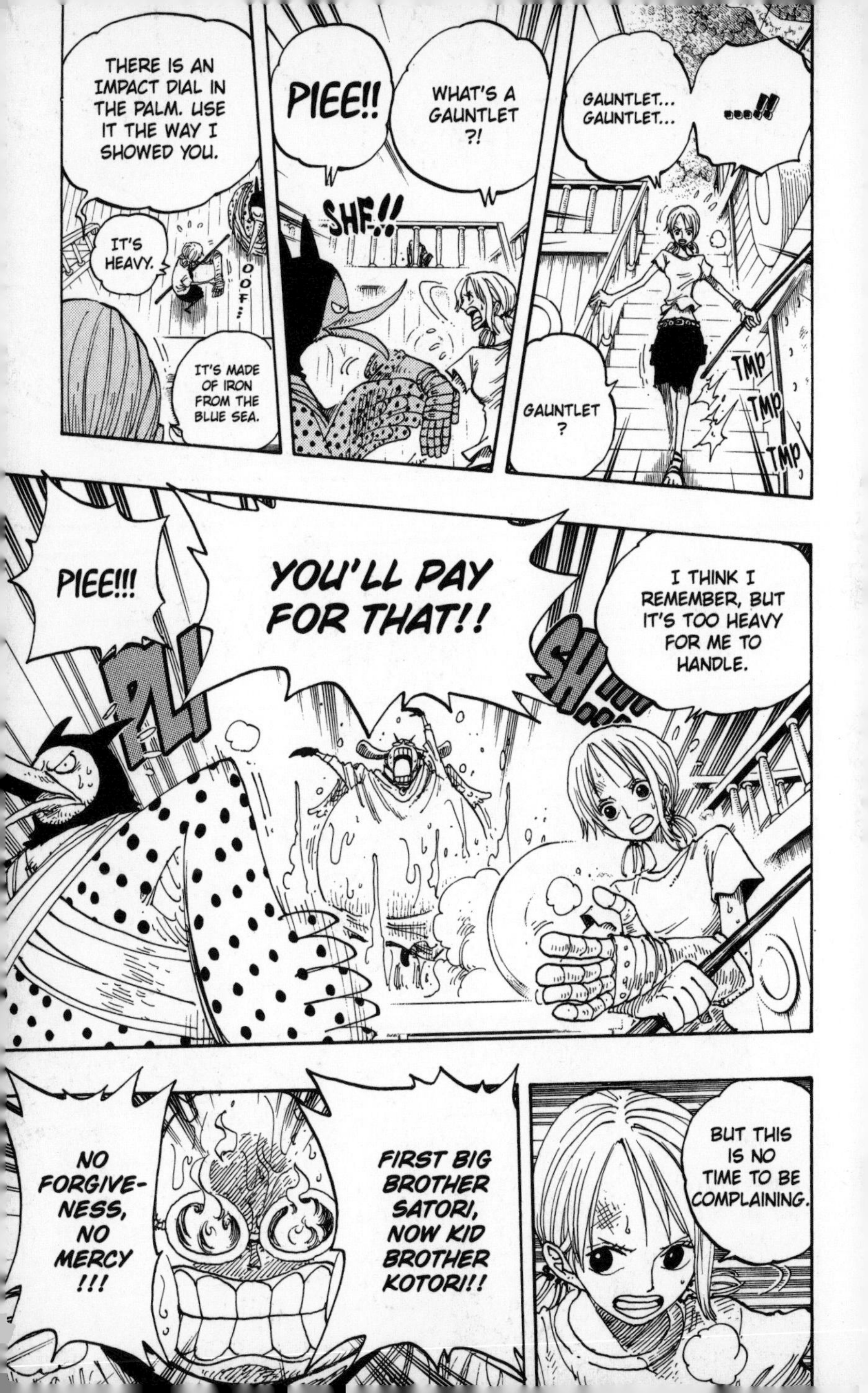
...!!
GAUNTLET... GAUNTLET...
TMP
TMP
TMP
GAUNTLET ?
WHAT'S A GAUNTLET ?!
PIEE!!
SHF!!
THERE IS AN IMPACT DIAL IN THE PALM. USE IT THE WAY I SHOWED YOU.
OOF...
IT'S HEAVY.
IT'S MADE OF IRON FROM THE BLUE SEA.
I THINK I REMEMBER, BUT IT'S TOO HEAVY FOR ME TO HANDLE.
YOU'LL PAY FOR THAT!!
PIEE!!!
BUT THIS IS NO TIME TO BE COMPLAINING.
FIRST BIG BROTHER SATORI, NOW KID BROTHER KOTORI!!
NO FORGIVE-NESS, NO MERCY!!!

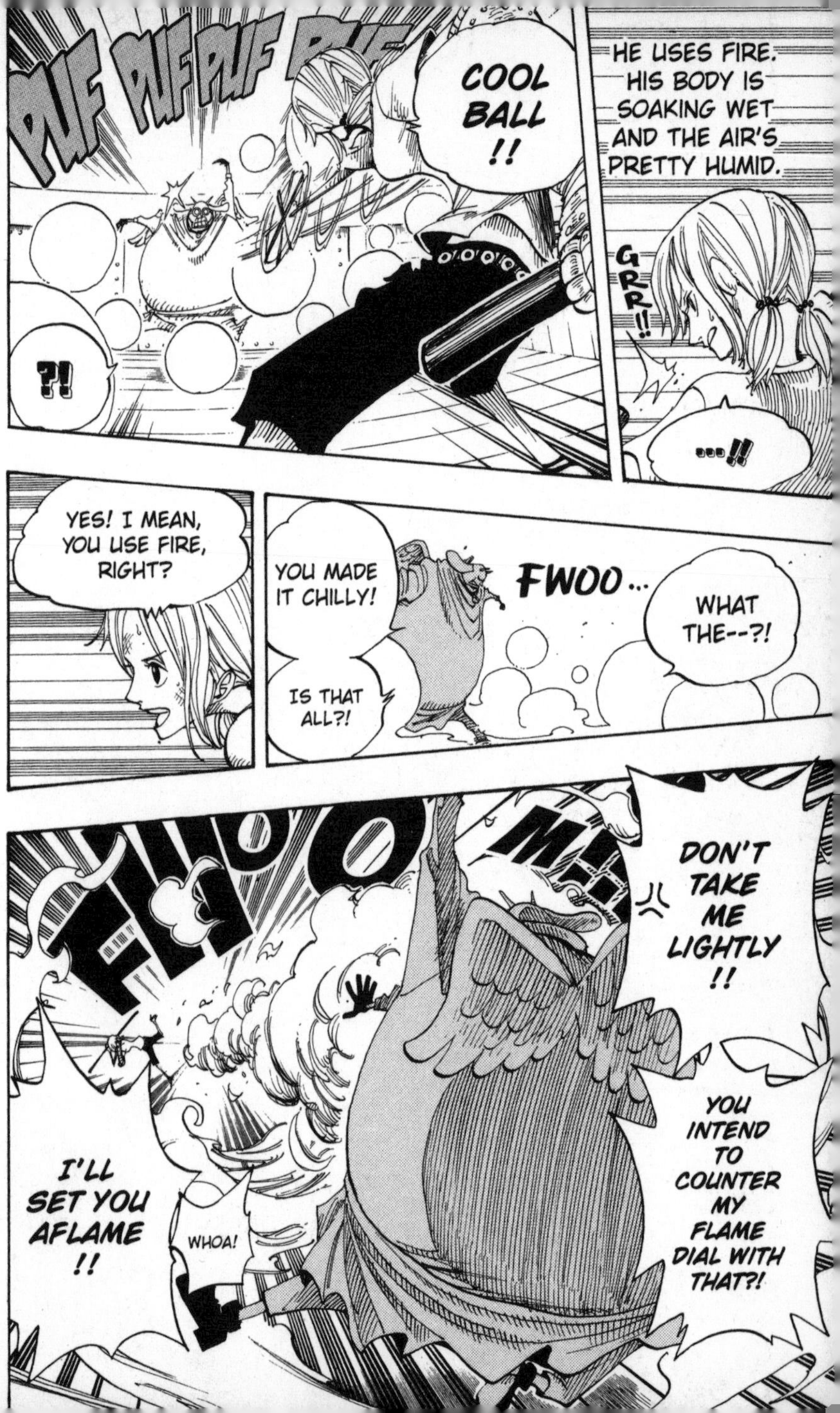
HE USES FIRE. HIS BODY IS SOAKING WET AND THE AIR'S PRETTY HUMID.
GRR!!
...!!
PUF PUF PUF PUF
COOL BALL!!
?!
WHAT THE--?!
FWOO...
YOU MADE IT CHILLY!
IS THAT ALL?!
YES! I MEAN, YOU USE FIRE, RIGHT?
DON'T TAKE ME LIGHTLY!!
YOU INTEND TO COUNTER MY FLAME DIAL WITH THAT?!
FWOOM
I'LL SET YOU AFLAME!!
WHOA!

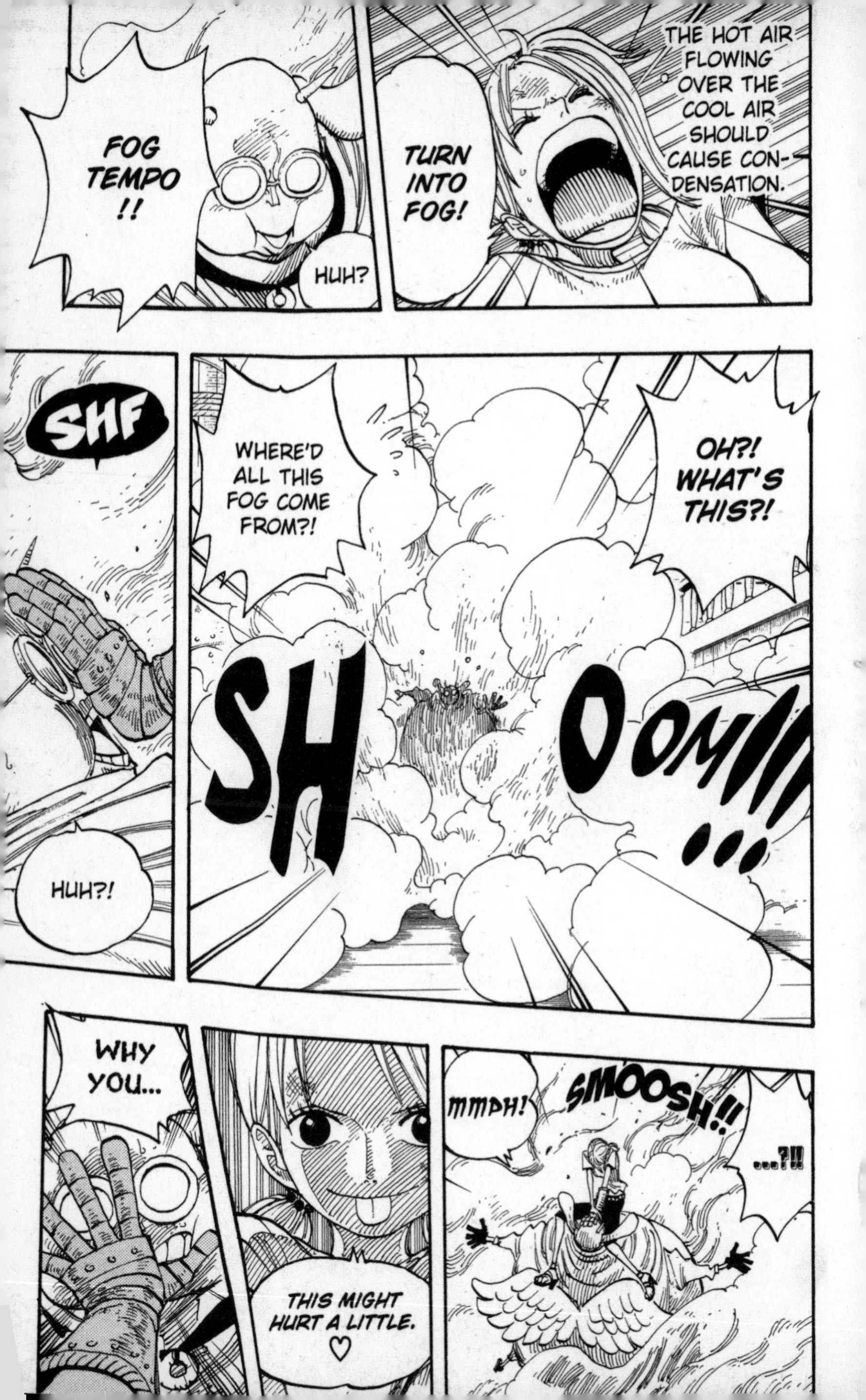
THE HOT AIR FLOWING OVER THE COOL AIR SHOULD CAUSE CON-DENSATION.
TURN INTO FOG!
FOG TEMPO !!
HUH?
OH?! WHAT'S THIS?!
WHERE'D ALL THIS FOG COME FROM?!
SHOOM!!!...
SHF
HUH?!
SMOOSH!!
MMPH!
...?!!
THIS MIGHT HURT A LITTLE. ♥
WHY YOU...

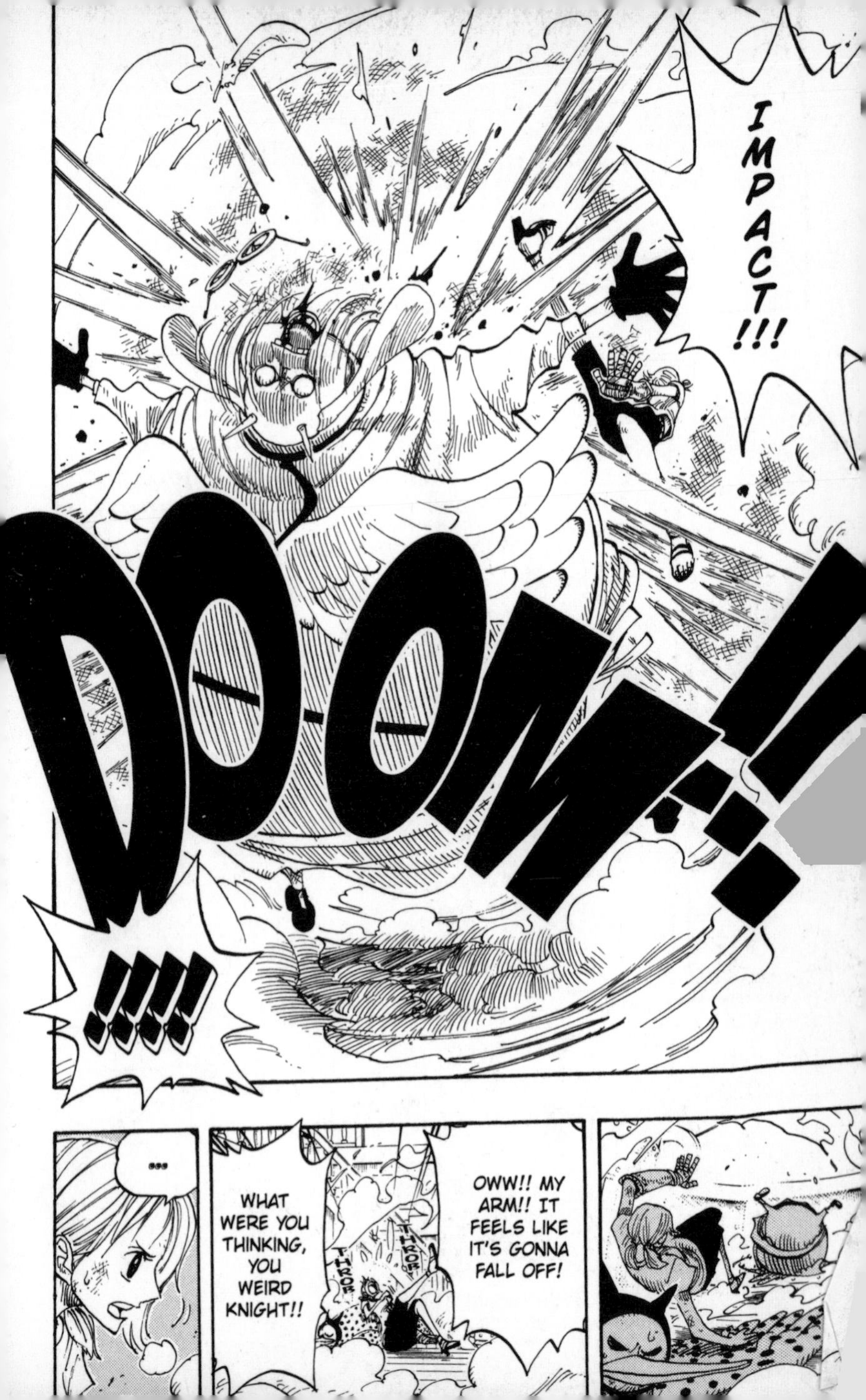
IMPACT!!!
DO-ON!!
!!!!
OWW!! MY ARM!! IT FEELS LIKE IT'S GONNA FALL OFF!
WHAT WERE YOU THINKING, YOU WEIRD KNIGHT!!
THROB
THROB
...

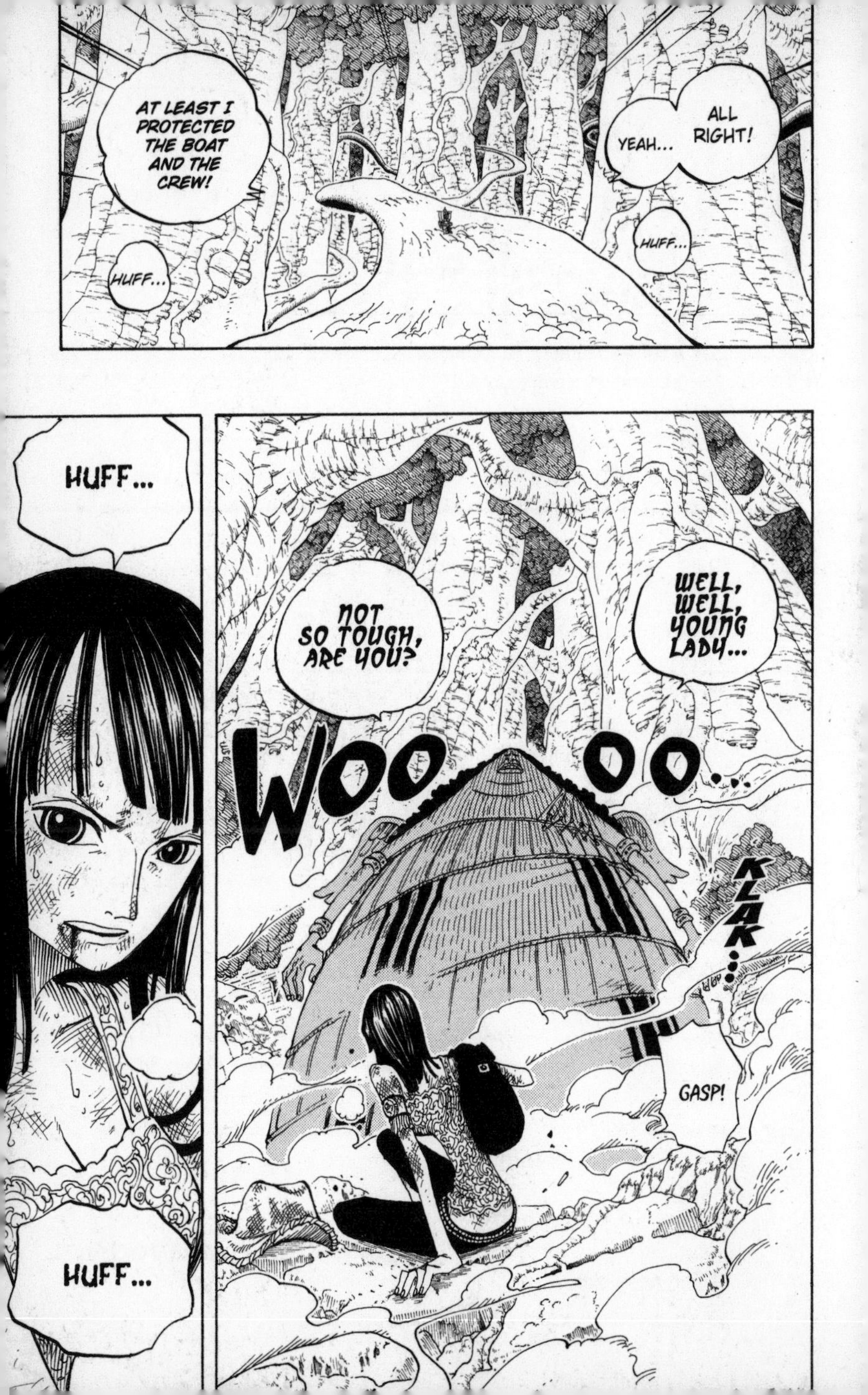
YEAH... ALL RIGHT!
HUFF...
AT LEAST I PROTECTED THE BOAT AND THE CREW!
HUFF...
WELL, WELL, YOUNG LADY...
NOT SO TOUGH, ARE YOU?
WOO...OO...
KLAK...
GASP!
HUFF...
HUFF...

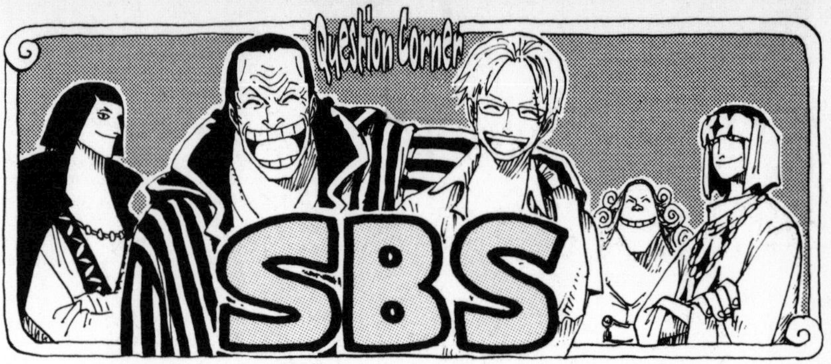
Question Corner
SBS

Q: Am I an ape or a prime ape?

-- Masira the Odd Jobs Pirate

A: You're a prime ape. All One Piece readers are prime apes! Wait, wait, everyone, don't run away. "Prime ape" is a compliment! Even if it doesn't really make sense...

Q: Hi!! Eicchi! Eicchi, in volume 27, you had the nerve to say that the Jaya arc was about "a man's dreams." Well, I'll have you know that for 18 years I've lived my life as a woman! So what do you make of my "passionate love for adventure" and my "infinite dreams"?! Sheesh! Every page, every panel of your manga makes my blood boil!!! Take responsibility!! Please.♡ It's time to step up and take responsibility! Start putting "woman" in there instead!

-- Her new eye co.

A: A "woman's dreams"?! No, no, you're taking me too literally! I often use the word "manly" as an adjective. Even the most feminine woman has manly sides to her. In days past, such a woman has been called a "true woman." So let me shout it out--for both men and women, it's a "man's dreams"!! That includes women!

Q: How do you do, Oda Sensei.♡ I'll get right to the question. For my high school admissions interview, when asked the question, "Who do you respect?" I was going to answer, "Luffy," but my parents said that I'll make a fool of myself. But I really do admire and respect Luffy! Oda Sensei, please say something to my parents!

-- Usagi Ko♡

A: Hey now, Mom and Dad!! You sure don't mince words. You think admiring my Luffy makes someone a fool?!! That may be...

Anyway, see you in the next volume.

Chapter 264:
WARRIOR KAMAKIRI VS. KAMI ENERU

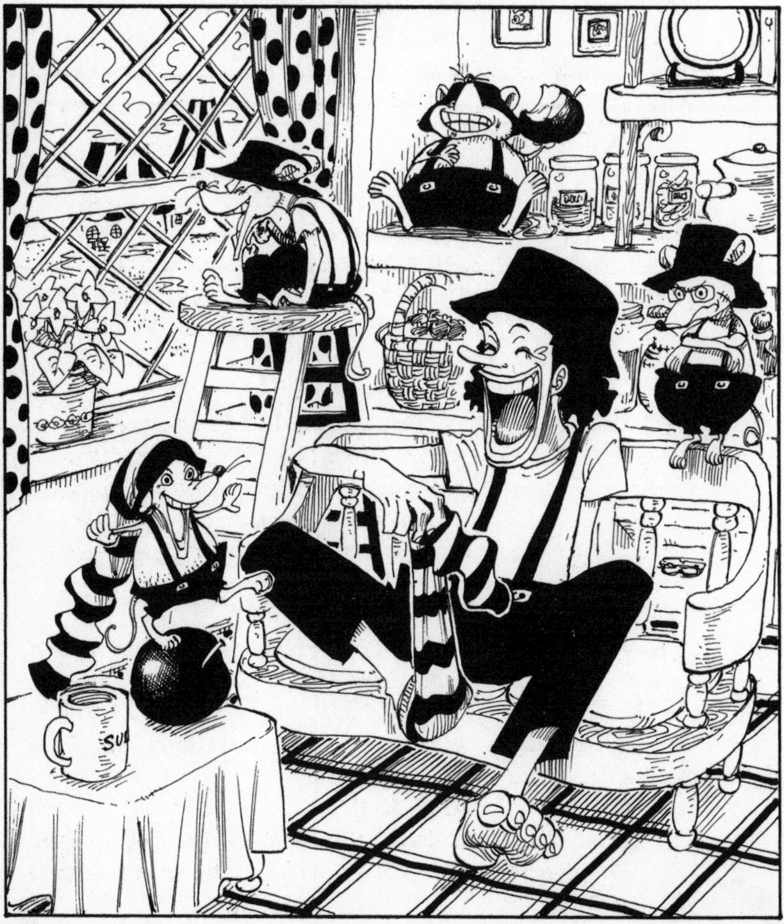

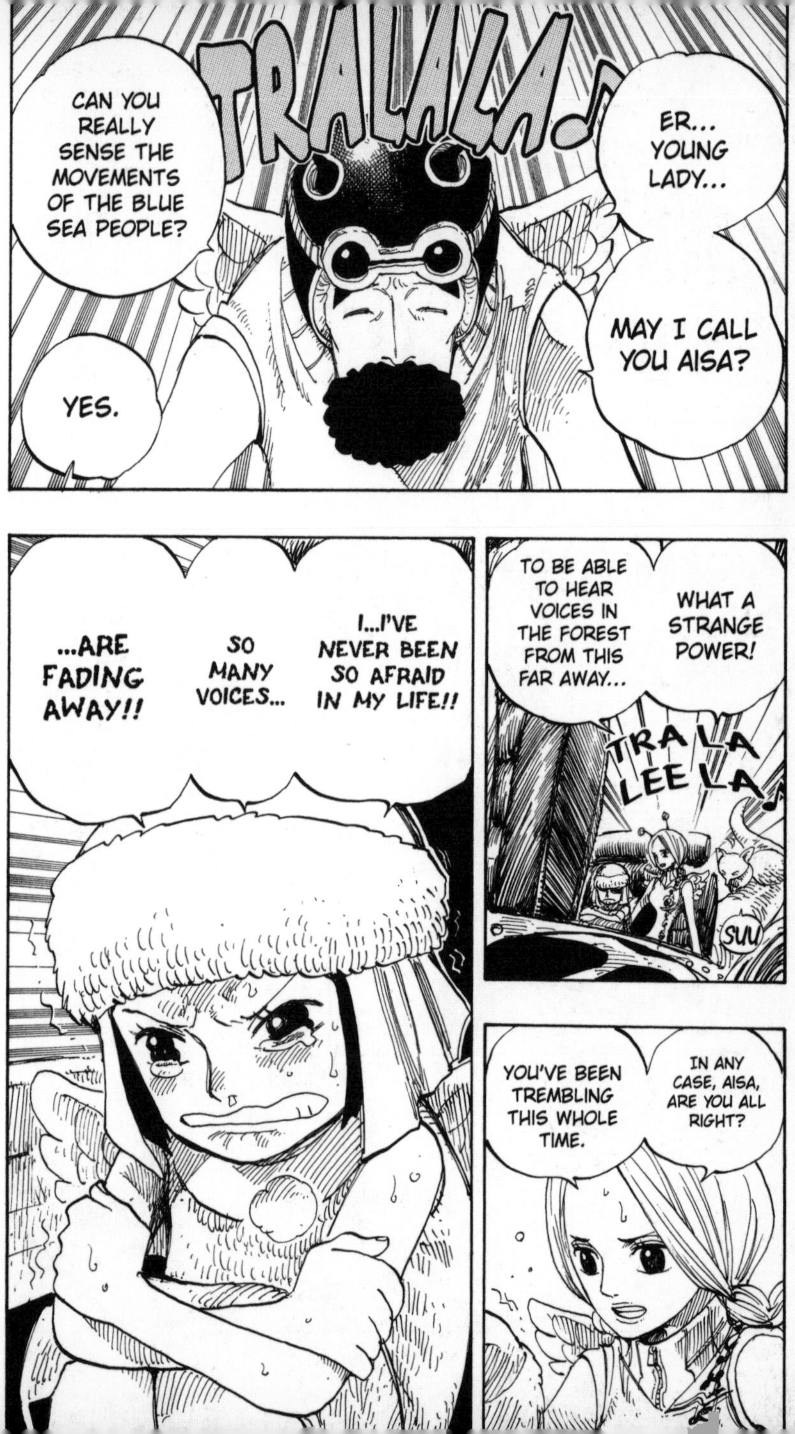
ER... YOUNG LADY...
TRALALA♪
CAN YOU REALLY SENSE THE MOVEMENTS OF THE BLUE SEA PEOPLE?
MAY I CALL YOU AISA?
YES.
WHAT A STRANGE POWER!
TO BE ABLE TO HEAR VOICES IN THE FOREST FROM THIS FAR AWAY...
TRA LA LEE LA♪
SUU
IN ANY CASE, AISA, ARE YOU ALL RIGHT?
YOU'VE BEEN TREMBLING THIS WHOLE TIME.
I...I'VE NEVER BEEN SO AFRAID IN MY LIFE!!
SO MANY VOICES...
...ARE FADING AWAY!!

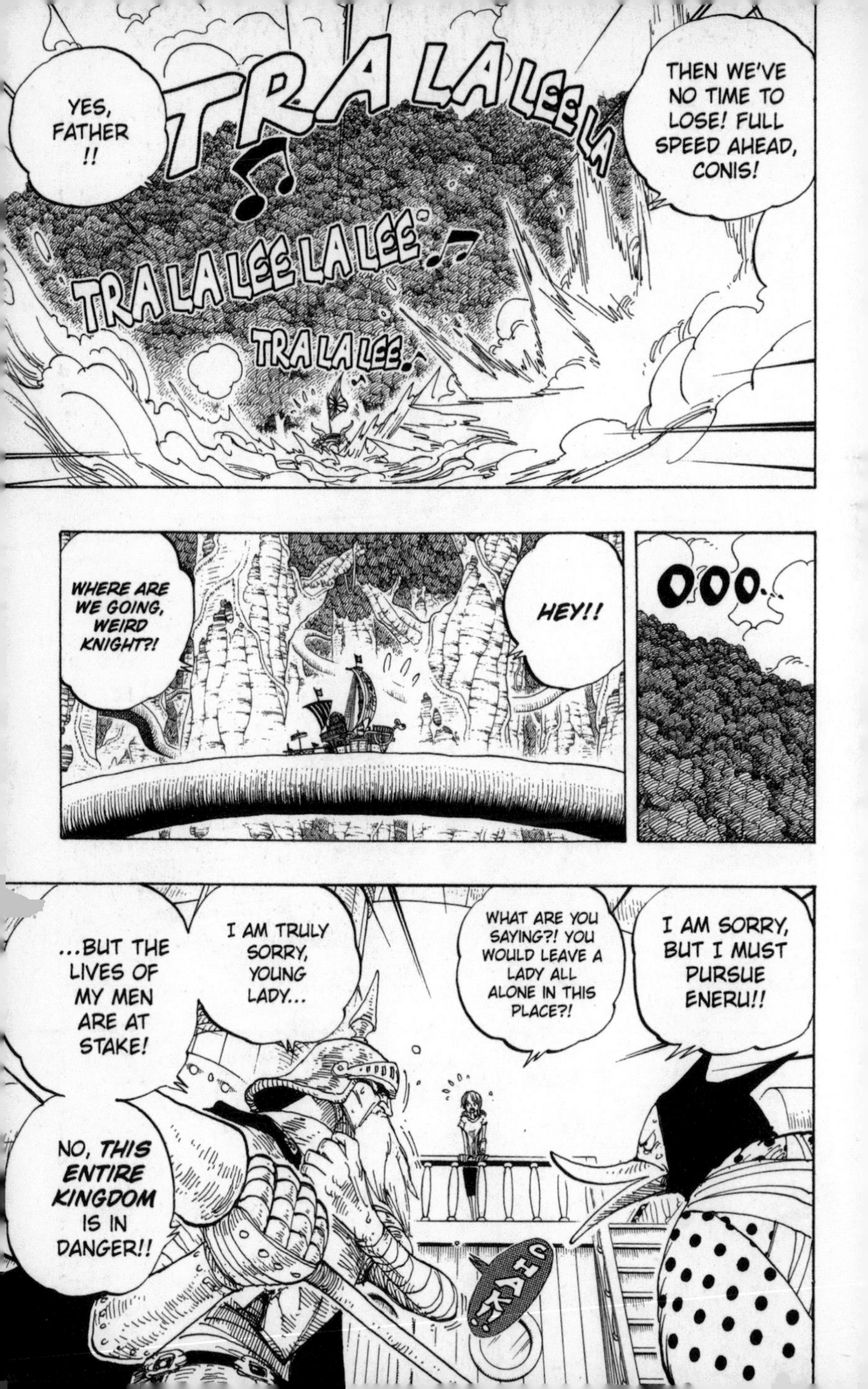
THEN WE'VE NO TIME TO LOSE! FULL SPEED AHEAD, CONIS!
TRA LA LEE LA
YES, FATHER !!
TRA LA LEE LA LEE
TRA LA LEE
OOO...
HEY!!
WHERE ARE WE GOING, WEIRD KNIGHT?!
I AM SORRY, BUT I MUST PURSUE ENERU!!
WHAT ARE YOU SAYING?! YOU WOULD LEAVE A LADY ALL ALONE IN THIS PLACE?!
I AM TRULY SORRY, YOUNG LADY...
...BUT THE LIVES OF MY MEN ARE AT STAKE!
NO, *THIS ENTIRE KINGDOM* IS IN DANGER!!
CHAK

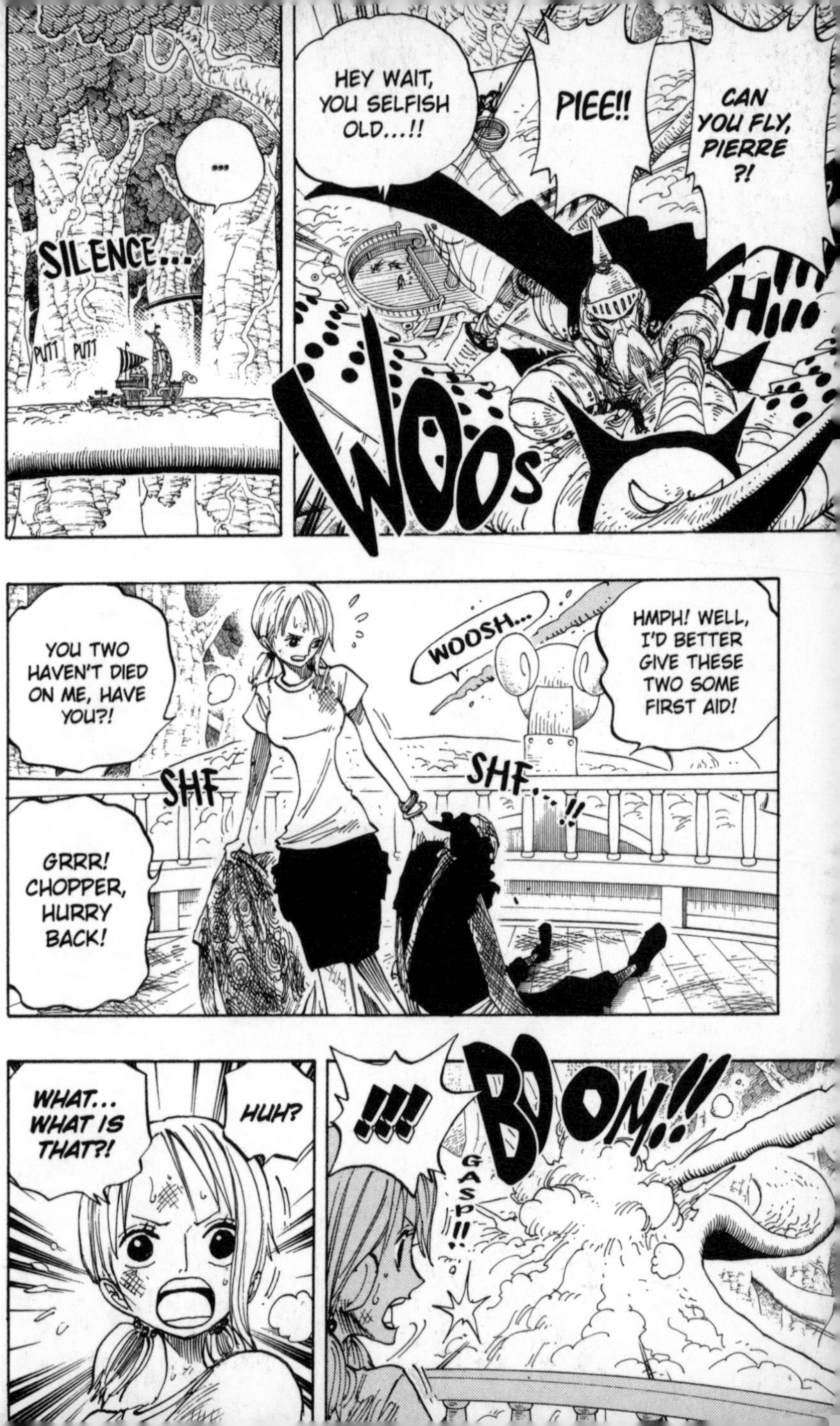
CAN YOU FLY, PIERRE ?!
PIEE!!
HEY WAIT, YOU SELFISH OLD...!!
WOOS
...
SILENCE...
PUTT PUTT
HMPH! WELL, I'D BETTER GIVE THESE TWO SOME FIRST AID!
WOOSH...
YOU TWO HAVEN'T DIED ON ME, HAVE YOU?!
SHF...!!
SHF
GRRR! CHOPPER, HURRY BACK!
BOOM!!
!!!
GASP!!
HUH?
WHAT... WHAT IS THAT?!

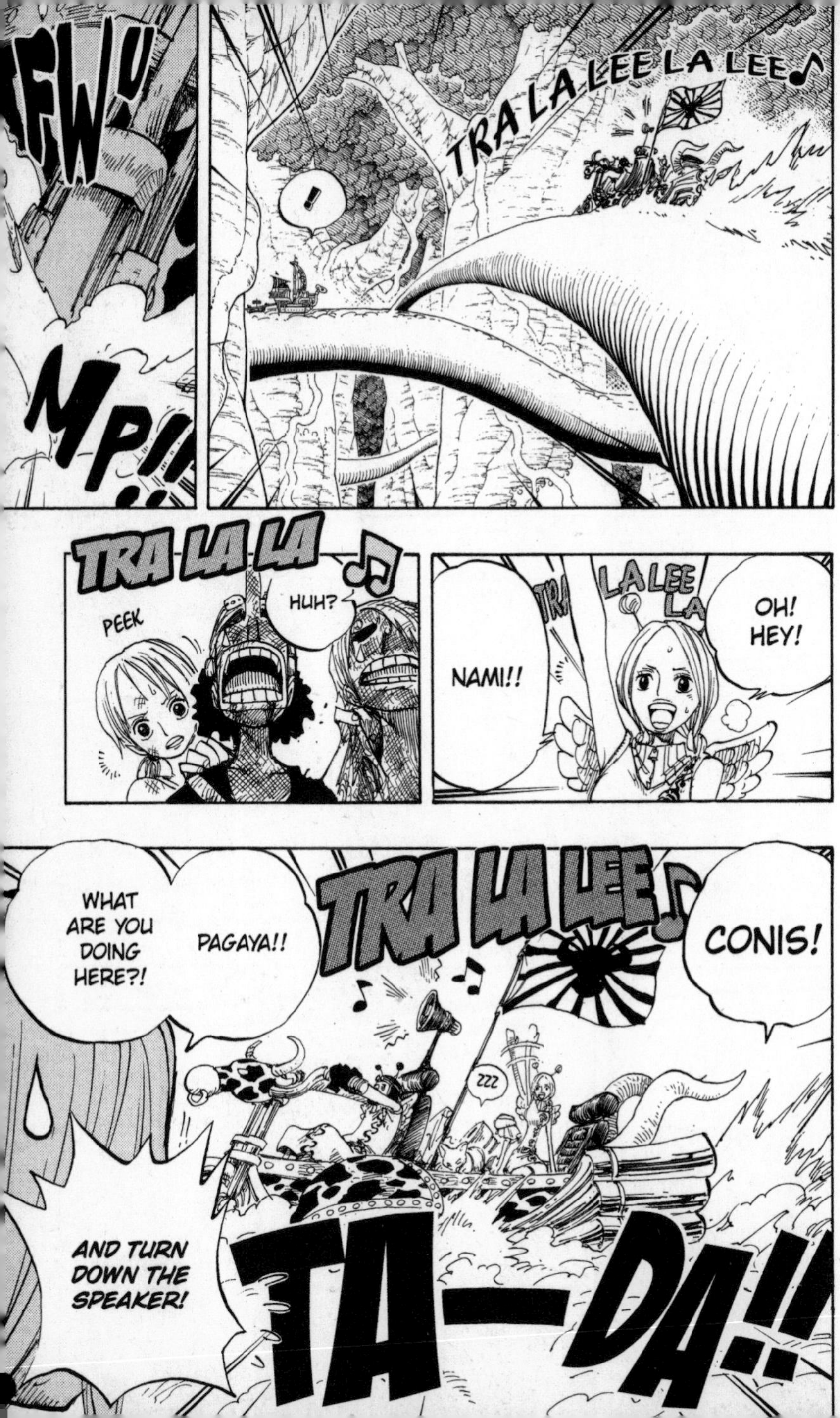

TRA LA LEE LA LEE♪
!
FWU!
MP!!
TRA LA LEE LA
OH! HEY!
NAMI!!
TRA LA LA ♪
HUH?
PEEK
TRA LA LEE♪
CONIS!
PAGAYA!!
WHAT ARE YOU DOING HERE?!
ZZZ
AND TURN DOWN THE SPEAKER!
TA-DA!!

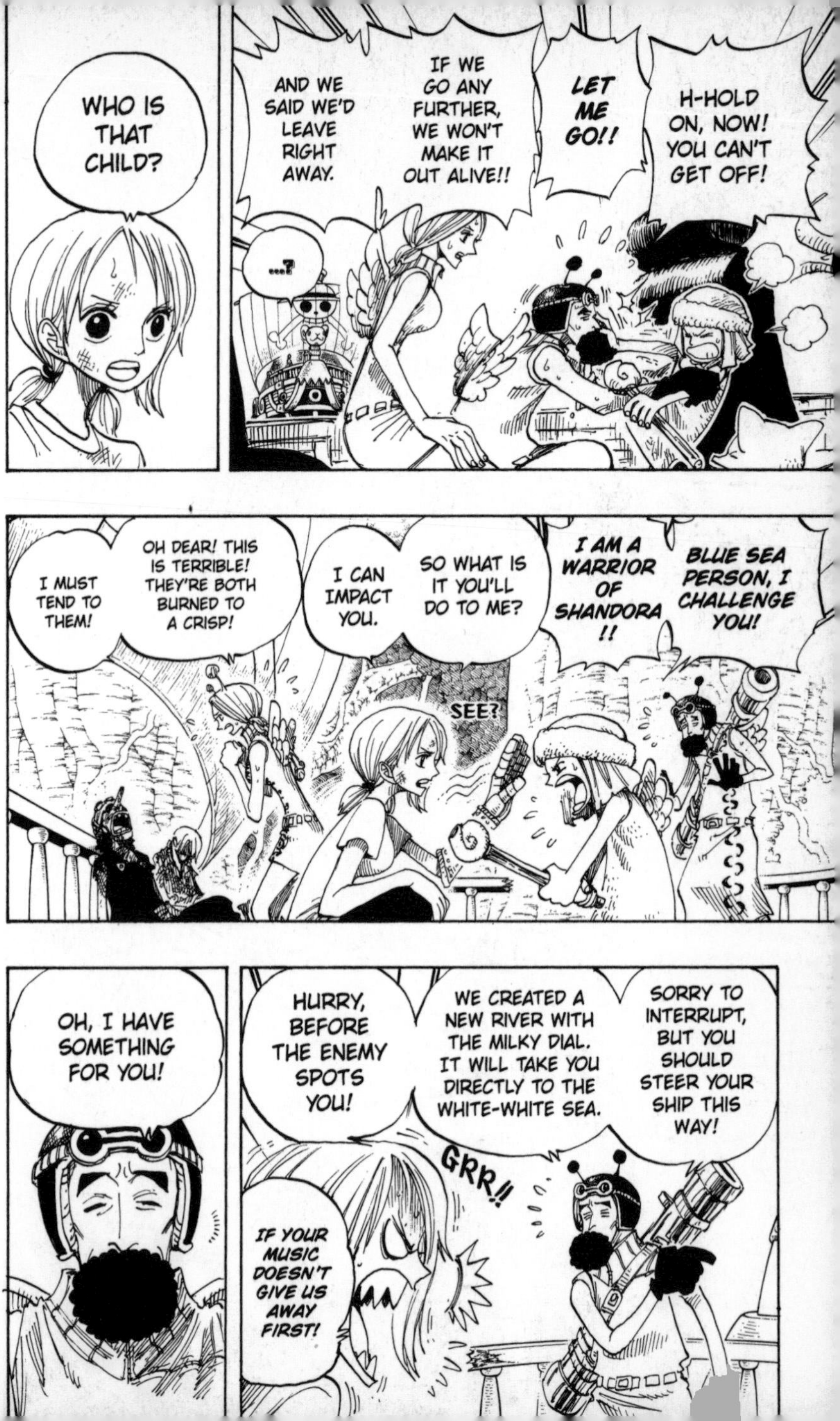
H-HOLD ON, NOW! YOU CAN'T GET OFF!
LET ME GO!!
IF WE GO ANY FURTHER, WE WON'T MAKE IT OUT ALIVE!!
AND WE SAID WE'D LEAVE RIGHT AWAY.
...?
WHO IS THAT CHILD?
BLUE SEA PERSON, I CHALLENGE YOU!
I AM A WARRIOR OF SHANDORA!!
SO WHAT IS IT YOU'LL DO TO ME?
I CAN IMPACT YOU.
SEE?
OH DEAR! THIS IS TERRIBLE! THEY'RE BOTH BURNED TO A CRISP!
I MUST TEND TO THEM!
SORRY TO INTERRUPT, BUT YOU SHOULD STEER YOUR SHIP THIS WAY!
WE CREATED A NEW RIVER WITH THE MILKY DIAL. IT WILL TAKE YOU DIRECTLY TO THE WHITE-WHITE SEA.
HURRY, BEFORE THE ENEMY SPOTS YOU!
GRR!!
IF YOUR MUSIC DOESN'T GIVE US AWAY FIRST!
OH, I HAVE SOMETHING FOR YOU!

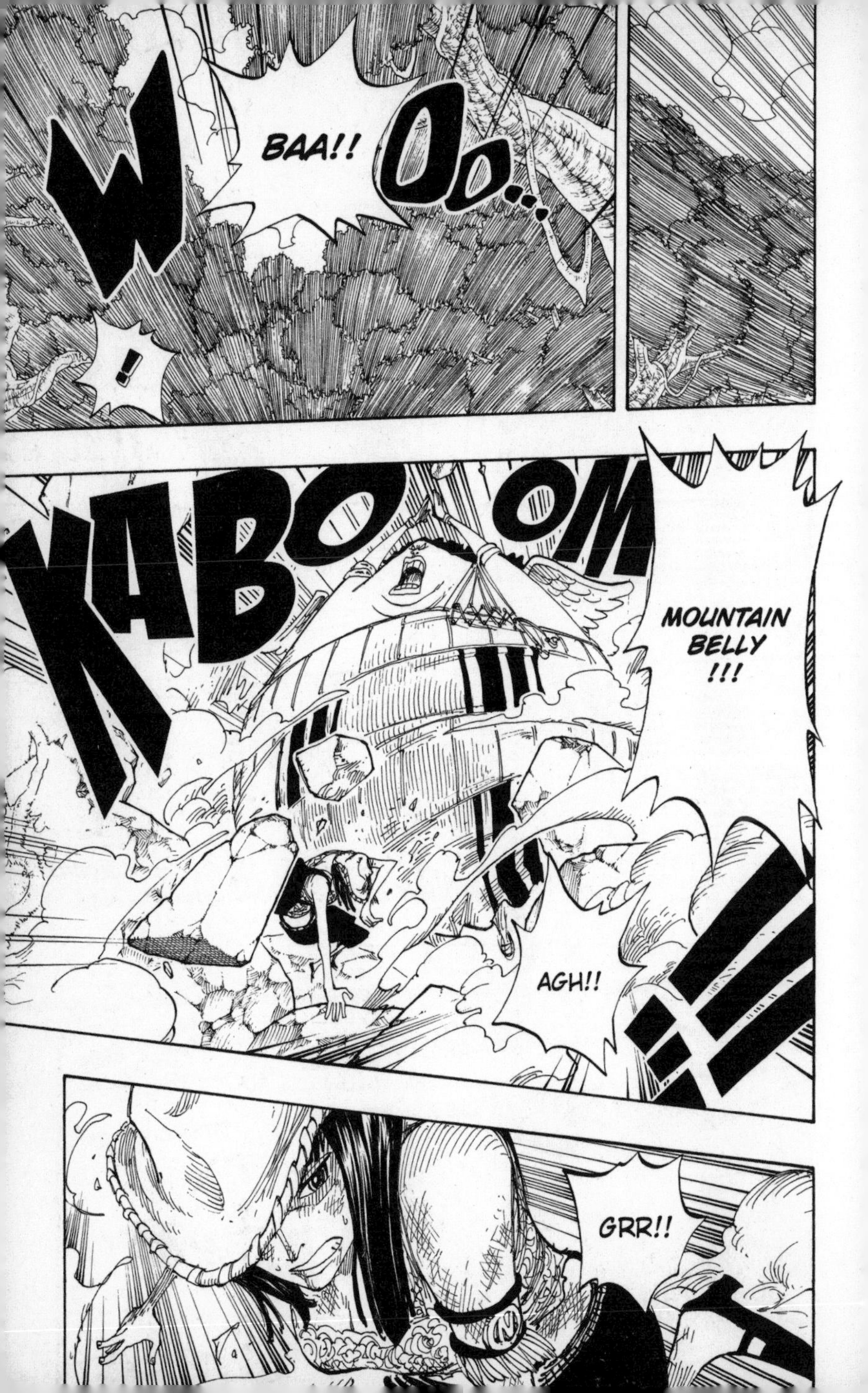
WOO...
BAA!!
!
KABOOM
MOUNTAIN BELLY !!!
!!
AGH!!
GRR!!

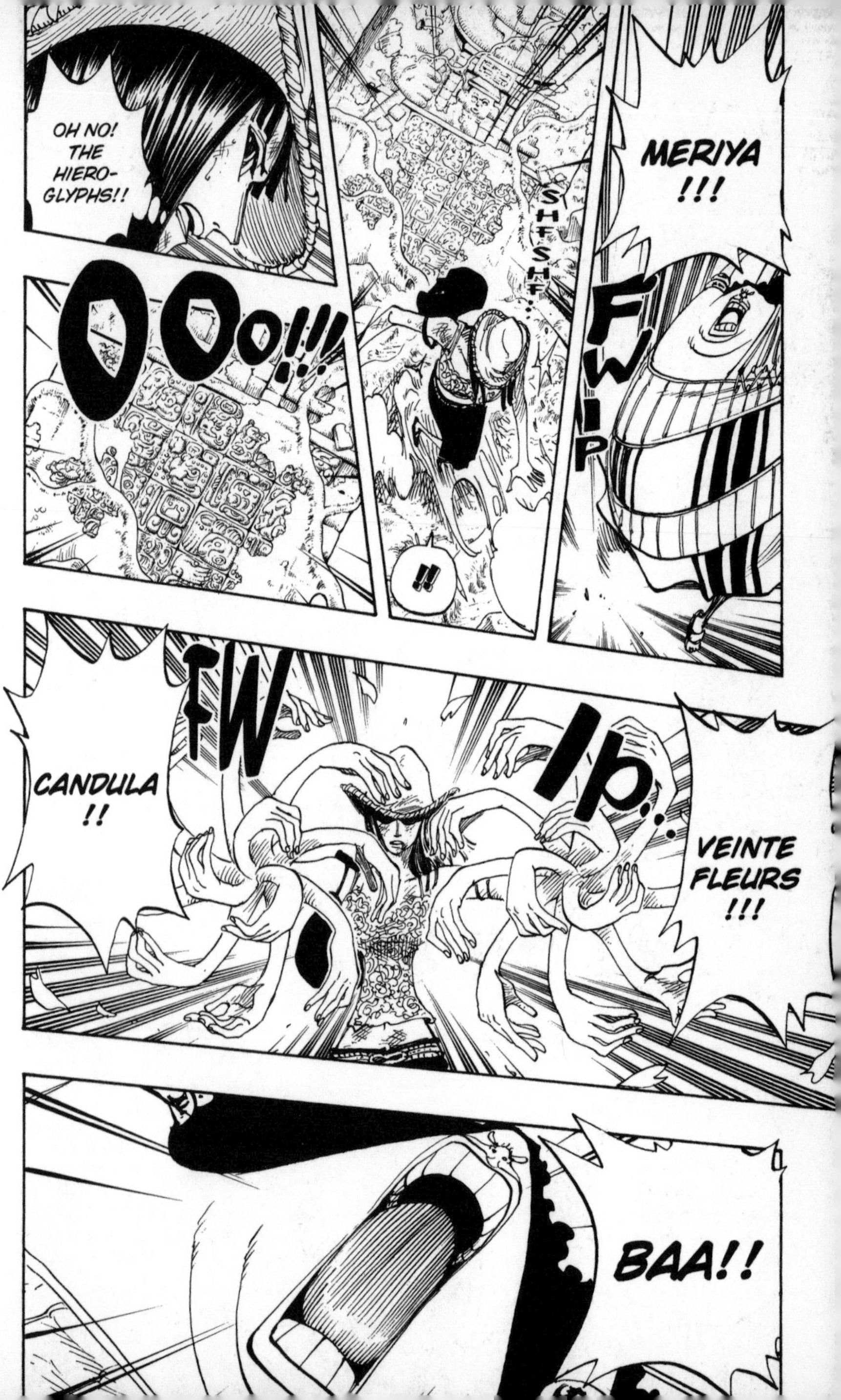
MERIYA !!!
FWIP
SHFSHF...
!!
OH NO! THE HIERO-GLYPHS!!
OOO!!!
VEINTE FLEURS !!!
FW Ip..
CANDULA !!
BAA!!

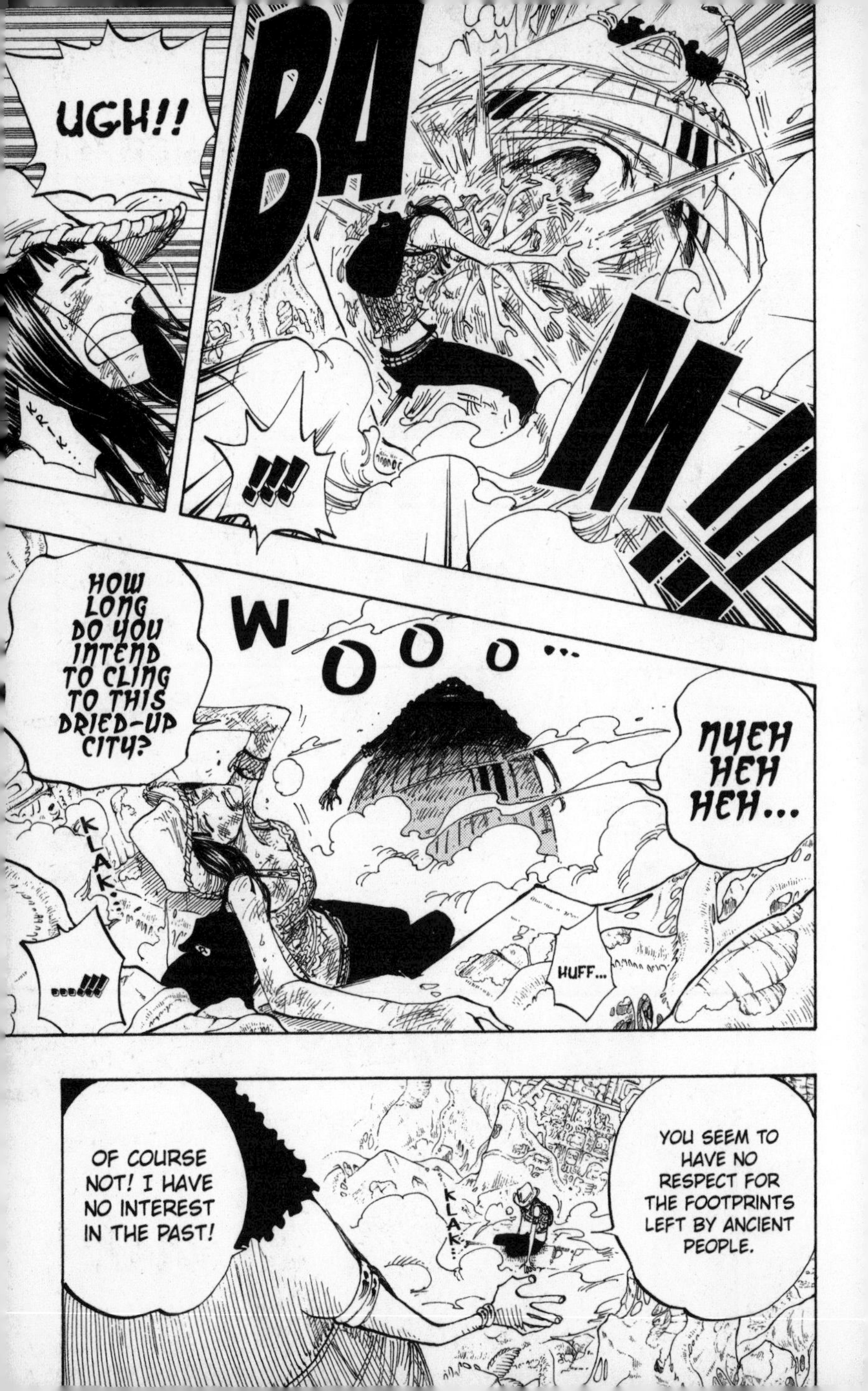
BAM!!
!!!
UGH!!
KRIK...
WOOO...
NYEH HEH HEH...
HOW LONG DO YOU INTEND TO CLING TO THIS DRIED-UP CITY?
KLAK...
HUFF...
...!!!
YOU SEEM TO HAVE NO RESPECT FOR THE FOOTPRINTS LEFT BY ANCIENT PEOPLE.
KLAK...
OF COURSE NOT! I HAVE NO INTEREST IN THE PAST!

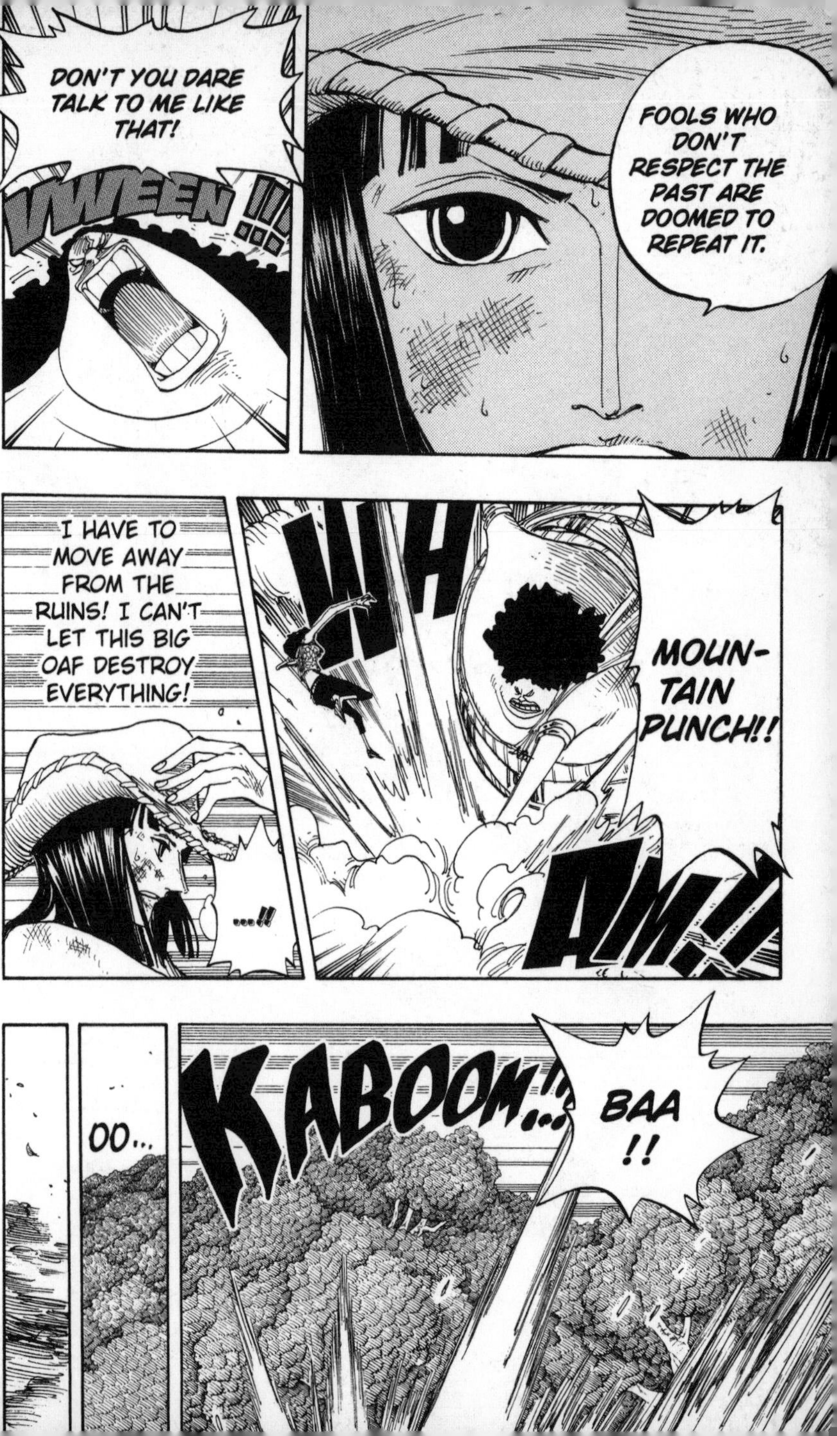
FOOLS WHO DON'T RESPECT THE PAST ARE DOOMED TO REPEAT IT.
DON'T YOU DARE TALK TO ME LIKE THAT!
VWEEN !!!
MOUN-TAIN PUNCH!!
AM!!
I HAVE TO MOVE AWAY FROM THE RUINS! I CAN'T LET THIS BIG OAF DESTROY EVERYTHING!
...!!
BAA !!
KABOOM...!!
OO...

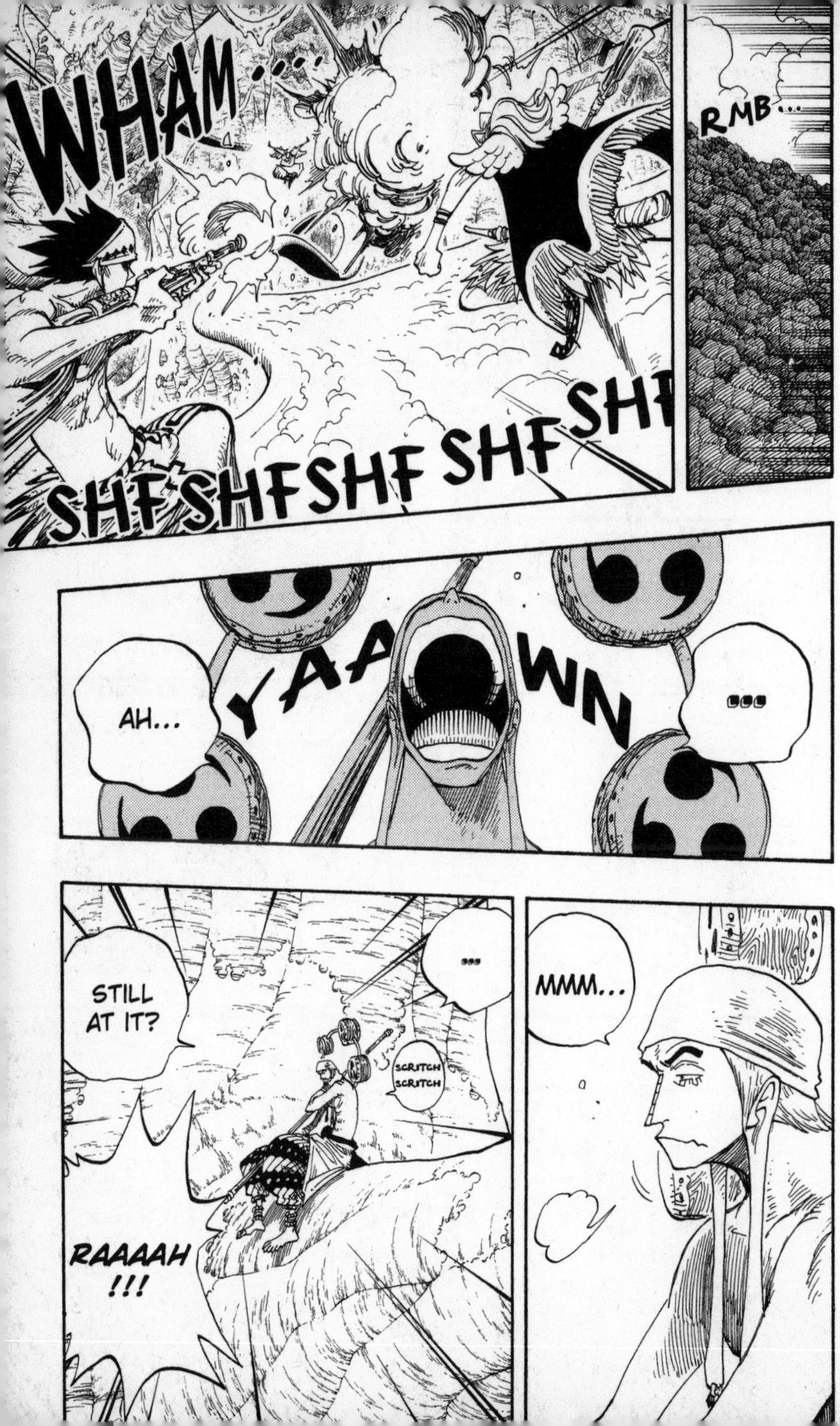
RMB...
WHAM...
SHFSHFSHF SHF SHF
...
YAAWN
AH...
MMM...
...
SCRITCH SCRITCH
STILL AT IT?
RAAAAH!!!

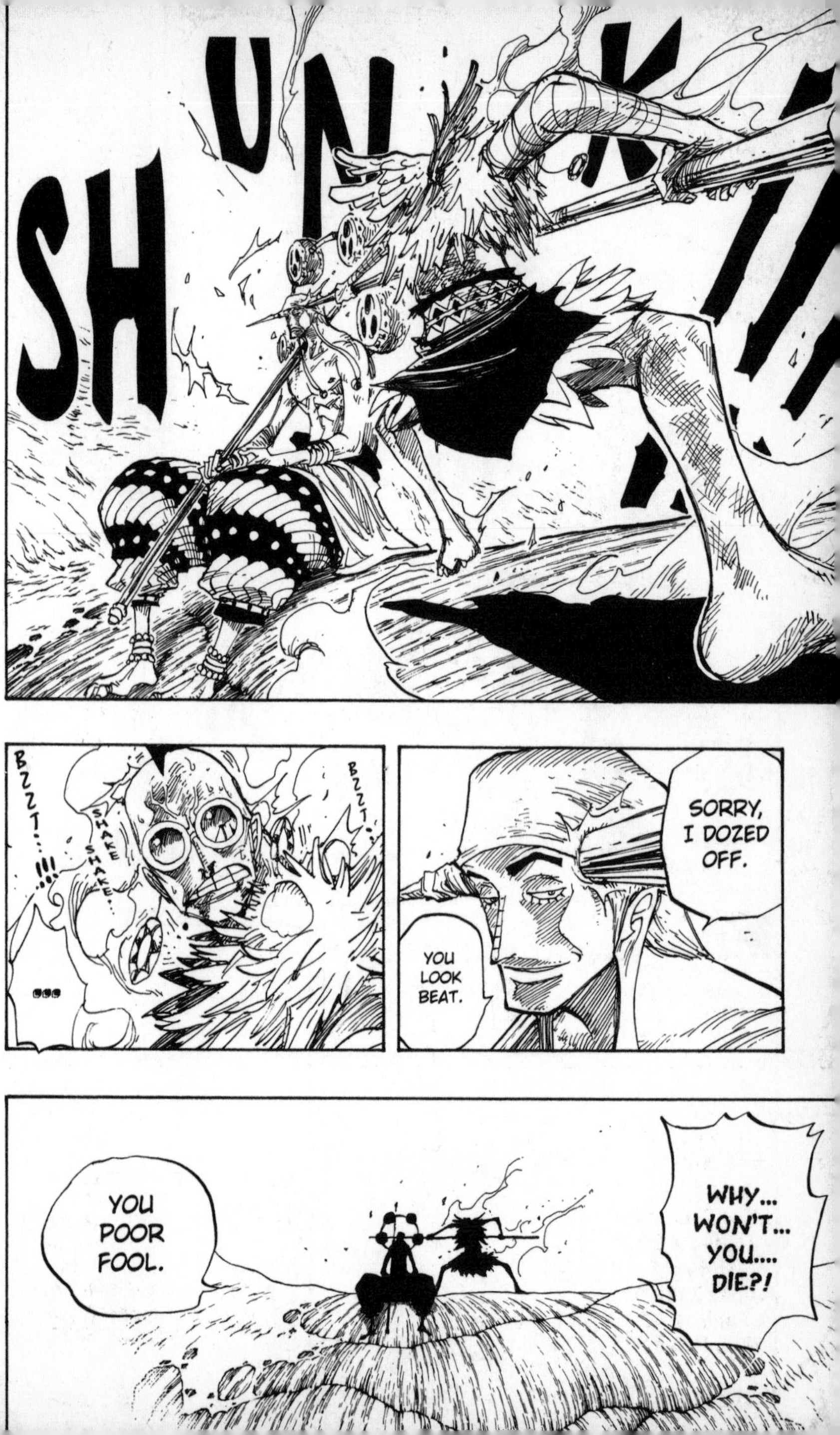
SHUNK!!!
SORRY, I DOZED OFF.
YOU LOOK BEAT.
BZZT...
SHAKE SHAKE...
BZZT...!!!
...
WHY... WON'T... YOU.... DIE?!
YOU POOR FOOL.

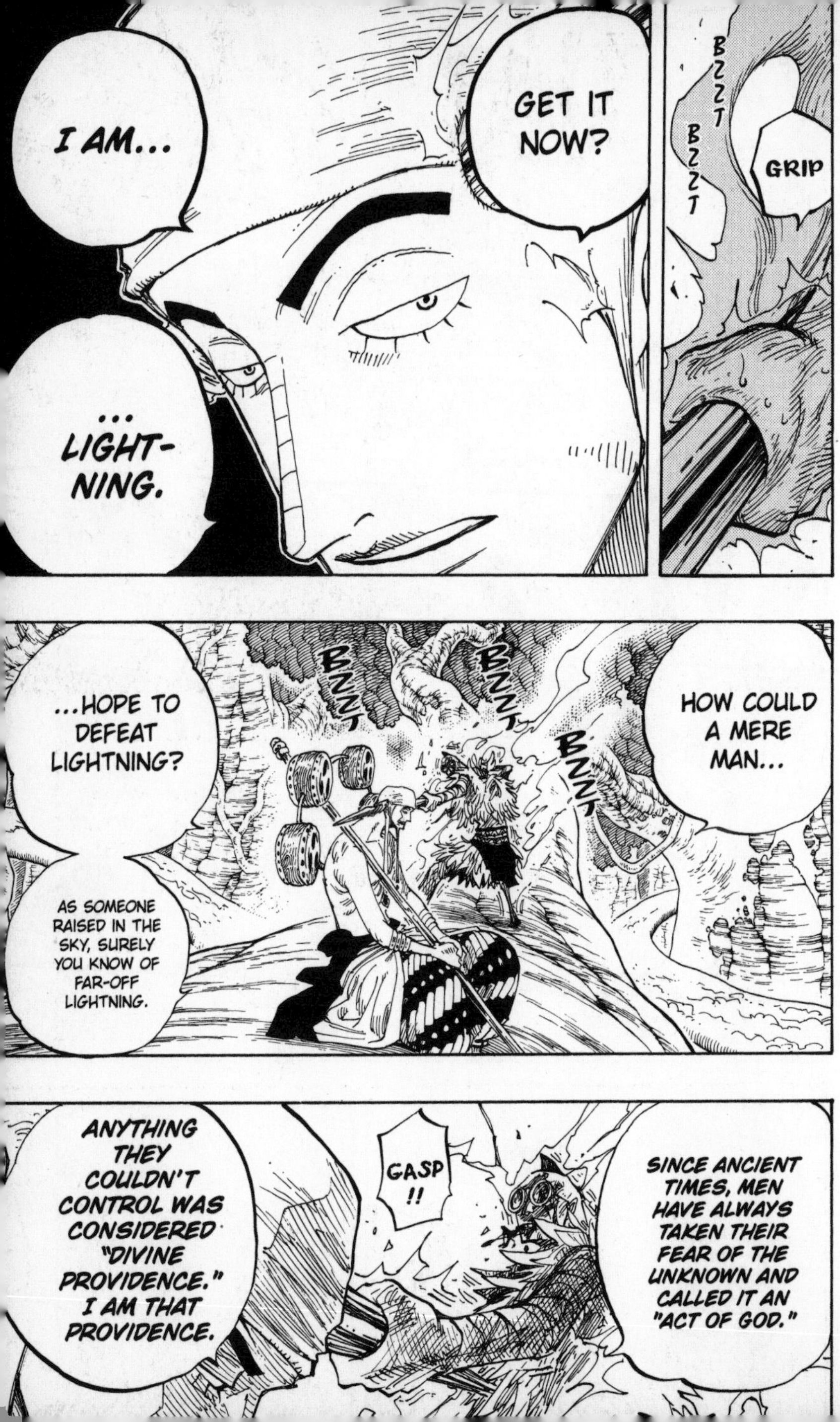
BZZT
BZZT
GRIP
I AM...
...LIGHTNING.
GET IT NOW?
HOW COULD A MERE MAN...
BZZT
BZZT
BZZT
...HOPE TO DEFEAT LIGHTNING?
AS SOMEONE RAISED IN THE SKY, SURELY YOU KNOW OF FAR-OFF LIGHTNING.
SINCE ANCIENT TIMES, MEN HAVE ALWAYS TAKEN THEIR FEAR OF THE UNKNOWN AND CALLED IT AN "ACT OF GOD."
GASP!!
ANYTHING THEY COULDN'T CONTROL WAS CONSIDERED "DIVINE PROVIDENCE." I AM THAT PROVIDENCE.

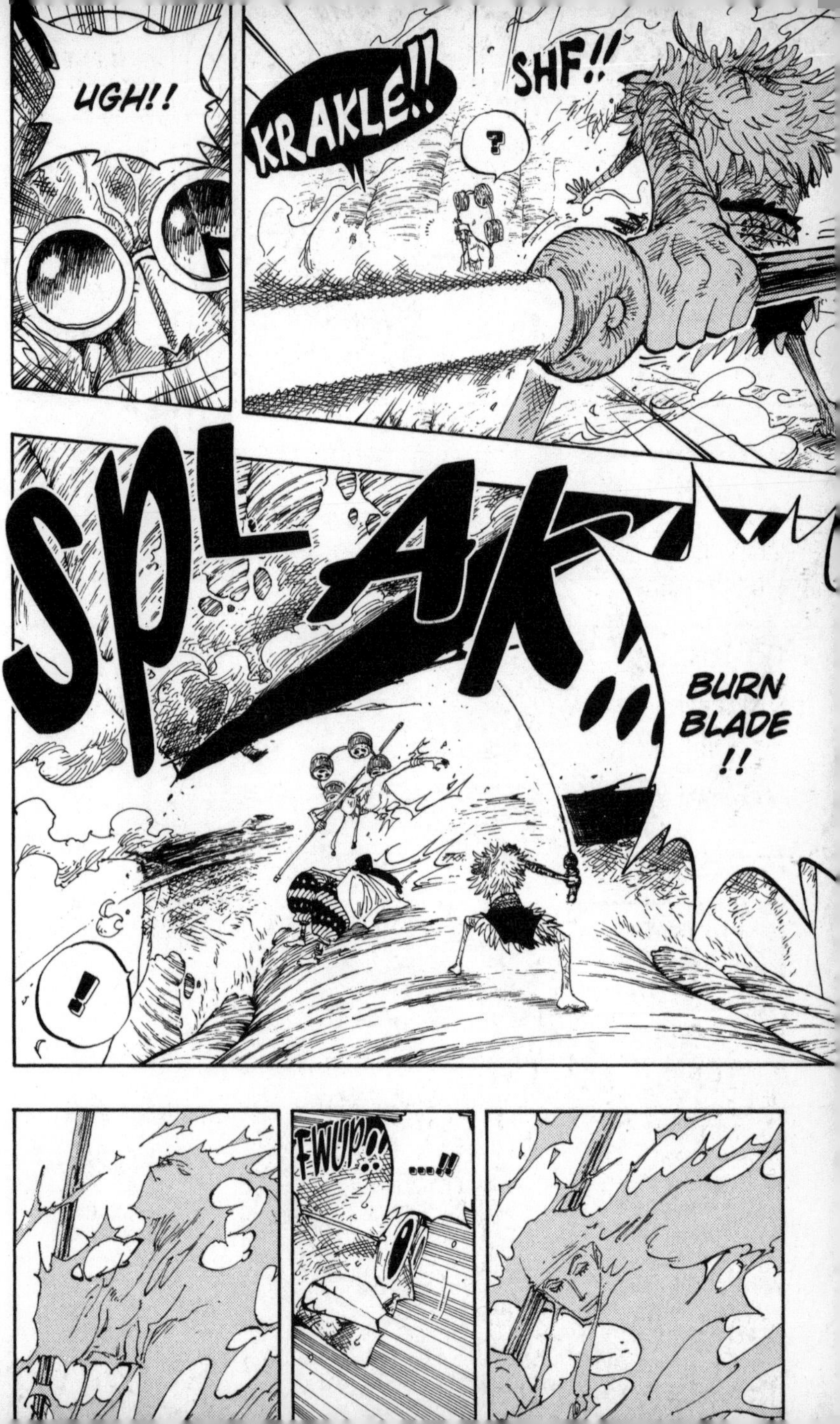
SHF!!
?
KRAKLE!!
UGH!!
BURN BLADE !!
SPLAK!!
!
...!!
FWUP!!

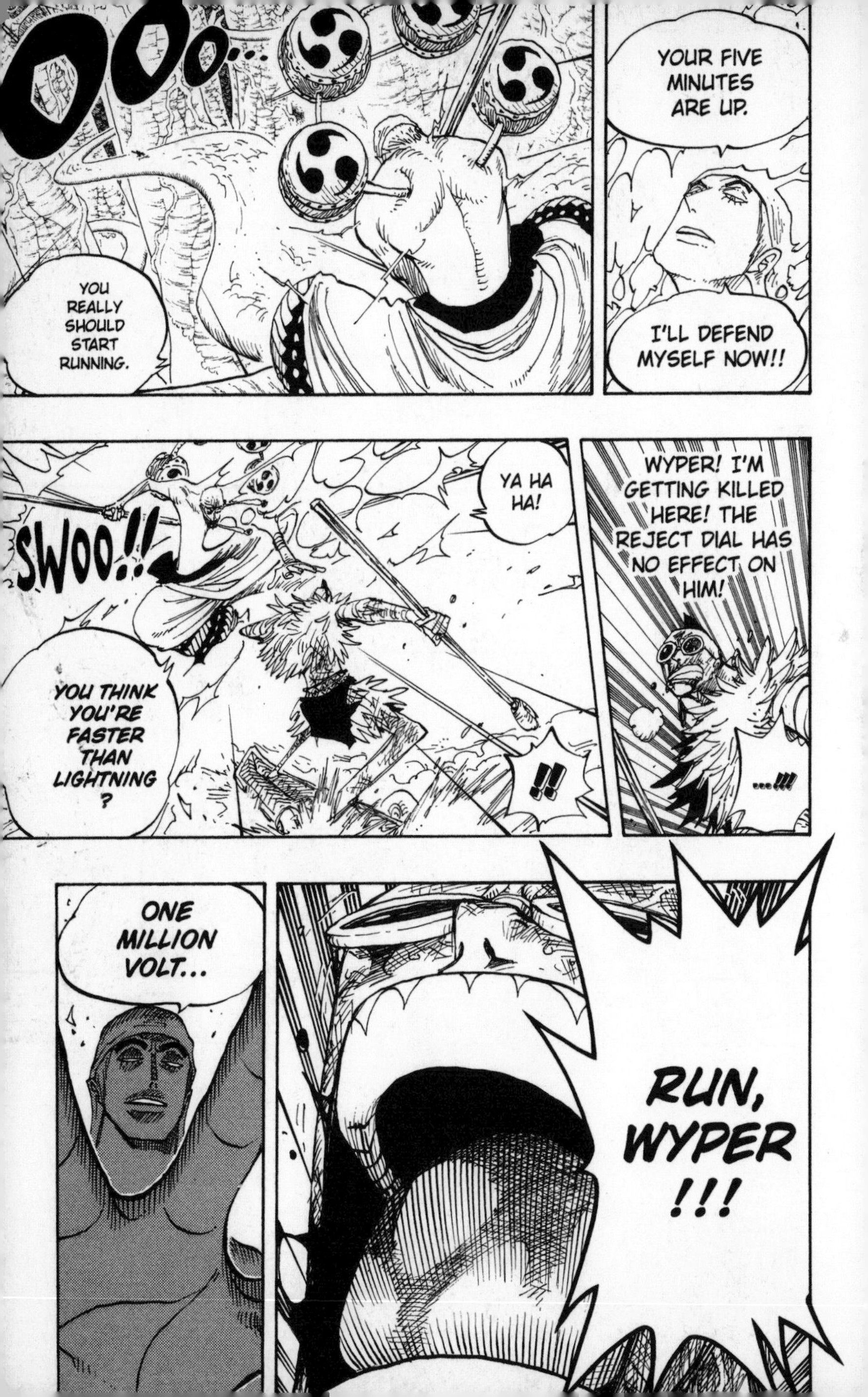
YOUR FIVE MINUTES ARE UP.
I'LL DEFEND MYSELF NOW!!
OOO...
YOU REALLY SHOULD START RUNNING.
WYPER! I'M GETTING KILLED HERE! THE REJECT DIAL HAS NO EFFECT ON HIM!
...!!!
YA HA HA!
SWOO!!
YOU THINK YOU'RE FASTER THAN LIGHTNING?
!!
RUN, WYPER!!!
ONE MILLION VOLT...

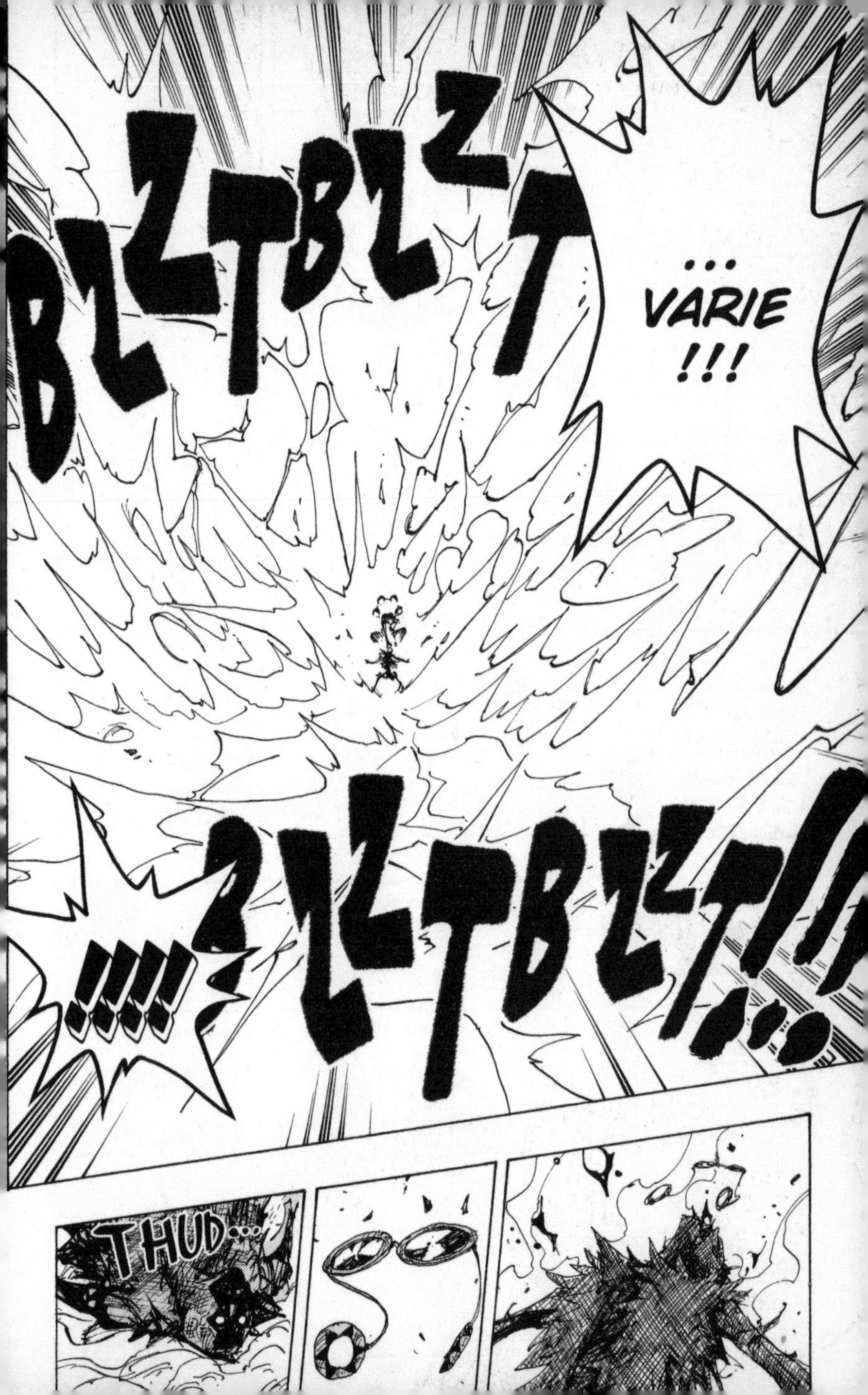
... VARIE !!!
BZZTBZZT
!!!!! BZZTBZZT!!
THUD...

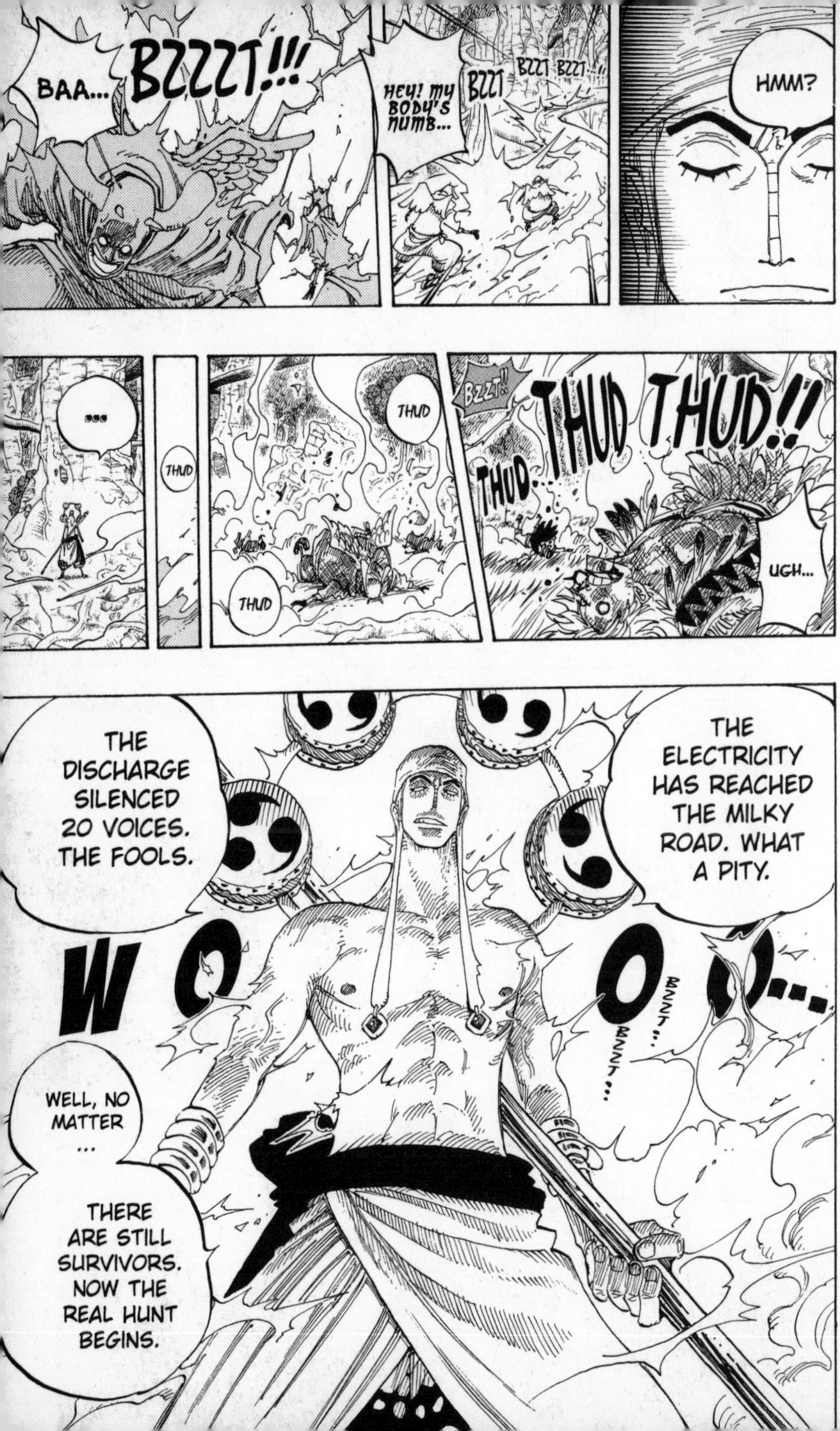
HMM?
BZZT BZZT...
BZZT
HEY! MY BODY'S NUMB...
BZZZT!!!
BAA...
BZZT!!
THUD THUD!!
THUD...
UGH...
THUD
THUD
THUD
...
THE ELECTRICITY HAS REACHED THE MILKY ROAD. WHAT A PITY.
THE DISCHARGE SILENCED 20 VOICES. THE FOOLS.
WOOO...
BZZT... BZZT...
WELL, NO MATTER...
THERE ARE STILL SURVIVORS. NOW THE REAL HUNT BEGINS.

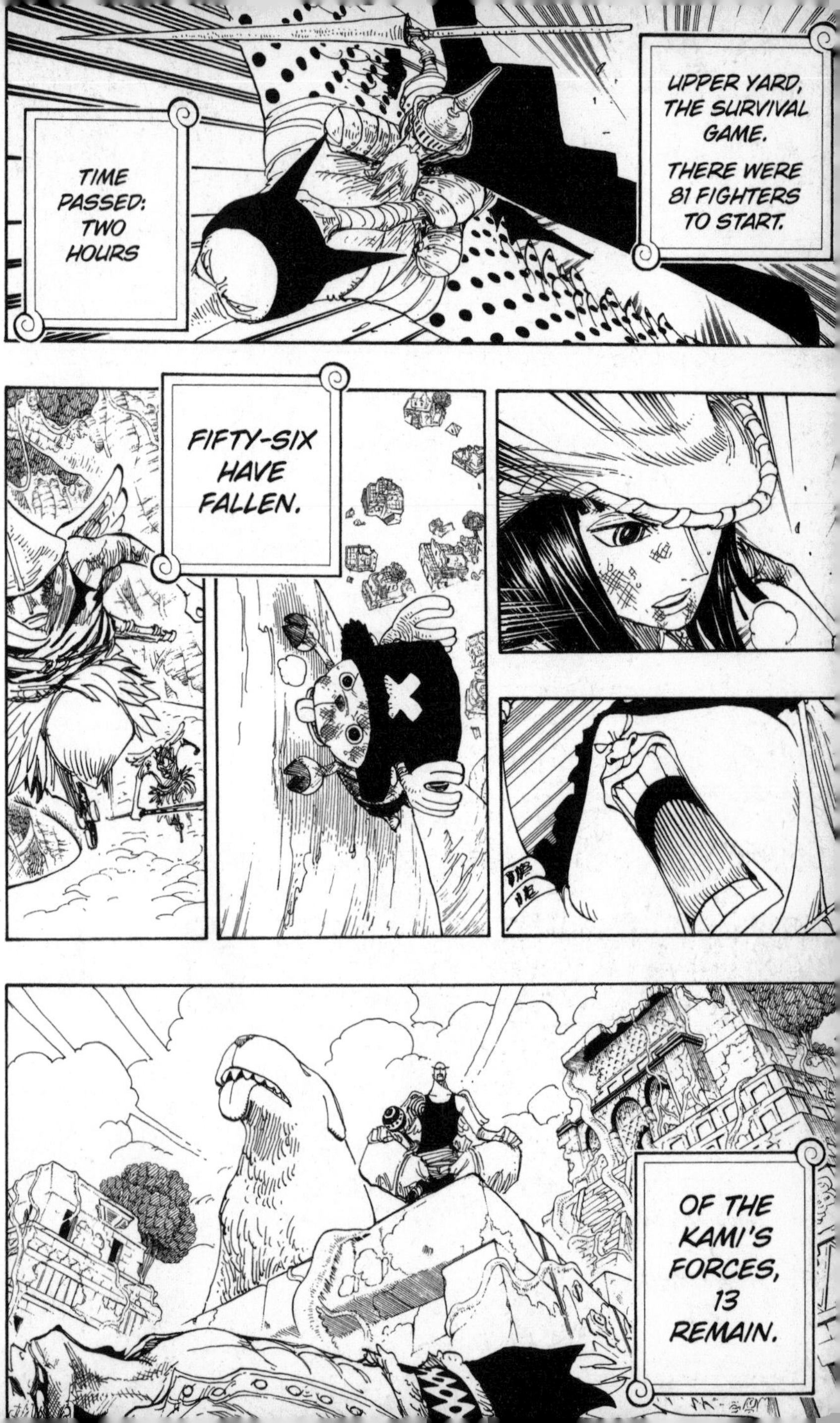
UPPER YARD, THE SURVIVAL GAME.
THERE WERE 81 FIGHTERS TO START.
TIME PASSED: TWO HOURS
FIFTY-SIX HAVE FALLEN.
OF THE KAMI'S FORCES, 13 REMAIN.

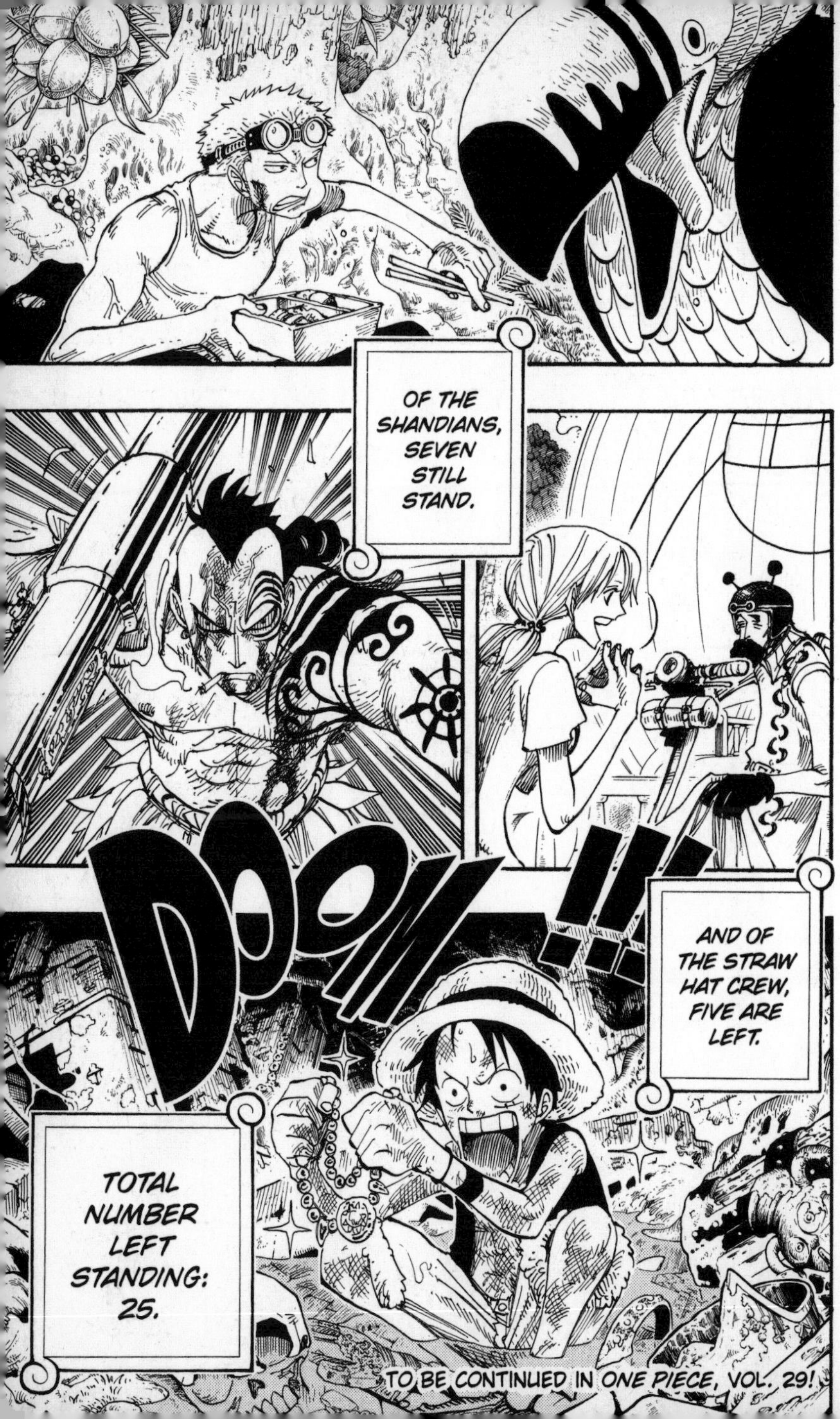
OF THE SHANDIANS, SEVEN STILL STAND.
DOOM!!
AND OF THE STRAW HAT CREW, FIVE ARE LEFT.
TOTAL NUMBER LEFT STANDING: 25.
TO BE CONTINUED IN ONE PIECE, VOL. 29!

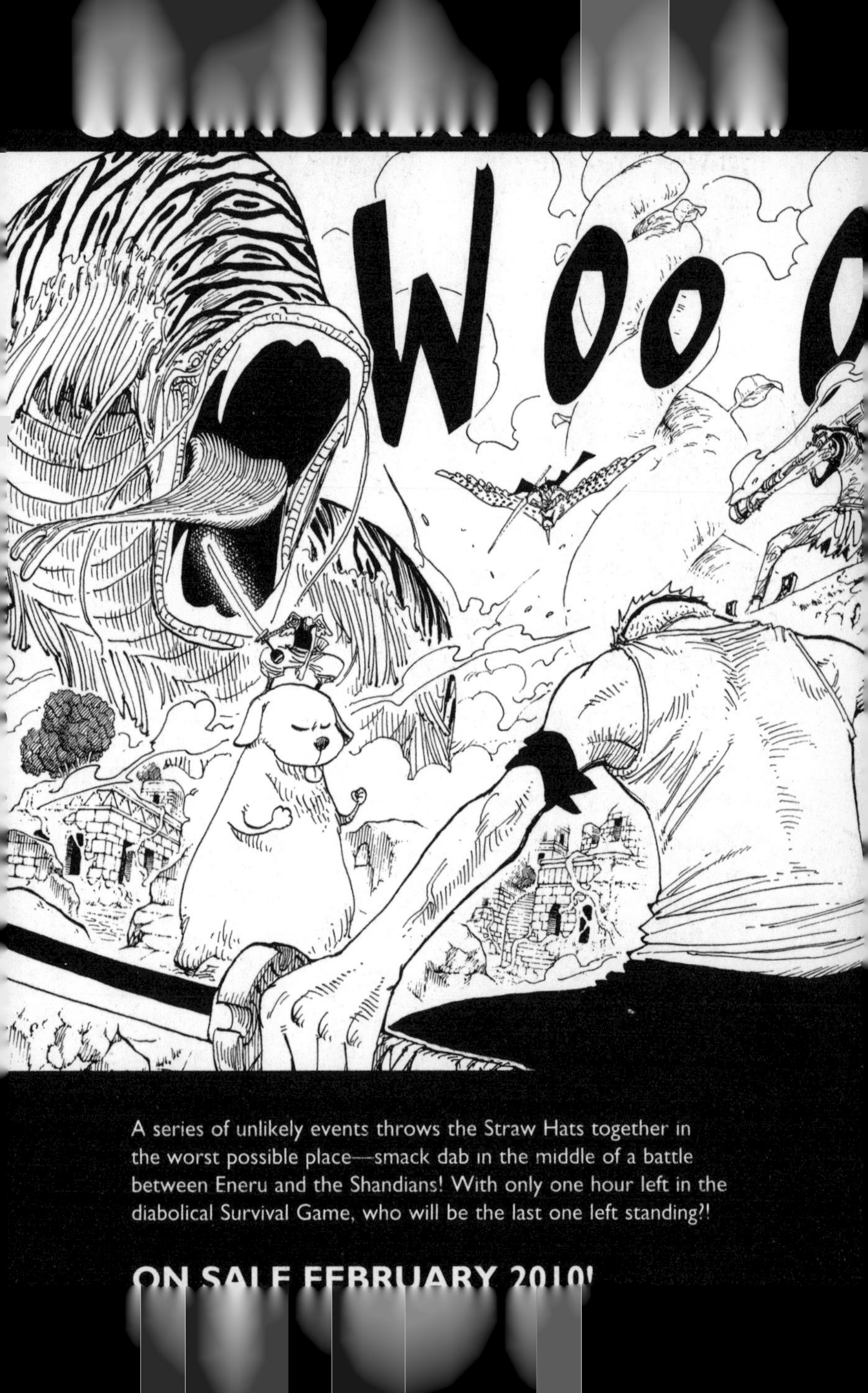
WOO

A series of unlikely events throws the Straw Hats together in the worst possible place—smack dab in the middle of a battle between Eneru and the Shandians! With only one hour left in the diabolical Survival Game, who will be the last one left standing?!

ON SALE FEBRUARY 2010!

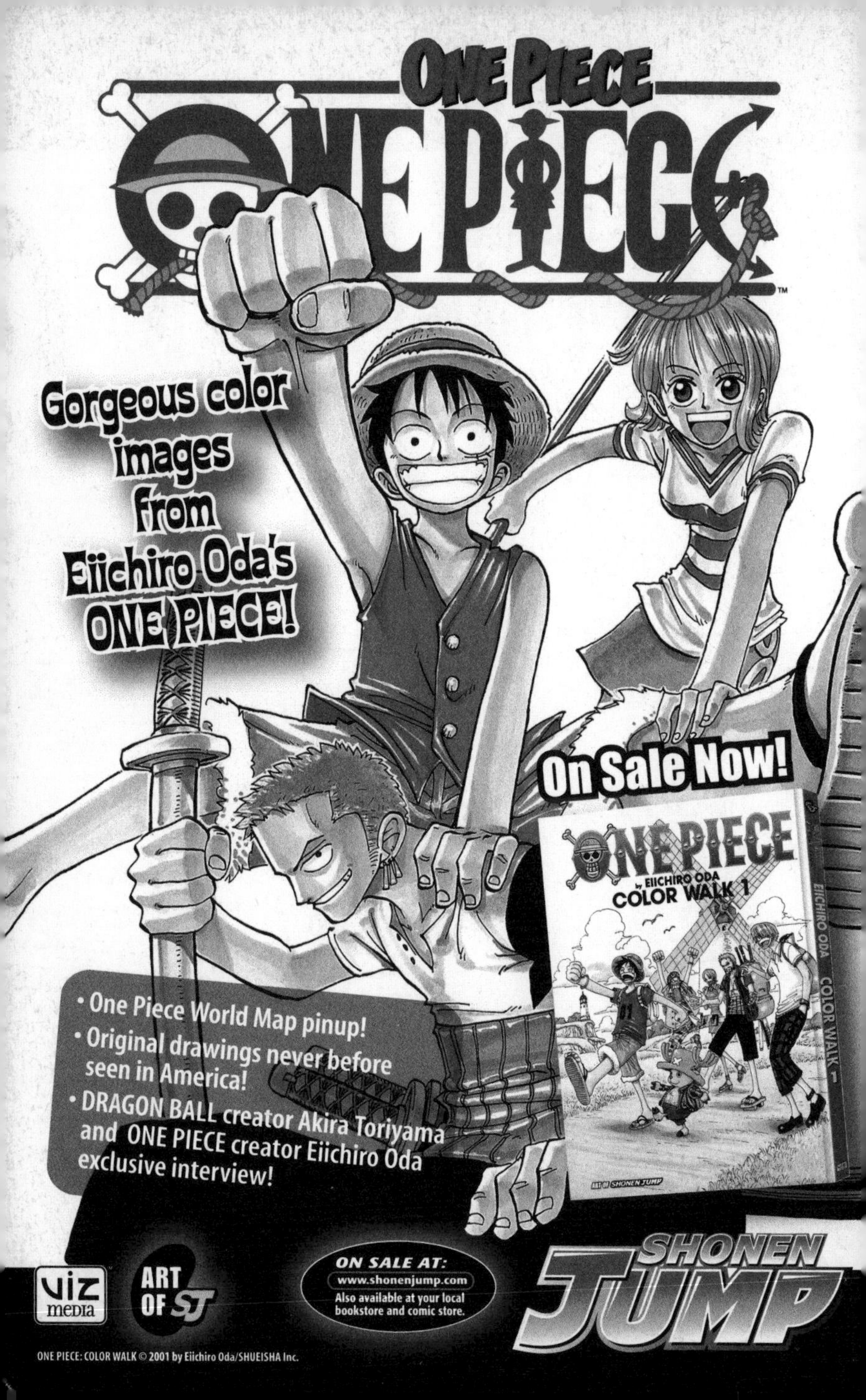

BOBOBO-BO BO-BOBO

BEWARE THE FIST OF THE NOSE HAIR!

MANGA SERIES ON SALE NOW
by Yoshio Sawai

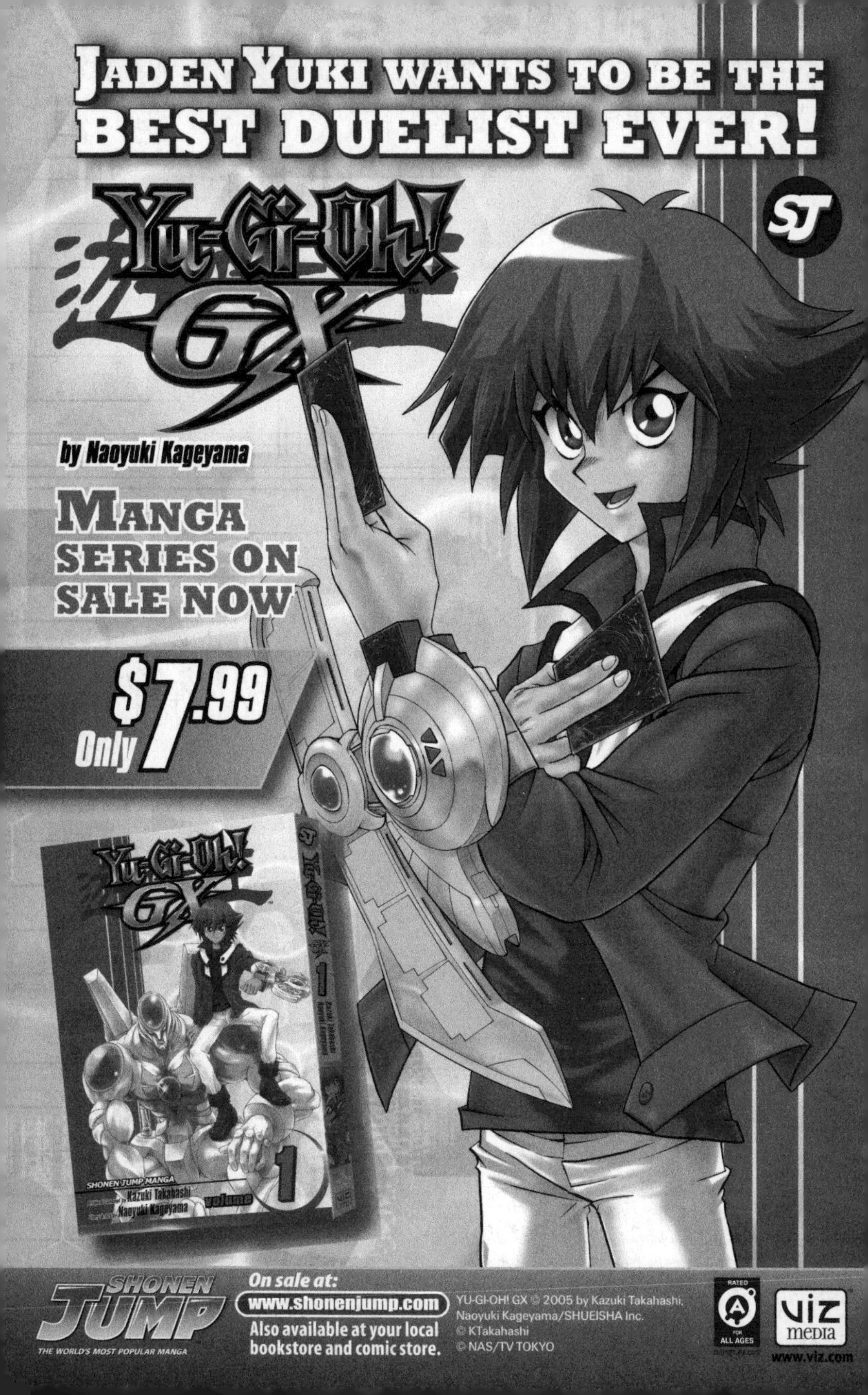
JADEN YUKI WANTS TO BE THE
BEST DUELIST EVER!
SJ
YU-GI-OH! GX
by Naoyuki Kageyama
MANGA
SERIES ON
SALE NOW
Only $7.99
YU-GI-OH! GX
SHONEN JUMP MANGA
Kazuki Takahashi
Naoyuki Kageyama
volume 1
SHONEN JUMP
THE WORLD'S MOST POPULAR MANGA
On sale at:
www.shonenjump.com
Also available at your local
bookstore and comic store.
YU-GI-OH! GX © 2005 by Kazuki Takahashi,
Naoyuki Kageyama/SHUEISHA Inc.
© KTakahashi
© NAS/TV TOKYO
RATED A FOR ALL AGES
VIZ media
www.viz.com

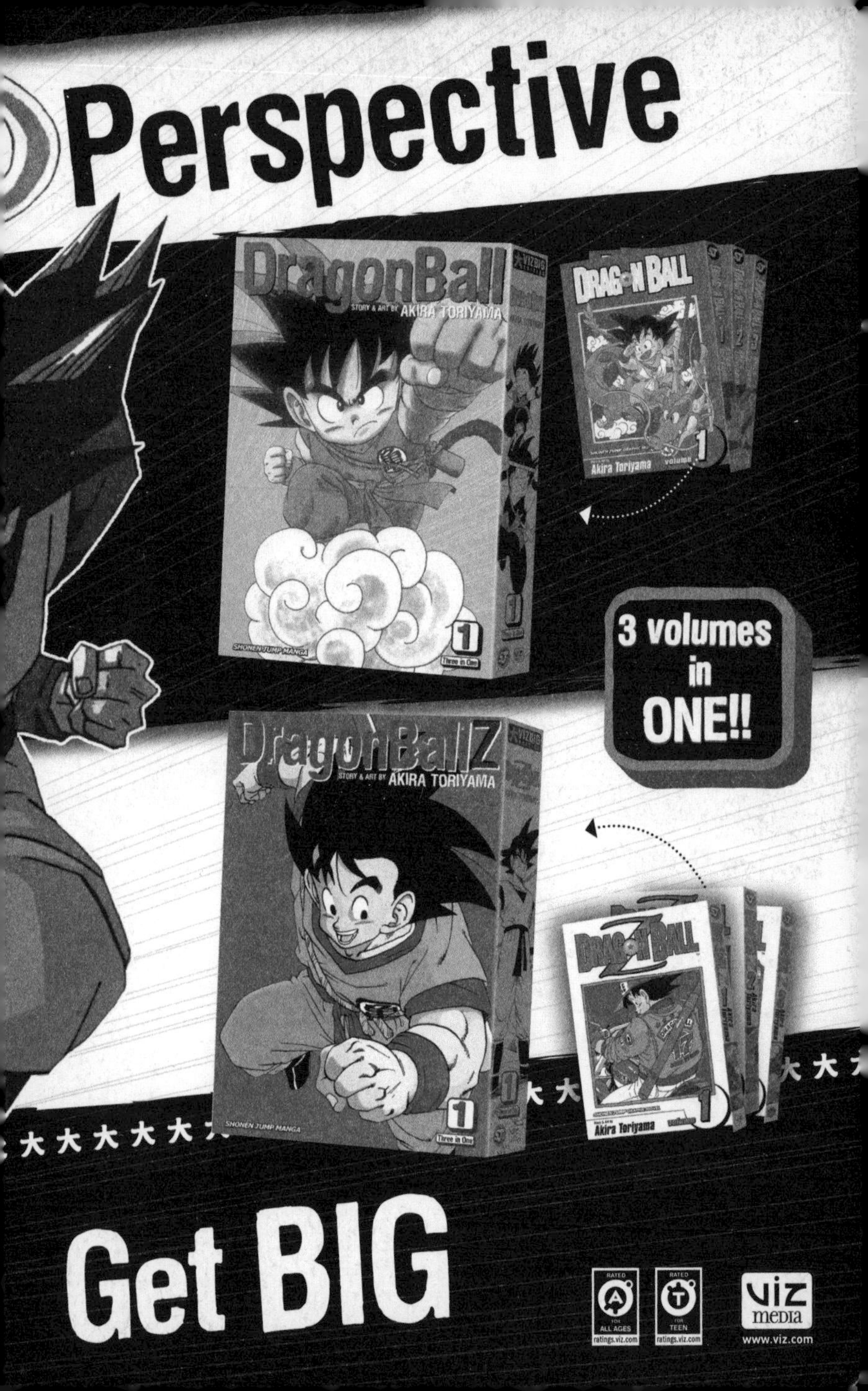
Perspective
DragonBall
STORY & ART BY AKIRA TORIYAMA
SHONEN JUMP MANGA
Three in One
DRAGON BALL
Akira Toriyama
volume 1
3 volumes in ONE!!
DragonBallZ
STORY & ART BY AKIRA TORIYAMA
SHONEN JUMP MANGA
Three in One
DRAGON BALL Z
Akira Toriyama
Get BIG
RATED A FOR ALL AGES ratings.viz.com
RATED T FOR TEEN ratings.viz.com
viz media
www.viz.com

Change Your

From Akira Toriyama, the creator of *Dr. Slump*, *COWA!*, and *SandLand*

Relive Goku's quest with the new VIZBIG Editions of *Dragon Ball* and *Dragon Ball Z*! Each features:

- Three volumes in one
- Exclusive cover designs
- Color manga pages
- Larger trim size
- Color artwork
- Bonus content

And more!

* * * * * * * * * * * * * * * * * * * *

On sale at:
www.shonenjump.com
Also available at your local bookstore and comic store